MW01257553

Report on

THE ENIAC

(Electronic Numerical Integrator and Computer)

Developed under the supervision of the
Ordnance Department, United States Army

TECHNICAL MANUAL
by
Adele K. Goldstine

UNIVERSITY OF PENNSYLVANIA

Moore School of Electrical Engineering

PHILADELPHIA, PENNSYLVANIA

June 1, 1946

Please note: this publication was made from
an original mimeograph copy of the master
typescript manuscript prepared in 1946.
As a result, some pages lack legibility.

About the author:
Adele Goldstine (1920 – 1964) was a graduate of the University of Chicago
and a pioneer woman in the field of computer science. Born Adele Katz,
she married mathematician and computer scientist Herman Goldstine in
1941. A short time later her husband took over the Moore School of
Electrical Engineering at the University of Pennsylvania. Subsequently
Adele and two other women became the instructors of ballistic classes
at the School, and Adele was tasked with recruiting additional female
"computers". When her husband took on the role of military liaison
and administrator for the ENIAC, Adele Goldstine learned to program
the machine. She also trained some of the female programmers, an
experience which made her the leading candidate to write this
ENIAC technical manual. Goldstine died of cancer at the age of 43.

A REPORT ON THE ENIAC

(Electronic Numerical Integrator and Computer)

Report of Work under Contract No. W-670-ORD-4926

Between

Ordnance Department, United States Army
Washington, D. C.

and

The University of Pennsylvania
Moore School of Electrical Engineering
Philadelphia, Pa.

PREFACE

The Report on the ENIAC consists of five separately bound parts, as follows:

1. ENIAC Operating Manual

2. ENIAC Maintenance Manual

3. Part I, Technical Description of the ENIAC

   Volume I (Chapters I to VI)

4. Part I, Technical Description of the ENIAC

   Volume II (Chapters VII to XI)

5. Part II, Technical Description of the ENIAC

Included with the Operating Manual and Parts I and II of the Technical Description are all drawings (see table 0.3 below) which are required for understanding these reports. The Maintenance Manual assumes access to the complete file of ENIAC drawings.

Part I of the Technical Description is intended for those who wish to have a general understanding of how the ENIAC works, without concerning themselves with the details of the circuits; it assumes no knowledge of electronics or circuit theory. Part II is intended for those who require a detailed understanding of the circuits. Its organization, to a great extent, duplicates that of Part I so as to make cross referencing between the two parts easy.

The ENIAC Operating Manual contains a complete set of instructions for operating the ENIAC. It includes very little explanatory material, and hence assumes familiarity with Part I of the Technical Description of the ENIAC. The ENIAC Maintenance Manual includes description of the various test units and procedures for testing, as well as a list of common and probable sources of trouble. It assumes a complete understanding of the circuits of ENIAC, i.e. a knowledge of both Parts I and II of the Technical Description of the ENIAC.

The Report on the ENIAC and the complete file of ENIAC drawings constitute a complete description and set of instructions for operation and maintenance of the machine. The drawings carry a number of the form PX-n-m. The following tables give the classification according to this numbering system.

	TABLE 0.1
Values of n	Division
1	General
2	Test Equipment
3	Racks and Panels
4	Trays, Cables, Adaptors, and Load Boxes
5	Accumulators
6	High Speed Multiplier
7	Function Table
8	Master Programmer
9	Cycling Unit and Initiating Unit
10	Divider and Square Rooter
11	Constant Transmitter
12	Printer
13	Power Supplies

	TABLE 0.2
Values of m	Subject
101-200	Wiring Diagrams
201-300	Mechanical Drawings
301-400	Report Drawings
401-500	Illustration Problem Set-Ups.

The reader of this report will be primarily interested in the types of drawings listed in the following paragraphs. A table on page 4 gives the corresponding drawing number for each unit of the ENIAC.

1) Front Panel Drawings. These drawings show in some detail the switches, sockets, etc., for each panel of each unit. They contain the essential instructions for setting up a problem on the ENIAC.

2) Front View Drawings. There is one of these drawings for each kind of panel used in the various units of the ENIAC. These show the relative position of the trays and the location of the various neon lights. Since these drawings show the neon lights, they can be used to check the proper operation of the various units.

3) Block Diagrams. These drawings illustrate the logical essentials of the internal circuits of each unit. That is, resistors, condensers, and some other electrical details are not shown; but complete channels (paths of pulses or gates representing numbers or program signals) are shown in all their multiplicity. These drawings will be of interest to those who are interested in Parts I and II of the Technical Report.

4) Cross-section Diagrams. These drawings are electronically complete except that only one channel is shown where there is more than one. Thus, these drawings show every resistor and condenser and any other electronic elements belonging to any circuit. These drawings will be of particular interest to the maintenance personnel and to those reading Part II of the technical report.

5) Detail Drawings. All other drawings of the ENIAC come under this heading. A complete file of drawings is available at the location of the ENIAC.

Table 0.3
ENIAC DRAWINGS

Unit	Front Panel	Front View	Block Diagram	Cross – Section
Initiating Unit	PX-9-302 9-302R	PX-9-305	PX-9-307	
Cycling Unit	PX-9-303 9-303R	PX-9-304	PX-9-307	
Accumulator	PX-5-301	PX-5-305	PX-5-304	PX-5-115
Multiplier	PX-6-302 6-302R 6-303 6-303R 6-304 6-304R	PX-6-309	PX-6-308	PX-6-112A 6-112B
Function Table	PX-7-302 7-302R 7-303 7-303R	PX-7-305	PX-7-304	PX-7-117 7-118
Divider and Square Rooter	PX-10-301 10-301R	PX-10-302	PX-10-304	
Constant Transmitter	PX-11-302 11-302R 11-303 11-303R 11-304 11-304R	PX-11-306	PX-11-307	PX-11-116 11-309 (C.T. and R.)
Printer	PX-12-301 12-301R 12-302 12-302R 12-303 12-303R	PX-12-306	PX-12-307	PX-12-115
Master Programmer	PX-8-301 8-301R 8-302 8-302R	PX-8-303	PX-8-304	PX-8-102

Other drawings of particular interest:

Floor Plan	PX-1-302	IBM Punch and	PX-12-112
A.C. Wiring	PX-1-303	Plugboard	PX-12-305
IBM Reader and	PX-11-119	Pulse Amplifier and	PX-4-302
plugboard	PX-11-305	Block Diagram	PX-4-301

Interconnection of Multiplier and Accumulators   PX-6-311
Interconnection of Divider and Accumulators   PX-10-307

The front view drawings and the large front panel drawings (whose numbers do not end with "R") are bound as a part of the Operator's Manual.

Included with the report is a folder containing all the drawings listed in the above table except the large front panel (see above). A complete file of drawings is available at the location of the ENIAC.

PART I

TECHNICAL DESCRIPTION OF THE ENIAC

by

Adele K. Goldstine

Moore School of Electrical Engineering
University of Pennsylvania

TABLE OF CONTENTS

I. INTRODUCTION

1.1. BRIEF DESCRIPTION OF THE ENIAC   1

    1.1.1. What the ENIAC does   1

    1.1.2. The Units of the ENIAC   2

    1.1.3. Representation of Digits by Pulses   4

    1.1.4. Programming by Means of Pulses,

         Switches, and Cables   6

    1.1.5. Synchronized System   8

1.2. ELECTRONIC ELEMENTS   10

    1.2.1. Single Tube Elements   11

        1.2.1.1. Buffers and Cathode Followers   11

        1.2.1.2. Inverters   12

        1.2.1.3. Gate Tubes   12

    1.2.2. Multi-Tube Elements   12

        1.2.2.1. Flip-flops   12

        1.2.2.2. Counters   13

        1.2.2.3. Standard Transmitters   15

        1.2.2.4. Receivers and Transceivers   15

        1.2.2.5. Plug-in Units   18

1.3. CLASSIFICATION OF ENIAC CIRCUITS: Numerical and
                                               Programming   18

    1.3.1. Program Controls   19

    1.3.2. Common Programming Circuits   19

1.4.   PROGRAMMING THE ENIAC   20

        1.4.1.   Preparatory Formulation of the Problem   20

        1.4.2.   Planning the Programs and Program Sequences   21

        1.4.3.   Programming on Higher Levels   22

        1.4.4.   Special Linking of Program Sequences by
                 Magnitude Discrimination   23

1.5.   EQUIPMENT ASSOCIATED WITH THE ENIAC   23

        1.5.1.   Ventilating Equipment   23

        1.5.2.   Power Equipment   24

        1.5.3.   Special Test Equipment   24

II.   INITIATING UNIT

2.1.   STARTING, STOPPING AND INITIAL CLEARING   1

        2.1.1.   Starting and Stopping the ENIAC   2

        2.1.2.   Initial Clearing   10

2.2.   READER AND PRINTER PROGRAM CONTROLS ON THE INITIATING UNIT 15

        2.2.1.   Reader Program Controls   15

        2.2.2.   Printer Program Controls   17

2.3.   INITIATING PULSE FOR A COMPUTATION: Reader Start Button and 17
                                            Initiating Pulse Button.

2.4.   SELECTIVE CLEAR CONTROLS   20

2.5.   DEVICES FOR TESTING THE ENIAC   20

III. CYCLING UNIT

3.1. PULSES AND GATES AND THEIR SOURCES   2

    3.1.1. The Pulses and Gates   2

    3.1.2. Sources of the Pulses and Gates   3

3.2. METHODS OF OPERATION   6

3.3. THE CYCLING UNIT OSCILLOSCOPE   10

IV. ACCUMULATOR

4.0. GENERAL SUMMARY OF THE ACCUMULATOR   2

4.1. PROGRAM CONTROLS AND THE SIGNIFICANT FIGURES AND
      SELECTIVE CLEAR SWITCHES   4

    4.1.1. The Operation Switch   5

    4.1.2. The Clear-Correct Switch   5

    4.1.3. Repeat Switch   7

    4.1.4. The Significant Figures Switch   8

    4.1.5. The Selective Clear Switch   10

4.2. COMMON PROGRAMMING CIRCUITS   10

    4.2.1. The Receive Circuits   10

    4.2.2. The Transmit Circuits   10

    4.2.3. The Clear Circuits   11

    4.2.4. Circuit for Admitting the 1'P to Units Decade   12

    4.2.5. Repeater Ring Common to Repeat Program Controls 12

4.3. NUMERICAL CIRCUITS   12

    4.3.1. Operation of the Numerical Circuits in
           Transmitting a Number and/or its Complement   12

    4.3.2. Operation of the Numerical Circuits in Re-
           ceiving a Number   15

    4.3.3. Static Communication Between an Accumulator
           and Another ENIAC Unit   18

4.4. USE OF ACCUMULATORS FOR FEWER THAN OR MORE THAN TEN DIGITS   20

    4.4.1. Use of an Accumulator to Store Two Numbers   20

    4.4.2. Interconnection of Two Accumulators to Form
           a Twenty Decade Accumulator.   20

4.5. ILLUSTRATIVE PROBLEMS   22

    4.5.1. Computation in Accumulators   25
    4.5.2. Dummy Programs   27
    4.5.3. Magnitude Discrimination Programs   28

V. HIGH-SPEED MULTIPLIER

5.0. GENERAL SUMMARY   1

5.1. PROGRAM CONTROLS   7

    5.1.1. The Multiplier and Multiplicand Accumulator
           Receive Switches   7

    5.1.2. Multiplier and Multiplicand Accumulator
           Clear Switches   11

5.1.3. The Significant Figures Switch 11

5.1.4. Places Switches 12

5.1.5. Product Disposal Switch 12

5.2. COMMON PROGRAMMING CIRCUITS 13

5.2.1. Argument Accumulator Receive Circuits 13

5.2.2. Program Ring and Associated Circuits 14

5.2.3. Argument Accumulator Clear Circuits 18

5.2.4. Product Disposal Circuits 18

5.3. NUMERICAL CIRCUITS 19

5.4. INTERRELATION OF THE HIGH-SPEED MULTIPLIER AND ITS
     ASSOCIATED ACCUMULATORS 22

5.4.1. Interconnections for Numerical and Programming
       Data 22

5.4.1.1. Programming Connections for
         "Receive Argument" Instructions 24

5.4.1.2. Connections for Partial Product
         Reception 24

5.4.1.3. Connections for Complement Correction 24

5.4.1.4. Connections for Final Product Collection 25

5.4.1.5. Programming Connections for Product
         Disposal Instructions 26

5.4.2. Position of Decimal Point in Product Accumulator 26

5.5. ILLUSTRATIVE PROBLEMS   27

      5.5.1. One Program Control Devoted to Each

           Multiplication   28

      5.5.2. One Program Control Used Repeatedly   29

      5.5.3. Isolation of Program Sequences which

           Stimulate Transmission of Arguments, to

           Argument Accumulators, Multiplication

           Programs, and Reception of Products from

           Product Accumulators   30

VI. DIVIDER AND SQUARE ROOTER

6.0. GENERAL SUMMARY   1

6.1. PROGRAM CONTROLS   11

      6.1.1. The Numerator Accumulator and Denominator

           Accumulator Receive Switches   12

      6.1.2. The Numerator Accumulator and Denominator

           Accumulator Clear Switches   13

      6.1.3. The Divide-Square Root and Places Switch   14

      6.1.4. The Round Off Switch   15

      6.1.5. The Answer Disposal Switch   16

      6.1.6. The Interlock Switch   17

6.2. COMMON PROGRAMMING CIRCUITS   19

      6.2.1. Status of the Circuits before a Transceiver

           is Stimulated   19

6.2.2. The Program Ring Circuit   20

6.2.3. The Interlock and Clear Circuit   22

6.2.4. The Overdraft and Sign Indication Circuits   23

6.2.5. The External — Internal Programming Circuits   26

6.2.6. The Divide Flip-flop   29

6.2.7. Chronological Description of the Common

      Programming Circuits   30

6.3. NUMERICAL CIRCUITS   31

6.4. INTERRELATION OF DIVIDER AND SQUARE ROOTER AND ITS

      ASSOCIATED ACCUMULATORS   34

6.4.1. Interconnections for Numerical Data   34

6.4.2. Interconnections for Programming Instructions   37

6.4.3. Relationship Between Alignment of the Arguments

      and the Answer   39

6.5. ILLUSTRATIVE PROBLEM SET-UP   43

VII. FUNCTION TABLE

7.0. GENERAL SUMMARY OF THE FUNCTION TABLE   1

7.1. PROGRAM CONTROLS   5

7.1.1. The Operation Switch   6

7.1.2. Argument Clear Switch   7

7.1.3. The Repeat Switch   8

7.2. COMMON PROGRAMMING CIRCUITS   8

7.3. NUMERICAL CIRCUITS   12

    7.3.1. Storage: Portable Function Table, Master
           PM Switches, Digit Delete and Constant
           Digit Switches, Subtract Pulse Switches   12

    7.3.2. Input to the Portable Function Table:
           Argument Counters and Table Input Gates   16

    7.3.3. Function Output   19

        7.3.3.1. Transmission of Information Stored
                on Portable Function Table Switches   19

        7.3.3.2. Transmission of Information Stored on
                Constant Digit Switches   21

        7.3.3.3. Role of the Subtract Pulse Switches   21

7.4. STORAGE OF PROGRAMMING DATA BY MEANS OF THE FUNCTION TABLE   21

7.5. ILLUSTRATIVE EXAMPLES OF THE USE OF THE FUNCTION TABLE IN
      INTERPOLATION   24

    7.5.1. Quadratic Lagrangian Interpolation   26
    7.5.2. Biquadratic Lagrangian Interpolation   30
    7.5.3. The Drag Function of the Exterior Ballistics
           Equations   34

      VIII. CONSTANT TRANSMITTER AND IBM READER

8.0. GENERAL SUMMARY OF THE READER AND CONSTANT TRANSMITTER   2

8.0.1. IBM Cards   2

8.0.2. The Card Reader   3

8.0.3. Card Reading   4

8.0.4. Storage of Card Data in the Constant Transmitter 6

8.0.5. Transmission of Data from the Constant Trans-
        mitter   7

8.1. PROGRAM CONTROLS OF THE IBM READER
                                                            9

8.1.1. Program Input and Output Circuits   10

8.1.2. Emergency Start Switch   11

8.1.3. Initial Start Switch   12

8.2. POLARITY SWITCH AND PLUG BOARD   15

8.3. PROGRAMMING CIRCUITS OF THE READER   21

8.3.1. Reset Control Circuits   21

8.3.2. Group Selection Circuits   23

8.3.3. Reset and Finish Signal Circuits   24

8.4. NUMERICAL CIRCUITS OF THE READER   26

8.5. PROGRAM CONTROLS AND PROGRAMMING CIRCUITS OF THE CONSTANT
      TRANSMITTER   26

8.6. NUMERICAL CIRCUITS OF THE CONSTANT TRANSMITTER   30

8.6.1. Storing Information from Cards in the
        Constant Transmitter   30

8.6.2. Transmitting Information from the Constant

    Transmitter   32

    8.6.2.1. Constants read from a card   32

    8.6.2.2. Constants set up on set switches   34

8.7. ILLUSTRATIVE PROBLEM   34

IX. PRINTER

9.0. GENERAL SUMMARY OF THE IBM PUNCH AND PRINTER   1

9.1. PROGRAMMING CIRCUITS OF THE PRINTER AND IBM PUNCH   5

9.2. IBM GANG PUNCH PLUG BOARD   8

9.3. NUMERICAL CIRCUITS OF THE PRINTER AND PUNCH   10

9.4. UNITS CONNECTED TO THE PRINTER   13

9.5. ILLUSTRATIVE PROBLEM SET-UP   16

X. MASTER PROGRAMMER

10.0. GENERAL SUMMARY   2

10.1. DECADE ASSOCIATOR SWITCHES   3

10.2. MASTER PROGRAMMER DECADES   4

    10.2.1. Decade Counter: Input and Carry-over Circuits   4

    10.2.2. Decade Switches and Decade Counter Clear Circuits   5

10.3. STEPPERS   6

10.3.1. Stepper Input and Output Circuits   6

10.3.2. Cycling a Stepper Counter   8

  10.3.2.1. Stepper Direct Input   8

  10.3.2.2. Stepper Cycling Gates   8

10.3.3. Clearing a Stepper Counter   9

  10.3.3.1. Stepper Clear Switch   9

  10.3.3.2. Stepper Clear Direct Input   10

10.4. PROGRAMMING THE MASTER PROGRAMMER   11

10.5. USES OF THE MASTER PROGRAMMER   11

  10.5.1. Link Program Control   11

    10.5.1.1. The Stimulation of Sequences   12

    10.5.1.2. Iteration of the Sequences of a Chain 12

    10.5.1.3. The Stimulation of Program Hierarchies 13

  10.5.2. Digit Program Control   13

  10.5.3. Accumulating Values of an Independent Variable 17

  10.5.4. Extending the Program Control Facilities of
           Other Units   18

10.6. ILLUSTRATIVE PROBLEM SET-UPS   20

  10.6.1. Problem 1   21

  10.6.2. Problem 2   23

    10.6.2.1. Sequences 1, 2, and 3.   26

    10.6.2.2. Clearing the Decades which Store
               the Independent Variable:-Sequence 4 28

    10.6.2.3. Sequence 5   30

    10.6.2.4. Tests on y and y'   30

XI. SYNCHRONIZING, DIGIT, AND PROGRAM TRANSMISSION SYSTEMS AND SPECIAL EQUIPMENT

11.1. SYNCHRONIZING TRUNK   2

11.2. DIGIT TRANSMISSION   2

      11.2.1. Digit Trunks   2

      11.2.2. Shifters, Deleters, and Adaptors   3

      11.2.3. Load Units for Digit Trunks   5

      11.2.4. Special Uses of Digit Trays Without Load Boxes   6

11.3. PROGRAM TRANSMISSION   7

      11.3.1. Program Lines   7

      11.3.2. Special Program Cables   8

      11.3.3. Load Units for Program Trays   8

      11.3.4. Special Program Lines Without Load Resistor   9

11.4. PULSE AMPLIFIER   9

11.5. SPECIAL INTERCONNECTION OF UNITS   10

      11.5.1. Connections to the Printer   10

      11.5.2. The High-Speed Multiplier and Its Associated
                  Accumulators   10

      11.5.3. The Divider and Square Rooter and Its
                  Associated Accumulators   11

      11.5.4. Interconnection of Accumulators   11

11.6. PORTABLE CONTROL BOX   11

TABLE OF FIGURES

		chapter	page
1-1	Schematic Diagram of Program Sequence for Generating n, n^2, n^3	I	8
3-1	Duration in μs.	III	4
4-1	Set-Up Diagram Symbols for Accumulators	IV	25
4-2	Set-Up Diagram for Generating n, n^2, n^3	IV	26
4-3	Use of Dummy Programs to Isolate Program Pulses	IV	28
4-4	Magnitude Discrimination Program	IV	29
5-1	Set-Up Diagram Conventions for High-Speed Multiplier	V	27
6-1	Set-Up Diagram Conventions for Divider and Square Rooter	VI	43
6-2 (a-g)	Set-Up Diagram for Computation of $x = \dfrac{\sqrt{a} + \sum_{i=1}^{3} x_i^3}{b} + cd$	VI	47
7-1	Use of Unmodified Function Table to Store Programming Information	VII	23
7-2	Set-Up Diagram Conventions for Function Table	VII	25
7-3 (a-e)	Quadratic Lagrangian Interpolation - Set-Up Diagram	VII	26
7-4	Storage of the G Function and Programming Instructions Regarding Use of the Tabulated Function	VII	35
8-1	Set-Up Diagram Conventions for Constant Transmitter	VIII	35
8-2	Master Programmer Links for Evaluation of N_k	VIII	38
8-3	Set-Up Diagram for Sequences 1 and 2.1	VIII	39
9-1 (a-c)	Set-Up Diagram for Sequence 5 - Evaluation of N_k (a-c)	IX	17
10-1	To stimulate Pi	X	16
10-2	Set-Up Diagram	X	16

		chapter	page
10-3	Use of Master Programmer to Delay a Program Pulse	X -	20
10-4	Master Programmer Set-Up Diagram Conventions	X -	21
10-5	Master Programmer Links - Problem 1	X -	21
10-6	Set-Up Diagram - Problem 1	X -	23
10-7	Subsequence of Sequence 2 - Problem 2	X -	25
10-8	Master Programmer Links - Problem 2	X -	26
10-9	Set-Up Diagram for Tests of $y'-c_1$ and $y'+c_1$.	X -	30
11-1	Digit Trays Connected by Pulse Amplifier	XI -	10
11-2	Bidirectional Communication in Pulse Amplifier Connected Trays	XI -	10
11-3	Isolation of Programs through the use of a Pulse Amplifier	XI -	10

TABLE OF TABLES

		chapter	page
1-1	Units of the ENIAC	I	4
2-1	Chronological Description of Initiating Sequence	II	9
2-2	Initial Clearing of the ENIAC	II	13
4-1	A and S Transmission	IV	13
4-2	Reception Involving Delayed Carry Over	IV	17
4-3	Set-Up Table for Generating n, n^2, n^3	IV	26
5-1	Correction Terms for Negative Ier and/or Icand	V	6
5-2	Multiplication of M 8 198 630 400 by P 2 800 000 000	V	8
5-3	Multiplication of M 8 198 630 400 by M 2 800 000 000	V	9
5-4	Chronological Operation of High Speed Multiplier's Programming Circuits	V	14
5-5	Partial Products Emmited by Multiplication Tables for Ier = 2	V	21
5-6	Selection of Products by Icand Selectors when Icand M 8 198 630 400 is multiplied by First Digit of Ier P 2 800 000 000	V	22
6-1	Extraction of Square Roots by Divider and Square Rooter- Period II	VI	5
6-2	Division - Illustrative Problem	VI	6
6-3	Square Rooting - Illustrative Problem	VI	6
6-4	Division - Initial Sequence - Period I	VI	30
6-5	Division - Period II - Basic Division Sequence and Shift Sequence	VI	30
6-6	Division - Period III - Round Off or No Round Off	VI	30

		chapter	page
6-7	Square Root - Period I	VI	- 30
6-8	Square Root - Period II - Basic Square Root Sequence and Shift Sequence	VI	- 30
6-9	Square Root - Period III - Round Off or No Round Off	VI	- 30
6-10	Division or Square Root - Period IV - Interlock or No Interlock	VI	- 30
6-11	Possible Placement of Radicand	VI	- 40
6-12	Incorrect Placement of Radicand	VI	- 40
6-13	Set-Up Table for Computation of	VI	- *

$$x = \frac{\sqrt{a} + \sum_{i=1}^{3} x_i^{3}}{b} + cd$$

7-1	Chronological Operation of the Function Table	VII	- 10
7-2	Function Output Terminal Leads and Associated Switches	VII	- 14
7-3	Illustrations of the Use of Switches on Panel 2 of the Function Table	VII	- 17
7-4	Quadratic Lagrangian Interpolation Set-Up Table	VII	- .*
7-5	Tabulation of Biquadratic Lagrangian Interpolation Coefficients on the Portable Function Table	VII	- 32
8-1	Reader Program Controls	VIII	- 10
8-2	Correspondence between Storage Relay Hubs and Points on Constant Selector Switches	VIII	- 16
8-3	Gates Controlled by Points on First Six Constant Selector Switches	VIII	- 28
8-4	Activation of Constant Transmitter Storage Relays	VIII	- 31
8-5	Use of Digit Output Leads for Constant Selector Switch Settings, L, R, or LR	VIII	- 32

		chapter	page
8-6	Simultaneous Stimulation of Two Constant Transmitter Program Controls	VIII -	33
8-7	Terms of N_k	VIII -	35
8-8	Computation to form the terms of N_k	VIII -	35
8-9	Storage of Constants	VIII -	37
8-10	Set- p Analysis for the Evaluation of the Numbers N_k	VIII -	37
8-11	Set-Up Table (for Sequence 1)	VIII -	38
8-12	Analysis of Multiplication Sequence	VIII -	40
8-13 (a-b)	Set-Up Table (for Sequence 2.1)	VIII -	*
8-14	Set-Up of Function Tables for Programming Transmission of Constants	VIII -	40
9-1	Chronological Operation of Punch	IX -	6
9-2	Operation of Numerical Circuits of Printer and Punch	IX -	12
9-3	Set-Up for Sequence 5 - Solution of Systems of Equations by Determinants	IX -	17
10-1	Properties of Master Programmer Input	X -	10
10-2	Set-Up for Stimulating Program Pi	X -	16
10-3	Set-Up Analysis - Problem 1	X -	22
10-4	Set-Up Analysis -Problem 2	X -	24
10-5	Set-Up Table for Tests of y and y'	X -	30

*In an envelope attached to the back cover.

PX DRAWINGS REFERRED TO IN

TECHNICAL DESCRIPTION OF ENIAC, PART I

Drawings bound with the text are given with a page reference. Those contained
in a separate folder are listed without a page reference. Drawings referred to,
but not included, in this report are marked with an asterisk. The last category
of drawings are a part of the complete file of drawings at the ENIAC location.

PX-1-302	I-2	PX-7-302	VII-1	PX-12-112	
1-303	II-2	7-303	VII-1	12-114*	
1-304*		7-304		12-301	IX-1
		7-305	VII-1	12-302	IX-1
PX-2-123*				12-303	IX-1
		PX-8-301	X-1	12-305	IX-8
PX-4-102	XI-1	8-302	X-1	12-305R1	IX-9
4-103*		8-303	X-1	12-305R2	IX-10
4-104a	XI-3	8-304		12-305R3	IX-17
4-104b-e*				12-306	IX-1
4-109	XI-5	PX-9-302	II-1	12-307	
4-111*		9-303	III-1		
4-114a-d*		9-304	III-1		
4-115*		9-305	II-1		
4-117*		9-306	I-3		
4-119		9-307			
4-301	XI-9				
		PX-10-301	VI-1		
PX-5-105*		10-302	VI-1		
5-109*		10-304			
5-110*		10-307	VI-34		
5-121*					
5-131*		PX-11-116			
5-134*		11-119			
5-135*		11-302	VIII-1		
5-136*		11-303	VIII-1		
5-137*		11-304	VIII-1		
5-301	IV-1	11-305	VIII-16		
5-304		11-305R1	VIII-19		
5-305	IV-1	11-305R2	VIII-20		
		11-305R3	VIII-20		
PX-6-302	V-1	11-305R4	VIII-21		
6-303	V-1	11-306	VIII-1		
6-304	V-1	11-307			
6-308		11-308	VIII-25		
6-309	V-1	11-309			
6-311	V-23				

I. INTRODUCTION

1.1. BRIEF DESCRIPTION OF THE ENIAC

1.1.1. What the ENIAC Does

The Electronic Numerical Integrator and Computer (ENIAC) is a high-speed electronic computing machine which operates on discrete variables. It is capable of performing the arithmetic operations of addition, subtraction, multiplication, division, and square rooting on numbers (with sign indication) expressed in decimal form. The ENIAC, furthermore, remembers numbers which it reads from punched cards, or which are stored on the switches of its so called function tables, or which are formed in the process of computation, and makes them available as needed. The ENIAC records its results on punched cards from which tables can be automatically printed. Finally, the ENIAC is automatically sequenced, i.e., once set-up (see Sections 1.1.4. and 1.4. and subsequent chapters) to follow a routine consisting of operations in its repertoire, it carries out the routine without further human intervention. When instructed in an appropriate routine consisting of arithmetic operations, looking up numbers stored in function tables, etc., the ENIAC can carry out complex mathematical operations such as interpolation and numerical integration and differentiation.

The speed of the ENIAC is at least 500 times as great as that of any other existing computing machine. The fundamental signals used in the ENIAC are emitted by its oscillator at the rate of 100,000 per second. The interval between successive signals, 10 micro-seconds, is designated by the term pulse time. The time unit in which the operation time for various parts of the ENIAC is reckoned is the addition time. An addition time is 20 pulse times or 200 micro-seconds (1/5000 th of a second). An addition time is so named because it is the time required to complete an addition. Other operations require an integral number of addition times (see Table 1-1).

1.1.2. The Units of the ENIAC

The ENIAC proper consists of 40 panels arranged in U shape, 3 portable function tables, a card reader, and a card punch (see PX-1-302). The term unit of the ENIAC is used to refer to one or more panels and associated devices (such as the portable function tables, for example) containing the equipment for carrying out certain specific related operations.

The units of the ENIAC can be classified functionally into 4 categories: arithmetic, memory, input and output, and governing. The arithmetic units include 20 accumulators (for addition and subtraction), 1 high-speed multiplier, and 1 combination divider and square rooter. There are two primary memory aspects in the ENIAC: memory for numbers and memory for programming instructions. The constant transmitter, 3 function tables, and the 20 accumulators provide numerical memory. The constant transmitter with its associated card reader reads from punched cards, numbers that are changed in the course of a computation and makes these numbers available to the computer as needed. Numbers that remain constant throughout a computation are stored on the switches of the constant transmitter or of the portable function tables and emitted when needed. The accumulators, not only function arithmetically, but also can be used to store numbers which are computed in one part of a computation and required in other parts. All units have program controls (see Sections 1.1.4. and 1.3.1.) which contribute to the programming memory in the following ways:

1) by recognizing the reception of a program input signal which
   stimulates the unit to perform

ONE ADDITION TIME (200μS)

CENTRAL PROG. PULSE (CPP)

10 P (10 μS PULSES)

9 P (9 μS PULSES)

1 P   —290   —345

2 P   —290   —345

2' P   —290   —345

4 P   —290   —345

1' P   —290   —345

                —290   —345V

~290

RESET PULSES (RP)   0

CARRY-CLEAR GATE (CCG)   +50   —345

MOORE SCHOOL OF ELECTRICAL ENGINEERING
UNIVERSITY OF PENNSYLVANIA

CYCLING UNIT
PULSES & GATES
PX-9-306

2) by causing the programming circuits (see Section 1.3.) to operate (as specified by the setting of program switches when there are options regarding the operation to be performed)

and 3) on the completion of the operation, by emitting a program output signal which, by means of program cable connections to program lines (see Section 1.1.4.) is brought to other units to cause them to operate. The program cable connections and switch settings are established before the computation begins.

The kind of programming described in points 1, 2, and 3 above is described as local programming memory because it is taken care of locally at each unit for that unit. The master programmer provides a certain amount of centralized programming memory by coordinating the local programming of the other units.

The input devices for the ENIAC consist of the card reader and the constant transmitter mentioned above in connection with numerical memory. The printer and card punch record computed results.

The governing units of the ENIAC are the initiating unit and the cycling unit. The initiating unit has controls for turning the power on and off, starting a computation, initial clearing, and other special functions. The cycling unit converts 100 kc sine waves emitted by its oscillator into a fundamental train of signals repeated every addition time (i.e. repeated 5000 times per second). These signals include various sequences of pulses and a gate. The term pulse is used to refer to a voltage change (either positive or negative) from some reference level and the restoration to the reference level which takes place in a short time, between 2 and 5 micro-seconds. The term gate also refers to a voltage change and the restoration to the reference level but differs from a pulse in duration. In the ENIAC a gate lasts for at least 10 micro-seconds.

TABLE 1-1
UNITS OF THE ENIAC

UNIT	TOTAL NO.	OPERATIONS	OPERATION TIME (1 addition time = 1/5000 of a second)
Accumulator	20	1. Stores a 10 digit signed number. 2. Receives a number and adds it to its contents. 3. Transmits its contents and/or the negative.	1. Continues to do so until instructed to clear. 2. } r addition times. 3. }
High Speed Multiplier	1	Multiplies a signed multiplicand having as many as 10 digits by a signed multiplier of p digits (where $2 \leq p \leq 10$).	$p + 4$ addition times.
Divider and Square Rooter	1	Finds a p (where p = 4, 7, 8, 9, 10) digit quotient or square root for arguments with up to 10 digits.	Approximately 13 p addition times (also see p. VI (31)).
Function Table (including an associated portable function table)	3	1. Each function table stores by means of switch settings a total of 1248 variable digits and 208 signs in such a way that 12 digits and 2 signs are associated with an argument between -2 and 101. In addition, 8 digits constant throughout the range of the argument can be remembered. 2. Function table selects and transmits the functional value (12 variable digits, 2 signs, and 8 constant digits) or the negative of the functional value associated with a particular value of the argument. The transmission may be done r times ($1 \leq r \leq 9$) in succession.	 2. $4 + r$ addition times for looking up the functional value and transmitting it r times.
Constant Transmitter and Reader	1	1. Constant transmitter stores 80 digits and 16 signs which the reader reads from punched cards and stores 20 digits and 4 signs set up manually on its switches. 2. Constant transmitter emits a signed 5 or 10 digit number.	1. The reader scans a card and causes 80 digits and 16 signs punched on the card to be stored in the constant transmitter in approximately 1/2 second. 2. 1 addition time.
Printer and Punch	1	The printer receives information for 80 digits and 16 signs from accumulators and the master programmer and causes this information to be punched on cards from which it can be printed.	80 digits and 16 signs are punched on a card in approximately 0.6 second.
Master Programmer	1	Coordinates the local programming of the other ENIAC units.	1 addition time.
Cycling Unit	1	Emits the fundamental train of pulses and the gate upon which other ENIAC units operate and which, thus, keeps them in synchronism with one another.	In each addition time (also see Chapter III).
Initiating Unit	1	Has controls for turning power on and off, starting the ENIAC, clearing the ENIAC, and other special functions.	

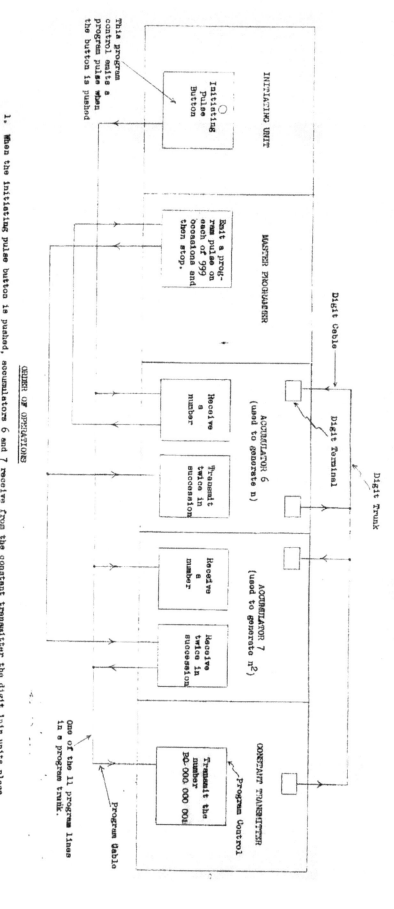

ORDER OF OPERATIONS

1. When the initiating pulse button is pushed, accumulators 6 and 7 receive from the constant transmitter the digit 1 in units place.

2. The master programmer determines whether to continue or to terminate the computation.

3. Accumulator 6 transmits its contents twice and accumulator 7 receives twice so that when this operation is completed, accumulator 6 holds the No. 1 and accumulator 7 holds the No. 3.

4. Accumulators 6 and 7 each receive 1 unit from the constant transmitter so that, as a result of this operation, accumulator 6 holds the No. 2 and accumulator 7 holds the No. 4.

5., 6., 7., Repeat items 2., 3., 4., respectively, etc.

SCHEMATIC DIAGRAM OF PROGRAM SEQUENCE FOR GENERATING n, n^2, for $1 \leq n \leq 1000$

Figure 1-1

The nomenclature for and the temporal order of the cycling unit pulses and gate are shown on PX-9-306.

Table 1-1 lists the units of the ENIAC, their operations, and operation times.

1.1.3. Representation of Digits by Pulses

With a few exceptions digits are communicated from one unit of the ENIAC to another in pulse form. Digit trays stacked above the front panels running from accumulator 1 to the second panel of the constant transmitter are used for this transmission. A digit tray has 11 wires and a ground. Each of ten wires carries the pulses for one place of a 10 place decimal number. To represent the digit n (where $0 \leqslant n \leqslant 9$) in a particular decimal place, n pulses are transmitted over the wire associated with that particular decimal place. The 11th wire is used for the transmission of sign information. No pulses are transmitted for sign plus and 9 pulses for sign minus (see the discussion of complements below). Pulses are transmitted over all 11 conductors simultaneously.

Each digit tray is 8 feet long and runs past 4 panels of the ENIAC. A 12 point terminal at each end of a tray makes it possible to connect a number of trays serially by means of jumper cables so as to form a digit trunk passing as many units of the ENIAC as desired. Spaced at two foot intervals on the digit trays are additional 12 point terminals. Units which are to communicate with one another in the course of a computation have their digit input and/or output terminals connected by means of digit cables to these 12 point terminals on a digit trunk. A resistance load box is plugged into an unused terminal on either the first or last tray of a digit trunk. This makes it possible to connect varying numbers of units in parallel into a digit trunk. At any given time, only one 10 digit number with its sign may be transferred over a particular digit trunk. More than 1 unit may listen to this number. Through the use of more than one digit trunk, several different numbers may be transferred simultaneously. (also Section 1.1.5.).

The units of the ENIAC transmit numerical information by emitting appropriate numbers of the 9 pulses or of the 1, 2, 2' and 4 pulses and the 1' pulse (see PX-9-306) which they receive from the cycling unit. Addition is performed in accumulators by means of 10 decade counters (see Section 1.2.2.), one counter for each decimal place of a 10 digit number, and a binary counter for sign plus (P) or minus (M). These counters are advanced one step by each pulse received. The decade counters and PM counter of an accumulator are so interconnected that provision is made for carry over. Subtraction is performed by adding the negative of the subtrahend to the minuend.

In order to avoid the necessity for cycling counters backwards, the negative of a number is represented as a complement with respect to a power of ten. Let us consider the decimal point to be located at the extreme right of an accumulator. Then the complement with respect to 10^{10} of the positive number stored in an accumulator as $P + \sum_{i=0}^{9} a_i \cdot 10^i$ is formed by transmitting 9 pulses for sign M and by transmitting the digit pulses for $10^{10} - \sum_{i=0}^{9} a_i \cdot 10^i$. Similarly, the complement with respect to 10^{10} of the negative number stored as $M + \sum_{i=0}^{9} b_i \cdot 10^i$ is formed by transmitting no pulses for sign P and by transmitting the digit pulses for $10^{10} - \sum_{i=0}^{9} b_i \cdot 10^i$. For example, the complement with respect to 10^{10} of PO 000 023 407 is M9 999 976 593; the 10^{10} complement of M9 307 504 000 is PO 692 495 000. As will be shown in the chapter dealing with the accumulator (Chapter IV), the mechanics of transmitting the digit pulses for a complement with respect to 10^{10} actually consist of transmitting first the pulses for $\sum_{i=0}^{9} (9-a_i) \cdot 10^i$ and then of transmitting one more pulse in the 10^0 decade place. The terms $9-a_i$ are called nines complements.

If desired, operations may be performed on n digits where n $\leqq$ 10. Here, we consider the significant figures to be located as far to the left as possible in the accumulator with the decimal point to the immediate right of the last significant figure at the right. Then, the digits for a complement with respect to 10^n are formed by emitting nines complements in all decade places and then by emitting an additional pulse in the nth decade place from the left.

Because the counters in an accumulator are so connected that there is carry over not only from each decade counter to the one on its left but also from the 10th decade counter to the binary counter for sign, the usual arithmetic properties obtain when complements are used in addition and subtraction. In this connection, it should be noted that even though, in the above discussion, we implied that sign P indicates a positive number and sign M a negative number, these signs may have another meaning. For example, if an accumulator holds P9 999 999 999, the carry-over to the PM counter which results when a positive number not in excess of 10^{10} is added to this number, causes the accumulator to register sign M. Here the M indicates that the sum is off scale.

1.1.4. _Programming by Means of Pulses, Switches and Cables_

Before a computation can be performed on the ENIAC, not only must the digit input and output terminals of the units be connected into digit trunks for the communication of numerical data, but also the units must be set up so as to recognize when they are to operate and which particular operations are to be performed. Program controls and program trays and cables are used to instruct the ENIAC in the programming requirements for a particular computation.

Each unit of the ENIAC has one or more program controls. These
controls are either of the repeat or non-repeat type. Non-repeat program
controls have an input terminal for a program signal and a receiver(see below
and Section 1.2.4.). Repeat controls have both an input and an output terminal
for a program signal and a transceiver (see below and Section 1.2.4.) or some
logically equivalent device. Each program control on a unit which is capable
of more than one operation or which is capable of performing operations in a
variety of ways has a set of program switches.

Receivers and transceivers alike have the following properties:
1) they have two stable states which will be referred to as the normal and
abnormal states; 2) when a program input signal is received, they are set into
the abnormal state; 3) they are so connected (through the program switches,
if any) to the programming circuits (see Section 1.3.) that, in the abnormal
state, they cause the programming circuits to function appropriately; and 4)
when the required routine has been completed, they are reset to the normal state
so that activity in the unit ceases. When the set of instructions either set up
on the program switches of a repeat control or built into the programming circuits
have been completed, moreover, the transceiver of a repeat program control causes
a central programming pulse (CPP on PX-9-306) to be emitted as a program output
pulse from the program control's output terminal.

The program trays, like the digit trays are 8 feet long, contain 11
wires and a ground, and have 12 point terminals at each end, so that as many
trays as desired can be jumper connected to form a program trunk. As in the case
of digit trunks, too, a resistance load is plugged into an unused terminal at
one end of a program trunk. Each of the 11 lines running the length of a program
trunk is referred to as a program line. The program trays differ from the digit

trays only in that at two foot intervals the program trays have a set of 11
two point program terminals (1 wire and a shield) instead of a 12 point digit
terminal. Input and output terminals of program controls are connected to the
program lines by means of program cables.

The procedure for instructing the ENIAC in its routine, then, consists
of setting program switches on the units so that, when stimulated by a program
input pulse, the program controls will cause the units to carry out a set of
specific operations. The temporal order in which the operations are to follow
one another is determined by the manner in which program pulse input and output
terminals are connected to program lines. All program controls whose program
pulse input terminals are connected into the same program line start to operate
simultaneously when that program line carries a program signal. If one of the
program controls thus stimulated is a repeat program control and if its program
pulse output terminal is connected to a second program line all program controls
whose program input terminals are connected to this second program line start to
operate when the routine set up on the repeat program control has been completed.

The schematic diagram of Figure 1-1 illustrates the method of setting
up an extremely simple computation. Each rectangle within the square that
symbolizes a unit of the ENIAC represents a program control with program pulse
input terminal and output terminal and possibly program switches. The instructions
set up on the program switches of a program control are described inside the box
representing the program control.

1.1.5. Synchronized System

All units of the ENIAC operate in synchronism with one another, i.e.,
all units that start to operate at the same time complete their operations either
at the same instant or at times that differ by an integral number of addition

times. The phrase "complete an operation" covers not only finishing the numerical processes involved in the operation but also the emission of a program output signal.

The basis of this synchronization is the fundamental train of pulses and a gate emitted by the cycling unit and delivered to all units of the ENIAC by means of a set of jumper connected trays called the synchronizing trunk. These trays are physically the same as the digit trays. The central programming pulse (CPP) emitted by the cycling unit in pulse time 17 of every addition time cycle plays a major role in such synchronization since the program output pulse which a repeat program control emits upon the completion of a program results from allowing a CPP to pass. The units of the ENIAC, moreover, have been so designed that in order to complete their operations they require the pulses and gate of either one addition time cycle or of an integral number of addition time cycles.

Even though the electromechanical devices used with the ENIAC, the reader and the card punch, do not take an absolutely definite number of addition time cycles to complete their operations, these units have been integrated into the synchronized system since they have been provided with program controls which emit a CPP as a program output pulse. Units of the ENIAC can even operate in parallel with the card reader since t h e reader does not emit a program output pulse signifying the completion of reading until it has received as an interlock pulse a program output pulse from some other unit of the ENIAC to indicate that the sequence carried on in parallel with reading has been completed.

In this report, incidentally, we will follow the convention that an addition time has its origin 3 pulse times after the CPP as shown on PX-9-306. This means that we will talk about a program's being stimulated at the end of addition time i and being carried out in addition time i + l by means of the cycling unit pulses and gate emitted during addition time i + l.

Because the units of the ENIAC operate in synchronism with one another and because multiple digit and program trunks have been provided, the operator can schedule parallel operations when planning the set-up of a problem. For example, the multiplier can be operating while several accumulators are performing additions and subtractions and while the divider is finding a quotient. Naturally, the scheduling of parallel operations requires that the operator plan for the use of separate digit trunks for the various operations and, in some cases, requires that attention be given to the number of addition times needed for the operations.

1.2. ELECTRONIC ELEMENTS

The circuits of the ENIAC are designed around a relatively small number of basic electronic elements. The following discussion, while wholly inadequate to convey any real knowledge of vacuum tubes or their action, is intended to enable the reader to obtain a formal acquaintance with some of the phenomena and terminology connected with the ENIAC.

The simplest tube used is the triode, so called because it has 3 characteristic elements, namely the cathode (surface which gives off electrons), the plate or anode (surface which receives electrons), and the grid (which controls the current passing through the tube). In addition, there is a heater to bring the cathode to the temperature required for it to emit electrons. Sometimes, 2 triodes are housed in one envelope. We shall refer to these as two tubes. Other tubes used in the ENIAC are multigrid tubes, for example, the pentode which has 3 grids.

To say that a tube is "on" or conducting means that with the usual convention of sign, current is flowing from the plate to the cathode. This implies that the plate is at a slightly higher voltage than the cathode, but that this voltage drop is trifling compared to the drop when the tube is "off" or non-conducting. Thus, if a tube is turned "off", i.e. changes from conducting to non-conducting, the voltage of the plate is raised and that of the cathode is lowered. Hence the plate emits a positive signal and the cathode one that is negative. If the tube is turned on these signs are reversed. Within appropriate limits, a tube is conducting if its grid (or grids) is (or are) kept above a certain voltage, non-conducting if below that voltage. Thus a tube is turned on by applying a positive signal to its grid (or grids), turned off by a negative signal.

In all cases, vacuum tubes in the ENIAC circuits are used only as on-off devices instead of as amplitude sensitive devices, i.e., the presence or absence of a signal depends on whether a tube is conducting or not-conducting and not on any measured magnitude of current and voltage. Furthermore, the machine has been so designed that signals are not constantly being degenerated but instead are regenerated from time to time out of the fundamental train of pulses and a gate emitted by the cycling unit.

1.2.1. Single Tube Elements

1.2.1.1. Buffers and Cathode Followers

Buffers and cathode followers are normally non-conducting tubes with a single input and a single output. When a positive signal is applied to the grid of a buffer, the output, taken off the plate side, is negative. In the cathode follower, where the output is taken off the cathode, the application of a positive signal to the grid results in the emission of a positive signal.

When the outputs of a number of buffers or cathode followers are connected together to a common load resistor, the resulting circuit provides for the logical "or" since when any one of the buffers or cathode followers receives a positive signal, the circuit emits a negative or positive signal respectively.

1.2.1.2. Inverters

An inverter is a tube whose grid is normally at a positive potential so that the tube is conducting. When a negative signal, applied to the grid, drives the tube to cut off, the output taken off the plate, is a positive signal. A positive signal is necessary to operate a gate tube as will be described in Section 1.2.1.3.

1.2.1.3. Gate tubes

A gate tube is a multiple grid tube with two inputs and an output normally taken off the plate. A gate tube emits a negative signal when both of its input grids are brought from a negative cut off voltage to a positive voltage. Thus, a gate tube is used to note the coincidence of two positive signals and hence corresponds to the logical "and".

A positive signal applied to one grid of a gate tube is said to "open the gate", since when this happens a positive signal reaching the other grid makes the tube conduct and hence emit a signal. The term "gate" is used in two senses: In one it means a gate tube (as described above) and in the other, the signal, lasting 10 μs or longer, which is used to open a gate tube (see Section 1.1.2.).

1.2.2. Multi-Tube Elements

1.2.2.1. Flip-Flops

The basic electronic memory device of the ENIAC is the flip-flop. A flip-flop consists essentially of a pair of triodes so connected that at any given time only one of the pair can be conducting. When a certain one of the tubes is conducting (and the other is not), the flip-flop is said to be in the normal state; when the other tube is conducting (and the first is not), the flip-flop is in the abnormal state. A flip-flop has two inputs and two outputs. A pulse received on one input (the set input), throws the flip-flop into the abnormal state in which state it remains until restored to the normal state by a pulse received at its second (or reset) input. When the flip-flop is in the normal state, one output is positive and the other negative. In the abnormal state, the polarity of its outputs is reversed.

Corresponding to each flip-flop in the ENIAC, there is a neon lamp. The neon lamp is so connected to its corresponding flip-flop that, with the exception of some neons in the divider and square rooter, the neon is lit when the flip-flop is in the abnormal state. Drawing PX-10-302 indicates when the neons in the divider and square rooter are lit.

These neons provide one of the most important visual checks on the operation of the ENIAC. In addition to the continuous mode of operation at the 100 kc rate, the ENIAC has 2 special modes of operation, 1 addition time and 1 pulse time operation, which permit the operator without disturbing the flip-flop memory, to stop the ENIAC at some point to examine the neons and, thus, to determine whether or not the proper sequence of events is taking place.

1.2.2.2. Counters

The counters of the ENIAC, in general, consist of a number of flip-flops arranged in sequence and interconnected so that the following characteristics result:

1) At any given time, only one flip-flop can be in the abnormal state and all others must be in the normal state.

2) The reception of a pulse at the input to the counter causes the flip-flop which is in the abnormal state to be reset and causes its successor to be set.

3) The counter can be cleared so that a specific stage comes up in the abnormal state and all others in the normal state.

Each flip-flop of a counter is called a stage and the reception of a pulse at a counter is said to advance the counter to the next stage. All counters in the ENIAC are ring counters, i.e., the first and last stages are so connected that if the counter is in its last stage and a pulse is received, the last stage is reset and the first stage is flipped into the abnormal state.

In accumulators, a 10 stage (decade) ring counter is used for each place of a 10 place number. Each stage of a decade counter corresponds to one of the digits between 0 and 9 inclusive.

The sign of a number is handled by means of a PM counter which differs somewhat from the other ENIAC counters. The PM counter has 2 tubes, one for sign P and for sign M. Each tube, here, is called a stage. The two tubes are so connected that only one of them can be conducting at a given time. Each pulse received cycles the PM counter 1 stage. Notice, that while the PM counter uses 2 tubes as does a flip-flop, it differs from an ordinary flip-flop in that it has but one input. The PM counter is also a ring counter.

Since each stage of a counter (other than the PM counter) is a flip-flop, one or both of its outputs are available for controlling other circuits. In the decade counters mentioned above, for example, one set of such outputs (which are referred to as the static outputs) can be used to deliver to the counter information about the number stored in a given accumulator. Ring counters are also used in the programming circuits of most ENIAC units. Here the outputs of the various stages are taken to gates.

1.2.2.3. Standard Transmitters

To meet the power needs resulting from the large capacitance associated with the interconnection circuits (digit trays, program trays, digit cables, etc.) and the high speed with which pulses are transmitted in the ENIAC, and also to provide positive output pulses (since positive pulses are required to operate gate tubes in the receiving units), the pulse outputs of all units (except the digit pulse output of the high-speed multiplier and the divider and square rooter) are passed through standard transmitters. A transmitter consists essentially of an inverter tube whose output is fed to the grids of 2 amplifying tubes which have their plates connected in parallel. The cathodes of the amplifier tubes are connected in parallel to ground through a resistor and the output of the transmitter is taken off between cathode and ground. As previously mentioned, varying numbers of output transmitters can be connected to the same program line or digit trunk since a load resistor is not built into each transmitter but is instead plugged into the trunk line.

The answer output circuits of the high-speed multiplier and of the divider and square rooter consist of inverter tubes with built-in load resistance. Therefore, the answer output terminals on these units are connected directly to the appropriate digit input terminals through a cable without resistance load or through a digit tray with no load box plugged into it. No other units may be connected in parallel into such a digit tray.

1.2.2.4. Receivers and Transceivers

Receivers and transceivers are used in the ENIAC to note the reception of a program pulse and to activate the programming circuits when a program pulse is received. As mentioned earlier, receivers are found in non-repeat program controls and transceivers in repeat program controls. In the divider and square rooter and in the high speed multiplier, however, there are a few examples of receivers which are not parts of program controls. Also, the reader, printer, and initiating pulse program controls are exceptional repeat program controls in that they do not contain transceivers.

To describe and illustrate the use of receivers and transceivers we shall refer to the program controls of an accumulator in which these devices are used in typical fashion (see drawing PX-5-304).

The receiver consists of an input buffer (66), a flip-flop (64, 65), an inverter (the left hand tube numbered 62), a cathode follower (63), a buffer (62), and a reset gate (61). An input pulse received at the program pulse input terminal associated with a receiver, passes through buffer 66 and sets the flip-flop of the receiver. The normally positive output of the flip-flop passes through the inverter and cathode follower and then through a program switch which routes it to a set of gates. Similarly, the normally negative output of the flip-flop, through buffer 62, is routed through program switches to another set of gates. Notice that before the reception of a program pulse, the outputs of the receiver are such that the gates remain closed; when the receiver is set, its output signals open the gates to which they are delivered and cause the unit to carry out the routine specified on the associated program switches. The CPP, which occurs 20 pulse times after the program input pulse which sets the receiver, passes through gate 61 (held open by the normally negative output of the flip-flop through buffer 62) and resets the receiver. Thus, a receiver is always reset one addition time after it has been set. Notice that the same receiver must not be stimulated on successive addition times since one addition time after a receiver is set it attempts to reset itself.

A transceiver, like a receiver, has an input buffer (69), a flip-flop

(66, 67), an inverter (65), cathode follower (64), and a reset gate (68). The transceiver, however, has several additional buffers (61), and (63), an extra gate (62) and inverter (65) and a standard transmitter (70, 71, 72). The transceiver elements which resemble receiver elements function in precisely the same fashion. The resetting of a transceiver, however, differs from that of a receiver. Transceivers usually operate in conjunction with a program ring counter or, as in the accumulator case, with a repeater ring counter. In the illustrative example being discussed here, one output of the transceiver is taken to gate K50. When the transceiver is set, gate H50 is open so that a CPP is allowed to pass through and cycle the repeater ring (64-72) each addition time that the transceiver remains in the abnormal state. Each point on the repeat switch (used to specify the number of times in succession that an operation is to be repeated) of an accumulator repeat program control is connected to one stage of this ring. When the repeater ring reaches the stage specified on the repeat switch, gate 62 receives a positive signal from that stage of the ring. The coincidence of a signal from the repeater ring and from the normally negative output of the flip-flop causes gate 62 to emit a signal which is inverted into a positive signal by inverter 65. The output of tube 65, through the buffers 63, goes on to stimulate certain clearing actions in the accumulator, and delivered to gate 68, allows the next CPP to pass through this gate. The output of gate 68 not only resets the transceiver but also passes through the standard transmitter (70, 71, 72) to be emitted from the program pulse output terminal of the program control. Notice that a transceiver remains set throughout the number of addition times required to complete the program specified on its associated switches, is reset at the end of the addition time in which the program is completed and emits a program output pulse when it is reset. At least one addition time should intervene between the transmission of a program output pulse and the next stimulation of a repeat program control in order to allow the control's transceiver to reset itself.

1.2.2.5. Plug-In Units

Wherever possible the design of elements of the ENIAC has been standardized and these elements have been used repeatedly in various units. Furthermore, to increase the ease of testing and replacing faulty components, many of these standardized elements have been designed as plug-in units.

The receivers and transceivers are of this nature. Each receiver plug-in unit has two receivers. A transceiver plug-in unit has just one transceiver. Another type of plug-in unit is the accumulator decade plug-in unit which consists of a decade ring counter, a pulse standardizer for shaping pulse input to the decade, carry over circuits, output transmitters, etc. In all, there are a total of 20 different types of plug-in units. These are enumerated on PX-2-123 where references are also made to detailed drawings of the plug-in units.

1.3. CLASSIFICATION OF ENIAC CIRCUITS: Numerical and Programming

The circuits of most ENIAC units can be conveniently described according to 2 classifications, numerical and programming. The numerical circuits are those which operate on the pulses or static signals which represent digits or sign. For example, in an accumulator the decade and PM counters or in the printer the tubes which are set up by the static outputs of counters whose information is to be punched on a card are classified as numerical circuits. The programming circuits are concerned with the following activities:

1) Recognizing when and how a unit is to function.

2) Stimulating the numerical circuits to operate appropriately.

3) Emitting a program output pulse to signify completion of a program.

In the case of certain units a further subdivision of the programming classification into program controls (see Section 1.1.4.) and common programming circuits
is desirable. The program controls, then, are charged with activities 1 and 3
above and the common programming circuits with activity 2.

1.3.1. Program Controls

The accumulator, high speed multiplier, divider and square rooter, and
function table have multiple sets of program controls. These program controls
include not only a receiver or transceiver, program pulse input terminal and
possibly program pulse output terminal but also program switches for describing
the procedure to be followed when the program control is stimulated. In each of
these units, any one of the program controls, when stimulated by the reception of
a program input pulse, can activate the common programming circuits. The buffers
and cathode followers in the receivers and transceivers of these program controls
serve to isolate one program control from the others. In the constant transmitter,
which has a total of 30 program controls each consisting of a transceiver, program
pulse input and output terminals, and a program switch, each group of six program
controls operates a set of programming circuits in common. In the remaining ENIAC
units the program controls and programming circuits are closely integrated with
one another.

If a unit has more than one program control, in general, only one
control should be operating at any given time so that inconsistent demands are
not made on the common programming circuits or the numerical circuits of the unit.

1.3.2. Common Programming Circuits

In the previous section it was pointed out that the stimulation of a
program control of a unit results in activating the unit's common programming
circuits. It should be pointed out that in a few cases the common programming

circuits of a unit can be entered without going through a program control.
For example, several accumulators are used in conjunction with the high speed
multiplier. These accumulators receive components of the product as they are
emitted from the multiplier. Ordinarily, to stimulate reception of a number,
a program input pulse must be delivered to an accumulator program control having
its program switch set to a receive setting. Then, the output of the receiver
or transceiver of the program control activates the programming circuits so that
reception takes place. The multiplier, however, has been designed so that it
contains receivers which are set when the associated product accumulators should
receive components of the product. These receivers in the multiplier are directly
connected to the common programming circuits of the associated accumulators so
that reception is stimulated when the multiplier's receivers are set even though
no program controls on the accumulators are stimulated. Several such examples
of direct entry into the common programming circuits of accumulators are to be
found in the chapters dealing with the high speed multipler and the divider and
square rooter.

1.4. PROGRAMMING THE ENIAC

In this portion of the Technical Manual for the ENIAC, Part I, much
emphasis will be given to the planning of computations to be performed.

1.4.1. Preparatory Formulation of the Problem

Starting with the mathematical equations which describe a problem,
such as the total or partial differential equations for example, the operator
must first break the equations down into a form involving the arithmetic operations
of which the ENIAC is capable. Another necessary preliminary step consists of
planning for the storage of numerical data. The initial conditions and other

constants basic to the computation will be given to the ENIAC by means of punched cards and the setting of switches on the constant transmitter. Arbitrary functions and other constants can be stored in the function tables. Numbers formed in the course of a computation and required in subsequent parts of a computation can be stored in accumulators. Should the quantity of numbers to be stored for further computation exceed the accumulator storage capacity, such numbers can be punched on cards by the printer unit and later can be inserted into the ENIAC again by means of the card reader and constant transmitter.

1.4.2. Planning the Programs and Program Sequences

For each arithmetic operation in the computation, one or more of the ENIAC's program controls will have to be set-up by the connection of program cables and possibly the setting of program switches. For example, if the numbers a and b are each stored in an accumulator and if a+b is to be formed in the accumulator containing b, then the accumulator which stores a, must be instructed to transmit and the one storing b, must be instructed to receive the transmitted number.

The instructions given to a single program control are referred to as a program. It is possible for a number of programs to be carried out in different units simultaneously. In general, however, only one program at a time can be performed in a given unit.

A unit carries out the program set up on one of its program controls when a pulse is delivered to the program control's program pulse input terminal, i.e., when the program control is stimulated. If a number of programs are to be performed in parallel, all of the program controls involved must be stimulated either by a pulse carried on the same program line or by pulses from different program lines which are activated at the same time.

The operator ties individual programs together into a program sequence in which one collection of programs is automatically stimulated upon the completion of another collection of programs by delivering the program output pulse of the program control used for a program of the first collection to a given program line and by picking up the stimulating pulse for all programs of the second collection from that same program line (see Section 1.1.4.)

1.4.3. Programming on Higher Levels

Certain program sequences of a computation may have to be iterated a number of times. The iteration of a program sequence into a program chain is accomplished through the use of the master programmer. This unit can also link together a number of chains or chains and sequences into a new program sequence which itself is to be iterated into a chain, etc.

The master programmer has a number of program controls each of which has a single input for program pulses and multiple program pulse output terminals. Each time a program input pulse is received, a pulse is emitted from one of the output terminals. The circuits of each control cause a pulse to be emitted from a given terminal a certain number of times which may be specified by the setting of a switch or in some other way and then to be emitted from another output terminal. Thus, the iteration of a program sequence into a chain can be accomplished by delivering the final program pulse of the sequence to a master programmer control and by picking up the initial pulse for the sequence from the program line to which the appropriate master programmer output terminal is connected. Another sequence or chain is linked to the first chain by picking up its initial pulse from the program line to which a second output terminal of the master programmer is connected, etc.

1.4.4. Special Linking of Program Sequences by Magnitude Discrimination

Not only can programs be linked together sequentially as described above in Sections 1.4.2, and 1.4.3 but, in addition, the ENIAC can be instructed to choose one of several program sequences depending on the magnitude of some number. This type of programming is referred to as magnitude discrimination.

In one form of magnitude discrimination, two numbers, a and b, are compared. If a $\geqq$ b, one program sequence is followed and in the opposite case, a second program sequence is stimulated. It is also possible to carry out more extensive magnitude discrimination programs in which the choice of program depends on a particular digit in some decimal place of a number.

Magnitude discrimination is accomplished by means of an accumulator and the master programmer. In such programs which will be discussed in greater detail in chapters IV and X, sign or digit pulses are used to stimulate program controls.

1.5. EQUIPMENT ASSOCIATED WITH THE ENIAC

In addition to the 40 panels, the portable function tables, the card reader and card punch which constitute the ENIAC proper, the ENIAC has certain associated ventilating, power, and testing equipment.

1.5.1. Ventilating Equipment

The ENIAC's 18,000 vacuum tubes generate a considerable amount of heat. An elaborate system of fans and blowers is used to drive off this heat. Each panel, moreover, has a thermostat which prevents the temperature inside the panel from exceeding 115°F by turning off the power to the ENIAC if this limit is exceeded. The ventilating system uses 240 V, three phase unregulated power.

1.5.2. Power Equipment

In addition to the a-c power for the heaters of its tubes and for the card reader and card punch, the ENIAC requires 78 different d-c voltages. These requirements are met in the following way:

Two hundred forty volt, three phase, regulated a-c is taken to power and auto-transformers which convert it into 110 V, 3 phase a-c. This power is carried on 3 buses in a power trough located along the front and bottom of the ENIAC panels. From this trough, the heaters and also the outlets below constant transmitter panel 3 and printer panel 2 are supplied with a-c power as long as the ENIAC's a-c power is turned on. The outlets below the other ENIAC panels are always alive.

The 240 V, 3 phase, regulated a-c is also taken to gas rectifier tubes in the ENIAC's 29 power supplies. The filaments of these tubes use 240 V, 3 phase, a-c. Through the use of bleeders the 78 d-c voltages are obtained. These voltages are carried to the ENIAC units by means of the d-c cables in the power trough mentioned above.

The power equipment is housed in 7 panels apart from the ENIAC and electrolytic condensers for filtering the d-c from the rectifier circuits are located in three condenser cabinets.

Only the control circuits for the power supplies are discussed at any length in this report (see Chapter II). The ENIAC MAINTENANCE MANUAL can be consulted for further details.

1.5.3. Special Test Equipment

A number of special testing devices are used with the ENIAC. These include a tube tester, a hi-pot test unit, a static tester, and a test table with its own power supplies, synchronizing unit, variable oscillator, and oscilloscope.

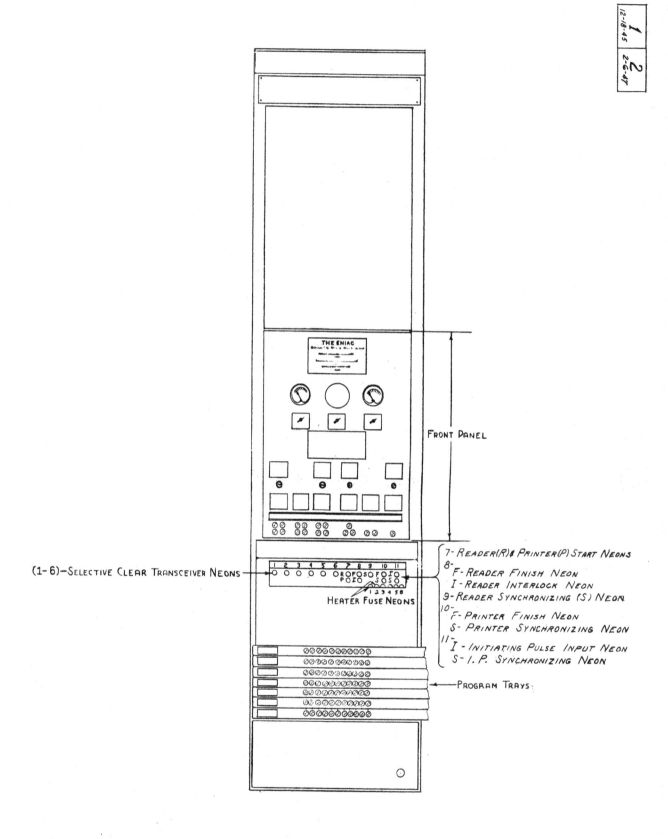

12-18-45
2-6-47
1
2

THE ENIAC

FRONT PANEL

(1-6)—SELECTIVE CLEAR TRANSCEIVER NEONS

1 2 3 4 5 6 7 8 9 10 11

HEATER FUSE NEONS
1 2 3 4 5 6

7- READER(R) & PRINTER(P) START NEONS
8-
  F- READER FINISH NEON
  I - READER INTERLOCK NEON
9- READER SYNCHRONIZING (S) NEON
10-
  F- PRINTER FINISH NEON
  S- PRINTER SYNCHRONIZING NEON
11-
  I - INITIATING PULSE INPUT NEON
  S- I. P. SYNCHRONIZING NEON

PROGRAM TRAYS

MOORE SCHOOL OF ELECTRICAL ENGINEERING
UNIVERSITY OF PENNSYLVANIA

INITIATING
UNIT
FRONT VIEW
PX-9-305

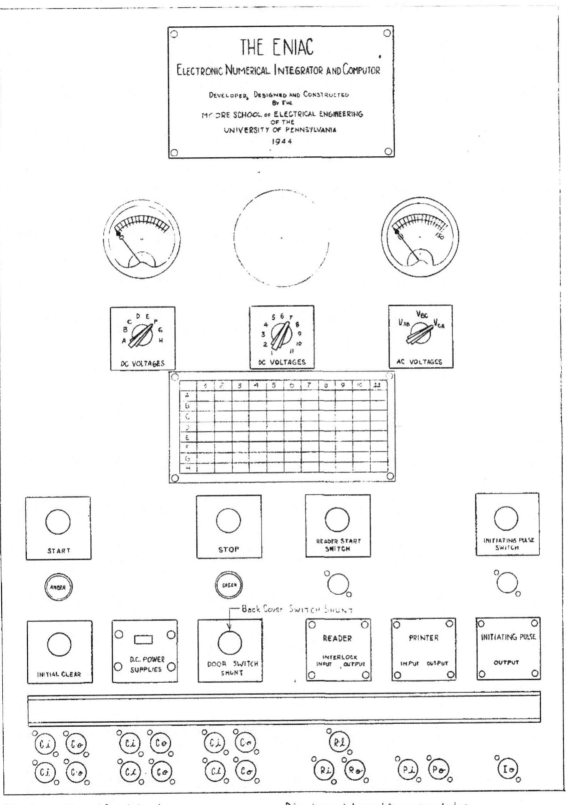

THE ENIAC

Electronic Numerical Integrator and Computor

Developed, Designed and Constructed
By the
Moore School of Electrical Engineering
of the
University of Pennsylvania
1944

DC VOLTAGES

DC VOLTAGES

AC VOLTAGES

START

STOP

READER START SWITCH

INITIATING PULSE SWITCH

AMBER

GREEN

Back Cover Switch Shunt

INITIAL CLEAR

D.C. POWER SUPPLIES

DOOR SWITCH SHUNT

READER
INTERLOCK
INPUT   OUTPUT

PRINTER
INPUT   OUTPUT

INITIATING PULSE
OUTPUT

Ci - pulse input terminal for selective clearing

Co - pulse output terminal for selective clearing

Ri - pulse input terminal for reader interlock signal.

Ri - pulse input terminal for reader.

Ro - pulse output terminal for reader

INITIATING DEVICE
FRONT PANEL
PX-9-302 P

II. INITIATING UNIT

The initiating unit of the ENIAC is the device which contains controls for turning the power on and off, for initiating a computation, for initial clearing, and for selective clearing a group of accumulators, as well as program controls for the reader and printer. Certain devices for testing the ENIAC are also located on the initiating unit.

The following topics are discussed in this chapter: Section 2.1, starting and stopping the ENIAC power and initial clearing; Section 2.2, reader and printer program controls on the initiating unit; Section 2.3, initiating a computation; Section 2.4, selective clear program controls; and Section 2.5, testing features. The following drawings are referred to in this section:

Initiating Unit – Front View	PX-9-305
Initiating Unit – Front Panel	PX-9-302
Cycling Unit and Initiating Unit	
Block Diagram	PX-9-307
Power System Block Diagram	PX-1-303
A-C Power Distribution Rack	PX-1-304

2.1. STARTING, STOPPING AND INITIAL CLEARING

Nearly all the characteristic functions of the ENIAC depend on d-c power. This, however, is derived from 240 volt, 3 phase, a-c. The latter has some immediate uses in addition to furnishing the d-c. There are in all five principal uses for the a-c power. These are as follows:

1) for the heaters of the numerous tubes of the ENIAC units.
2) for the heaters of the rectifier tubes in the ENIAC's power supplies which convert a-c into the different d-c voltages.

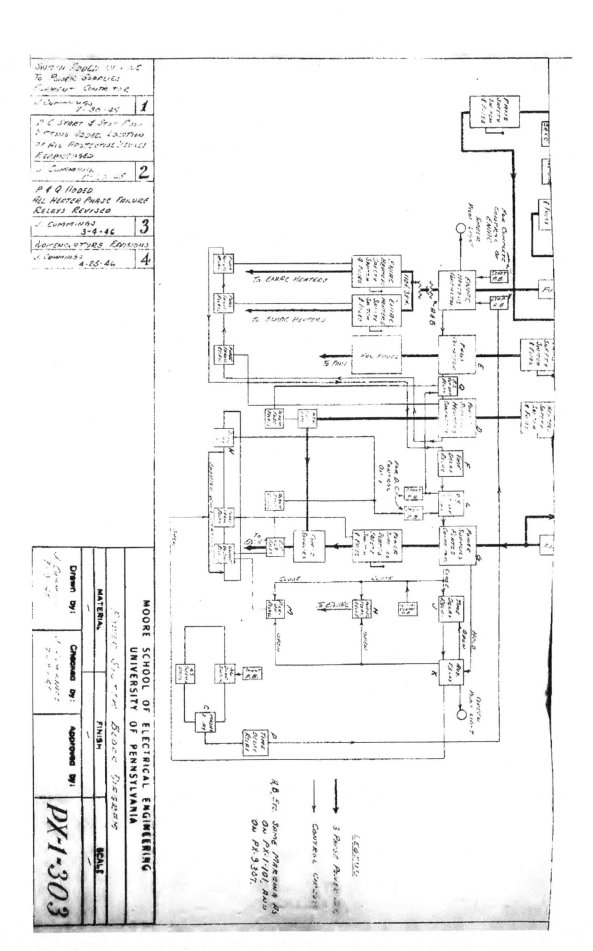

3) for the plates of the rectifier tubes.

4) for the fans which dispel the great amount of heat generated by the preceding

5) for the control circuits needed in starting and stopping the ENIAC power, in furnishing protection to various circuits, and in initial clearing.

The first four items referred to above are identified by the corresponding numbers on PX-1-303. The last item is noted there as control circuits and is more explicitly dealt with on PX-9-307. The control circuits govern the connection of the other items to the a-c lines, cause d-c to be supplied to the units of the ENIAC, and control the initial clearing of these units.

Program controls for these circuits are found on the initiating unit. Other auxiliary program controls and elements of the control circuits are found on the power distribution rack, the condenser cabinets, and the units of the ENIAC themselves. In this section we shall discuss the events involved in starting and stopping the ENIAC (Section 2.1.1.) and in initial clearing (Section 2.1.2.)

2.1.1. <u>Starting and Stopping the ENIAC</u>

In this discussion it is assumed that the main a-c safety switch is closed. By a "safety switch" is meant one whose opening not merely cuts off power, but actually opens all lines of the circuit controlled by the switch. We also assume here that the 2 safety switches for the ENIAC heaters and those for the fans and for the heaters and plates of the power supplies are all on. With the last 2 switches off, only the a-c circuits can operate; with any of the others off, neither a-c nor d-c can.

When the start button on the initiating unit (see PX-9-302) is

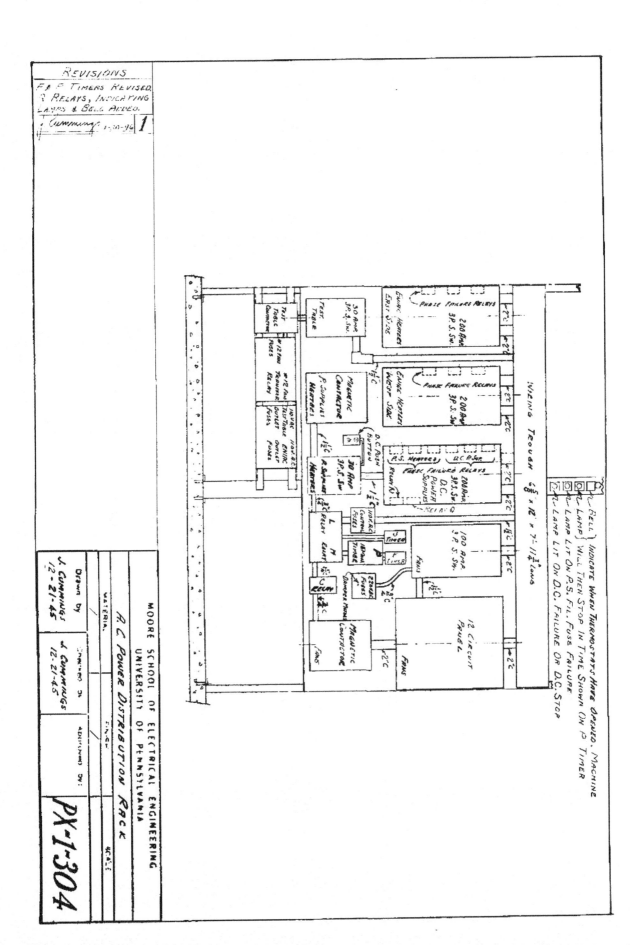

REVISIONS

F & F TIMERS REVISED,
8 RELAYS, INDICATING
LAMPS & BELL ADDED.

J. Cummings 1-30-96 1

MOORE SCHOOL OF ELECTRICAL ENGINEERING
UNIVERSITY OF PENNSYLVANIA

A.C. POWER DISTRIBUTION RACK

Drawn by
J. CUMMINGS
12-21-45

CHECKED BY
J. CUMMINGS
12-21-45

APPROVED BY:

MATERIAL

FINISH

SCALE

PX-1-304

depressed, the amber pilot light goes on immediately and the following sequence of events takes place: the ENIAC heaters and the power supply heaters are connected to the a-c and the ventilating system is turned on. One minute later, after the heaters have had an opportunity to warm up, the plates of the power supply tubes are connected to the a-c. Simultaneously, initial clearing, which lasts for 10 seconds, begins. After the ENIAC has been initially cleared, the green pilot light on the initiating unit goes on and the ENIAC is ready to operate.

The heaters clock on the front of the initiating unit, which keeps count of the number of hours that the power supply heaters are on, starts to record as soon as the start button is pushed. On each of the remaining 39 panels of the ENIAC, there is also a heaters clock and an on-off switch for the heaters. When the a-c is turned on, the heaters in a panel go on only if the switch for that panel is in the "on" position. The associated heaters clock records the number of hours that the heaters of the panel are turned on.

Before a more detailed discussion of the starting sequence is given, the elements involved in various phases of starting will be pointed out on the schematic diagram of the a-c control circuits shown on PX-9-307. The elements enclosed within the heavy lines are not in the initiating unit. The 28 under-voltage release relays and their 14 associated pick-up relays (designated by M) are located in the condenser cabinets. In the Moore School installation the power supply heater fuse relays and the d-c fuse relays are in a cabinet beside the d-c fuse cabinet and relays A, B, and K are located in the machinery laboratory. The remaining items, except for the door switches and thermostats which are in the ENIAC panels, are on the power distribution rack in the ENIAC room (see PX-1-304).

Relays A and B connect the heaters of the ENIAC units to the 3 phase a-c power. Relay D is the power supply heaters contactor. F, an adjustable timer which has been set for 1 minute, provides for the delay between the turning on of the power supply heaters and plates. When timer F has counted the specified period of time, relay G is activated. This relay connects the plates of the power supplies to the a-c so that the d-c is turned on when relay G is activated. Timer J which has been set for 10 seconds and relay H, the main initial clear relay, are activated after the d-c is turned on. Relays 3 and 4, auxiliary initial clear relays, are each responsible for the emission of one of the signals involved in initial clearing (see Section 2.1.2.). Ten seconds after timer J starts to count, relay K is activated and the initial clear period is terminated, thus bringing the starting sequence to an end.

It can be seen on PX-9-307 that in addition to the start and stop buttons on the initiating unit which operate both the a-c and d-c circuits, separate d-c start and stop buttons have been provided. Through the use of the d-c stop button, only the d-c circuits (controlled by relay G), can be turned off, leaving the a-c circuits unaffected. With the a-c power on, pushing the d-c start button connects in the d-c circuits and causes initial clearing to take place. Isolation of the d-c from the a-c circuits has been provided in order to make possible leaving the heaters turned on even when the ENIAC is not to be operated or when there is a failure (see the discussion of protective circuits below) in the d-c circuits. This has been done because it is hoped that, by cutting down the number of times that the heaters are turned on and off, tube life will be lengthened.

It is to be noted that the operation selector switch on the cycling unit must be set at continuous when the power is turned on. In Section 2.1.2.

where initial clearing is discussed, it is pointed out that when the power is first turned on, a number of flip-flops may come up in the abnormal state and it is also remarked that the resetting of these often depends on the pulses and gates emitted by the cycling unit. These pulses are not given out immediately unless the ENIAC is in continuous operation. The danger of having these flip-flops remain in the abnormal state is that, as a result, a number of tubes that should be off most of the time and on only a short period of time (i.e. tubes in circuits that have been designed for a low duty cycle) remain on for a long time and thus cause damage to themselves and other elements.

Certain protective devices included in the control circuits are also shown on PX-9-307. Of these the most important are relays C, Q, N, and L. The action of these will be discussed in the following paragraphs. Their distinguishing characteristics are as follows: under proper operating conditions C and N are on; L and Q are off. C may be turned off by a thermostat or a door switch. Since it is believed undesirable to turn off the heaters unless it is absolutely necessary, C acts through a timer P which may be set between 5 and 15 minutes. When this time has elapsed and the trouble has not been remedied, both a-c and d-c circuits are turned off. The other three relays act without any delay but affect only the d-c. Relay Q is turned on by the blowing of any heater fuse. This cuts off the d-c power supply including its heaters. Relay N is turned off by phase in the plate supply or under-voltage in the output of a d-c power supply. The effect is to turn on L. This is also accomplished by the d-c stop button or the failure of a d-c fuse. When L is turned on or when there is any phase failure in the heaters, the plate supply to the rectifiers is cut off, but the heaters are left on. The distinction between N and L is that there is a provision for inhibiting the action of N during starting. These actions will now be discussed in more detail.

Relay C is a master relay which controls both a-c and d-c circuits. This relay, which is activated when the a-c safety switch is closed, operates in conjunction with the door switches (see below), thermostats, and timer P. Found at the back of each ENIAC panel and at the front of the power supply and condenser cabinets, is a door switch. When the cover of a panel or cabinet is removed, the door switch on the panel opens,* causing relay C to be deactivated. If, however, the door switch shunt button on the initiating unit (see PX-9-302) is held down while the cover is off, relay C is not deactivated. Relay C is also deactivated when a thermostat opens as a result of the overheating of a unit. When relay C is not activated contact C_1 closes and timer P which is set for 5 minutes starts to operate. First its clutch (CL) is thrown in, and next the motor (M) is connected into the circuit through contact CL_1. A warning lamp above the power distribution rack (see PX-1-304) also lights. Necessary repairs can be made on the machine during this 5 minute period, (which may be adjusted to as much as 15 minutes if more repair time is required). If, at the end of 5 (or 15) minutes, the condition which caused relay C to be deactivated has not been corrected, then contact P_1 opens and relay A is deactivated. This turns off both the a-c and d-c circuits. The start button on the initiating unit is used to turn the power on again after the fault has been corrected.**

The door switches have been provided as a safety measure for both personnel and the machine since the opening of a panel exposes dangerous voltages

*At the present time, there is a permanent shunt for the door switches so that removing a cover does not cause relay C to be deactivated. The description in the text above applies to the intended method of operation of the door switches.
**If both the amber and green pilot lights are off, the start button on the initiating unit must be used. If only the green pilot light is off, the power may be turned on through the use of the d-c start button.

(as much as 1500 volts in the case of the d-c) and also, by drawing air from the ventilating system to the open panel, may cause another unit to overheat.

Relay Q protects the d-c circuits and the power supplies. When Q is activated, contact Q_1 opens so that relay D is de-energized. This turns off the power supply heaters and causes contact D_1 to open. With contact D_1 open, F is de-energized so that contact F_1 opens and relay G, the d-c contactor is deactivated. Relay Q is activated when a contact on one of the power supply heater fuse relays closes. This latter event takes place if a power supply heater fuse blows. If the d-c is turned off because Q has been activated, the d-c start button on the power distribution rack must be used to turn the power on again.

The remaining protective devices shown on PX-9-307, relays L and N with their associated devices, control only the d-c circuits, leaving all heaters turned on in case of a failure. If one of these circuits detects a failure and turns the machine off, the power can be turned on again through the use of the d-c start button. The main and power supply heater phase failure relays connected in series with timer F detect faults in the three phase which goes to the heaters of the ENIAC and of the power supplies. These phase failure relays are activated so that the contacts shown on PX-9-307 are closed under proper operating conditions. In the event of a phase failure, F is de-energized so that contact F_1 opens and relay G drops out. As soon as the fault is repaired, timer F is again activated and, one minute later, contact F_1 closes.

Relay L is the d-c cut-off relay. When this relay is activated, contact L_1 opens so that relay G is de-energized. This results in cutting off the d-c power. With the a-c on (so that contact A_4 is closed), relay L can be picked up through the closing of the d-c stop button, the activation of the d-c fuse relays when a d-c fuse blows, or the non-activation of relay N (see the discussion of relay N in the next paragraph).

Relay N operates in conjunction with the power supply phase failure relays and the under-voltage release relays. The power supply phase failure relays in this circuit detect faults in the three phase a-c which goes to the plates of the power supply tubes. These relays are activated and their contacts closed under proper operating conditions. There is an under-voltage release relay for each power supply. During the starting sequence while initial clearing takes place, relays M are activated. These relays provide the high voltage required to pick up the under-voltage release relays. After the starting sequence is completed, the under-voltage release relays remain activated and their contacts are closed unless the voltage emitted by a d-c power supply drops below a specified level. During the initial clear period while the under-voltage release relays are being picked up, contact K_2 of relay K provides a circuit which shunts the under-voltage release relays and the power supplies phase failure relays.[*] Thus, relay N is activated and contact N_1 is open at all times unless a fault is selected.

The starting sequence which takes place when the start button in the initiating unit is pushed is described chronologically in Table 2-1. In some cases, a contact is classified as both a pick up and hold contact for a circuit, since the contact must close for the circuit to operate and since the circuit continues to operate only so long as the contact remains closed. In other cases, the pick up and holding functions are performed by separate contacts.

When the stop button on the initiating unit is pushed, the ENIAC is

---

[*]Timer J should not be set for less than 10 seconds since this delay is required when turning the d-c on to permit the under-voltage release relays to pick up before the shunt across them is removed.

TABLE 2-1

CHRONOLOGICAL DESCRIPTION OF STARTING SEQUENCE

Activated Relay or Circuit Element	Pick Up Contact (contact whose closing causes circuit to operate)	Hold contacts (contacts which must remain closed for circuit to continue to operate).
A-auxiliary start relay	Start switch – closed when start button is pushed	Stop switch – normally closed P_1 – closed unless timer P has been activated for 5 minutes.* B_1 – closes immediately after A is activated.
B-main start relay and ENIAC heaters contactor.	A_1	A_1 B_1
E-fans contactor	A_3	A_3
D-power supply heaters contactor	E_1	E_1 Q_1 – closed unless Q is activated.*
Amber start pilot and power supply heaters. clock.	A_4	A_4
F-one minute timer	D_1	D_1 Main and power supply heaters phase failure relays – closed unless a fault is detected.*
G	F_1 – closes after F has counted out 1 minute	F_1 L_1 – closed unless L is activated.*
H-Main initial clear relay J-10 sec. timer M-under voltage release pick-up relays	G_1	G_1 K_4 – closed until K is activated.
K-relay which terminates initial clear period.	J_1 – closes after timer has counted 10 seconds.	K_1 G_1 Initial clear switch – remains closed unless I.C. button is pushed.
Green ready pilot	K_3	K_3

*See discussion of protective devices included in Section 2.1.1.

completely turned off. Relay A, then B, E, D, G, H, and K are de-energized.

When only the a-c circuits are on, and the d-c start button is pushed, the following events take place: Relay L is deactivated, and through contact F_1 (closed provided that the a-c is on and there is no phase failure in the power for the ENIAC and power supply heaters) and L_1 (closed when L is deactivated), relay G is picked up. This turns the d-c on and then initial clearing follows as indicated on Table 2-1.

When the d-c stop button is pushed, relay L is activated. Since contact L_1 then opens, relay G drops out and the d-c is disconnected. Contact G_1 also opens, causing relay K to drop out.

With regard to the matter of interrupting a computation, it might be pointed out that it is not necessary to push the stop button on the initiating unit or the d-c stop button for this purpose. Even though the power is turned on, a computation can be stopped in a number of different ways. If a program cable which delivers a program output pulse to a program tray is removed, the computation in progress ceases with the program whose program output pulse is eliminated in this way. If the card reader exhausts the cards in its magazine (see Section 8.3.) the computation is terminated with the program just before the one in which reading would take place. A computation ceases, similarly, when the cards in the magazine of the card punch are exhausted (see Section 9.1.).

2.1.2. Initial Clearing

When the ENIAC is turned on, it is a matter of chance as to which flip-flops in the various counters, both numerical and program ring, or which program flip-flops (in receivers, transceivers and common programming circuits) will come up in the abnormal state. It is obvious that a computation must start with the numerical and program rings in the clear position and with program flip-flops in the normal state in order that the correct answer may be obtained. Furthermore, if a flip-flop in a transceiver or a program control flip-flop such as the printer start flip-flop (see Section 9.1.) comes up in the abnormal state, not only is the associated program commenced, but also, upon the completion of the program, an output pulse is transmitted which, in turn, may stimulate another program control, etc. Thus, it is also necessary before starting a computation to break program chains or sequences which are accidentally begun when the ENIAC is turned on. Furthermore, it is convenient to be able to stop a computation at a certain point (without turning the ENIAC power off), erase all data stored in accumulators and the master programmer, and then start afresh.

The initial clear circuits in the ENIAC provide for the contingencies mentioned above. The initial clear circuits consist of the initial clear push button on the initiating unit, relays H and K which were referred to in Section 2.1.1. and initial clear relays 3 and 4 (see PX-9-307). When the ENIAC's power is turned on, initial clearing takes place automatically immediately after the d-c goes on (see Section 2.1.1.). The initial clear push button is pushed when, with the power already on, it is desired to clear the accumulators and the master programmer. It is to be noted, that the <u>operation selector switch on the cycling unit must be set at continuous</u> for initial clearing to take place. Relay H is the main initial clear relay. When activated, this relay causes initial clearing to take place. Relay K terminates the initial clear period. Initial clear relay 4 is responsible for emitting the initial clear gate (ICG) which, in general, clears the counters used for either numerical or programming purposes. Initial clear relay 3 causes the master programmer clear gate (MPC) to be emitted. The MPC is used in the master programmer to break program sequences (see the discussion in the latter part of this section.)

When the start button on the initiating unit or the d-c start button is pushed, relay K is not activated so that relay H and the ten second timer J are picked up through contacts G_1 and K_4. At the end of 10 seconds, contact J_1 on the timer closes. Through J_1, relay K is picked up. From then on, relay K holds through contact K_1 and the initial clear switch which is normally closed.

When the power has been on and the initial clear button is pushed, relay K is de-energized so that K_4 closes. Since G_1 remains closed as long as the d-c is on, relay H and timer J are then picked up through G_1 and K_4.

When relay H picks up, contact H_1 closes, thus activating relay 3. Contact 3-1 then closes and the MPC is emitted. As a result of the activation of relay 3, contact 3-3, which is normally closed, opens. Now with 3-3 closed, there is a circuit which allows a small amount of current to flow through the coil of relay 4 but not enough to pick this relay up, and very little passes through the large resistor to the condenser. While 3-3 is open, however, the condenser is charged.

Ten seconds after relay H is activated, K is activated. Contact K_4 opens and H is, thus, deactivated. This causes contact H_1 to open and relay 3 to drop out. At this time, contact 3-3 closes. This allows the condenser to discharge through the coil of relay 4. In this way, relay 4 is activated and contact 4-1 is closed. With contact 4-1 closed, the initial clear gate is emitted. Initial clear relay 4 is restored to the normal state with contact 4-1 again open in about 1/2 a second when the condenser has discharged.

As can be seen from the discussion above, the 10 second period (when the green light is off and when timer J is operating) designated by the phrase initial clear period, is actually devoted to the master programmer clear signal. The initial clear gate comes on after the MPC goes off and lasts for about 1/2

TABLE 2-2 - INITIAL CLEARING OF ENIAC UNITS

UNIT	ITEM	MANNER OF INITIAL CLEARING OR RESETTING
Accumulator	Flip-flops in receivers and transceivers.	No provision for direct reset of receivers or transceivers. However, if a F.F. comes up in the abnormal state, the program set up on the associated switches is carried out and, in a maximum of 9 add. times, the F.F. is reset.
	Decade flip-flops	Normally negative output of decade F.F. gates RP through gate 18 so that a decade F.F. in abnormal state is reset.
	Repeater ring	CPP gated through K50 by ICG resets repeater ring.
	Decade counters and PM counter	CCG gated through L44 by ICG clears counters.
Multiplier	Flip-flops in transceivers	Reset in maximum of 14 add. times (see Accumulator).
	Program ring	If program ring is not in stage 1, CPP is gated through J'44. ICG holds G'44 open so that output of J'44 is passed to prog. ring. Thus the ring is cycled to stage 1. When prog. ring is in stage 1, J'44 is closed so that no other CPP are admitted to cycle the ring.
	Reset flip-flops	Normally negative output of a reset F.F. which comes up in abnormal state opens G49 or L'50 so that a CPP is passed to reset the F.F.
	L and R receivers	ICG gates CPP through E'47 to reset these receivers.
	Ra-R8, Da-D8, and answer disposal receivers	Reset by CPP.
Divider and Square Rooter	AT PRESENT, ICG gates a CPP through E50. The output of E50 gives rise to CL and CL' pulses so that clearing is accomplished as follows:	
	Flip-flops in transceivers	No provision for direct reset, since the reset signal for transceivers in the divider comes from the clear F.F. and the present method of init. cl. does not ensure that the clear F.F. will be set during init. cl. Since a divider program may last longer than init. cl. finishing cannot be depended on for resetting program controls in this unit.
	Program ring	Cleared to stage 1 by CL' signal.
	Pulse source flip-flop	Reset by CL'.
	D'γ, +1, and -1 receivers	Reset by CL'.
	Program ring flip-flop	Reset by CL.
	Numerator Binary Ring	Cleared to stage 0 by CL.
	Denominator flip-flop	Reset by CL.
	Answer Place Ring	Cleared to stage 1 by CL.
	Clear flip-flop	Reset by CL.
	Interlock flip-flop	Reset by CL' gated through K48 by ICG.
	Interlock coincidence flip-flop	NOT RESET by the present method.
	S_{AC}, H'γ, S_{α}, H_{AC}, D_γ, Q_α, +2, -2 answer disposal and argument accumulator receivers.	Reset by CPP.
	H_γ, D_A, D_S	Reset by GP emitted after pulse source flip-flop is reset.
	It is planned to modify the design of the divider in such a way that the interlock coincidence F.F. will be eliminated and also so that the transceivers will be reset during the init. cl. period.	
Function Table	Flip-flops in transceivers	Reset in a maximum of 13 add. times (see Accumulator).
	Argument flip-flop and Add. and Sub. flip-flops	Reset by CPP gated through C48 by ICG.
	Program ring	Cleared to stage -3 by CPP gated through B48 held open by ICG.
	Units and tens argument counters	Cleared by CPP gated through A48 by ICG.
Constant Transmitter	Flip-flops in transceivers	Reset in 1 add. time (see Accumulator).
Reader	Start flip-flop	Reset by CPP gated through 63 by ICG.
	Interlock flip-flop Finish flip-flop Synchronizing flip-flop	Reset by CPP gated through 71 by ICG.
Printer	Start flip-flop	Reset by CPP gated through 71 by ICG.

Under the present method of initial clearing, a card may be fed to the reader or punch in the period between the turning on of the power and the resetting of the start flip-flop.

	Finish F.F. is set by CPP gated through 71 by ICG. Then CPP gated through 66 sets synchronizing F.F. Normally negative output of synchronizing F.F. gates CPP through 69 so that Finishing and Synchronizing flip-flops are reset by the output of gate 69.	
Master Programmer	MPC holds stepper output gates closed so that master programmer cannot emit a program output pulse.	
	Stepper input flip-flops	Reset by CPP gated through 69 if F.F. is in abnormal state.
	Stepper Counters	Cleared to stage 1 by CPP gated through C47 by ICG.
	Master programmer decade counters	Cleared to stage 0 by CPP gated through B44 by ICG.

a second. Both the MPC and ICG are carried to the other units of the ENIAC
in the d-c voltage cable.

At the time of writing of this report, the MPC is taken only to the
master programmer's stepper output gates (see Section 10.3.1.). The MPC, a
negative signal closes down these gates so that no program output pulse can be
emitted by the master programmer while the MPC is on. Although a program
sequence may be initiated because the flip-flop of some transceiver comes up
in the abnormal state, it is impossible for a program sequence lasting 10 seconds
(of continuous operation) not to go, at some time in that period, to the master
programmer. Since the master programmer, however, cannot transmit a program output
pulse while the MPC is on, program sequences which have started accidentally are
broken here.

The way in which the initial clear gate is used in the units of the
ENIAC to prepare them for computation is shown on Table 2-2. The reader will
probably find it convenient to refer to this table in connection with Chapters
IV-X. The circuit elements referred to in Table 2-2 can be identified on the
block diagrams for the various units. The reader will notice that in many cases
clearing depends on the carry clear gate and the central programming pulse emitted
by the cycling unit. It is for this reason, that the cycling unit must be in
continuous operation for initial clearing to be accomplished.

On Table 2-2, two difficulties inherent in the present method of
initially clearing the divider and square rooter are noted. One of these difficulties, that the flip-flops in the transceivers may not be reset by the end of
the initial clearing period, arises from the fact that in the divider and square
rooter, as in the other units of the ENIAC, no special provision has been made
for directly resetting the transceivers. In other units of the ENIAC, this causes

no difficulty. For, suppose that a transceiver in the high-speed multiplier comes up in the abnormal state when the power is turned on. The multiplier then proceeds, during the time that the MPC is on, to carry out the program set-up on the switches associated with that transceiver. In a maximum of 14 addition times the program is completed and the transceiver is reset.

In the divider and square rooter, however, there is no upper limit on the length of time required for a division program (division by zero, for example, requires an infinite length of time). Therefore, if a division program is started because a transceiver comes up in the abnormal state when the ENIAC is turned on or because an accidentally begun program sequence stimulates it, there is no certainty that the program will be completed and the transceiver be reset by the end of the initial clear period.

Plans have been made to revise this initial clearing difficulty by causing the clear flip-flop in the divider and square rooter to be set during the initial clear period. Since the clear flip-flop in the abnormal state causes the CL and CL' signals to be emitted, any flip-flops now reset by CL and CL' will also be reset by the modified method of initial clearing. The CL signal also resets the clear flip-flop. The normally negative output of the clear flip-flop provides a reset signal for the divider and square rooter's transceivers.

Until the initial clearing process for the divider and square rooter is modified, the operator can circumvent this first difficulty by setting the operation switches on this unit at square root instead of divide and the inter-lock switches at NI (no interlock). Since the maximum time for a square rooting program is 400 addition times (less than a tenth of a second), an accidentally begun square rooting program is certain to be completed by the end of the initial clear period. The reason for setting the interlock switches on the program controls at NI is that, even though a program were completed, a program output pulse would not be emitted and the transceivers would not be reset unless the interlock flip-flop also came up in the abnormal state or unless some program sequence, accidentally started, provided for an interlock pulse.

The second difficulty, that no provision has been made for resetting the interlock coincidence flip-flop, is also to be remedied. Plans have been made for making a small modification in the divider and square rooter's common programming circuits which will eliminate the need for this flip-flop. Until this modification is made, the operator must pay particular attention to the interlock coincidence flip-flop neon (see PX-10-302) before starting a computation. When the interlock coincidence flip-flop is in the normal state, this neon is off. If this flip-flop comes up in the abnormal state at the end of initial clearing, initial clearing should be repeated until this flip-flop does come up in the normal state.

2.2. READER AND PRINTER PROGRAM CONTROLS ON THE INITIATING UNIT

2.2.1. Reader Program Controls

Certain reader program controls are found on the initiating unit (see PX-9-302 and 9-307). These include the reader start flip-flop and program pulse input terminal (Ri), the reader interlock flip-flop and interlock pulse input terminal (Rl), the reader finish flip-flop, the reader synchronizing flip-flop and program pulse output terminal (Ro), and associated gates, buffers, and inverters. The reader start button is also on the initiating unit.

The reader start flip-flop is flipped into the abnormal state either when Ri is pulsed or when, at the beginning of a computation (see Section 2.3.), the reader start button is pushed. When the start flip-flop is in the abnormal state, a start relay in the constant transmitter is activated so that the reader is stimulated to read a card and cause information read from the card to be stored in the constant transmitter. A little less than half way through the card reading cycle (see Chapter VIII), a reset signal from the reader resets the start flip-flop, so that, even though reading is not yet completed, the start flip-flop is capable of again being flipped into the abnormal state (by the reception of a pulse at Ri) to remember that reading is to take place again.

When reading is completed, the reader emits a finish signal which causes the reader finish flip-flop to be flipped into the abnormal state. The interlock flip-flop is flipped into the abnormal state when an interlock pulse arrives at Rl or, at the start of a computation, when the reader is stimulated to read by the reader start button. The reader interlock flip-flop makes it possible to carry on a sequence of programs in parallel with reading and then to stimulate the next program sequence when both reading and the parallel sequence have been completed since no program output pulse is emitted from terminal Ro unless the interlock flip-flop is flipped into the abnormal state (see below). If a computation does not call for a sequence in parallel with reading, the operator can provide an interlock pulse by sending the pulse which goes to Ri also to Rl.

The coincidence of signals from the interlock and finish flip-flops causes gate 69 to emit a signal. The output of gate 69 gates a CPP through gate 62 which then sets the reader synchronizing flip-flop. The CPP gated · through 68 by the normally negative output of the synchronizing flip-flop gates a CPP through 68 and, thus, provides a reader program output pulse which is emitted from terminal Ro. The reason that the synchronizing flip-flop and gate 68 are used after gate 62 is to ensure a program output pulse of the proper shape and in synchronism with other program pulses.

Neons correlated with the flip-flops mentioned above are shown on PX-9-305. Program controls for the reader in addition to those on the initiating unit are discussed in Chapter VIII.

2.2.2. Printer Program Controls

The printer program controls on the initiating unit include the printer start flip-flop and program pulse input terminal, the printer finish flip-flop, the printer synchronizing flip-flop and program pulse output terminal, and associated gates, buffers, and inverters. Neons correlated with the flip-flops appear on PX-9-305.

A program input pulse received at Pi flips the printer start flip-flop into the abnormal state. This causes a start relay in the punch to be activated so that the tubes in the printer are set up for the data to be printed and so that a card punching cycle is initiated (see Chapter IX). About 1/4 way through the card punching cycle, the punch emits a finish signal which resets the start flip-flop and sets the printer finish flip-flop. The output of the finish flip-flop in the abnormal state gates a CPP through gate 66. The output of 66 sets the printer synchronizing flip-flop whose output gates a CPP through gate 69. The output of gate 69 is transmitted from PO as a program output pulse.

The printer program controls are discussed in greater detail in Chapter IX.

2.3. INITIATING PULSE FOR A COMPUTATION: Reader Start Button and Initiating Pulse Button.

Once the starting sequence is completed (amber and green pilot lights are on), the ENIAC is ready to begin computing. To stimulate the computation to begin, however, a program pulse must be delivered to the input terminals of the program controls on which are set up the programs that begin in the first addition time of the computation. Two alternative methods exist for stimulating the beginning of a computation.

If the first event of a computation consists of the reading of a card, the computation can be started by pushing the reader start button on the initiating unit (see Section 2.2.1.). When reading is completed, then, a program output pulse is emitted from terminal Ro. This pulse can be used to stimulate the programs of the computation which immediately follow reading. As was noted in Section 2.2.1, pushing the reader start button also results in setting the reader interlock flip-flop so that no interlock pulse need be provided for a reading initiated by the reader start button.

The terminal marked R_s on PX-9-302 parallels the reader start switch and is used for remote control (see Section 2.2.1.).

The second procedure for initiating a computation is to connect the terminal marked Io (see PX-9-302) to the same program line as the input terminals of the program controls used for the first programs of the computation. When the initiating pulse button is pushed, the initiating pulse input flip-flop (see PX-9-307) is set. Its output allows a CPP to pass through gate 66 and set the synchronizing flip-flop. The output of the synchronizing flip-flop gates a CPP through gate 69 which resets the input and synchronizing flip-flops and causes a program pulse to be emitted from terminal I_o. Neons correlated with the flip-flops mentioned above are shown on PX-9-305.

The initiating pulse button has a second important use in connection with testing the ENIAC. One of the chief techniques for localizing errors in either the machine or the set-up of the machine is to operate the ENIAC in the one addition time mode or in the one pulse time mode. Here, the pulses for one addition time or 1 pulse time at a time respectively are given out in sequence every time the 1 pulse - 1 addition time button on the cycling unit is pushed (see Chapter III). In this way, there is an opportunity to observe the numerical and programming neons. Frequently, it is more convenient to proceed through a portion of the computation with the ENIAC operating in its normal or continuous mode and then to switch to 1 addition time or 1 pulse time operation than it is to progress through the entire computation non-continuously. This may be arranged by disconnecting the program cable which delivers the pulse used to initiate the programs which are to be examined non-continuously. We call this point where the program cable is removed a break point. When the initiating pulse button is pushed, the computation begins and progresses to the break point. With the necessary switch made in the cycling unit (see Chapter III), computation in the non-continuous mode can be stimulated by delivering the initiating pulse from terminal I_o to the program line from which the program cable was removed. The reader will notice that after the initiating pulse button is pushed, two addition time cycles, one in which a CPP passes through gate 66 and one in which a CPP passes through gate 69, are required before the initiating pulse is delivered.

The emission of the initiating pulse may also be stimulated by remote control. The terminal marked I_s on PX-9-302 is used to parallel the initiating pulse switch with a switch which may be carried anywhere around the ENIAC room and which is connected to I_s via a program line which has no load box.[*]

---

[*] Also see the discussion of the portable control box in Section 11.6.

2.4. SELECTIVE CLEAR CONTROLS

There are 6 selective clear program controls on the initiating unit.
Each control consists of a transceiver with a program pulse input (Ci) and output (Co) terminal on the front panel. The six selective clear transceiver outputs are connected in parallel to a line of the synchronizing trunk. When a
selective clear transceiver is stimulated, its flip-flop emits a signal called
the selective clear gate (SCG). One addition time later, the transceiver is
reset by a CPP and a program output pulse is emitted. Neons associated with the
selective clear program controls are shown on PX-9-305.

The selective clear gate is delivered by the synchronizing trunk to
the 20 accumulators. When the SCG is given out, any accumulator whose selective
clear switch is set at SC clears in accordance with the setting of its significant
figures switch (see Section 4.2.3.). Notice that selective clearing lasts but
one addition time and clears only the decade and PM counters of accumulators.
The selective clear feature provides a convenient means of clearing the group
of accumulators which store data for the printer (see Chapter IX) after printing
takes place (see the illustrative problem discussed in Sections 8.7 and 9.5.).

2.5. DEVICES FOR TESTING THE ENIAC

Located on the initiating unit (see PX-9-302) are the following
devices for testing the ENIAC: d-c voltage meter and associated voltage selector
switches, d-c voltage hum oscilloscope, and a-c voltage meter and voltage selector switch.

The d-c voltage meter together with the two d-c voltage selector
switches provide a means of examining any of the ENIAC's 78 d-c voltages. The

d-c voltage chart below the selector switches indicates which voltage is measured as a result of the combination of settings on the switches.

The a-c voltage meter and switch are used to measure the three phases of one of the two bus systems supplying 110 volt a-c to the filament transformers of the various units. Further details concerning the use of the testing devices mentioned above as well as others not located at the initiating unit are to be found in the ENIAC MAINTENANCE MANUAL.

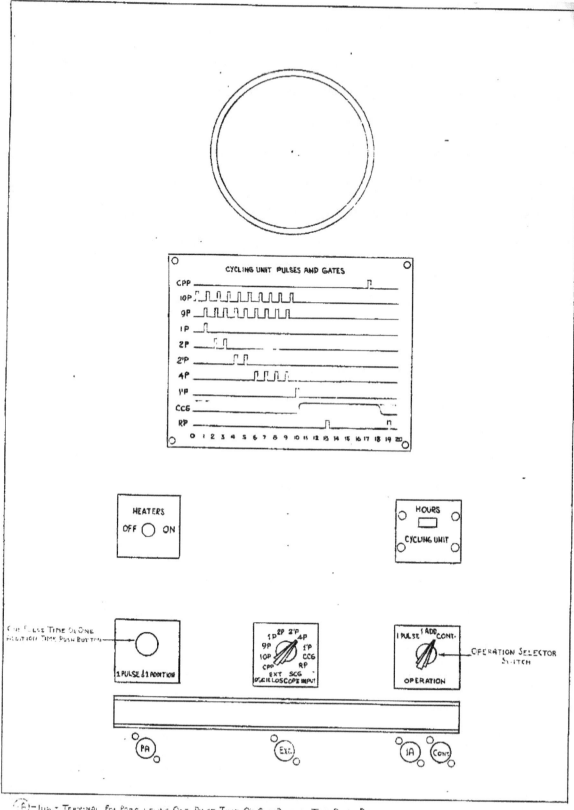

CYCLING UNIT PULSES AND GATES

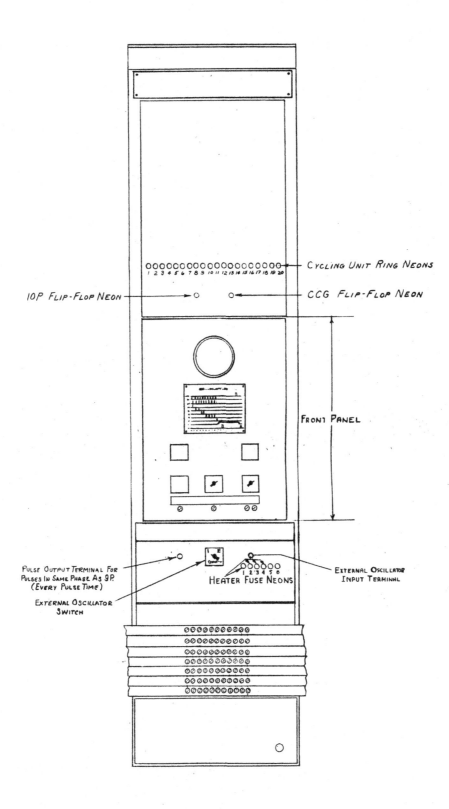

CYCLING UNIT RING NEONS

1 2 3 4 5 6 7 8 9 10 11 12 13 14 15 16 17 18 19 20

IOP FLIP-FLOP NEON

CCG FLIP-FLOP NEON

FRONT PANEL

PULSE OUTPUT TERMINAL FOR
PULSES IN SAME PHASE AS 9P.
(EVERY PULSE TIME)

EXTERNAL OSCILLATOR
SWITCH

1 2 3 4 5 6
HEATER FUSE NEONS

EXTERNAL OSCILLATOR
INPUT TERMINAL

MOORE SCHOOL of ELECTRICAL ENGINEERING
UNIVERSITY of PENNSYLVANIA

CYCLING UNIT
FRONT VIEW
PX-9-304

III CYCLING UNIT

The cycling unit of the ENIAC is the device which provides pulses and a gate for the other units to operate on and which, thus, keeps the units operating in csynchronism with one another.

Normally a quartz crystal oscillator emits 100 kc sine waves which are converted into pulses spaced at a 10 μs interval by a pulse standardizer. The fundamental time unit for the ENIAC, a pulse time, is thus 10 μs. The output of the pulse standardizer goes to the so called on beat circuit which contains another pulse standardizer and tubes for power amplification. The on beat circuit emits pulses (through one of its 3 outputs) to the off beat circuit. The off beat circuit shapes, amplifies and delays the pulses which it receives. One output of the off beat circuit, delayed 1.25 μs after the on beat pulses, is taken to a 20 stage ring counter (neons correlated with the stages of the ring are shown on PX-9-304) which controls certain gates and flip-flops. The off beat pulses, delayed 2.5 μs after the on beat pulses, are taken to a gate which is controlled by a flip-flop, in turn, controlled by the ring. Other gates associated with the ring pass on beat pulses. The ring with its associated flip-flops and gates is responsible for producing a pattern of pulses repeated every 20 pulse times (or every addition time). The gate and each of the 9 different kinds of pulses (see PX-9-306) emitted every addition time are each carried on one of the 11 leads of the synchronizing trunk (see Chapter II for the use of the 11th lead). The various units of the ENIAC are connected into the synchronizing trunk so that they can pick up the pulses needed for their operation.

The pulses generated by the cycling unit or pulses from some external source can be viewed on the screen of an oscilloscope built into the cycling unit.

This chapter will cover the following topics: sources of pulses and gates, Sec. 3.1; methods of operation of the cycling unit and ENIAC, Sec. 3.2;

cycling unit oscilloscope, Sec. 3.3. Reference will be made to the following
drawings:

Front Panel of the Cycling Unit   PX-9-303

Front View of the Cycling Unit   PX-9-304

Block Diagram of the Cycling Unit

    and Initiating Unit   PX-9-307

Cycling Unit Pulses and Gates   PX-9-306

3.1. PULSES AND GATES AND THEIR SOURCES

3.1.1. The Pulses and Gates

The nine different kinds of pulses and the gate emitted by the
cycling unit every 200 μs are shown on PX-9-306. The 10P are classified as
off beat pulses; all other pulses as on beat. Each of the 10P, 9P, 2P, 2'P,
4P, the 1P, 1'P and CPP are roughly the same in shape and alike in duration
(namely, 2 μs). They differ from one another in the line of the synchronizing
trunk over which they are transmitted, the part of the addition time cycle in
which they are emitted, and the purposes for which they are used in the ENIAC.

The 9P, the 1'P, the 1, 2, 2', and 4P are commonly used as digit
pulses. An accumulator transmits the number stored in it or the complement of
the number stored in it by gating appropriate numbers of the 9P over the various
lines of the digit output. In the transmission of complements from an
accumulator, the 1'P is gated and allowed to pass over the lead which carries
the extreme right hand significant figure being stored in the accumulator to
make a tens instead of nines complement. The 1, 2, 2', and 4 pulses are used
particularly where information stored in static form is converted into pulse
form, e.g. in the high speed multiplier, the function table, the divider-square-
rooter, and the constant transmitter. By suitable combinations of the 1, 2, 2',
and 4 pulses any number between 1 and 9 can be formed. The 10P are used only
in accumulators. They serve to cycle each counter around back to the position

it starts from when the transmission of a number and/or its complement from an accumulator takes place (see Sec. 4.3.1).

The carry clear gate (which lasts from pulse time 11 to 17) is used to cause the clearing of accumulators which, at the operator's option, may or may not take place after transmission from an accumulator (see Sec. 4.2.3.). The carry clear gate also allows a carry over pulse to pass from a decade counter to the decade counter immediately to the left if carry over takes place in the reception of a number by an accumulator (see Sec. 4.3.2). Carry over can take place in two ways: delayed or direct. In delayed carry over, the first reset pulse passed through a gate (which is controlled by a flip-flop that remembers that carry over is to take place) is gated by the carry clear gate so that it can reach the next decade. The second reset pulse resets this flip-flop. Direct carry over takes care of carry overs which result from carry over. In this latter form, the pulse which necessitates carry over (and not the reset pulse, as above) is the one which the carry clear gate allows to pass to the next decade counter. The reset pulse is emitted twice, once during the emission of the carry clear gate for delayed carry over and once after the carry clear gate to reset carry over flip-flops which may be set after delayed carry over takes place. The first reset pulse is also used to reset a flip-flop (the same one used for carry over in reception) which is set in the process of transmitting from an accumulator.

The principal uses of the central program pulse (emitted at pulse time 17) are the provision of the program pulses needed to stimulate program controls and the resetting of the receivers and transceivers in these program controls.

3.1.2. Sources of the Pulses and Gates

A block diagram of the circuits of the cycling unit which are involved in generating the pulses and gates emitted by this unit appears on the left hand half of PX-9-307.

The oscillator (61, 63) emits 100 KC sine waves which the pulse standardizer (K, L26) converts into pulses spaced at 10 μs intervals.

In continuous operation (see Sec. 3.2.) each pulse from the oscillator and pulse standardizer circuit is delivered to the on beat circuit. A special pulse standardizer in this circuit (tubes 61 and 62 and the 1 μs delay line) produces rectangular pulses 2 μs broad. The on beat circuit has 3 outputs. One of the outputs is brought to a terminal labelled on beat pulse output terminal (see PX-9-304). For every pulse received by the on beat circuit, a pulse in phase with the 9P is emitted from this terminal. These pulses are used in the test equipment of the ENIAC (see ENIAC MAINTENANCE MANUAL). Another output of the on beat circuit delivers pulses to gates associated with various stages of the cycling unit ring and the third output delivers pulses to the off beat circuit.

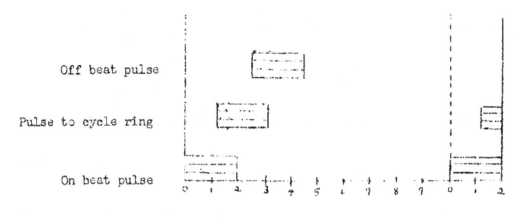

Off beat pulse

Pulse to cycle ring

On beat pulse

Duration in μs

Figure 3-1

The off beat circuit routes these pulses through a 2.5 μs delay line. This delay line is tapped at half its length, for the pulses which cycle the ring counter. The pulses delayed the full 2.5 μs, called the off beat pulses, are delivered to gate L30 (see Fig. 3-1 for a chronological comparison of the on beat and off beat pulses and the pulses which cycle the ring).

The off beat pulses pass through L30 to produce the 10P as long as gate L30 is held open by the 10P flip-flop (L29) in the abnormal state. This flip-flop is flipped into the abnormal state when the ring counter is in stage zero and remains in this state until reset by a signal from gate A30 (which is controlled by stage 10 of the ring). The 10P neon correlated with this flip-flop is shown on PX-9-304.

Stage 1 of the ring controls gate K30. The on beat pulse passed through gate K30 gives rise to the 1P and the first of the 9P. Stage 2 of the ring controls gate J30. The on beat pulse passed through gate J30 gives rise to the first of the 2P and the second of the 9P, etc. In this way, the 1, 2, 2', and 4P, and the 1'P are generated in the chronological order shown on PX-9-306.

When the cycling unit ring reaches stage 11, gate B27 opens to pass an on beat pulse. This signal sets the carry clear gate flip-flop, E27 (see PX-9-304 for the associated neon). This flip-flop remains in the abnormal state for the next 7 pulse times, being reset by an on beat pulse gated through gate H27 which is controlled by stage 18 of the ring. The signal from the carry clear gate flip-flop in the abnormal state produces the CCG.

While the carry clear gate is on, an on beat pulse gated through gate C27 (which is controlled by stage 13) produces a reset pulse. The second reset pulse is produced when the ring is in stage 19.

A signal from stage 17 of the ring gates an on beat pulse through gate 27 to produce a CPP.

All of the cycling unit pulses and gates shown on PX-9-306 are passed through cycling unit transmitters (61-70, 21-30, or 3-12) for power amplification before transmission from the cycling unit.

It is expected that most of the time the ENIAC's oscillator circuit with its 100 kilocycle rate will be used in the cycling unit. If for any reason it is desired to operate the ENIAC at some other rate, a different oscillator can be plugged in and used to supply pulses to the on beat circuit. When the oscillator switch (see PX-9-304) is set at Ext. and an external oscillator is plugged into the external oscillator input terminal at the right of this switch, the fundamental pulses for the cycling unit are derived from the external oscillator. When the cycling unit's oscillator supplies the fundamental pulses, the oscillator switch is set at Int. It is to be noted that the time constants for the ENIAC's circuits have been designed for a frequency of 100 KC and certain safety factors have been included on this basis. If a higher frequency is used, these safety factors will be lost so that the reliability of the ENIAC will be decreased.

3.2. METHODS OF OPERATION

The cycling unit can be set up so that the ENIAC operates in one of 3 modes:

1) continuous operation at the fundamental frequency of the oscillator used.

2) one addition time operation in which the cycling unit supplies the pulses for only one addition time cycle at the oscillator rate with a wait of any length desired by the operator between addition times.

3) one pulse time operation in which the cycling unit supplies the pulses of the addition time cycle one at a time with a wait of any length desired by the operator between pulses.

Continuous operation is the natural method of operation of the ENIAC. One addition time or one pulse time operation is used for testing and checking purposes. One addition time operation is particularly useful in checking a set-up that is put on the ENIAC. Before actually running through a complete computation continuously, the operator can cause the ENIAC to progress through one cycle of the computation addition time by addition time. By observing the neon bulbs in the various units, he can then check to see that the units are operating properly and that switch settings and cable connections have been made correctly to carry out the contemplated set-up. To test whether or not a particular unit is functioning properly, 1 addition time, or, for finer discrimination, one pulse time operation can be used.

The cycling unit controls which are used for the various modes of operation are the operation selector switch and the 1 pulse time-1 addition time push button (see PX-9-303). When the operation selector switch is set at Cont., the cycling unit emits the pulses and gates continuously. When this switch is set at 1 Add, the pulses and gates for 1 complete addition time cycle are given out every time the 1P-1A button is pushed. With the switch set at 1 Pulse, the pulses or gates of the addition time cycle are given out in chronological sequence, one each time the 1P-1A button is pushed. It might be mentioned that all three modes of operation are possible whether the ENIAC's oscillator or an external oscillator is used to supply the fundamental pulses.

Continuous or non-continuous operation is accomplished by allowing all pulses or only certain pulses from the oscillator circuit to reach the on beat circuit (and then the off beat circuit, and the ring with its associated gates). The continuous relay, the 1 addition time relay, gates L 28 and L 27 and the 1 pulse - 1 addition time push button (see PX-9-307) are used for this purpose. It might be pointed out that gate L 27 is connected to the normally positive output of stage zero of the ring. Thus L 27 is closed when the ring is in stage zero and open at all other times.

In continuous operation, the requirements are that the circuit containing gates L 27 and L 28 shall pass all of the pulses from the oscillator and that accidentally pushing the 1 pulse - 1 addition time push button shall have no effect. The requirements are met in the following way: with the operation switch set at continuous (as shown on PX-9-307) the continuous relay is activated so that contacts 1 and 3 are closed and the 1 addition time relay is not activated so that contact 6 is closed. Now with contact 1 closed, the cathode of tube 70 (at the left) floats and the tube is, therefore, inoperative. Since this tube is not conducting, a positive voltage is applied to gate L 28. The circuit through contact 3 delivers to the pulse standardizer K-L 26 and then to gate L 28 the oscillator pulses which then pass through gate L 28.

When the operation switch is set at 1P or 1A respectively, only the pulse which results from pushing the 1 pulse - 1 addition push button or only 20 oscillator pulses immediately following the pushing of the button are to reach the on beat circuit. Let us, therefore, consider the circuit containing the 1 pulse - 1 addition push button. Tubes 68 are normally on and tubes 69 constitute a flip-flop with but one stable state (a non-standard flip-flop for the ENIAC). The normally positive output of this flip-flop is taken to tube 70 and the normally negative output is used to reset the flip-flop immediately after it is set. When the push button is pushed, tubes 68 go off and the flip-flop is set momentarily; otherwise, this flip-flop remains in the normal state.

When the operation switch is set at 1^P, neither the continuous nor the 1 addition time relay is activated so that contacts 6, 4, and 2 are closed. The circuit through contact 2 connects the cathode of tube 70 (at the left) to -40V so that, with the flip-flop (69) in the normal state, tube 70 is on. The negative output of this tube holds L 28 closed. Only when the push button is pushed is tube 70 turned off so as to open gate L 28. The positive pulse from tube 70 (at the left) also passes through the other tube of the same number and, through contacts 6 and 4, is delivered to the pulse standardizer and, finally, gate L 28.

In 1 addition time operation, contacts 5, 4, and 2 are closed.
The circuit through contact 2, as described above, causes gate L 28 to be opened momentarily when the 1 pulse - 1 addition time button is pushed. The circuit through contacts 5 and 4 delivers the oscillator's pulses to the pulse standardizer and the gates L 27 and L 28. The first oscillator pulse passes through gate L 28. This pulse results, finally, in cycling the ring from stage zero to stage 1 so that the subsequent 19 pulses from the oscillator pass through gate L 27. When the ring reaches stage zero again, L 27 is closed and L 28 does not open again unless the 1 pulse - 1 addition button is pushed. In case the cycling unit has been running in the 1 pulse time mode and is switched into the one addition time mode in the midst of an addition time cycle, the pulses and gates for the remainder of the addition time are given out immediately (since gate L 27 is open), whether or not the 1 pulse - 1 addition button is pushed.

Controls are provided which enable the operator to control the method of operation of the cycling unit when he is standing near some unit different from the cycling unit. The PA, 1A, and Cont. input terminals (shown on PX-9-303) make this possible. Portable push buttons may be used in connection with these terminals by plugging them into program lines (with no load box) which are in turn connected to each of the terminals PA, 1A, and Cont.

A push button connected to terminal PA parallels the 1 pulse - 1 add addition time push button. Portable push buttons connected to the 1A or Cont. terminals can be used only when the operation selector switch is set at 1 Pulse, since, with either of the other settings, the mode of operation circuits are locked so that they cannot be entered except from the operation selector switch. Closing the button connected to terminal 1A causes the 1 addition time relay to be activated; closing the button connected to the Cont. terminal causes the continuous relay to be activated.

A more convenient method of operating the 1 pulse time - 1 addition time push button and the operation selector switch from any place in the ENIAC room is provided by the portable control box. This box, which parallels certain controls found on both the initiating unit and the cycling unit, is discussed in Section 11.6.

3.3. THE CYCLING UNIT OSCILLOSCOPE

An oscilloscope whose screen is shown on PX-9-303 is built into the cycling unit. The oscilloscope input switch with its 12 positions makes it possible to view any of the groups of cycling unit pulses or gates, the selective clear gate, or any external signal brought to the cycling unit through terminal Ext. below the switch.

It might be noted that the main purpose of the oscilloscope is to make possible verification of the presence of the pulses and to provide a rough check on their amplitudes. When viewed on the screen, the cycling unit pulses and gates should be approximately an inch high as indicated by the line on the oscilloscope screen. Because of their reflection in the lines of the synchronizing trunk, the cycling unit pulses and gates seen on the oscillo-scope screen do not have the symmetrical square shape shown on the chart below the screen.

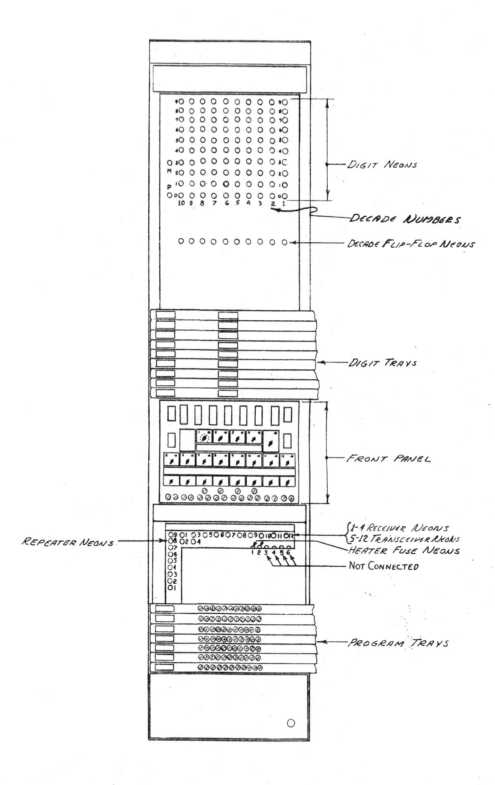

Digit Neons

Decade Numbers

Decade Flip-Flop Neons

Digit Trays

Front Panel

Repeater Neons

1-4 Receiver Neons
5-12 Transceiver Neons
Heater Fuse Neons
Not Connected

Program Trays

MOORE SCHOOL of ELECTRICAL ENGINEERING
UNIVERSITY of PENNSYLVANIA

ACCUMULATOR
FRONT VIEW
PX-5-305

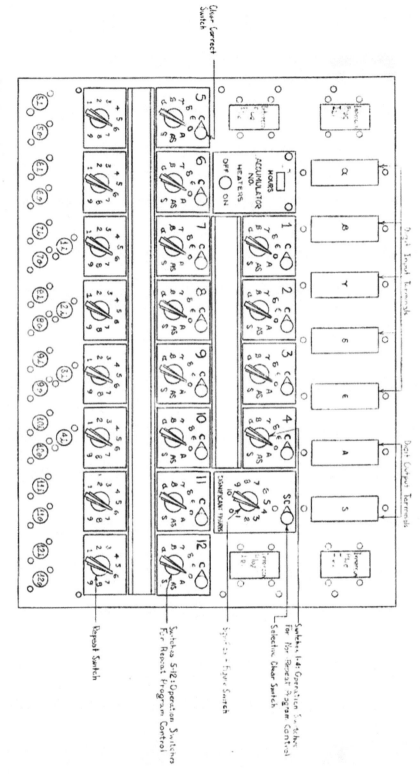

Clear Correct Switch

Digit Input Terminals

Digit Output Terminals

TERMINALS 1i, 2i,...,12i
Program pulse input terminals

TERMINALS 5o, 6o,...,12o
Program pulse output terminals

Repeat Switch

Switches 5-12: Operation Switches
For Repeat Program Control

Significant Figure Switch

Selective Clear Switch

Switches 1-4: Operation Switches
For Non-Repeat Program Control

ACCUMULATOR
FRONT PANEL
PX-S-304 R

The accumulator serves as a memory and arithmetic unit. Each accumulator can store and operate on a number having as many as 10 digits with its sign indication. Two accumulators can be interconnected by special plugging of their interconnector terminals so that they can store and operate on a signed number with as many as 20 digits. Programming memory is provided by the transceivers of the accumulator's 8 repeat program controls. Repeat switches included in the repeat program controls make it possible for an accumulator to remember that it is to transmit a program output pulse 1 to 9 addition times after receiving a program input pulse. In addition to 8 repeat program controls, the accumulator has 4 non-repeat program controls which have receivers and can, therefore, receive but not transmit a program pulse.

Because an accumulator is capable of receiving a number or of transmitting the number and/or the complement of the number stored in it, an accumulator is capable of performing the operations of addition or subtraction. Repeat program controls on the ENIAC make it possible for the accumulator to receive or transmit repetitively from one to nine times when a given repeat program control is stimulated. Each accumulator has 5 digit input channels through any one of which it can receive a 10 digit signed number. Mechanical shifters plugged into these input terminals make it possible to receive the incoming number shifted to the right or left. Thus, the accumulator, through repeated addition, can carry out the multiplication of a number by a constant having one or more digits.

The ability to do addition and subtraction and the presence of transceiver units in the accumulator also make it possible for the ENIAC to compare the magnitudes of two numbers in accumulators and, on the basis of this discrimination, choose which of 2 alternative program courses is to be followed.

The accumulator can clear its contents to zero in all decades or can clear so that zero remains in all decades but one and a five remains in that one (clear to 5). The ability to clear to 5 in a given decade combined with the possibility of plugging a deleter into an accumulator's digit output terminal or terminals makes it possible to use the accumulator to round off numerical results.

The static outputs of various stages of the 10 decade counters and the binary PM counter of an accumulator can be connected to other units such as the high speed multiplier or printer so that these units can receive information about the number stored in a given accumulator statically. (see Sec. 4.3.3.).

The following topics regarding the accumulator will be discussed in this chapter: Sec. 4.1, program controls; Sec. 4.2, common programming circuits; Sec. 4.3, numerical circuits; Sec. 4.4, use of accumulators for fewer or more than 10 digit computations; and Sec. 4.5, problems illustrating the use of accumulators. Reference will be made to the following diagrams:

Accumulator Front View	PX-5-305
Accumulator Front Panel	PX-5-301
Accumulator Block Diagram	PX-5-304

4.0. GENERAL SUMMARY OF THE ACCUMULATOR

Each accumulator has 12 program controls (see PX-5-301). Four of these are non-repeat program controls; eight are repeat.. Each of the 12 program controls has an operation switch for specifying the operation (receive, transmit, or neither) which the accumulator is to perform and a clear-correct switch. In addition, each non-repeat control has a receiver with a program pulse input terminal; each repeat program control has a transceiver with program pulse input and output terminals and a repeat switch. Neons associated with the 4 receivers and 8 transceivers are shown on PX-5-305.

The 12 program controls operate common programming circuits (see PX-5-304) the receive circuits, the transmit circuits, the clear circuits (including the significant figures switch and selective clear switch), and a circuit which enables the accumulator to pick up the l'P. The repeat switches of the 8 repeat program controls also operate in conjunction with the 9 stage repeater ring circuit. The repeater neons (see PX-5-305) are correlated with the stages of the repeater ring.

The programming circuits common to all 12 program controls operate the accumulator's numerical circuits (see PX-5-304). The accumulator's numerical circuits consist of 10 decade plug in units and a PM-clear plug in unit. Each decade plug in unit consists of a decade (10 stage ring) counter, a decade flip-flop (16, 17), a stage nine gate (14), reset pulse gate (18), carry over gates (19 and 20), A and S output gates (21 and 22 respectively) and transmitters, a pulse standardizer and several inverter tubes. Each decade counter stores 1 digit of a number and plays a part in the reception or transmission of one digit of the total of 10 digits that the accumulator can handle. The decade flip-flop has 2 purposes: (1) In reception it remembers if carry over is to take place; (2) in transmission it controls the A and S output gates. Gates 14, 18, 19, and 20 participate in the carry over process. Gate 18, moreover, controls the resetting of the decade flip-flop. The decades are numbered from right to left so that units decade counts as decade 1 and the 10^9 decade, as decade 10. There is a neon bulb associated with each stage of a decade counter and with the decade flip-flop (see PX-5-305).

The PM-clear unit contains a binary ring (PM) counter, A and S output gates and transmitters, a pulse standardizer, and amplifier tubes for the clear signal. There is also a special transmitter for the l'P used when the accumulator transmits subtractively. The PM counter has stage P for positive numbers, and stage M for negative numbers (which are treated as complements in the ENIAC). It should be noted that pulse input to the PM counter can come not only from the PM lead of a digit input terminal, but also can result from carry over from the 10th decade. This latter fact makes possible the correct addition or subtraction of signed numbers. Neons correlated with the stages P and M of the PM counter are shown on PX-5-305.

When storing the number +2 345 098 765, the accumulator's face will have the appearance shown on PX-5-305 (a) where a darkened circle denotes a lit neon bulb, and the corresponding stages of the various counters will be in the abnormal state.

The negative of a number is represented in the ENIAC by the complement of the number with respect to 10^{10*}. An accumulator stores the number -2 345 098 765 in the form M+$(10^{10}$-2 345 098 765) or M+(7 654 901 235). When an accumulator is storing -2 345 098 765, the digit neons appear as in Px-5-305 (b) and the corresponding stages of the counters are in the abnormal state.[**]

The decade counters and PM counter transmit their digit output through either or both of 2 terminals, the A (add) and S (subtract) output terminals. The number stored in an accumulator is emitted over the A terminal; the complement, over the S terminal. The counters can receive their inputs from any one of 5 input terminals identified by the letters α, β, γ, δ, ε. The decade counters and the PM counter of an accumulator receive or transmit the information for all 10 digits and sign simultaneously (the transmission of the pulses for each digit is, however, serial).

4.1. PROGRAM CONTROLS AND THE SIGNIFICANT FIGURES AND SELECTIVE CLEAR SWITCHES

As stated earlier, each accumulator has 12 program controls: four non-repeat controls (consisting of receiver with program pulse input terminal, operation switch and clear-correct switch) and 8 repeat controls (consisting of transceiver with program pulse input and output terminals, operation switch, clear-correct switch, and repeat switch). In this section the possible settings

---

* Also see Sec. 4.1.4.
**When two accumulators are interconnected to form one 20 decade accumulator, complements are taken with respect to 10^{20}.

and uses of program control switches will be described. The significant figures switch and selective clear switch which are more properly classified as part of an accumulator's common programming circuits are also described here. The switches are shown on PX-5-301. Neons correlated with the 12 program controls are shown on PX-5-305.

4.1.1. The Operation Switch

The operation switch has 9 positions: α, β, γ, δ, ϵ, 0, A, S, AS. If the operation switch of a stimulated program control is set at one of the settings α, β, γ, δ, or ϵ, the accumulator receives the pulses representing any number transmitted over the digit tray to which the corresponding digit input terminal is connected. Obviously, if that input terminal is not connected to a digit tray or is connected to a tray not carrying pulses at the time the control is stimulated, the accumulator receives no pulses. This point will be referred to in Sec. 4.1.2, in connection with the clear-correct switch.

If the operation switch is set at A, S, or AS, the accumulator transmits its contents, the complement of its contents, or both respectively when the control is stimulated.

The setting 0 instructs the accumulator to neither receive nor transmit. This setting is useful on non-repeat or repeat control operation switches when it is desired to clear an accumulator without receiving or transmitting (see Sec. 4.1.2.). When set on the operation switch of a repeat program control, the setting 0 provides a means of obtaining a program output pulse delayed from 1 to 9 addition times without, however, disturbing the contents of the accumulator. (See the discussion of dummy programs in Sec. 4.5.).

4.1.2. The Clear-Correct Switch

The clear-correct switch can be set at either C or 0. The accumulator's interpretation of the setting C depends on the setting of the associated operation switch.

If a stimulated program control's operation switch is set at one of the transmit settings (A, S, or AS) or is set at 0, the accumulator clears either to zero in all decades or to zero in all decades except one in which it clears to 5. The setting of the significant figures switch (see Sec. 4.1.4) determines whether clearing is to zero or 5 and, if to 5, in which decade the 5 appears.

With the operation switch set to a receive setting α, β, γ, δ, or ε, the setting C of the clear-correct switch gives the instruction "pick up the 1'P from the synchronizing trunk and put it in the first decade". If there are no digit pulses coming to the digit input terminal when the control set up in this way is stimulated, the accumulator simply picks up the 1'P. If there are actually pulses coming to the digit input terminal, these are first received and then, when the cycling unit emits the 1'P, this pulse also is picked up and put into the first decade. A "receive - C" program in which digits are received and the 1'P is picked up is, however, not possible when the digits are being transmitted as a complement from another unit in such a way that the 1'P from the digit tray also arrives in units place. (See Sec. 4.3.1.)

There are at least three occasions when the "receive -C" setting of a program control proves useful. If a given accumulator is being used to store the independent variable, the accumulator can be programmed to pick up the 1'P whenever it is desired to increase the value of the independent variable by one (see the illustrative problem of Chapter VIII). In some problem set-ups, an accumulator may receive from the S output terminal of the product, quotient, or two root accumulator, a complement with respect to 9 in all decades instead of a 10^{10} complement (see Chapters V and VI and Sec. 4.3.1.). Also, an accumulator may receive a number transmitted as a complement by a second accumulator and shifted to the right enroute so that the original 1'P needed to make a tens complement (see Sec. 4.3.1.) is lost. The missing pulse, in either case, can be picked up through a "receive -C" program.

4.1.3. Repeat Switch

The repeat switch (which is found only on repeat program controls) can be set to any number between one and nine inclusive. The accumulator carries out whatever operation is set on the associated operation switch as many times as is specified by the setting of the repeat switch. Each repetition requires one addition time so that if the repeat switch of a control is set at r ($1 \leqslant r \leqslant 9$), r addition times must be allowed for the program set up on that control. The transceiver of a repeat program control emits a program output pulse at the end of r addition times.

It is to be noted that if the clear switch of a repeat program control is set at C in connection with an O or transmit setting of the operation switch, clearing of the accumulator takes place but once, at the end of the rth addition time. The setting C in connection with a receive setting of the operation switch of a repeat program control causes the accumulator to pick up the 1'P in each of r addition times.

If the number a is stored in one accumulator and the number b in another accumulator, $a \pm rb$ (where $1 \leqslant r \leqslant 9$) may be formed in the first accumulator through the use of a repeat program control on each accumulator. The operation switch of the control on the first accumulator should be set at a receive setting and the repeat switch, at r. The operation switch of the second accumulator's control should be set at A (if $a+rb$ is to be formed) or at S (if $a-rb$ is to be formed) and the correlated repeat switch, at $R \geqslant r$. (see Problem 1, Sec. 4.5.)

In a similar fashion, it is possible to form $a \pm b \sum r_i \, 10^{k-i}$. In this case where the coefficient of b has more than one digit, shifters (see Secs. 4.5 and 11.2) are used to effect multiplication by powers of 10.

Notice that if the coefficient of b has p digits, p program controls will usually have to be used on the receiving accumulator but fewer than p may suffice on the transmitting accumulator. For example, 234b may be formed in an accumulator through the use of one program control (set-up to transmit additively 9 times) on the transmitting accumulator. Three program controls must be used on the receiving accumulator: one set up to receive, say on α, 4 times; another set up to receive on β, 3 times; a third set up to receive on γ, twice. A shifter which shifts numerical data 1 place to the left should be used at the β input terminal and one which shifts numbers two places to the left, at the γ input terminal of the receiving accumulator. As an example of the circumstances under which fewer than p program controls suffice on the transmitting accumulator, consider the case of forming 998b. This can be done by programming the accumulator which stores b to transmit subtractively twice and then additively once and by programming the receiving accumulator to receive twice thru an input terminal without a shifter and once thru an input terminal with a shifter that displaces data 3 places to the left (i.e. form 998b as $10^3 b - 2b$).

4.1.4.   The Significant Figures Switch

The significant figures switch is a part of the common programming circuits which function when the accumulator transmits subtractively or when the accumulator clears. The significant figures switch has eleven positions, 0, 1, ..., 10. These numbers refer to the number of significant figures, counted toward the right from the PM counter, to be retained in the accumulator.

If the significant figures switch on an accumulator is set at s ($0 \leqslant s \leqslant 10$), when clearing takes place, decade 10-s (i.e. the $s+1^{st}$ decade from the left) clears to five and all other decades to zero. When a single accumulator is used, this means that the accumulator is cleared to zero in all decades if its significant figures switch is set at 10. If two accumulators (see Sec. 4.4.2.) are interconnected to form a 20 decade accumulator, the setting s●10 on the left hand accumulator causes it to clear to zero in all decades; the right hand accumulator then clears in accordance with the setting of its significant figures switch. For example, if 11 significant figures are to be stored in the 11 left hand decades of a 20 decade accumulator, the significant figures switches of the left and right hand accumulators respectively are set at 10 and 1.

The setting of the significant figures switch also determines the decade place into which the 1'P is put when an accumulator transmits subtractively. With the significant figures switch of an accumulator set at s, the 1'P is transmitted over the lead for decade place 11-s, i.e., the sth decade place from the left. If the significant figures switch of an accumulator is set at 0, this means that the 1'P is not transmitted when subtractive transmission takes place. It is to be noted that the 1'P is picked up and put into units decade of an accumulator (which, in the case of 2 interconnected accumulators, mean the 20th decade from the left) when a "receive-C" program control is stimulated regardless of the setting of the significant figures switch.

Notice, that as far as rounding off a number in an accumulator is concerned, the setting of the significant figures switch provides only for getting the correct s digits from the left. The significant figures switch setting has nothing to do with deleting the non-significant digits at the right. The operator provides for the deletion of non-significant figures by placing a deleter at the output* terminal or terminals of the accumulator storing s significant figures (see Secs. 4.5 and 11.2). When printing of an s significant figure result is to take place from an accumulator and the non-significant figures at the right have not been deleted, deletion can be

---

* The deleters constructed at present can be used only at digit output terminals. Special deleters, however, can be constructed for use at digit input terminals.

provided for in the set up of the IBM punch plug board (see Sec. 9.4 for an illustration).

4.1.5. The Selective Clear Switch

The selective clear switch has two positions, SC and O. When the selective clear signal is transmitted from the initiating unit (see Chapter II), all accumulators whose selective clear switches are set at SC clear; those accumulators whose selective clear switches are set at O do not clear.

4.2. COMMON PROGRAMMING CIRCUITS

4.2.1. The Receive Circuits

When the receiver or transceiver of a program control whose operation switch is set at a receive setting (α, β, γ, δ, or ε) is stimulated, a signal from the normally positive output of the flip-flop is delivered (after passing thru an inverter and a buffer) by way of one deck of the operation switch to the receive circuits of the accumulators. The receive circuits include gates A through E 47, buffer tubes (A-C 48, A, C. E, G, and J 46, and A-D 49), and the 5 sets of receive gates A-L 41, ..., A-L 45 for the digit input terminals α through ε respectively.

The signal from the deck of the operation switch (referred to above) applied to the set of receive gates corresponding to the setting of the switch, opens the 11 receive gates for that digit input channel. Simultaneously, then, the digit pulses for the 10 decade places and the PM place are received in the accumulator. The pulses for each place are routed to the appropriate counter with each pulse received at a counter cycling it one stage.

The signal applied to one of the gates A-E 47 allows the carry clear gate to enter the accumulator and play its role in the carry over process (see Sec. 4.3.1.).

4.2.2. The Transmit Circuits

If a stimulated program control is set up for transmission (operation switch set at A, S, or AS), a signal from the normally positive output of the flip-flop opens one of the gates F, G, or H47 so that the 10 P are admitted to each of the decades of the accumulator. The role played by the 10 P in transmission is described in Sec. 4.3.1. The signal from the flip-flop also opens gate F49 (if S), J49 (if A) or gates G and H49 (if AS) so that the 9P can pass to the A and/or S output gates of the 10 decades and the PM unit. In S or AS transmission, moreover, gate M42 or M41 is opened to pass the 1'P. The 1'P passing through deck 3 of the significant figures switch is routed to the lead of the S output terminal specified by the setting of the significant figures switch. The manner in which the A and S gates are controlled so that the correct number of digit pulses (or 9P) are emitted over each decade place lead is described in Sec. 4.3.1.

4.2.3. The Clear Circuits

The clear circuits include gate M44, decks 1, 2, 1A, and 2A of the significant figures switch and the clear tubes in the PM unit.

If an accumulator is stimulated to transmit and clear, a signal from **buffer 62 of receivers or buffer 63 of transceivers is applied to** gate M44 so that the carry clear gate (CCG) is passed to the PM-Clear unit. The clear signal from the PM tubes goes directly to the upper connections of stages 1, 2, 3, 4, 6, 7, 8 and 9 in all decades causing these stages to be flipped into the normal state. With the significant figures switch set at s, the signal from the clear tubes is routed through deck 2A to the upper lead of the zero stage in decade 10-s and through deck 1 to the upper connection to stage 5 in all decades except decade 10-s. Decks 1A and 2 of the significant figures switch are return circuits from the flip-flops. Thus, stage zero is left in the abnormal state in all decades except decade 10-s in which stage 5 is left in the abnormal state.

Notice that gate M44 can be opened to pass the CCG either by the initial clear gate (see Chapter II) or by the selective clear gate (provided that the accumulator's selective clear switch is set at SC.), as well as by the flip-flop mentioned above.

4.2.4. Circuit for Admitting the 1'P to Units Decade

A signal from the normally negative output of a transceiver's flip-flop, through a buffer and then passing through the clear correct switch and one of the receive points on the operation switch reaches gates E49 and E50 after passing through the inverter G50. These gates, when opened, allow the 1'P to pass through to units decade of the accumulator.

4.2.5. Repeater Ring Common to Repeat Program Controls

The eight repeat program controls on an accumulator operate the 9 stage repeater ring circuit in common. A signal from the normally negative output of the flip-flop of such controls and then through buffer 61 opens gate H50 so that a CPP can reach the repeater ring to cycle it one stage per addition time. When the ring reaches stage r, the output signal from this stage, passing through point r on the repeat switch, causes gate 62 in the transceiver to emit a signal. The signal from 62 opens gate 68 which passes a CPP. The resulting pulse resets the transceiver's flip-flop and passes through the transmitter as a program output pulse. The signal from gate 62 also opens gate K50 so that a CPP passing through it clears the repeater ring back to stage 1 at the same time as the transceiver is emitting a program output pulse.

4.3. NUMERICAL CIRCUITS

4.3.1. Operation of the numerical circuits in transmitting a number and/or its Complement.

When an accumulator is stimulated to transmit its contents and/or the complement of its contents, the 10P are routed simultaneously to each of the 10 decade ring counters of the accumulator. Each of the 10P cycles the counter one stage. Thus, if the stage corresponding to 7 is in the abnormal state before any of the 10P is received, after receiving one pulse, the stage

TABLE 4-1

A and S TRANSMISSION

Accumulator stores P 0 000 000 007 – Significant figures switch is set at 10

Pulse Time	9P emitted over A leads PM 10 987 654 321	9P emitted over S leads PM 10 987 654 321	As result of receiving 10P acc. registers	Comment
0-17				Program input pulse is received.
18				
19				
1-0		1 1 111 111 111	P 1 111 111 118	
1		1 1 111 111 111	P 2 222 222 229	
2			P 3 333 333 330 *	*Indicates that decade flip flop is in abnormal state.
3	0 0 000 000 001	1 1 111 111 110	P 4 444 444 441*	
4	0 0 000 000 001	1 1 111 111 110	P 5 555 555 552*	
5	0 0 000 000 001	1 1 111 111 110	P 6 666 666 663*	
6	0 0 000 000 001	1 1 111 111 110	P 7 777 777 774*	
7	0 0 000 000 001	1 1 111 111 110	P 8 888 888 885*	
8	0 0 000 000 001	1 1 111 111 110	P 9 999 999 996*	
9	0 0 000 000 001	1 1 111 111 110	P 0 000 000 007 * *** ***	I'P is emitted over the lead for units decade because s = 10.
10		0 0 000 000 001		
11				
12				
13				Reset pulse resets all decade flip-flops.
14				
15				
16				
17				Program output pulse is transmitted if repeat control is used. Receiver (of non-repeat control) or transceiver (of non-repeat control) is reset.

corresponding to 8 is in the abnormal state, and stage 7 not. After receiving

10 pulses, the stage corresponding to 7 is in the abnormal state again (See

Table 4-1).

Meanwhile the accumulator changes the 9P into digit pulses in

the following way: Let d be the digit stored in a given decade counter

before the reception of any of the 10P. Then as the 10P are received, 9-d of

the 9P pass through gate 22 to be emitted over a lead of the subtract output

terminal. That one of the 10P which cycles the decade counter from stage 9

to zero, also passes through gate 14 and sets the decade flip-flop. With the

decade flip-flop in the abnormal state gate 22 is closed and 21 open so that

the subsequent d pulses of the 9P group are passed over the corresponding decade

place lead of the add output terminal. The first of the RP resets the decade

flip-flop.

So far in this discussion mention has been made of transmitting

through the subtract output terminal the complement of a number stored in an

accumulator with respect to 9 999 999 999. Complements with respect to 10^{10}

are provided by the accumulator's transmitting over the subtract output lead

corresponding to decade s from the left (where s is the number of significant

figures stored in the accumulator), the 1'P.

The transmission of sign indication is accomplished in a somewhat

different manner. The S and A gates, 16 and 15 respectively, of the PM unit

are controlled by stages P and M respectively of the PM counter. When a

positive number is stored in an accumulator which is transmitting, a positive

voltage from stage M holds gate 16 open so that the 9P are emitted over the

PM lead of the subtract output terminal; no pulses are transmitted over the

PM lead of the add output terminal since gate 15 is closed. If the sign of

the stored number is M, gate 16 remains closed and 15 is opened so that no

PM pulses are transmitted through the subtract output terminal, while 9 pulses are transmitted through the add output terminal.

4.3.2. Operation of the Numerical Circuits in Receiving a Number

The digit pulses received through the 11 input gates (see Sec. 4.2.1.) are routed simultaneously to the PM counter and the ten decade counters. Each pulse a decade counter receives cycles it one stage. The PM counter receives zero sign pulses for a positive number and 9 for a negative number. Each pulse received by the PM counter cycles it one stage so that the reception of an even number of pulses leaves the PM counter unchanged while the reception of an odd number of pulses has the effect of cycling the PM counter to the opposite stage.

If a given counter stores the digit d before reception and p $(9-d < p \leq 10)$ digit pulses are received, carry over takes place from that counter to the next one at the left (whether the PM or a decade counter). So called delayed carry over takes care of such carry-overs which result from incoming digit pulses. If a given counter, c, is in stage 9 and there is a carry over from the counter c-1, then, it is also necessary for carry over to take place from counter c to counter c+1. Carry overs which result from carry overs in this way are effected by a direct carry over process.

When a given counter is cycled to stage 9, a signal from this stage opens gate 14 so that the next pulse received by the decade (whether digit or carry pulse) not only cycles the counter back to stage zero but also passes through gate 14 and sets the decade flip-flop (16, 17). In delayed carry over, the decade flip-flop continues to remember that a carry over must take place but no further action is taken while the digit pulses (the 9P and the 1'P) are being received. The signal from the normally negative output of the decade flip-flop opens gate 18 so that the reset pulse is passed (in pulse time 13 of the addition time cycle). This pulse resets the decade flip-flop and also goes to gate 20. Now, in receive programs, the receive programming circuits allow the carry clear gate to reach and open gate 20, so that the pulse from gate 18 passes through to the next decade at the left.

The need for direct carry over arises after the first reset pulse is emitted by the cycling unit (since it is this reset pulse which gives rise to the need for direct carry over) so that carry over resulting from carry over must be treated differently. The carry pulse which passes through gate 14 goes to gate 19. Since the carry clear gate remains on for 7 pulse times, gate 19 is held open to pass this pulse to the next decade at the left. The carry clear gate, as a matter of fact remains on long enough for a carry pulse to proceed from units decade to the PM counter of 2 interconnected accumulators (with a safety factor). Notice, that even in direct carry over, the decade flip-flop is flipped into the abnormal state. The 2nd reset pulse, which is emitted after the carry clear gate goes off, resets the flip-flop in this case (see PX-9-306)

A number may be received in an accumulator so that a digit appearing in the i decade of the transmitting unit is received in the i decade of the receiving unit by connecting the digit output terminal of the transmitting unit to some digit trunk by the standard cable for that purpose, and then connecting the same digit trunk to one of the 5 digit input terminals of the receiving accumulator by a standard cable. However, if it is desired to receive a number transmitted from   decade i of the transmitting unit in decade i + k of the receiving accumulator (where k may be either positive or negative), the number must be passed through a shifter enroute from the transmitting to the receiving unit. It is usually most convenient to plug ordinary shifters into a digit input terminal of the receiving unit. A number may be <u>shifted to the left</u>

TABLE 4-2

RECEPTION INVOLVING DELAYED CARRY OVER

Accumulator Stores M 9 832 104 707 and Receives P 0 000 000 004

Pulse Time	Accumulator Receives PM 10 987 654 321	Accumulator Stores After Receiving PM 10 987 654 321	Comment
0-17			Program input pulse received.
-18			
-19			
1-0	0 0 000 000 001	M 9 832 104 708	
1	0 0 000 000 001	M 9 832 104 709	
2	0 0 000 000 001	M 9 832 104 700*	*Decade flip-flop in abnormal state.
3	0 0 000 000 001	M 9 832 104 701*	
4			
5			
6			
7			
8			
9			
10			
11			
12			
13	0 0 000 000 010	M 9 832 104 711	Reset pulse resets decade flip-flop and causes carry pulse.
14			
15			
16			
17			Program output pulse emitted if repeat control is used, and program control is reset.

either by an ordinary shifter plugged into a digit input terminal or by a
special shifter plugged into a digit output terminal. A number may be shifted
to the right only through an ordinary shifter plugged into a digit input terminal (see Sec. 11.2).

Table 4-2 illustrates the way in which an accumulator receives a
number and also the delayed carry over process.

4.3.3. Static Communication Between an Accumulator and Another ENIAC Unit

The high-speed multiplier receives its arguments and the printer
data to be printed in static form from accumulators. The divider and square
rooter also receives information about the signs of the arguments statically.
The term static is used to distinguish this kind of communication between an
accumulator and another unit from the usual dynamic transmission in which an
accumulator transmits d pulses for the digit d and 0 or 9 pulses for sign P
or M respectively.

A unit which receives the static outputs of an accumulator has an
array of vacuum tubes[*] corresponding to the flip-flops of the counters in an
accumulator. For example, the ier selectors in the high-speed multiplier
(see Sec. 5.3) which receive the multiplier from the multiplier accumulator
statically consist of a 10 by 10 array of vacuum tubes. Each of the tubes
in a column of the array corresponds to one of the flip-flops in a decade
counter of an accumulator; each column in the array, to a decade counter in
an accumulator. Two standard 55 conductor cables (carried in the static
cable trough which runs along the tops of the ENIAC units) are used to deliver
the static outputs of the accumulator which stores the multiplier to the ier
selectors. The normally negative output of the flip-flop representing digit d

---

[*]Two double triodes in one envelope are referred to here as 2 tubes.

in decade counter c is connected by one of the leads in these cables to the corresponding tube in the ier selectors. Thus, 100 of the 110 leads are used. An additional lead in one of the cables goes from the flip-flop for stage M in the accumulator's PM counter to a tube in the high-speed multiplier which represents sign M of the multiplier. In this way, when flip-flop d of counter c is in the abnormal state (because that counter stores the number d) the tube in row d and column c of the ier selectors is turned on. The other tubes in column c of the ier selectors do not go on.

Similar connections are made to tubes in the printer from the counters of accumulators which store data for printing (see Sec. 9.4). In some cases data is printed from only 5 decades and the PM of an accumulator so that only 1 cable connects such an accumulator to corresponding tubes in the printer. The master programmer also has decade counters which are similar in some respects to the decade counters of an accumulator (see Sec. 10.2.). These, too, can be connected statically to the printer.

In the case of the divider and square rooter only sign indication is communicated statically from the accumulators which store the numerator (or radicand) and denominator.

The length of time required for the information stored in an accumulator to be communicated in static form to another unit depends on the length of the leads from the accumulator to the unit. Approximately an addition time is required to turn on the tubes in the high-speed multiplier and in the divider and square rooter because the accumulators statically connected to these units are near them. A somewhat longer time is required in the case of the printer.

4.4. USE OF ACCUMULATORS FOR FEWER THAN OR MORE THAN TEN DIGITS

4.4.1. Use of an Accumulator to Store Two Numbers

In some problems it may be desirable to put emphasis on the number of different numbers which can be stored in accumulators so that they will be readily available for computations rather than on the number of significant figures carried in the computation. While the accumulator has been designed to handle 10 digit numbers, it is possible to store in an accumulator two numbers with the same sign if their combined number of digits is 10 or fewer or with different signs if their combined number of digits is fewer than 10. In the first case the PM counter is used for the common sign. In the second case, one of the decade counters is used as a PM counter for the purpose of registering sign indication for one of the numbers with stage 0 representing sign P and stage 9, sign M.

When the numbers are transmitted to other units for computational purposes, they can be isolated from one another by the use of special deleters, adaptors, and/or shifters. It is to be noted, however, that if subtractive transmission takes place from an accumulator storing two numbers, only one of the numbers will be a correct tens complement since the other will lack the 1'P needed to make such a complement.

An example involving the use of an accumulator to store two different numbers simultaneously is given in the illustrative problem of Sec. 8.7.

4.4.2. Interconnection of Two Accumulators to Form a Twenty Decade Accumulator

Another option available to the operator is whether an accumulator is to be used alone as a 10 decade accumulator with 12 program controls or as a 20 decade accumulator with controls for 24 programs. This option results from the fact that certain of the accumulator's circuits have been left open at the accumulator's interconnector terminals (indicated on PX-5-304 by the symbol $\longrightarrow$ $\square$ $\square$ $\longrightarrow$). The circuits so treated include the receive, transmit, clear, and pick up the l'P circuits, and the input to units decade and the carry over input to the PM counter from decade 10. By special connections of the accumulator's interconnector terminals (I_{L_1}, I_{L_2}, I_{R_1}, and I_{R_2} on PX-5-301), these circuits are closed in one way to make the accumulator function as a 10 decade accumulator and in a different way to interconnect two accumulators so that they form a 20 decade accumulator.

If a single accumulator is used as a 10 decade accumulator, the following interconnections must be made:

      (a) vertical interconnector cable must be plugged from interconnector terminal I_{L_1} to I_{L_2}

      (b) load box must be placed at interconnector terminal I_{R_1}.

If two accumulators U and U' (where U is assumed to be the left hand accumulator) are to be used as a 20 decade accumulator, the required interconnections are:

      (a) vertical interconnector cable from I_{L_1} to I_{L_2}

      (b) horizontal interconnector cables from I_{R_1} to I'_{L_1} and from I_{R_2} to I'_{L_2}

      (c) load box at I'_{R_1}.

The significant figures switch of the left hand accumulator should be set to 10 and in the right hand accumulator to s' where $0 \leq s' \leq 10$ if $10 + s'$ significant figures are desired. If fewer than 10 significant figures are desired, the left hand switch is set to this number and the right hand switch to 10.

For a given program only 1 program control is used. In reception, each accumulator receives its ten digits over one of its 5 digit input terminals. If the standard jumper cable for interconnecting accumulators is used, each accumulator receives its 10 digits through the digit input terminal on its front panel bearing the same designation (α-ϵ) as the setting of the operation switch used to program the reception. Each accumulator transmits its digit output through its own digit output terminals. In the transmission of complements the 1' pulse is emitted over the decade place lead of the last significant figure being retained. The 20 decade accumulator clears to zero in all decades except possibly one where clearing is to 5. Clearing is to zero in all decades if both s and s' are 10. In "receive -C" programs, the 1' pulse is put into the 20th decade from the left.

More than 2 accumulators should not be interconnected with one another as described above since the carry clear gate does not last long enough to provide safely for direct carry over across more than 20 decades; nor are the program control buffers designed to operate more than 2 accumulators.

4.5. ILLUSTRATIVE PROBLEMS

Matters relevant to setting up accumulators for certain specific purposes will be discussed in the following pages. Sec. 4.5.1. illustrates the set-up for a very simple computation involving only accumulators. Sec. 4.5.2. treats of the use of dummy programs, and Sec. 4.5.3. deals with the use of accumulators for magnitude discrimination programs. Examples of the use of accumulators in conjunction with other ENIAC units are found at the end of Chapters VI - IX.

The examples will be described with the aid of set-up tables and set-up diagrams. The set-up table is designed to give a comprehensive plan of the computation showing the programs the units will perform and their numerical contents at various addition times in the computation. The set-up diagrams show the cable connections which must be made between the units and program or digit trays to carry out the computations and also indicate the settings of switches which are parts of the common programming circuits.

The set-up tables are given with addition times as the independent variable. A double column is devoted to each unit. In the left hand half the program is described; in the right hand half, the contents of the unit as a result of the program are shown. For accumulator programs, symbols appear on three levels, e.g.

$$1\text{-}8 \quad ⑤ \qquad\qquad\qquad\qquad ⑥$$
$$A\ C\ 1 \qquad\qquad\text{or.}\qquad\qquad 0\ 0\ 1$$
$$1\text{-}9 \qquad\qquad\qquad\qquad 1\text{-}10\quad 1\text{-}11$$

The symbols have the following interpretations:

(1) ⓘ at the upper right of the first level indicates that the program is set-up on program control i

(2) j-k designates a program pulse with j representing the tray and k the line in the tray on which the program pulse is carried. A program input pulse which occurs, say, at pulse time 17 (CPP time) of addition time 0, is written at the left on the first level of the addition time I line. A program input pulse which is derived from a digit pulse so that it occurs, not at CPP time, but at some other time in the addition time cycle, let us say pulse time 5 of addition time 1, is written at the left of the third level on the line corresponding to addition time 1. A program output pulse is always written at the right of level

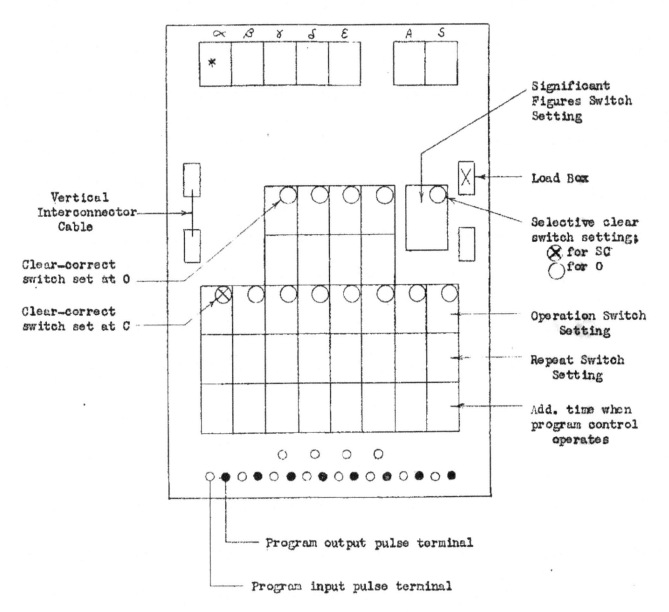

*A shifter, deleter, or adaptor plugged into a digit terminal is described in the digit terminal box as follows:

A shifter which shifts numerical data k places to the left or right respectively by the symbol +k or −k.

A deleter which eliminates the digits carried on certain decade places leads by the letter d followed by the numbers of the decade place leads deleted.

An adaptor by the letter a. A description of the adaptor appears in a convenient place on the diagram.

Fig. 4-1

SET-UP DIAGRAM SYMBOLS FOR ACCUMULATOR

three. An arrow ending on the addition time line in which

the program is completed and program output pulse is trans-

mitted intervenes between level 2 and level 3 for programs

lasting more than one addition time. In such cases, the

program output pulse is written at the right of the arrow

tip on the line for the addition time at the end of which

the program is completed and the program output pulse is

transmitted.

(3) The symbols in the second level represent the settings of

the operation, clear-correct, and repeat switches reading

from left to right.

Thus, the illustrative group of symbols above at the left, has

the following meaning: A program pulse (derived from a CPP) which is picked

up from line 8 in program tray 1 stimulates program control 5 to cause the

accumulator to transmit additively one time and then to clear. Upon completion

of the program, a program output pulse is emitted to line 9 in program tray 1.

On some occasions, as noted above, digit pulses will be used in lieu

of program pulses. A program in which such a digit pulse is generated might

be written as in the sample below.

$$2\text{-}3 \qquad \textcircled{8}$$
$$\begin{array}{|l|} \hline A\ 0\ 1 \\ A(3)\ \text{to} \\ 1\text{-}5 \\ \hline \end{array}$$
$$2\text{-}4$$

This group of symbols describes the following program: The program pulse

delivered to the program input terminal of control 8 causes the accumulator

to transmit additively once without clearing. The digit pulses carried on

the add output lead for decade place 3 are delivered to line 5 of program tray 1.

The program output pulse from control 8 is carried on line 4 of program tray 2.

The symbol $\sim\sim\sim$ in the contents column is used to indicate that an accumulator is cleared. It is always written on the line corresponding to the addition time at the end of which clearing takes place.

The conventions on the set-up figures for accumulators are described in Figure 4-1.

4.5.1. Computation in Accumulators

The computation described here consists of generating n, n^2, and n^3 respectively in accumulators 6, 7, and 8. It is desired to terminate the computation when $n^3 \geq 9\ 000\ 000\ 000$.

The basic computation which is repeated until the limit specified on n^3 is reached is arrived at inductively. Assuming that n, n^2, and n^3 are stored in accumulators 6, 7, and 8 respectively we can proceed to $(n+1)^3$ and $(n+1)^2$ by adding $3n^2$, 3n, and then 1 to n^3 and by adding 2n and then 1 to n^2 (see Table 4-3).

To terminate the computation at the desired point we make use of the fact that the complement of 9 in a decade place other than that of the extreme right hand significant figure is zero. Now, we stimulate repetition of the computing cycle each time by the program output pulse of a dummy program control whose program input pulse is derived from the digit pulse or pulses on the subtract output lead for decade 10 of accumulator 8. As long as the digit in the 10th decade is different from 9, this control receives and therefore, transmits a program output pulse which stimulates the iteration. When 9 appears in the 10th decade, this dummy program control receives and, therefore, emits no program output pulse so that the computation is terminated.

The question as to why the S digit output of the 10th decade is

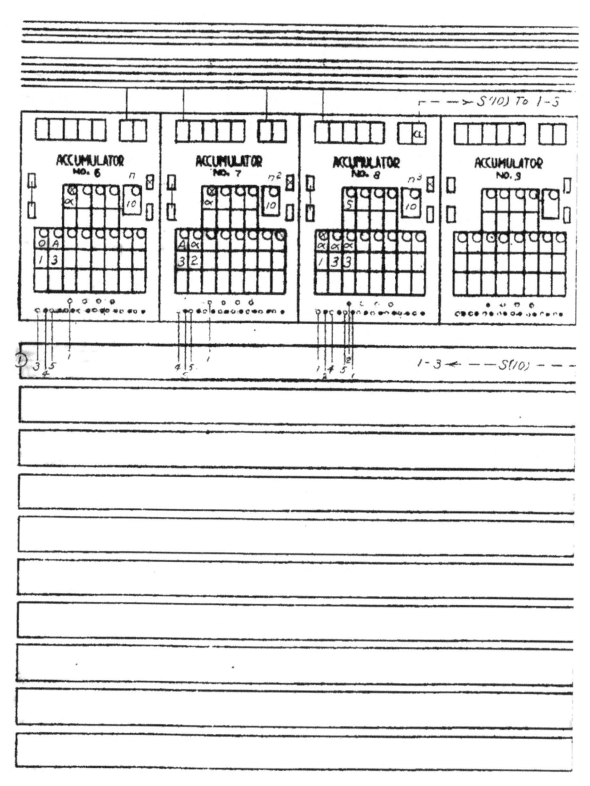

Fig. 4-2

Set-Up Diagram for Problem of Generating n, n^2, and n^3 as long as $n^3 < 8\ 000\ 000\ 000$

TABLE 4-3

SET-UP TABLE FOR GENERATING n, n^2, n^3

Computation is terminated when $n^3 \geq$ 9 000 000 000

Unit Add Time	Accumulator No. 6		Accumulator No. 7		Accumulator No. 8		
0	Initiating Pulse from initiating unit to program line 1-1						↑
1	1-1 ① α C 1	1	1-1 ① α C 1	1	1-1 ⑤ α C 1 1-2	1	Initial Sequence
2	1- 0 0 1 ⑤ 1-3 1-4				1-2 ① S 0 1 S (10) to 1-3		↓
3	.		1-4 ⑤ ʌ 0 3		1-4 ⑥ α 0 3	2	↑
4						3	
5			↓ 1-5			4	Basic Computing Sequence Repeated as long as $n^3 <$ 9 000000000
6	1-5 ⑥ ʌ 0 3		1-5 ⑥ α 0 2	2	1-5 ⑦ α 0 3	5	
7				3		6	
8					1-1	7	
9	1-1 ① α C 1	2	1-1 ① α C 1	4	1-1 ⑤ α C 1 1-2	8	
10	0 0 1 ⑤ 1-3 1-4				1-2 ① S 0 1 S (10) to 1-3		↓

delivered to a program control which does nothing but transmit a program output pulse instead of being delivered to one of the controls used for computing may be raised at this point. The answer lies in the fact that the digit pulses do not begin to pour out of the S output terminal until pulse time 1 in the addition time cycle. This would mean that a computing program initiated by a digit pulse would start after at least one of the 10P and one of the 9P had been emitted by the cycling unit. Since these pulses play a vital role in computing programs, such programs must be initiated before the digit pulses are emitted. For this reason digit pulses may be used to initiate computing programs only under certain restricted conditions. Instead digit pulses should be converted into a true program pulse through the use of a dummy program (see Sec. 4.5.2.) and the computing program can then be initiated by the program pulse which results from the dummy program.

4.5.2. Dummy Programs

A dummy program is defined as one in which the operation and clear-correct switches are set at 0 and the repeat switch at r where $1 \leq r \leq 9$. Dummy programs are always set-up on repeat program controls. The dummy program has at least 3 important functions: 1) conversion of digit pulses into program pulses, 2) delay of a program pulse, and 3) isolation of programs from one another.

The discussion in Sec. 4.5.1. regarding use 1) may be summarized as follows: To ensure that units receive all of the pulses needed for arithmetic operations, computational programs must usually be initiated by program pulses occuring at the time of the CPP. Where the stimulation of subsequent programs depends on digit pulses, the digit pulses should be converted into a program pulse by being brought to a dummy program control. The program output pulse

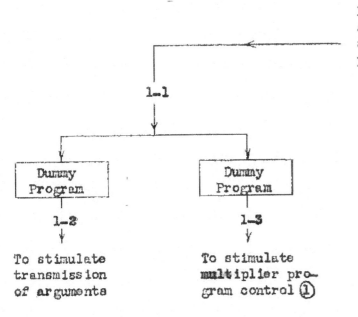

Program pulse available to
stimulate transmission of
arguments and first multiplication program.

1-1

Dummy
Program

Dummy
Program

1-2

1-3

To stimulate
transmission
of arguments

To stimulate
multiplier pro-
gram control ①

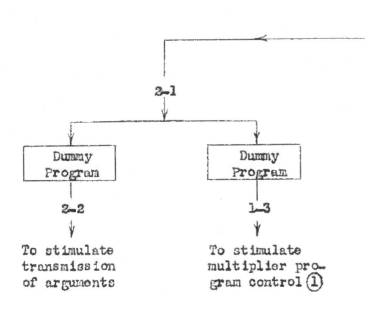

Program pulse available to
stimulate transmission of
arguments and second multiplication program.

2-1

Dummy
Program

Dummy
Program

2-2

1-3

To stimulate
transmission
of arguments

To stimulate
multiplier pro-
gram control ①

Fig. 4-3

USE OF DUMMY PROGRAMS TO ISOLATE PROGRAM PULSES

from the dummy program control can then be used to stimulate computing programs.

The need for the second contribution (delay) of dummy programs becomes apparent in setting up a fairly complicated problem in which a number of programs are carried out in parallel. As an example of this need, the reader is referred to the illustrative problem of Sec. 8.7.

Suppose that at some point in a computation one program pulse is available to stimulate a multiplier program control and also to stimulate the transmission of the arguments for the multiplication program. Let us suppose further that the same multiplier program control is to be stimulated at some later time but that the arguments for the multiplication program, this time, are to be obtained in a different way. Obviously, the program pulse that stimulates transmission of the arguments must be isolated from the pulse that stimulates the multiplier program control for, otherwise, the units which transmit the arguments for the first multiplication cannot be suppressed from transmitting when the second multiplication program takes place.

The desired isolation can be provided for through the use of dummy programs in the manner suggested in Figure 4-3. The lines which carry program pulses have been labelled with program tray and line numbers for illustrative purposes.

4.5.3. Magnitude Discrimination Programs

As mentioned in the opening paragraphs of this chapter, the ENIAC is capable of discriminating between program sequences by examining the magnitude of some numerical result. In this section one possible method of carrying out such a magnitude discrimination program in an accumulator is discussed.

Let us assume that the critical quantity upon whose magnitude the choice of subsequent programs depends is x so that when $x < b$, program P_1 is

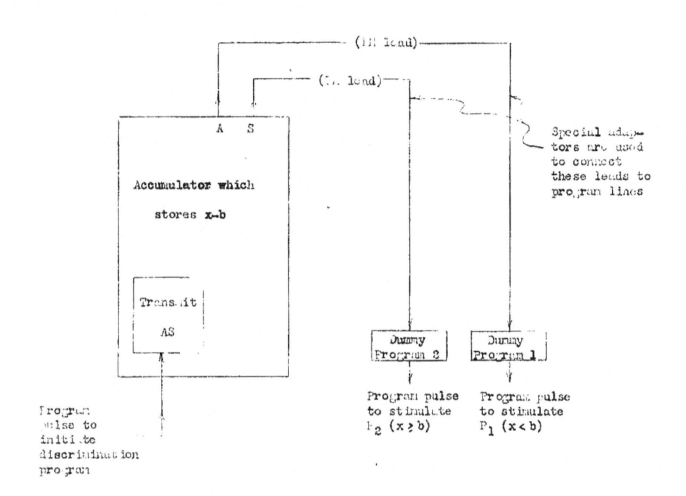

Fig. 4-4

MAGNITUDE DISCRIMINATION PROGRAM

to be stimulated and that when $x \geqslant b$, program P_2 is to be stimulated. The magnitude discrimination program is possible because 9 digit pulses are transmitted for sign indication M and none for sign indication P.

Let us form the quantity x-b in some accumulator. Then, using a special adapter, connect the PM lead of the A output terminal of this accumulator to the program pulse input terminal of one dummy program control and the PM lead of the S output terminal to the program pulse input terminal of a second dummy program control as indicated on the schematic diagram of Figure 4-4.

Obviously when $x < b$, a positive number is emitted over the S terminal and a negative over the A terminal so that only dummy program control 1 is stimulated to emit a program pulse. Similarly, when $x > b$, the number emitted over the A terminal is positive and that over the S terminal, negative so that only dummy program control 2 is stimulated to emit a program pulse.

Even though both the number zero and its complement are represented in the ENIAC by P 0 000 000 000, the case $x = b$ (or $x - b = 0$) can still be treated in the same way as $x > b$ (or $x - b > 0$). For recall, when a positive number is transmitted from an accumulator, the A output gate of the PM counter remains closed and the S gate opens to allow the 9P to pass to the PM lead of the S output terminal.[*] These 9P received at the program pulse input terminal of dummy program control 2 cause the emission of a program output pulse to stimulate P_2.

---

[*]Notice that when an accumulator which stores zero transmits subtractively to a second accumulator, this second accumulator receives, at first, M 9 999 999 999. Later, in the pulse time of the 1'P, the transmitting accumulator emits this pulse so that the receiving accumulator then stores P 0 000 000 000 after direct carry over proceeding from units decade to the PM counter has taken place.

In a problem in which accumulators are not urgently needed for storage or computational purposes, this set-up of a magnitude discrimination program is satisfactory. However, in general, this method has the disadvantage that no numerical programs other than one magnitude discrimination program can be carried out in an accumulator so set up, since both digit output terminals of the accumulator are completely associated with the magnitude discrimination program. The same magnitude discrimination can be effected without completely tying up either digit output terminal of an accumulator if the master programmer is used. A magnitude discrimination program involving the master program is described in Sec. 10.6.2. of the master programmer chapter.

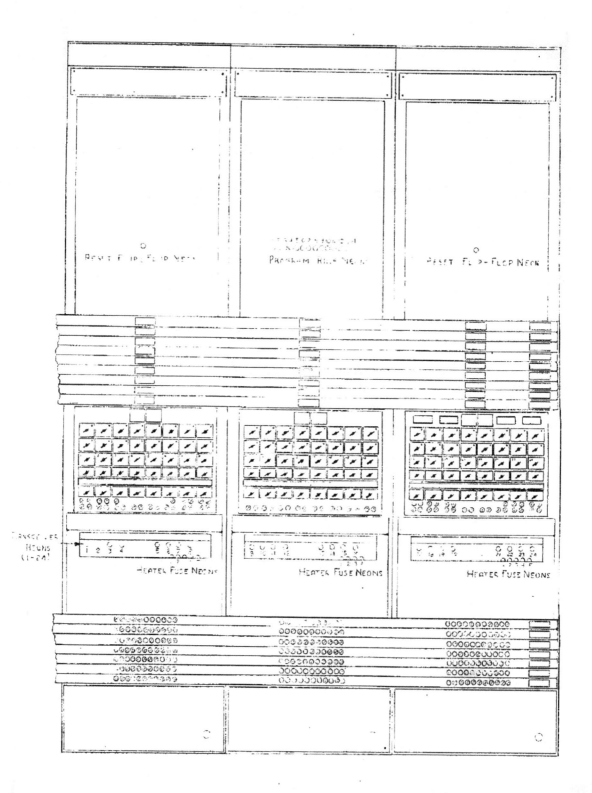

RESET FLIP-FLOP NEONS

PROGRAM RING NEONS

RESET FLIP-FLOP NEONS

TRANSFER
NEONS
(1-24)

HEATER FUSE NEONS

HEATER FUSE NEONS

HEATER FUSE NEONS

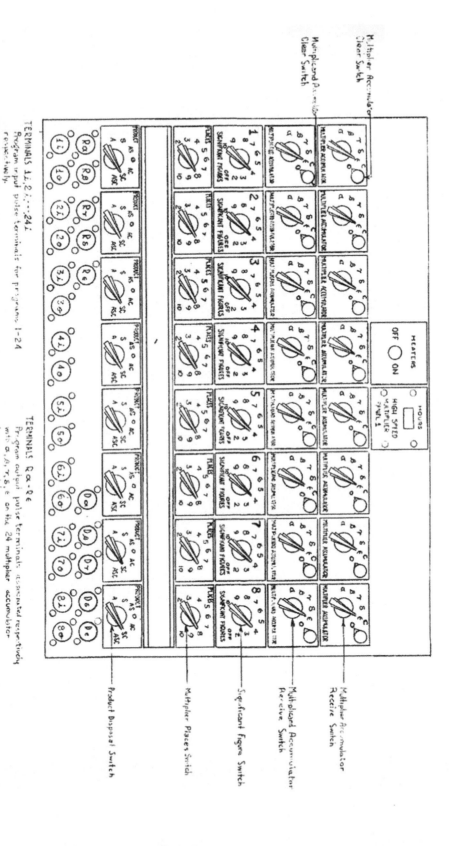

HIGH SPEED MULTIPLIER
FRONT PANEL NO. 1
PX-6-302R

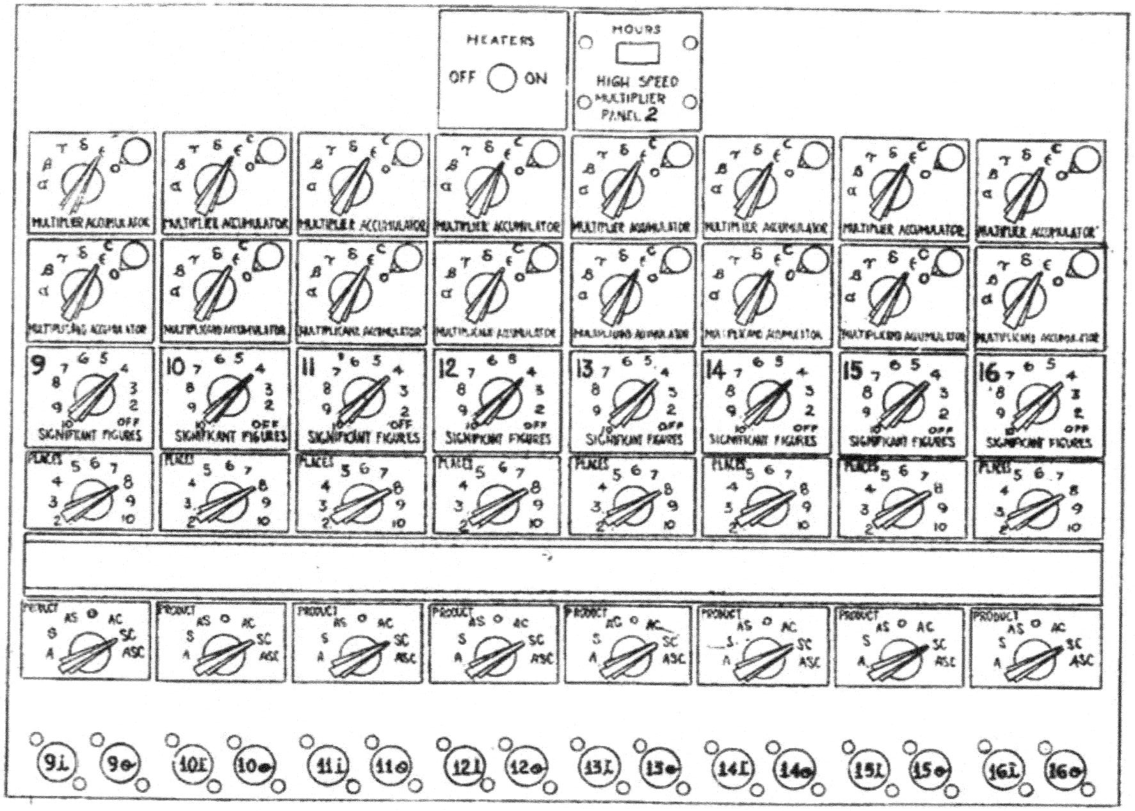

HIGH SPEED MULTIPLIER
FRONT PANEL No. 2
PX-6-303R

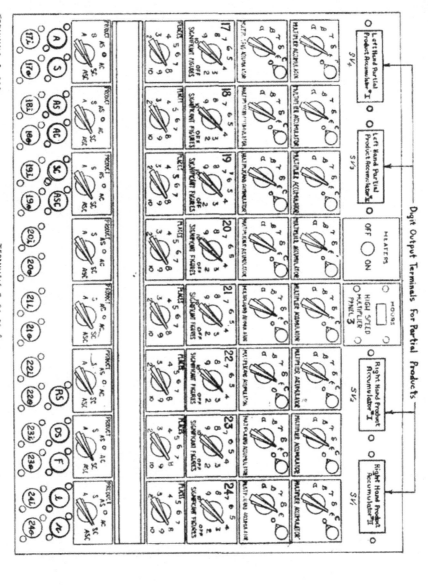

TERMINALS A-ASC

Program output pulse terminals associated respectively with A,S,AS,AC,Sc,ASc, on product disposal switch.

TERMINALS F, RS, DS, ℓ, ~

Program output terminals for transmitting following signals which occur during multiplication cycles:

ℓ and ~ - left and right hand accumulators respectively receive partial products

RS and DS - correct for negative multiplicand and/or multiplier respectively

F - left hand accumulator transmit contents to right hand accumulator (or vice versa).

Digit Output Terminals for Partial Products

HIGH SPEED MULTIPLIER
FRONT PANEL No.3
PX-6-304R.

V   HIGH-SPEED MULTIPLIER

The high-speed multiplier finds the product of a signed multiplicand with as many as 10 digits by a signed multiplier of p digits (p $\leq$ 10) in p+4 addition times. This high-speed is possible because products are obtained through the use of a multiplication table rather than by repeated addition.

Not only does the high-speed multiplier find products, but it also has facilities for controlling certain programming features in accumulators associated with it: 1) It can instruct the argument accumulators to receive and clear or not clear at the end of the multiplication; 2) It can signal the final product accumulator to dispose of the product; 3) It delivers to associated accumulators programming signals used in the multiplication process.

The following topics will be discussed in this chapter: Sec. 5.1, program controls; Sec. 5.2, common programming circuits; Sec. 5.3, numerical circuits; Sec. 5.4, Interrelation of high-speed multiplier and associated accumulators; Sec. 5.5, illustrative problem set-ups. Reference will be made to the following diagrams:

Front View	PX-6-309
Front Panels	PX-6-302, 303, and 304
Block Diagram	PX-6-308
Interconnection of High-Speed Multiplier with Associated Accumulators	PX-6-311

5.0. GENERAL SUMMARY

The high-speed multiplier operates in conjunction with 4 or, possibly, 6 accumulators. Two accumulators, the ier (multiplier) and icand (multiplicand) accumulators, store the arguments. The accumulators used for this purpose have the static outputs of their counters connected to the multiplier. Also, the PM-clear unit is statically connected to the multiplier so that these accumulators can be cleared by a signal from the multiplier at the end of a multiplication program and so that the high-speed multiplier may take proper cognizance of the signs. If products having 8 or fewer significant figures are required, two accumulators are used for storing the products which the multiplier emits in pulse form through the digit output terminals on panel 3. These accumulators are referred to as the LHPP (left hand partial products) and RHPP (right hand partial products) accumulators. Where products of more than 8 significant figures are desired, a pair of interconnected accumulators may be used as the LHPP accumulator and another pair as the RHPP accumulator. The role of the LHPP and RHPP accumulators will be discussed in greater detail below. Either the LHPP or RHPP accumulator may be used as the final product (FP) accumulator.

The high-speed multiplier has 24 program controls (8 on each of its 3 panels) on which can be set up 24 essentially different multiplication programs. In a problem in which there are more than 24 basic multiplications, each multiplier control can be used on a number of different occasions with the aid of the master programmer or sequences of dummy programs.

Each program control consists of a transceiver with program pulse input and output terminals, multiplier and multiplicand accumulator receive switches, multiplier and multiplicand accumulator clear switches, a significant figures switch, a multiplier places switch, and a product disposal switch. The argument accumulator receive switches enable the operator to specify the digit input terminals through which the ier and icand accumulators shall receive their

arguments for a given program. The significant figures switch setting
determines into which decade place of the LHPP five round off pulses are transmitted for a given program. The setting of the places switch determines how
many of the multiplier's digits are used for the program and, therefore, how
long the multiplication takes (see below and Sec. 5.2.). Instructions for the
transmission of the product from the final product accumulator can be set up
on the answer disposal switch.

The 24 program controls operate the common programming circuits
which include a 14 stage program ring with associated gates, inverters and
buffers, the ier accumulator and ic nd accumulator receive circuits with
program pulse output terminals Ra-Re and Da-De on front panel 1, argument
accumulator clear circuits, the product disposal circuit with program pulse
output terminals A, S, ..., ASC on front panel 3, and the argument accumulator
clear circuits.

The program ring with its associated tubes clocks the progress of
multiplication programs. Gates A'47 and A'46 which admit the 1'P and 4P are
the round off gates. Gates B'-K'46 operate in conjunction with the places
switch to terminate the program when the specified number of places of the
ier have been used and, in conjunction with gate F'48, to clear the ring to
stage 13 at this time. The program ring, ultimately, also controls a circuit
for correcting products if either or both of the arguments are negative (see
discussion below), the l and r receiver circuits which emit static signals
to program the partial products accumulators to receive, the circuit which
emits the F pulse to stimulate the collection of the partial products in the
final product accumulator, and the reset circuits for the program controls.

The outputs of stages 3 through 12, by means of the buffer tubes B'-L' 42, control the high-speed multiplier's numerical circuits so that multiplication by each digit of the ier takes place successively.

The numerical circuits consist of the multiplier selector gates, the multiplication table, the coding gates which pass the 1, 2, 2', and 4P, the multiplicand selector gates and the shifters. The multiplication table stores the products of numbers between 1 and 9 by numbers between 0 and 9 by means of a resistance matrix. The table actually consists of 2 tables, the tens and units tables, used for storing the tens and units digits of these products respectively. For example, the multiplication table remembers the product of 4 x 9 by storing 3 in the tens table and 6 in the units table.

The ier selector tubes are set up by the static outputs of the ier accumulator counters. Each column in this array of tubes is dedicated to 1 decade place of the ier; each row, to one of the digits between 0 and 9. When the program ring signals for multiplication by the ier digit in a particular decade place, the activated ier selector gate for that decade place emits a signal to the multiplication tables.

Static signals for the products of all digits between 1 and 9 by the particular ier digit are emitted from the multiplication table and converted into pulse form at the coding gates. The products from the tens and units tables respectively then go to the left and right hand sets of multiplicand selector gates. These gates are set up by the static outputs of the icand accumulator so that only the products appropriate to the digits of the icand are allowed to pass.

These partial products then go to the left and right hand shifters. Each set of shifters consists of a 10 by 10 array of gates. The gates on each row are controlled by one stage of the program ring and the outputs of the gates are connected diagonally so that products are shifted successively one place to the right as multiplication by the ier digits progresses from left to right. The products are emitted from the 4 digit output terminals on panel 3 of the high-speed multiplier with those from the tens table being emitted by the terminals LH partial products accumulators I and II and those from the units table, by the terminals RH product accumulators I and II. The terminals identified by II and I respectively take care of the digits for decade places $10^0 - 10^9$ and $10^{10} - 10^{19}$.

Notice, that the high-speed multiplier transmits only the digits of the product but not the sign. For positive arguments, this results immediately in the correct signed product. If either or both of the arguments are negative, certain correction terms are needed to produce the correct signed products. From Table 5-1 in which the correction terms for the various cases are tabulated, it can be seen that whenever an argument is negative, the product obtained from the multiplication tables must be corrected by 10^{10} times the complement of the other argument. In the case where both arguments are negative, moreover, the sign of the product must be corrected. The programming circuits (see Sec. 5.2.) provide for the last correction by causing the 1'P to be transmitted over the PM lead of the digit output terminal RH product accumulator I. The programming circuits provide for the other corrections by causing the emission of program output pulses at the RS and/or DS output terminals. The operator must interconnect the multiplier with its associated accumulators so that these pulses stimulate the corrections to take place (see PX-6-311 and Sec. 5.4.).

TABLE 5-1

CORRECTION TERMS FOR NEGATIVE IER AND/OR ICAND.
R and D represent the absolute values of the ier and icand respectively.

	Case 1 Ier positive Icand negative	Case 2 Ier negative Icand positive	Case 3 Ier and Icand both negative
ier	$P + (R)$	$M + (10^{10} - R)$	$M + (10^{10} - R)$
icand	$M + (10^{10} - D)$	$P + (D)$	$M + (10^{10} - D)$
Product obtained from multiplication tables	$P + (10^{10} R - RD)$	$P + (10^{10} D - RD)$	$P + 10^{20} + (RD - 10^{10}R - 10^{10}D)$ $= M + (RD - 10^{10}R - 10^{10}D)$
Correction term needed	$M + 10^{10}(10^{10} - R)$	$M + 10^{10}(10^{10} - D)$	$M + [P + 10^{10}(R)] + [P + 10^{10}(D)]$
Correct signed product	$M + (10^{20} - RD)$	$M + (10^{20} - RD)$	$P + (RD)$

To summarize the discussion of the previous pages, multiplication of a 10 or fewer digit icand by a p digit ier required p + 4 addition times. These addition times are used for the following purposes:

1. reception of arguments

2. setting up of selector tubes and round off in LHPP accumulator

3.
.
. obtaining the partial products (icand)x (1 digit of the ier) successively for the p digits of the ier
.
p+2.

p+3. correcting products in case either one or both of the arguments are negative

p+4. collecting the partial products so as to form the final product and clearing of the argument accumulators.

Tables 5-2 and 5-3 offer examples illustrating the operation of the high-speed multiplier. Although either the LHPP or RHPP accumulator can be used for forming the final product, we assume here, as in PX-6-311, that the RHPP accumulator is used for this purpose.

5.1. PROGRAM CONTROLS

Each of the high-speed multiplier's 24 program controls consists of a transceiver with program pulse input and output terminals, argument accumulator receive switches and clear switches, a significant figures switch, a places switch, and a product disposal switch. Neons correlated with the transceivers are shown on PX-6-309.

5.1.1. The Multiplier and Multiplicand Accumulator Receive Switches

Each of the argument accumulator receive switches has the positions α, β, γ, δ, ε, and 0. Associated with the points α-ε on the switch for the ier accumulators are the program pulse output terminals $R\alpha$-$R\varepsilon$ and, for the icand

TABLE 5-2

MULTIPLICATION OF M 8 198 630 400 by P 2 800 000 000

Description of Program: Multiply (read by 2 places of the ier)
Round answer off to 8 places
Clear ier and icand accumulators after multiplication
Transmit product from final product accumulator

Add. Time	Ier accumulator stores	Icand accumulator stores	LHPP Accumulator (I)		RHPP and PP Accumulator (I)	
			Receives	Stores after receiving	Receives	Stores after receiving
1	P 2 800 000 000	M 8 198 630 400	M 10 987 654 321	M 10 987 654 321	M 10 987 654 321	M 10 987 654 321
	M 8 198 630 400	M 10 987 654 321				
2			0 000 000 050	P 0 000 000 050		
3			1 011 100 000	P 1 011 100 050	0 628 626 080	P 0 628 626 080
4			0 607 642 030	P 1 618 742 080	0 048 248 402	P 0 676 874 482
5			X 7 209 000 000			
6				M 8 818 742 080	M 8 818 742 080	M 9 495 616 562
7						

Program output pulse and product disposal signal are emitted.

Product is transmitted from product accumulator.

TABLE 5-3

Multiplication of M 8 198 630 400 by M 2 800 000 000

Description of Program: Multiply Icand by 3 places of Ier
Do not round answer off
Clear Ier and Icand accumulators
Retain product in final product accumulator

Add. Time	Ier accumulator stores	Icand accumulator stores	LHPP accumulator (I) Receives	LHPP accumulator (I) Stores after receiving	RHPP and FP accumulator (I) Receives	RHPP and FP accumulator (I) Stores after receiving
M	2 800 000 000	M 8 198 630 400				
1	P: 10 987 654 321	P: 10 987 654 321	P: 10 987 654 321	P: 10 987 654 321		P: 10 987 654 321
2						
3			1 011 100 000	P 1 011 100 000	C 628 626 080	P 0 628 626 080
4			0 607 642 030	P 1 618 742 030	C 048 248 402	P 0 676 874 482
5			0 000 000 000	P 1 618 742 030	0 000 000 000 / 0 000 000 000	P 0 676 874 482 / M 0 676 874 482
6			P 7 200 000 000	P 8 818 742 030	P 1 801 369 600	M 2 478 244 082
7			Program output pulse is transmitted	P 8 818 742 030		P 1 296 986 112

accumulator, Da-De. If one of these switches is set at a receive point, a program pulse received on a program input terminal is retransmitted through the corresponding terminal Ra-Re or Da-De when the program control of which the switch is a part is stimulated. The operator sets up program controls on argument accumulators so that a pulse transmitted in this way will cause reception to take place as specified (see PX-6-311 and Sec. 5.4.).

The argument accumulator receive switches have been provided in order to simplify the programming of multiplications. Once the connections between some or all of the terminals Ra-Re, Da-De and the argument accumulators are made and switches have been set up accordingly on the argument accumulators, the operator does not need to provide the argument accumulators with a separate program pulse to stimulate them to receive whenever a multiplication is to take place. The one program pulse which stimulates the performance of the multiplication also stimulates the reception of the arguments provided that they can both be received during the first addition time of the multiplication.[*]

If an argument accumulator receive switch is set at 0, no pulse to stimulate reception of the corresponding argument is transmitted. The setting 0 is used for multiplication programs in which the argument is held over from the previous program (see Sec. 5.1.2.) or in programs in which it is desirable to stimulate the argument accumulator independently to receive its argument.

---

[*]If, for example, both the ier and icand are received directly from the constant transmitter, the argument accumulators cannot both receive their arguments in the same addition time because the constant transmitter transmits but one number in an addition time.

5.1.2. Multiplier and Multiplicand Accumulator Clear Switches

Clear circuits in the high-speed multiplier are connected to the PM-clear units of the ier and icand accumulators. If an argument accumulator clear switch is set at C, the high-speed multiplier's clear circuits emit a clear signal towards the end of addition time p+4 which causes the corresponding argument accumulator to clear. In programs for which a clear switch is set at O, no clear signal is transmitted to the corresponding accumulator.

5.1.3. The Significant Figures Switch

The setting of the significant figures switch determines to which decade place of the LHPP accumulator 5 pulses for round off are transmitted. If this switch is set at $2 \leq s \leq 9$, the five round off pulses are sent to decade 10-s of LHPP accumulator I. For s=10, the round off pulses are sent to decade 10 of LHPP accumulator II.[*] No round off pulses are emitted in a program for which the significant figures switch is set at "off".

The significant figures switch provides greater flexibility in the round off options for the 24 programs than would be possible if the only round off control available were the significant figures switch on the final product accumulator. If, however, the round off requirements on all multiplication programs are the same, the significant figures switches of the multiplier program controls can be set at off and the significant figures switch on the final product accumulator can be set appropriately.

Notice that the setting of the significant figures switch of a multiplier program control does not cause the final product accumulator to emit the 1'P (needed for a complement with respect to 10^{10}) when the product is disposed of subtractively. Whether or not this pulse is put in, and the

---

[*]Unless 2 pairs of interconnected accumulators are used to receive the partial products, the round off pulses emitted for s=10 are lost.

decade in which it is put, depend on the setting of the significant figures switch on the final product accumulator (see Sec. 4.1.4.).   If a product is disposed of subtractively in such a way that the l'P is not transmitted by the final product accumulator, the l'P can be put in at the receiving accumulator (see Sec. 4.1.2.).

5.1.4. Places Switches

If the places switch of a program control is set at p (where $2 \leqslant p \leqslant 10$), the high-speed multiplier multiplies the entire icand by the p left hand digits of the ier whenever this program control is used. Such a program lasts p+4 addition times and a program output pulse is emitted by the transceiver p+4 addition times after the reception of the program input pulse.

5.1.5. Product Disposal Switch

The points A, AS, ..., ASC on the product disposal switch together with the program pulse output terminals A, S, ..., ASC at the left of panel 3 of the high-speed multiplier make it possible for this unit to direct the transmission of the product from the final product accumulator.

At the end of addition time p+4 when the high-speed multiplier program control emits a program output pulse, a pulse is also emitted from the terminal A, S, ..., or ASC corresponding to the point at which the product disposal switch is set. The product disposal program pulse output terminals which are used should be connected to program pulse input terminals on the final product accumulator (see PX-6-311). If a product disposal switch of a given program control is set at O, the high-speed multiplier does not emit a product disposal pulse when this program control is used.

The program switches on the final product accumulator may, but need not necessarily, be set so as to correspond to the labelling of the product disposal terminal from which the stimulating pulse comes. For example, if in a given program it is convenient to dispose of some product subtractively twice, and then clear and, moreover, no multiplication program requires ASC disposal, then the ASC output terminal can be connected to a repeat program control on the final product accumulator set up for subtractive transmission repeated 2 times with clearing. Notice that with such a set-up the point ASC on the product disposal switch no longer has the meaning transmit A and S simultaneously and clear but, rather, the meaning established by the set up of the program control on the final product accumulator.

In a course like the previously described one care must be exercised to prevent conflicting programs. Since during the first two addition times of a multiplication program, the RHPP accumulator has a completely non-active role, product disposal lasting 2 addition times is possible (with the RHPP accumulator used as the FP accumulator) even though a new multiplication program is initiated when the product disposal signal is emitted. If the product is disposed of repetitively r times (where $r > 2$), the next multiplication program must be initiated no sooner than $r-2$ addition times following the product disposal signal. It might also be mentioned at this point that repetitive reception of an argument cannot be accomplished through the use of the terminals Ra-Rε or Da-Dε since the arguments must be received no later than the end of addition time 1 of a program in order to allow sufficient time for the selectors to set up.

5.2. COMMON PROGRAMMING CIRCUITS

5.2.1. Argument Accumulator Receive Circuits

A program input pulse delivered to a program control is routed

TABLE 5-4

CHRONOLOGICAL OPERATION OF HIGH SPEED MULTIPLIER'S PROGRAMMING CIRCUITS

Note: It is assumed here that ten-decade accumulators are used for the partial products.

Add. Time for 2 digit multiplier	Stage of Ring Counter	EVENT	
		In High Speed Multiplier's programming circuits	In associated accumulators
End of Add. Time 0	1	1) Program input pulse is received and re-transmitted to ier and/or icand accumulators	1) See addition time 1.*
1	1	1) Ring cycles to stage 2 at CPP time.	*Ier and icand accumulators receive arguments.
2	2	1) 1P passed by $\boxed{B'47}$ sets l and r receivers. 2) 1'P gated through $\boxed{A'47}$ and 4P through $\boxed{A'46}$ are delivered to round off gates. 3) Ring cycles to stage 3.	1) LHPP and RHPP accumulators' "receive on α" circuits are activated. 2) LHPP accumulator receives five round-off pulses.
3	3	1) Signal from stage 3 opens ier selector K gates so that multiplier tables are entered with first from the left ier digit. 2) Signal from stage 3 opens A" shifter gates. 3) Ring cycles to stage 4.	1 and 2) LHPP accumulator receives tens digits of "icand x first ier digit" in decade places 10 through 1. RHPP accumulator receives units digits of "icand x first ier digit" in decade places 9 through 1.
4	4	1) Signal from stage 4 opens ier selector J gates and shifter B" gates. 2) Signal from $\boxed{B'46}$ gates a 1'P through $\boxed{L'47}$. 3) Signal from $\boxed{B'46}$ gates CPP through $\boxed{B'46}$ to initiate RS and DS corrections if R and/or D are negative. 4) Signal from $\boxed{B'46}$ gates CPP through $\boxed{E'48}$ to provide reset signal for l and r receivers. 5) Signal from $\boxed{B'46}$ allows CPP to pass through F'48 to clear ring to stage 13.	1) LHPP accumulator receives tens digits of second P.P. in decade places 9 through 1. RHPP accumulator receives units digits of second P.P. in decade places 8 through 1. 2) PL counter of RHPP accumulator receives 1'P if both ier and icand are negative. 3) See addition time 5.** 4) LHPP and RHPP accumulators' "receive on α" circuits cease to be activated.
5	13	1) Signal from stage 13 allows CPP to pass through $\boxed{D49}$ and $\boxed{K'50}$ to the reset flip-flops for program controls 1-8 and 17-24. 2) Signal from stage 13 gates a CPP through $\boxed{A'47}$ so that F pulse is emitted 3) Ring cycles to stage 14.	**RS and/or DS corrections are made (see addition time 4). 2) See addition time 6.***
6	14	1) Signal from stage 14 goes to reset gates of program controls 9-16 to reset these controls. All other program controls are reset by signals from reset flip-flops. 2) Icand and ier accumulator clear signals are emitted. 3) Program output pulse and product disposal signal are emitted. 4) Ring cycles to stage 1.	***LHPP and RHPP are combined. 2) Argument accumulators clear.
7	1		Product is transmitted from final product accumulator.

immediately through buffers (61 and 62 on program control 1, for example) to the argument receive switches for that control. Each receive point on these switches connects to one of 5 output circuits consisting of buffer, inverter, standard transmitter, and program pulse output terminal (Rα-Rϵ or Dα-Dϵ on front panel 1). The program output pulse transmitted in this way is taken to a program control on the argument accumulator to stimulate reception of the argument (see Sec. 5.4.).

5.2.2. Program Ring and Associated Circuits

When a high-speed multiplier program control is stimulated, the signal derived ultimately from the normally negative output of the flip-flop holds gate F'44 open so that a CPP is admitted to cycle the program ring one stage per addition time. The effect of signals from various stages of the ring on the round off, partial product receiver, complement correction, final product collection (F pulse), and program control reset circuits are discussed in this section. Mention is also made of the effect of signals from the ring on the numerical circuits which are discussed in greater detail in Sec. 5.3. Table 5-4 summarizes the chronological operation of the programming circuits for the case of a 2 place multiplier.

The program ring is in stage 1 when a program input pulse is received by some program control at the end of, let us say, addition time zero. During addition time 1, the argument accumulators receive their arguments (see Sec. 5.2.1.) and, at the end of addition time 1, the ring cycles to stage 2.

A signal from stage 2 opens gate B'47. The 1P passed through this gate sets the l and r receivers early in addition time 2. These receivers are not reset until the end of addition time p+2 (see discussion below). As long as these receivers are set, a static signal is delivered to the l and r terminals on front panel 3. These signals, brought to interconnector terminals on the left and right hand partial products accumulators (see Sec. 5.4.), stimulate the reception, through the α input terminal, of the round off pulses (see discussion immediately following), the partial products emitted during the succeeding p addition times, and the l'P to correct the sign of the product when both the ier and icand are negative. Since the l and r signals are brought directly into the "receive on α" programming circuits of the product accumulators, no program controls need be set up to program the reception of the partial products.

The signal from stage 2 of the ring also opens gates A'47 and A'46 so that the l'P and 4P are passed. These five pulses, used for round off of the product, are delivered to the gates A"-H" and K" 45. Each of these gates is connected to a point on the significant figures switches as indicated on PX-6-308. The normally positive output of the activated program control's flip-flop through inverter 65, buffer 64, and point s on the significant figures switch, opens one of these gates so that the round off pulses are emitted over the lead for decade place 10-s of the left hand partial products digit output terminal I or over the lead for decade place 10 of the left hand partial products digit output terminal II.

In addition time 3, a signal from stage 3 through B'42 and inverter Ll is applied to the ier selector gates for the 10th decade place, K 2-11, and through inverter B'41, to the shifter gates A" 30-21 and 10-1. In this way, multiplication by the first digit of the ier takes place with the products being emitted on the leads for decades 10-1 of the digit output terminal LHPP accumulator I and on the leads for decades 9-1 of the digit output terminal RHPP accumulator I, and for decade 10 of RHPP accumulator II. Similarly, in addition times 4, 5, ..., p+2, the ring causes multiplication by successive digits of the ier and the emission of the products shifted over one place to the right each time.

The places gates numbered B'-K'46 emit a signal on the coincidence of a signal from the normally negative output of the flip-flop (and buffer 61) passing through point p on the places switch and a signal from stage p+2 of the ring. The signal emitted by one of these gates terminates the multiplications by successive ier digits, causes complement correction to take place, and resets the l and r receivers.

The phase of the multiplication program in which the tables are used is terminated as follows: A CPP passed through gate F'48 at the end of addition time p+2 clears the ring to stage 13. At the same time, a CPP passed through gate E'47 resets the l and r receivers.

During addition time p+2, the signal from one of the places gates allows a l'P to pass through gate L"47 and a CPP, through gate B"46. A static output signal from stage M of the ier accumulator's PM counter holds gate B"47 open so that gate B"47 passes the output of gate B"46 to the DS output terminal on panel 3. Similarly, if the icand is negative, the output of gate B"46 passes through gate C"47 to the RS terminal. The gates L"47, 45, and 43 are so arranged in series that the l'P is allowed to reach the PM lead of terminal RHPP accumulator I only if both the ier and icand are negative. This latter pulse is received in the right hand partial product accumulator because the r receiver is not reset until the end of addition time p+2 after this pulse has been emitted. With the associated accumulators set up as shown on PX-6-311, the pulses transmitted from terminals RS and DS stimulate the carrying out of the complement corrections (shown on table 5-3.) during addition time p+3.

At the end of addition time p+3, a CPP passes through gate A"47 which is held open by a signal from stage 13 of the ring. This pulse, transmitted through terminal F on panel 3, is used to stimulate the collection of the partial products into the final product (see PX-6-311 and Sec. 5.4.).

At the end of addition time p+4, the activated program control is reset and a program output pulse is transmitted. This resetting is accomplished in one way for program controls (9-16) on panel 2 and in a slightly different way for program controls (1-8 and 17-24) on the first and third panels.

The signal from stage 14, early in addition time p+4, is brought directly to gate 62 of transceivers on the second panel. This gate, controlled by the normally negative output of the flip-flop, then emits a signal which passes through inverter 65 and opens gate 68. The CPP passed through gate 68 at the end of addition time p+4 resets the flip-flop and is transmitted as a program output pulse.

Gate 62 of a transceiver on the first or third panel also gets a reset signal early in addition time p+4. This signal, however, is derived from one of the reset flip-flops (E, F 49 on panel 1 or L", K" 49 on panel 3). A signal from stage 13 opens gates D49 and K"50 to allow a CPP to pass and, thus, set the reset flip-flops on panels 1 and 3 respectively. The normally negative output of these flip-flops is then brought to gate 62 in the associated transceivers. Neons correlated with the reset flip-flops are shown on PX-6-309.

5.2.3. Argument Accumulator Clear Circuits

The reset signal, whether from stage 14 or from the reset flip-flops (see discussion immediately above), causes gate 62 of the stimulated transceiver to emit a signal early in addition time p+4. This signal, through inverter 65 and buffer 63, passes through the ier and/or icand accumulator clear switches to one or two of the argument accumulator clear gates B, D, F, and H30. The argument accumulator clear gates are so connected to points on the clear switches that gate H30 is opened if only the ier accumulator is to be cleared, gates D30 and F30 if both argument accumulators are to be cleared, and gate B30 if only the icand accumulator is to be cleared. Towards the end of addition time p+4, the carry clear gate (CCG) passes through the opened clear gate (or gates) to the PM-clear unit of the accumulator (or accumulators) to cause the clearing of the argument accumulators as specified by the settings of the argument accumulator clear switches.

5.2.4. Product Disposal Circuits

There are 6 product disposal circuits A, S, ..., ASC each consisting of a program pulse output terminal on panel 3, a transmitter, a gate D", E", ..., or J"47 and, a buffer D", E", ..., or J"46. Each of these circuits is connected to the corresponding point A, AS, ..., ASC on the product disposal switch.

The signal emitted by gate 62 of the stimulated program control when the reset signal arrives, passes through inverter 65, buffer 63 and the product disposal switch to the buffer of the appropriate product disposal circuit. Thus, the gate in such a circuit is held open to pass a CPP at the end of addition time p+4. This pulse, emitted from one of terminals A, S, ..., ASC at the end of addition time p+4, is used by the operator to stimulate disposal of the product (see Secs.5.1.5. and 5.4.) which takes place during addition time p+5.

5.3. NUMERICAL CIRCUITS

The numerical circuits of the high-speed multiplier consist of the ier selector gates, the tens and units multiplication tables, the coding gates, the left and right hand icand selector gates, the left and right hand shifters, and the 4 digit output terminals, LH partial products accumulators I and II and RH product accumulators I and II on panel 3 (see PX-6-308).

The ier selectors consist of a 10 by 10 array of gates. The ier selector gate in row i (i = 0 to 9 from bottom to top) and column j (j = 10 to 1 from left to right) receives, as one input, the static output of stage i in decade counter j of the ier accumulator and, as its second input, a signal from stage 13-j of the multiplier ring. The output signal from a gate in row i activates row i of the multiplication tables.

In the tens table there are eight groups of vertical conductors corresponding to icand digits 2 to 9 and in the units table, 9 groups of vertical conductors corresponding to icand digits 1 to 9. The basic products are remembered by means of a pattern of connections between the horizontal conductors (from the ier selectors) and the vertical conductors (to the coding gates). Each of the vertical conductors is labelled so as to indicate the pulses (1, 2, 2', or 4) which are brought to the coding gate to which it is connected. No conductor is needed for icand equal to one in the tens table since the tens digit of any one digit ier by icand equal to one is zero.

Now, a signal from a gate in row i of the selectors is delivered through the connections between row i of the tables and the vertical conductors

to the coding gates. Since the output of the ier selector gate is negative
the signals from the multiplication tables have an inhibitory effect on the
coding gates to which they are delivered. Notice that for ier equal to zero,
all coding gates are turned off. The 1, 2, 2', or 4P are allowed to pass
through only the coding gates which receive no signal from the multiplication
tables.

Suppose, for example, that the digit in the tenth decade place of
the ier is 2. Then during addition time 3, the tube K9 emits a signal. The
digit pulses passed by the coding gates as a result are shown in Table 5-5.

The pulses passed by the coding gates associated with the tens and
units multiplication tables are brought through buffers and inverters to the
left and right hand icand selector gates respectively. The left hand selectors
consist of a 10 by 8 array of gates with the tubes in row i (i = 2 to 9 from
bottom to top) corresponding to digit i of the icand and the tubes in column j
(j = 10 to 1 from left to right) to decade place j of the icand. Similarly,
the right hand icand selectors consist of a 10 by 9 array of gates with each
of the 9 rows corresponding to a digit of the icand between 1 and 9. The
static outputs of the icand accumulator's decade counters provide one input
for the icand selector gates. The second input for the icand selector gates
on row i consists of the pulses passed by the coding gates associated with
icand i. Out of the collection of products transmitted by the coding gates,
the icand selector gates select the products needed for the particular icand
set up in them. For example, when the icand M 8 198 630 400 is multiplied
by the first digit of the ier P 2 800 000 000 (see the illustrative problem
of table 5-2), the product pulses passed by icand selector gates are shown

TABLE 5-5

PARTIAL PRODUCTS EMITTED BY THE MULTIPLICATION TABLES FOR IER = 2

	Icand	Coding Gates which receive signals from multiplication tables	Pulses passed by coding gates.
TENS TABLE	2	G48	none
	3	G47, F46	none
	4	G46, F46	none
	5	F45, E45	1P by G45
	⋮	⋮	⋮
UNITS TABLE	1	G29, E29, D29	2P by F29
	2	R28, E28	4P by D28
	3	G27, F27	2'P by E27 and 44P by D27
	⋮	⋮	⋮

in Table 5-6.

Corresponding to each set of icand selector gates is a set of shifters. Each set of shifters consists of a 10 by 10 array of gates. The pulses for the partial product "ier"digit by icand digit in decade place j" are routed through buffers and inverters to the shifter gates in column j (j=10 to 1 from left to right). The second input for the gates in row i (i= 3 to 12) comes from stage i of the program ring. The outputs of the shifters are connected diagonally to the leads of the digit output terminals, LH partial products accumulators I and II and RH product accumulators I and II, in such a way that the partial products are emitted one decade place further to the right as multiplication by successive ier digits takes place. The partial products for icand by first ier digit are emitted over the leads for decade places 10-1 of the left hand partial products accumulator I, decade places 9-1 of right hand partial products accumulator I, and decade place 10 of right hand partial products accumulator II.

Notice that the pulses for the partial products are emitted from inverter tubes instead of standard transmitters. For this reason, the digit output terminals on panel 3 must be connected to input terminals on the partial products accumulators by means of digit trays or cables to which no other units are connected in parallel. No load boxes are used on these digit trays (see Sec. 5.4.).

5.4. INTERRELATION OF THE HIGH-SPEED MULTIPLIER AND ITS ASSOCIATED ACCUMULATORS

5.4.1. Interconnections for Numerical and Programming Data

The 10 decade counters of the ier accumulator (9) are connected statically to the ier selector gates. Similarly, the decade counters of the icand

TABLE 5-6

SELECTION OF PRODUCTS BY ICAND SELECTORS WHEN ICAND N 8 198 630 400

IS MULTIPLIED BY FIRST DIGIT OF IER P 2 800 000 000

Decade Place	Left Hand Icand Selector Gate	Pulses Passed	Right Hand Icand Selector Gate	Pulses Passed
10	L'22	1	L'2	6
9	——	0	K'9	2
8	J'21	1	J'1	8
7	H'22	1	H'2	6
6	G'24	1	G'4	2
5	F'27	0	F'7	6
4	——	0	——	0
3	D'26	0	D'6	8
2	——	0	——	0
1	——	0	——	0

MOORE SCHOOL of ELECTRICAL ENGINEERING
UNIVERSITY of PENNSYLVANIA

NOTE— HORIZONTAL LINES ABOVE THE UNITS REPRESENT DIGIT TRAYS.
THE DOTTED LINES REPRESENT TRAYS WHICH NEED BE USED
ONLY WHEN 20 DIGIT PRODUCTS ARE FOUND.

HIGH- SPEED MULTIPLIER

PANEL #1

PANEL #2

PANEL #3

THESE TRAYS TO BE USED ONLY TO
CARRY THE PARTIAL PRODUCTS
AND FOR NO OTHER PURPOSE

NO LOAD BOXES ARE TO BE
USED ON THESE LINES

SEE PX-5-131

LEFT HAND PARTIAL PRODUCT ACC. II

LEFT HAND PARTIAL PRODUCT ACC. I
IF 20 DIGIT PRODUCTS ARE FOUND.

Acc #1   Acc #10   Acc #11   Acc #12   Acc #13   Acc #14

INTERCONNECTION OF HIGH-SPEED MULTIPLIER WITH
ASSOCIATED ACCUMULATORS ~ PX-6-311

accumulator (10) are connected to both sets of icand selector gates. Stage M of the ier accumulator is statically connected to gates B"47 and L"45 and stage H of the icand accumulator, to gates C"47 and L"43 of the complement correction circuit (see Sec. 5.2.2.). Fifty leads in each of 4 55-conductor cables are used for the static outputs of the 20 decade counters involved. An additional lead in each of 2 of the cables carries minus sign data. These cables are brought from accumulators 9 and 10 to the selector gates in the high speed multiplier by way of the static cable trough which runs along the top of the ENIAC panels.

Only accumulators 9 and 10 which are next to the high-speed multiplier can be used as the ier and icand accumulators $\underset{\wedge}{\text{since}}$ only one addition time, the 2nd, is allowed (with a safety factor included) for the set-up of the arguments in the selectors. If longer static leads were used to deliver the arguments to the selectors, more time than has been provided would be needed to set up the arguments. As a matter of fact not even the ier and icand accumulators can be interchanged since the time constants have been measured on the basis that the further accumulator (9) is connected to the ier selectors on panel 1 and the nearer accumulator (10), to the icand selectors on panel 2 of the high-speed multiplier.

The outputs of gates B, D, F, and H50 in the clear circuits (see Sec. 5.2.2.) are also connected to the PM clear units of the argument accumulators.

All the other connections between the multiplier and its associated accumulators for numerical and programming purposes are made through digit or program trays or cables. These are shown on PX-6-311.

5.4.1.1. Programming Connections for "Receive Argument" Instructions

The terminals Rα-Rε are connected to program pulse input terminals on the ier accumulator. The program switches associated with these terminals are set up appropriately. Similarly terminals Dα-Dε are connected to program pulse input terminals on the icand accumulator. Although PX-6-311 shows all of the Rα-Rε Rα-Rε and Dα-Dε terminals connected, it is, of course, necessary to make connections only for the terminals which are used.

5.4.1.2. Connections for Partial Product Reception

The signals emitted through the l and r terminals on panel 3 of the high-speed multiplier during addition times 2 through p+2, are delivered to the "receive on α" programming circuits of the partial products accumulators by means of cables (see PX-5-131) running from the l and r terminals to interconnector terminals on the LHPP and RHPP accumulators respectively. The digit output terminals on panel 3 of the high-speed multiplier are connected to the α input terminals of the partial products accumulators. If products with 8 or fewer significant figures are required, the dotted digit connections may be omitted.

To repeat the statement made in Sec. 5.2.2, no other units can be connected in parallel to the trays used to carry the partial products and no load box should be used on these trays.

5.4.1.3. Connections for Complement Correction

The S output terminals of the ier and icand accumulators are connected to the β input terminals of LHPP Accumulator I and RHPP Accumulator I respectively for the purpose of delivering to these accumulators the correction terms required if either or both of the arguments are negative (see Table 5-1).

with these digit connections, the following program connections must be made:

1) from terminal RS on panel 3 to a control on the ier accumulator set up for subtractive transmission and to a control on the LHPP accumulator set up for reception on β.

2) from terminal DS on panel 3 to a control on the icand accumulator set up for subtractive transmission and to a control on the RHPP accumulator set up for reception on β.

A second method of making the complement correction connections is possible. The S output terminals of the ier and icand accumulators may be connected to the β input terminals of RHPP accumulator I and LHPP accumulator I respectively. In this case the program connections are as follows:

1) from terminal RS to the ier accumulator and to the RHPP accumulator

2) from terminal DS to the icand accumulator and to the LHPP accumulator.

5.4.1.4. Connections for Final Product Collection

PX-6-311 shows the partial product accumulators set-up so that the RHPP accumulator also serves as the final product accumulator. The A output terminal of the LHPP accumulator is connected to the β input terminal of the RHPP accumulator and the F terminal on panel 3 is connected to a control on the LHPP set up for reception on β. Since the RHPP accumulator is free for two addition times at the beginning of multiplication programs and the LHPP accumulator is free for only one addition time (see Sec. 5.1.5.), there is a slight advantage in using the RHPP accumulator as the final product accumulator if repetitive disposal of the product is contemplated. Otherwise, by suitable digit tray and programming connections, the LHPP accumulator can just as well be made to serve as the final product accumulator. Notice that it is not necessary to use a shifter at the β input terminal of the FP accumulator in collecting the partial products in one accumulator because the high-speed multiplier's shifters align the partial products so that they can be combined properly.

5.4.1.5. Programming Connections For Product Disposal Instructions

PX-6-311 shows several of the A, S, ..., ASC terminals on panel 3 connected to program controls on the final product accumulator which are set-up for transmission. As mentioned earlier in Sec. 5.1.5., the meanings taken on by the points A, S, ..., ASC on the product disposal switch depend entirely on the set up of the program controls on the final product accumulator to which the terminals A, S, ..., ASC are connected.

5.4.2. Position of Decimal Point in Product Accumulator

The position of the decimal point of the product can easily be deduced from the description of the way in which the shifters route the partial products (see Sec. 5.3.). If r, d, and f respectively represent the number of decade places that the decimal points of the ier, icand, and final product are removed from the PM place in their respective accumulators (r, d, and f are positive or negative according as they are counted toward the right or left of the PM counter), then

$$f = r + d$$

This formula is illustrated in the table below.

ier	r	icand	d	product	f
P 1. 000 000 000	1	P 1. 000 000 000	1	P 0 1.00 000 000	2
P 0 03.0 000 000	3	P.4 000 000 000	0	P 0 P1.2 000 000	3
P 0 03.0 000 000	3	10^{-2}(P.4 000 000 000	-2	P 0. 012 000 000	1

5.5. ILLUSTRATIVE PROBLEMS

Programs set up on the high-speed multiplier are described in the high-speed multiplier column of set-up tables as follows:

1) On the first level, i-j, at the left, represents the line from which the program input pulse comes and $(\overline{k})$, at the right, the program control

2) On the second level, the first pair of symbols (α, ..., ε, or O followed by C or O) represents the settings of the ier accumulator receive and clear switches; the second pair of symbols represents the settings of the icand accumulator receive and clear switches; the third symbol (n, ..., ASC, or O) the setting of the product disposal switch. A special meaning assigned to one of the points on the product disposal switch is indicated by an asterisk and an explanatory note at the top of the high-speed multiplier column.

3) On the third level, the first symbol (2, ..., 10, or off) specifies the significant figures switch setting; the second symbol, the places switch setting.

4) On the fourth level, located on the addition time line in which the program is completed, the symbol m-n designates the program output pulse.

Thus, the following symbols

1-3   ④
    αC βO A
    off, 8

    ↓   5-6

describe a program set up on high-speed multiplier control 4. The program
input pulse comes from line 3 of program tray 1. The ier accumulator receives
its argument through its α input terminal and the icand accumulator receives
the icand through its β input terminal. The ier accumulator is, and the icand
accumulator is not cleared at the end of the program. The product is transmitted additively from the final product accumulator. The product is not
rounded off and 8 multiplier places are used. The program output pulse is
transmitted to line 5-6. If the program input pulse 1-3 were received, say,
at the end of addition time 6, all the above symbols except the arrow and the
program output pulse would appear on the addition time 7 line. The arrow
would run from the line for addition time 7 to the line for addition time 18.
The program output pulse symbol would appear on line 18.

No symbols are written in the columns for accumulators associated
with the high-speed multiplier when these accumulators carry out programs
(receiving the arguments, for example) stimulated by the high-speed multiplier.
The set-up diagrams, however, indicate the semi-permanent connections made
between the high-speed multiplier and these accumulators.

For the symbols used on the set-up diagrams see Fig. 5-1 below.

5.5.1. Une Program Control Devoted to Each Multiplication

The problem of Sec. 7.5.1. which describes the way in which the ENIAC
can be set up to perform quadratic Lagrangian interpolation illustrates one
method of using the program controls on the high-speed multiplier. Here it is
assumed that the interpolation is carried out as part of a computation which
does not come anywhere near exhausting the program control facilities of the
high-speed multiplier. Since sufficient program controls are available, one
control is devoted to each multiplication program.

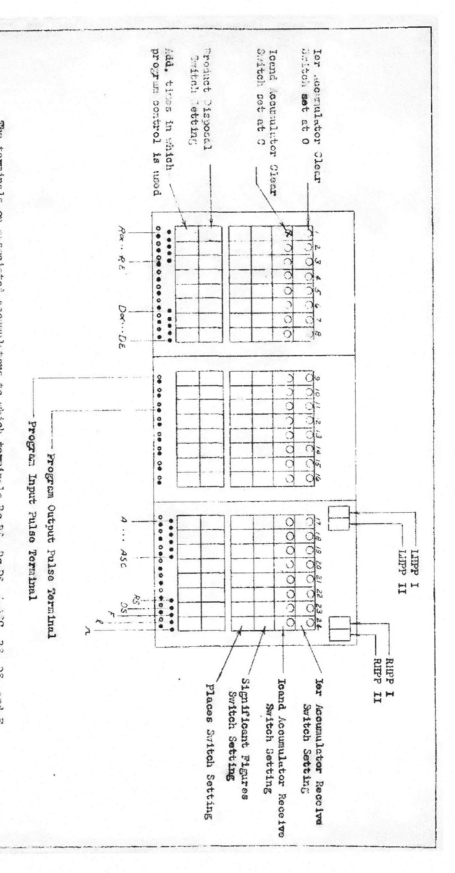

Ier Accumulator Clear
Switch set at 0

Icand Accumulator Clear
Switch set at 0

Product Disposal
Switch Setting

Add. times in which
program control is used

The terminals on associated accumulators to which terminals Ra-Rδ, Da-Dδ, ...ASC, RS, DS, and F
are connected are marked with a corresponding symbol.

Fig. 5-1

SET-UP DIAGRAM CONNECTIONS FOR HIGH-SPEED MULTIPLIER

Ra...Rδ

Da...Dδ

LHPP I
LHPP II

RHPP I
RHPP II

Program Output Pulse Terminal

Program Input Pulse Terminal

A ... ASC

RS

F

Ier Accumulator Receive
Switch Setting

Icand Accumulator Receive
Switch Setting

Significant Figures
Switch Setting

Places Switch Setting

The stimulating pulses for the various multiplication programs are derived directly from the main programming sequence and the multiplier's program output pulses go back to the main programming sequence (see Table 7-4).

5.5.2. <u>One Program Control Used Repeatedly</u>

The computation discussed in section 6.5 which consists of forming

$$x = \frac{\sqrt{a} + \sum_{i=1}^{3} x_i^3}{b} + cd$$

illustrates the repeated use of a given high-speed multiplier program control. In this computation, the three pairs of multiplications to form the terms x_i^2 and then x_i^3, while they involve different arguments, can be handled by one pair of multiplier controls. Here again the pulses which stimulate the multiplication programs as well as the ones which stimulate transmission of x_1, x_2, and x_3 to the argument accumulators are derived from the main program sequence. However, after each term x_i^3 is formed and received in another accumulator from the final product accumulator, the program sequence goes to the master programmer for instructions as to whether or not the multiplier program controls used repeatedly for the formation of x_i^2 and x_i^3 are to be used again and, if so, with which argument (see Table 6-13).

The problem of Sec. 6.5. also illustrates the use of one of the points on the product disposal switch to effect repeated transmission from the final product accumulator.

5.5.3. Isolation of Program Sequences Which Stimulate Transmission of Arguments to Argument Accumulators, Multiplication Programs, and Reception of Products From Product Accumulators.

In Sec. 8.7 is described a problem in which there is a basic computation sequence involving 17 multiplications. This basic sequence is repeated 10 times in the course of the problem. One program control is devoted to each of 12 of the multiplications and the remaining 5 multiplications are taken care of by either of 2 program controls. Each time the basic computation sequence is repeated, arguments stored in different units of the ENIAC are used. Also, within each sequence, the location of one of the arguments required in the 5 multiplication programs which are performed on 2 program controls, as mentioned above, varies. Furthermore, in alternate repetitions of the basic computing sequence, 6 of the 17 products are received by way of different input terminals in the accumulators to which the final product accumulator transmits.

The set up for this problem is summarized in Table 8-13. As much of the basic computing sequence as is constant for all 10 repetitions is handled in one predominant program sequence. In this predominant program sequence, the same program input pulse which stimulates a multiplication program also stimulates the accumulators which store arguments for the multiplication to transmit them and the program output pulse from a multiplier program control not only stimulates the reception of the product from the final product accumulator, but also initiates the next multiplication program. The program pulses for this predominant sequence are carried in program trays 7 and 8 (see Table 8-13.

Branching off the predominant program sequence and carried on in parallel with it are three sequences. The sequence whose stimulating program pulse is carried on program line 6-11 is concerned with procuring appropriate arguments in the cases where the location of argument varies from repetition to repetition. A second sequence whose program pulses are carried on program tray 9 is concerned with selecting which of 2 multiplier controls is to be used for 5 of the 17 multiplications and with stimulating the transmission of an appropriate argument. A third sequence whose program pulses are carried on trays 10 and 11 handles the reception of 6 of the 17 products from the final product accumulator.

The iteration of the predominant sequence with its branches 10 times is provided through the use of the master programmer.

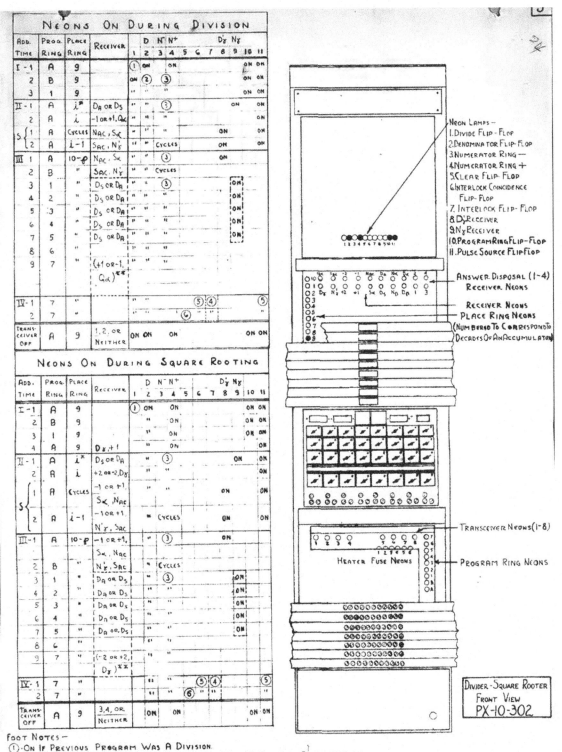

NEONS ON DURING DIVISION

Add. Time	Prog. Ring	Place Ring	Receiver	D (1)	N⁻ N⁺ (2)	(3)	(4)	(5)	Dᵧ Nᵧ (6)	(7)	(8)	(9)	(10)	(11)
I-1	A	9		①ON		ON							ON	ON
2	B	9		ON	②	③							ON	ON
3	1	9		"	"	"							ON	ON
II-1	A	iⁿ	Dₐ or Dₛ	"	"	③					ON			ON
2	A	i	-1 or +1, Qₐ	"	"	"								ON
S { 1	A	Cycles	Nₐc, Sₐ	"	"	"				ON				ON
{ 2	A	i-1	Sₐc, N'ᵧ	"	"	Cycles				ON				ON
III-1	A	10-ρ	Nₐc, Sₐ	"	"	③				ON				
2	B	"	Sₐc, Nᵧ	"	"	Cycles								
3	1	"	Dₛ or Dₐ	"	"	③				ON				
4	2	"	Dₛ or Dₐ	"	"	"				ON				
5	3	"	Dₛ or Dₐ	"	"	"				ON				
6	4	"	Dₛ or Dₐ	"	"	"				ON				
7	5	"	Dₛ or Dₐ	"	"	"				ON				
8	6	"		"	"	"								
9	7	"	(+1 or -1, Qₐ)**	"	"	"								
IV-1	7	"		"	"		⑤	④				⑤		
2	7	"		"	"			⑥	"	"				
Transceiver Off	A	9	1, 2, or Neither	ON	ON				ON			ON	ON	

NEONS ON DURING SQUARE ROOTING

Add. Time	Prog. Ring	Place Ring	Receiver	D (1)	N⁻ N⁺ (2)	(3)	(4)	(5)	Dᵧ Nᵧ (6)	(7)	(8)	(9)	(10)	(11)
I-1	A	9		①ON		ON							ON	ON
2	B	9		"		ON							ON	ON
3	1	9		"		ON							ON	ON
4	A	9	Dᵧ, +1	"		ON								ON
II-1	A	iˣ	Dₛ or Dₐ	"		③					ON			ON
2	A	i	+2 or -2, Dᵧ	"		"								ON
S { 1	A	Cycles	-1 or +1, Sₐ, Nₐc	"		"				ON				ON
{ 2	A	i-1	-1 or +1, N'ᵧ, Sₐc	"		Cycles				ON				ON
III-1	A	10-ρ	-1 or +1, Sₐ, Nₐc	"		③				ON				
2	B	"	N'ᵧ, Sₐc	"		Cycles								
3	1	"	Dₐ or Dₛ	"		"				ON				
4	2	"	Dₐ or Dₛ	"		"				ON				
5	3	"	Dₐ or Dₛ	"		"				ON				
6	4	"	Dₐ or Dₛ	"		"				ON				
7	5	"	Dₐ or Dₛ	"		"				ON				
8	6	"		"		"								
9	7	"	(-2 or +2, Dᵧ)**	"		"								
IV-1	7	"		"			⑤	④				⑤		
2	7	"		"				⑥	"	"				
Transceiver Off	A	9	3, 4, or Neither	ON		ON				ON			ON	ON	

Divider-Square Rooter Front View — PX-10-302

Diagram labels:

Neon Lamps —
1. Divide Flip-Flop
2. Denominator Flip-Flop
3. Numerator Ring —
4. Numerator Ring +
5. Clear Flip-Flop
6. Interlock Coincidence Flip-Flop
7. Interlock Flip-Flop
8. D'ᵧ Receiver
9. Nᵧ Receiver
10. Program Ring Flip-Flop
11. Pulse Source Flip-Flop

Answer Disposal (1-4) Receiver Neons

Receiver Neons
Place Ring Neons
(Numbered To Correspond To Decades Of An Accumulator)

Transceiver Neons (1-8)

Heater Fuse Neons

Program Ring Neons

FOOT NOTES —

① On If Previous Program Was A Division.

② On If Denominator Is Positive <u>When Received In Denominator Accumulator.</u>

③ If, Before Denominator Is Added To Or Subtracted From Numerator, The Numerator Is Positive, Neon #4 Is On; Otherwise Neon #3 Is On.

④ Goes On When Interlock Pulse Is Received.

⑤ Go On One Addition Time After III-9

⑥ Goes On: a - In NI Case, Two Addition Times After III-9.
b - In I Case, In Whichever Occurs Later: Two Addition Times After III-9 Or One Addition Time After Neon 7.

** Only If No Overdraft Results.

* $9 \geq i \geq 10-\rho$ Where ρ Is The Setting Of The Places Switch.

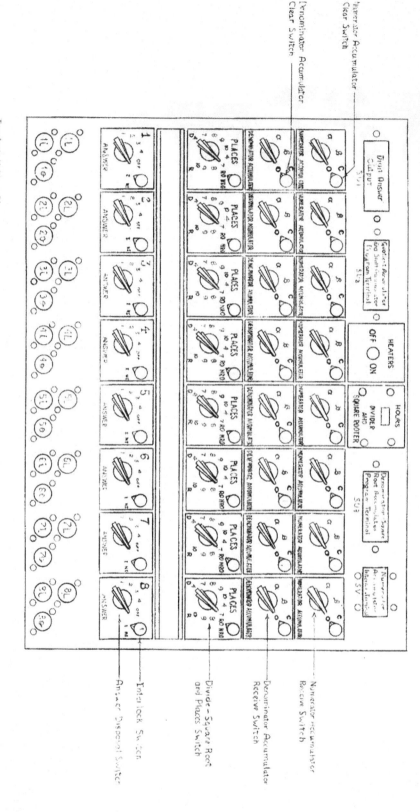

DIVIDER AND SQUARE ROOTER
FRONT PANEL
PX-10-301-Q

VI. DIVIDER AND SQUARE ROOTER

The divider and square rooter is the unit which enables the ENIAC to carry out the operations of division and square rooting. The time required to complete these operations depends on the number of places required in the answer and the digits in each place of the answer. If it is assumed that the average digit of the answer is 5 and if p designates the number of places in the answer, approximately 13 p addition times[*] are consumed in division or square rooting.

The first section of this chapter contains a general summary of the divider and square rooter. Sections 6.1, 6.2, and 6.3 respectively cover the program controls, common programming circuits, and numerical circuits of this unit. Information pertinent to the interrelation of accumulators associated with the divider and square rooter appears in Section 6.4, and 6.5 includes an illustrative set-up for computations involving the divider and square rooter. The following diagrams will be referred to in this chapter:

Front View of the Divider and Square Rooter	PX-10-302
Divider and Square Rooter Front Panel	PX-10-301
Divider and Square Rooter Block Diagram	PX-10-304
Interconnection of Divider and Square Rooter with its Associated Accumulators	PX-10-307

6.0. GENERAL SUMMARY

The divider and square rooter carries out a division or square rooting by operating as a central programming agent for a group of associated accumulators (see Section 6.4). In division the associated accumulators are the numerator (dividend) accumulator, the denominator (divisor) accumulator, shift accumulator,

---

[*]In Section 6.2 a formula for calculating exactly the number of addition times required for a given division or square root is given.

and quotient accumulator; in square rooting the associated accumulators are the numerator (radicand) accumulator, the shift accumulator, and the denominator (twice the root) accumulator. The divider controls these accumulators in the sense that at various periods of the operation cycle, it transmits to these accumulators program signals appropriate to the period of the computation and the quantities involved in the computation and in the sense that it provides the answer accumulator with the numerical data from which the answer is ultimately formed.

The operation cycle, whether for division or square rooting, divides itself rather clearly into 4 periods: period I in which the stage is set for the following periods, period II during which the operation itself proceeds, period III, the round off period, and period IV, the interlock and clear period. When a divider and square rooter program control is stimulated, the events which occur in the four periods mentioned above, depend, to some extent, on the way in which the program control is set up. (cf. Section 6.1 and the illustrative examples in Tables 6-2 and 6-3).

In addition to a transceiver with program pulse input and output terminals, each of the 8 program controls contains an interlock pulse input terminal and 8 program switches (see PX-10-301). The program switches provide the operator with options as to:

1) reception of the arguments by the argument accumulators (numerator and denominator accumulator receive switches)

2) clearing of one or both of the argument accumulators upon completion of the program (numerator and denominator accumulator clear switches)

3) choice between the operations of division and square rooting
   (divide-square root and places switch)

4) the number of places to be obtained in the answer (divide-square
   root and places switch)

5) round-off or no round-off of the answer (round-off switch)

6) whether or not the transmission of a program output pulse is to
   wait on the divider-square rooter's reception of an interlock
   input pulse (interlock switch)

7) transmission of the answer from the quotient or denominator
   accumulator (answer disposal switch).

During period I of a division, the divider and square rooter emits
signals which stimulate the argument accumulators to receive the arguments in
accordance with option 1 above and sets up certain of its common programming
circuits (see Section 6.2) in accordance with option 3.

Period II, for division, includes combinations of a basic division
sequence and a shift sequence. When the numerator and denominator have like
signs, the denominator is subtracted from the numerator and the quotient is
increased by one unit in a particular decade place; when the signs of the
arguments are unlike, the denominator is added to the numerator and the quotient
is decreased by one unit in a particular decade place. When the remainder from
the numerator after an addition or subtraction of the denominator shows an overdraft (i.e. a change in sign from the one which the remainder carried before the
addition or subtraction), the basic division sequence is interrupted. Then the
remainder is transmitted from the numerator accumulator to the shift accumulator
where it is received shifted over one place to the left. Next the numerator

accumulator again receives the numerator from the shift accumulator. The basic division sequence is repeated with the quotient respectively increased or decreased by one unit after every time a subtraction or addition of the denominator takes place. After a shift sequence, however, the unit is added to or subtracted from a decade place of the quotient one further to the right than before the shift sequence.[*]

Square roots in the ENIAC are obtained by a method which makes use of the fact that $\sum_{i=1}^{a} (2i - 1) = a^2$ and which is analogous to a method often used to find square roots on electric or manual desk computing machines.

Period I for square-rooting not only covers the reception of the numerator (or radicand) and the set-up of certain circuits in the divider and square rooter, but also provides for the reception of one pulse in the 10^8 decade of the denominator(twice the root) accumulator.

In the basic square-rooting sequence of period II, odd numbers successively increasing (and accumulated in the denominator accumulator) are subtracted from the radicand until an overdraft occurs. Then odd numbers successively decreasing are added to the radicand. The ENIAC finds by this procedure twice the square root (formed in the denominator accumulator) since the answer is increased or decreased by two units after each addition or subtraction takes place. Period II, in square rooting as in division, includes a shift sequence which takes place whenever the remainder from the radicand indicates a change of sign. The square root shift sequence provides for transmission of the radicand to the shift accumulator to shift it one place to the left and the return of the shifted radicand to the numerator or radicand accumulator. The shift sequence, further-

---

*From the time that period II begins until just after the first overdraft, one unit is added to or subtracted from the 10^8 decade of the quotient in the basic division sequence. After the first shift sequence, the 10^7 decade of the quotient is worked on by the divider etc.

TABLE 6-1

EXTRACTION OF SQUARE ROOTS BY THE DIVIDER AND SQUARE ROOTER - Period II

PROBLEM:
To find ... where ...

Assume ...

So that* ...

When the square rooting commences, the numerator accumulator holds R.

where the a_i are integers between 0 and 9

OPERATION PERFORMED ON CONTENTS OF NUMERATOR ACCUMULATOR	REMAINDER IN NUMERATOR ACCUMULATOR AS A RESULT OF OPERATION IN COLUMN 1.	CONTENTS OF DENOMINATOR (TWO-ROOT) ACCUMULATOR
In basic square rooting sequence before first overdraft, SUBTRACT		AFTER OVERDRAFT OCCURS BUT BEFORE SHIFT SEQUENCE
		AT END OF FIRST ADDITION TIME OF SHIFT SEQUENCE
		AT END OF SHIFT SEQUENCE
After first shift sequence, but before second overdraft, ADD		AFTER OVERDRAFT OCCURS BUT BEFORE SHIFT SEQUENCE
		AT END OF FIRST ADDITION TIME OF SHIFT SEQUENCE
		AT END OF SHIFT SEQUENCE

* Compare R with the column showing the contents of the denominator accumulator and note the displacement of the answer. (See Sec. 6.4.3.)

more, provides for the subtraction or addition respectively of one unit first in the decade place in which twice the root was previously increased or decreased by two units in the basic square root sequence and then in a decade place one further to the right. After a shift sequence the basic square root sequence is repeated until overdraft occurs. Table 6-1 shows the contents of the radicand accumulator and of the twice the root accumulator at various times in period II of square rooting.

Period II is terminated and period III initiated when an overdraft occurs and when the divider and square rooter has found the number of places (counting toward the right from the PM decade) of the answer specified by the setting of the divider-square root and places switch of the answer. In division, period III includes the shifting of the numerator one place to the left as in the shift sequence of period II. Then, if round-off is specified by the setting of the program control, the denominator is subtracted from or added to the numerator (if the numerator's remainder and the denominator have like or unlike signs respectively) five times. If overdraft does not result from these subtractions or additions, the quotient is respectively increased or decreased by one unit in the last place from the left required by the setting of the places switch. Period III of square rooting is similar to that for division except for two details. In square rooting this period covers the shifting of the radicand's remainder and the addition or subtraction of one unit in the decade place of twice the root which, in the previous basic square root sequence, was decreased or increased by two units. Also, in square-rooting as in division, if round-off is specified, the contents of the denominator accumulator are then subtracted from or added to the contents of the numerator accumulator. If no overdraft

TABLE 6-3
SQUARE ROOT - ILLUSTRATIVE PROBLEM

Problem: Find $\sqrt{0\ 061\ 360\ 400}$. Round answer off to 4 places. No interlock

Period	Add. Time	Numerator (addicand) Accumulator		Denominator (2 root) accumulator		Shift Accumulator	
		Receives	Stores after receiving	Receives	Stores after receiving	Receives	Stores after receiving
I	1	P 0 061 360 400	P 0 061 360 400				
	2						
	3						
	4						
	5	M 9 900 000 000	M 9 961 360 400	P 0 100 000 000	P 0 100 000 000		
	6						
shift	7						
shift	8	M 9 813 604 000	M 9 813 604 000	P 0 200 000 000	P 0 300 000 000	M 9 813 604 000	M 9 813 604 000
II	9	P 0 190 000 000	P 0 003 604 000	M 9 990 000 000	P 0 290 000 000		
	10			M 9 900 000 000	P 0 190 000 000		
	11			M 9 980 000 000	P 0 170 000 000	P 0 036 040 000	M 9 813 604 000
	12	P 0 036 040 000	P 0 036 040 000	P 0 010 000 000	P 0 160 000 000		
	13	M 9 819 000 000	M 9 855 040 000	P 0 001 000 000	P 0 181 000 000		
	14			P 0 002 000 000	P 0 183 000 000		
III	15			M 9 999 000 000	P 0 182 000 000	M 8 550 400 000	P 0 036 040 000
	16	M 8 550 400 000	M 8 550 400 000				
	17	P 0 182 000 000	M 8 732 400 000				
	18	P 0 182 000 000	M 8 914 400 000				
	19	P 0 182 000 000	M 8 996 400 000				
	20	P 0 182 000 000	M 9 278 400 000				
	21	P 0 182 000 000	M 9 460 400 000				
	22	P 0 182 000 000	M 9 460 400 000				M 8 550 400 000
	23						
IV	24						
	25		M 9 995 000 000				
	26				P 0 160 000 000		

Program output pulse and answer disposal signal is transmitted.

Answer is transmitted from accumulator accumulator.

TABLE 6-2

DIVISION - ILLUSTRATIVE PROBLEM

Problem: Divide P 0 2090070 000 by P 0 230 000 000. Round answer off to 4 places. No interlock.

Period	Add. Time	Quotient Accumulator Receives	Quotient Accumulator Stores after Receiving	Numerator Accumulator Receives	Numerator Accumulator Stores after receiving	Denominator Accumulator (Receives during period 1 and stores thereafter) Receives	Shift Accumulator Receives	Shift Accumulator Stores after Receiving
I	1			P 0 209 070 000	P 0 209 070 000	P 0 230 000 000		
	2							
	3							
	4							
	5	P 0 100 000 000	P 0 100 000 000	M 9 770 000 000	M 9 979 070 000		M 9 790 700 000	M 9 790 700 000
II	6							
shift	7		P 0 100 000 000	M 9 790 700 000	M 9 790 700 000			
shift	8							
	9	M 9 990 000 000	P 0 090 000 000		P 0 040 700 000		P 0 207 000 000	P 0 207 000 000
III	10							
shift	11			P 0 207 000 000	P 0 247 000 000			
	12							
	13	P 0 001 000 000	P 0 091 000 000	M 9 770 000 000	M 9 977 000 000		M 9 770 000 000	M 9 770 000 000
	14							
	15							
	16			P 0 230 000 000	P 0 000 000 000			
	17			P 0 230 000 000	P 0 230 000 000			
	18			P 0 230 000 000	P 0 460 000 000			
	19			P 0 230 000 000	P 0 690 000 000			
	20			P 0 230 000 000	P 0 920 000 000			
	21				M 9 770 000 000			
IV	22	P 0 000 000 000		P 0 000 000 000				
	23		P 0 091 000 000					
	24							
	25			Program output pulse and answer dispatch signal is transmitted				

Answer is transmitted from quotient accumulator.

results, twice the root is increased or decreased by two units.

Period IV is identical in both division and square rooting. In this period, ring counters (see below and Section 6.2,) in the divider and square rooter are cleared and certain flip-flops are reset so as to ready the divider and square rooter for the next program. A program output pulse is transmitted either to indicate the completion of the operation or the reception of an interlock input pulse as well at the completion of the operation. The divider-square rooter signals for the disposal of the answer in accordance with the setting of the answer disposal switch at the end of period IV and the numerator and denominator accumulators clear or do not clear in accordance with the settings of the numerator and denominator accumulator clear switches.

The events described above are motivated by the divider and square rooter's common programming circuits (see Section 6.2). The answer which is accumulated in the quotient accumulator in division or in the denominator accumulator in square rooting is supplied by the numerical circuits (see Section 6.3) of the divider and square rooter.

The common programming circuits of the divider-square rooter which are operated by the program controls may be divided roughly into 3 categories: circuits which are concerned solely with programming within the divider-square rooter (internal programming circuits); circuits which program the associated accumulators as well as other circuits within the divider (internal - external programming circuits); and circuits concerned solely with programming the accumulators associated with the divider and square rooter (external programming circuits).

The internal programming circuits (see PX-10-304) include the program ring circuit, the overdraft circuit, the sign indication circuit, the divide flip-flop, and the interlock and clear circuit.

The program ring circuit contains a flip-flop called the pulse source flip-flop which controls the emission of certain specialized pulses (see Section 6.2) used only in the divider and square rooter. Which pulses are emitted depends on whether division or square rooting is the operation and also on the period of the computation. The 9 stage program ring directs the progress of the computation by providing gates for particular signals suitable to the phase of the computation at various times. The cycling of the program ring is controlled by the program ring flip-flop and by certain of the special pulses whose emission in turn, is controlled by the pulse source flip-flop.

The overdraft circuit has for its purpose the sensing of overdrafts. It consists of a binary ring counter (called the numerator ring) for registering the sign of the numerator. This ring is cycled only during period I and just after the numerator is shifted to the shift accumulator in periods II and III. In addition to the numerator ring, the overdraft circuit has four gates each of which is connected to a stage of the numerator ring and statically to the PM counter of the numerator accumulator. As long as the remainder from the numerator remains the same as it was before an addition or subtraction of the denominator, this circuit emits an NO (no overdraft) signal. When the numerator's remainder changes sign an O (overdraft) signal is emitted.

The sign indication circuit compares the signs of the numerator and denominator emitting a like sign signal when numerator and denominator have the same sign and an unlike sign signal when the signs of the numerator and denominator differ. The denominator flip-flop in this circuit is set only if the denominator is negative. The denominator flip-flop feeds to each of four gates which have for their second input static leads from the PM counter of the numerator accumulator.

The divide flip-flop is used to remember whether the operation being performed is division or square rooting. This flip-flop affects programming only during the round off period at which time its intervention results in the emission of the instructions which distinguish period III for division from period III for square rooting.

The interlock and clear circuit which consists of the interlock flip-flop, the interlock coincidence flip-flop, the clear flip-flop and the various gates operated by these flip-flops, during period IV, emits signals which clear the divider and square rooter's rings and reset certain of its flip-flops.

The circuits which are both internal and external programming circuits are those containing the receivers which, when set, motivate the accumulators associated with the divider and square rooter to perform certain suboperations involved in division and square rooting and which also stimulate other programming circuits within the divider and square rooter to function (see Section 6.2). The receivers included in this category are the N_γ, D_A, D_S, Q_α, D_γ, D'_γ, S_α and N_{AC} and S_{AC} and N'_γ receivers. Signals from these receivers are delivered to the associated accumulators by means of special cables leading from the quotient accumulator and shift accumulator program terminal, the denominator and square root accumulator program terminal, and the numerator accumulator interconnector terminal (see PX-10-301) to interconnector terminals on accumulators corresponding to the names of the terminals on the divider and square rooter.

The N_γ receiver stimulates the reception, via the numerator accumulator's γ input channel, of the denominator or the complement of the denominator when either of these quantities is transmitted from the denominator accumulator as a result of the setting of the D_A or D_S receivers during the basic division or square rooting sequence of period II or in round off during period III.

The Q_α receiver controls the reception, via the quotient accumulator's α channel, of the units which are used to form the quotient and which are transmitted by the divider and square rooter whenever the basic division sequence of period II takes place or at the end of period III in round off programs if no overdraft results from the addition or subtraction of five times the denominator from the numerator.

The D_γ receiver controls the reception by the denominator accumulator via its γ channel of the +2 or -2 units transmitted by the divider and square rooter every time the basic square rooting sequence of period II occurs or in period III if no overdraft occurs after the addition or subtraction of 5 times twice the square root in period III of round off programs. Another receiver, the D'_γ receiver also controls reception via the denominator accumulator's γ channel of numerical data which ultimately forms twice the square root. This receiver, however, is used to program the reception of the single unit (+ or -) transmitted first in a given decade place and then in a decade place one further to the right during the square rooting shift sequence of period II and to program the reception of a single unit just once at the beginning of period III for square rooting.

The S_α, N_{AC}, S_{AC}, and N'_γ receivers control events which occur during the shift sequence of period II and at the beginning of period III for either division or square rooting. The first two receivers stimulate the transmission (with clearing) of the contents of the numerator accumulator to the shift accumulator which receives this data through its α channel. A shifter which shifts numerical data one place to the left is placed at the α input terminal to accomplish the shifting of the numerator. The numerator is then cleared out of the shift accumulator and returned to the numerator accumulator via the numerator accumulator's γ input channel as a result of the setting of the S_{AC} and N'_γ receivers.

The circuits which are used solely for external programming are the numerator and denominator accumulator clear circuits and the N_α, N_β, D_α, D_β, receivers and answer disposal receivers 1, 2, 3, and 4. Signals from the external programming circuits are delivered to the associated accumulators in exactly the same way as are the signals from the circuits which are both internal and external programming circuits.

The N_α and N_β receivers correspond respectively to the points α and β on the numerator accumulator receive switches and are used to stimulate the reception of the numerator (or radicand) by the numerator accumulator at the beginning of a program. The D_α and D_β receivers have a similar function. Whether these receivers actually stimulate reception through the α or β input channels or through some other channels depends, of course, on the manner in which the interconnector plugs of the cables leading from the divider and square rooter to the numerator and denominator accumulators are wired. The plugs, (see Section 6.A) used at present, however, stimulate reception in accordance with the labelling on the numerator accumulator and denominator accumulator receive switches.

The instructions given to the quotient or denominator accumulator as a result of the setting of one of the four answer disposal receivers depend on the wiring of the interconnector plugs used to deliver the divider and square rooter's programming instructions to the answer accumulators (see Section 6.4).

The answer is built up in the quotient accumulator (in division) or in the denominator accumulator (in square rooting) out of numerical data produced by the numerical circuits of the divider and square rooter. These circuits, which are discussed in greater detail in Section 6.3, include the +1, -1, +2, -2 receivers, gates controlled by the above mentioned receivers which pass the 1, 2, 2', 4, 9, or 1' pulses, the 10 stage place ring, and 10 pairs of digit output gates with each pair controlled by a stage of the place ring.

The answer is formed one unit (in division) or two units (in square rooting) at a time in a particular decade place from the digit pulses passed through the 1, 2, 2', 4, 9, and 1' pulse gates and routed into appropriate decade places by the 10 pairs of gates controlled by the places ring. Sign indication M belonging to any component of the answer is derived from the 9P delivered to the PM lead of the answer output terminal on the divider and square rooter front panel.

6.1. PROGRAM CONTROLS

The divider and square rooter has 8 program controls each consisting of a transceiver with program pulse input and output terminals on the divider and square rooter front panel, an interlock pulse input terminal, a numerator accumulator and a denominator accumulator receive switch, a numerator accumulator and denominator accumulator clear switch, a divide-square root and places switch, a round-off switch, an answer disposal switch, and an interlock switch.

6.1.1. The Numerator Accumulator and Denominator Accumulator Receive Switches.

The numerator accumulator and denominator accumulator receive switches of the divider and square rooter have the same purpose as the multiplier accumulator and multiplicand accumulator receive switches of the high-speed multiplier (see Section 5.1.). These two sets of switches on the divider-square rooter enable the operator to control the stimulation of the reception of the arguments entering into a divider and square rooter program centrally at the divider and square rooter instead of locally at the associated accumulators. The instructions specified by the setting of the receive switches on the divider and square rooter, however, are transmitted statically to the numerator and denominator accumulator via cables leading from the denominator-square root accumulator program terminal and the numerator accumulator interconnector terminal on the divider and square rooter's front panel to interconnector terminals respectively on the numerator accumulator and denominator accumulator. It is to be noted that in the case of the high-speed multiplier, the instructions set-up on the receive switches are transmitted in pulse form from pulse output terminals on front panel 1 of the high-speed multiplier to program pulse input terminals on the ier and icand accumulators. In the case of the high-speed multiplier it is necessary to set-up ier and icand accumulator program controls corresponding to the $R\alpha$—$R\epsilon$ and $D\alpha$—$D\epsilon$ terminals on the high-speed multiplier. In the case of the divider and square rooter it is not necessary to set up program controls on the numerator and denominator accumulators since the receive instructions are delivered directly into the common programming circuits of these accumulators.

The numerator accumulator and denominator accumulator receive switches differ also from the high-speed multiplier's receive switches in that the former offer the operator only two options as to the accumulator input channel through which reception is to take place. The cables used to connect the numerator accumulator interconnector terminal and the denominator and square root accumulator program terminal to the numerator and denominator accumulator interconnector terminals have been so wired that if either or both of the numerator or denominator accumulator receive switches be set to α or β, the corresponding accumulator receives its argument through the α or β input channel respectively (see Section 6.4.2.).

If it is not desired to stimulate the reception of an argument on any given program or if it is desired to control the reception of either or both arguments for a given program locally at the appropriate accumulator (by delivering a program input pulse to a suitably set up program control on the accumulator either before or simultaneously with the program input pulse that stimulates the divider and square rooter program control), then one or both receive switches can be set to 0 (off).

When the receive switch of a given program control is set to a setting different from 0, the divider and square rooter emits the receive instructions at the same time as the program control's transceiver is set by the program input pulse so that the accumulator correlated with the receive switch receives its argument during the 20 pulse times immediately following the reception of a program input pulse by the divider and square rooter (see Section 6.2).

6.1.2. The Numerator Accumulator and Denominator Accumulator Clear Switches.

The numerator accumulator and denominator accumulator clear switches control the clearing of the numerator and denominator accumulators respectively. These switches have two positions: C (clear) and 0 (off). If a clear switch is set to C, the clear circuits (see Section 6.2.) in the divider and square rooter emit a clear signal during the last addition time of a program just before the transmission of a program output pulse. This signal is delivered by means of static leads from the divider and square rooter to the PM-Clear Unit of the accumulator corresponding to the receive switch set at C in the addition time at the end of which the divider and square rooter emits a program output pulse.

Since the denominator accumulator is used as the answer accumulator in square rooting programs and since answer disposal takes place in the addition time following the transmission of a program output pulse (see Table 6-10), it is obvious that the answer would be lost before it could be transmitted to another unit if the denominator accumulator clear switch were set at C for square rooting programs. The answer disposal switch together with a suitable adaptor (such as the one shown on PX-4-114A or PX-4-114C-see Section 6.4.2) plugged into the denominator square root accumulator program terminal provide a correct method for clearing the denominator accumulator without loss of the answer in square rooting programs.

6.1.3. The Divide-Square Root and Places Switch.

The divide-square root and places switch provides a means of choosing which of the divider and square rooter's operations is to be performed on a given program and of specifying the number of places in the answer (counting from the PM counter toward the right as seen from the front of the unit) to be found. The five left hand positions of this switch specify division to 4, 7, 8, 9, or 10 places and the five right hand positions, square rooting to 4, 7, 8, 9, or 10 places (see Section 6.4.3.). The number of places chosen by the operator for a given program will depend on the accuracy requirements of the computation and on the alignment of the arguments in the argument accumulators.

See Section 6.4 for a discussion of the relationship between the location of the decimal point in the argument and answer accumulators.

The setting of the divide-square root and places switch like the setting of the significant figures switch of the high-speed multiplier, has no effect on the putting in of the 1'P pulse when the answer is disposed of subtractively from the answer accumulator. Which decade the 1'P is put into in subtractive disposal depends on the setting of the significant figures switch on the answer accumulator. If programs with different round off requirements are performed, it may be necessary to supply the 1'P at the accumulators which receive complements from the answer accumulator.

6.1.4. The Round Off Switch

The round off switch offers the operator a choice between obtaining an answer rounded off (RO) or not rounded off (NRO) to the number of places specified by the setting of the divide-square root and places switch. In general, division or square rooting programs in which 10 or fewer answer places are required will either be performed with round off or else round off will be taken care of in an accumulator after the divider has found more answer places than are required. To obtain answers with 11-19 places (see Sections 6.2 and 6.4), two programs are necessary. The first one, in which the first 10 left hand digits are found, should be performed without round off. The result of the second program should be rounded off whether as part of the second divider program or in an accumulator after the divider program.

It should be noted that under certain circumstances, twice the square root obtained through a round off program may be in error by 2 units in the last place found. For example, the divider and square rooter produces the answer

P0002 when $2\sqrt{0}$ is found to four places in a round off program. The reason for this slight inaccuracy becomes apparent when it is remembered that round off of square roots as carried out by the divider is only approximate. Let R represent the remainder from the radicand and let p + 2x be the number stored in the denominator accumulator at the end of addition time III - 2 where 2x is the extreme right hand digit of the answer found (so that, at this time p is the answer less 2x). Assume that k answer places have been found and, for simplicity, let us say that the decimal point in the numerator and denominator accumulator occurs k places from the left. If k is odd (so that R, the remainder from the radicand before round off, is greater than or equal to zero) the decision to change or not change the answer by 2 units in the last place depends on whether R-5p-10x does not or does show an overdraft. If round off were carried out exactly, the quantity R-5p-10x-2.5 would be examined instead. Thus, the rounded off answer is inaccurate when R-5p-10x $\geq$ 0 and when R-5p-10x-2.5 $<$ 0. It can easily be seen, then, that the rounded off answer obtained in square rooting programs is correct except when

$$0 \leq (5p + 10x) - |R| < 2.5 \quad \text{for an even number of places}$$
$$\text{or } 0 \leq |R| - (5p + 10x) < 2.5 \quad \text{for an odd number of places}$$

6.1.5 The Answer Disposal Switch.

The answer disposal switch on the divider and square rooter is comparable to the product disposal switch on the high-speed multiplier in that the former enables the operator to provide for the stimulation of the disposal of the answer from the answer accumulator without the necessity of delivering a program input pulse to the answer accumulator specifically for this purpose. The answer disposal switch on the divider and square rooter, however, offers the operator only 4 optional methods of disposal in contrast with the 6 options of the product disposal switch on the high-speed multiplier.

The answer disposal signals emitted by the divider and square rooter, moreover, are static signals which are delivered to the quotient and/or denominator accumulator by means of cables connecting the quotient accumulator and shift accumulator program terminal and/or the denominator-square root program terminal to interconnector terminals on the quotient and/or denominator accumulator. Points 1 and 2 of the answer disposal switch refer to the disposal of the quotient and points 3 and 4 to the disposal of twice the root. The exact meaning conveyed by their settings, however, depends on the wiring of the adaptors and interconnector cables used to carry instructions from the program terminals on the divider and square rooter to interconnector terminals on the associated accumulators (see Section 6.4.2) since the instruction signals are brought directly into the accumulators' common programming circuits. In the high-speed multiplier, on the other hand, the instructions specified by the settings A, S, AS, AC, SC or ASC of the product disposal switch, depend on the set-up of the product accumulator program controls which receive product disposal pulses from the A, S, AS, AC, SC, or ASC pulse output terminals on panel 3 of the high-speed multiplier.

6.1.6. The Interlock Switch.

The setting of the interlock switch determines the conditions for the occurrence of the final addition time of a divider and square rooter program (i.e. the addition time when a program output pulse, answer disposal signal, signal for clearing the argument accumulator's and signals for clearing certain circuits within the divider and square rooter are emitted). If the interlock switch is set at no interlock (NI), the final addition time occurs during the second addition time following the completion of the actual numerical operations involved in a division of square rooting (i.e. during the second addition time of period IV). If the interlock switch is set at I (interlock), not only must period III be completed, but also the divider and square rooter must have received an interlock input pulse before the divider and square rooter program can be considered completed. In the interlock case, the final addition time takes place during the second addition time following whichever of the 2 events hereinafter listed occurs later in the cycle of operations: 1) completion of period III; 2) the reception by the divider and square rooter of an interlock input pulse (see Table 6-10).

The interlock feature of the divider and square rooter is desirable when a division or square rooting program occurs simultaneously with another sequence of programs and is to be followed by a second sequence using either the same units as are used by the sequence in parallel with the division or square rooting or using results obtained from the parallel sequence and results of the division and square rooting.. By using the final program output pulse of the sequence in parallel with the division or square rooting as an interlock input pulse and then using the divider and square rooter's program output pulse as the initial program input pulse for the sequence which is to follow the division, the operator insures the completion of all of the programs of the parallel sequence before the commencement of the second sequence.

Had the interlock feature been omitted from the design of the divider and square rooter, the operator, under the same circumstances as those described in the previous paragraph, would have faced two equally disagreeable alternatives:

1) never to schedule a parallel sequence lasting between the minimum time to maximum time for completing a division or square rooting

2) to compute the maximum number of addition times required to complete the division or square rooting program and then to use the final program output pulse of the sequence in parallel with the division or square rooting to produce eventually (after a delay consistent with the maximum division or square rooting time) an initial program input pulse for the second sequence.

6.2. COMMON PROGRAMMING CIRCUITS

6.2.1. Status of the circuits before a transceiver is stimulated.

Before a program input pulse is received by a transceiver to stimulate a given program control, but immediately after initial clearing or the completion of a previous program, the status of certain important components of the divider and square rooter's common programming circuits may be summarized as follows:

In the program ring circuit, the pulse source flip-flop and the program ring flip-flop are in the so called normal state. The program ring (whose stages are designated by A, B, 1, 2, ..., 7) is in stage A. The observer viewing the divider and square rooter from the front (see PX-10-302) observes that the pulse source and program ring flip-flop neons are lit as is program ring neon A.

The numerator ring of the overdraft circuit is in stage P (the corresponding neon is lit) and the denominator flip-flop of the sign indication circuit is in the normal state (with the denominator flip-flop neon lit). If the previously completed program was a square rooting program, the divide flip-flop is in the normal state and the divide flip-flop neon is off. Otherwise this flip-flop is in the abnormal state and its corresponding neon is on. The interlock, interlock coincidence, and clear flip-flops are in the normal state (and their corresponding neons are off). The receivers of the internal and external-internal programming circuits are all in the normal state and the neons corresponding to them are off.

In the numerical circuits, the place ring is in stage 1 (and the place ring neon numbered 9 on PX-10-302 is on). The +2, -2, +1, and -1 receivers are in the normal state (and their corresponding neons are off).

6.2.2. The Program Ring Circuit.

As soon as a program control of the divider and square rooter is stimulated, period I is initiated. The characteristics of period I as evidenced in the divider and square rooter's program ring circuit are given in the following paragraphs.

The pulse source flip-flop remains in the normal state so that a 1'P is gated through F6 to produce a $1'P_1$ and a CPP is gated through F4 to produce a CP pulse every addition time. If the program control's divide-square root and places switch is set at a divide setting and the round-off switch at round-off or no round-off, then GP is gated through K6 or L6 respectively to produce a divide pulse (DP); if the divide-square root and places switch is set at a square root setting and the round off switch at RO or NRO, GP is gated through K3 or L3 respectively to produce a square root pulse (SRP).

During period I, also, the program ring flip-flop remains in the normal state so that DP or SRP is gated through A10 or A11 respectively to cycle the program ring 1 stage per addition time.

In the third addition time of period I, the program ring is in stage 1. A signal from this stage gates a GP through gates A7 and through B7 clearing the program ring back to stage A and flipping the program ring into the abnormal state at the end of addition time 3. This marks the termination of period I for division; period I for square rooting lasts one addition time longer. (See Table 6-4 and Table 6-7).

During period II the pulse source flip-flop remains in the normal state so that GP, $1'P_1$ and either DP or SRP continue to be emitted at the end of every addition time. Since the program ring flip-flop is in the abnormal state (and gates A10 and A11 are closed) neither DP nor SRP can cycle the program ring. The program ring, therefore, continues to register stage A throughout this period.

Period II is terminated and period III initiated when an S pulse (this is a pulse produced by the divider and square rooter when a shift sequence is about to begin - see below) is gated through E6 as a result of the coincidence of a signal from the stage of the place ring corresponding to the places setting of the divide-square root and places switch and a signal from this same switch. The pulse produced in this way is designated on PX-10-304 by the symbol SS. The SS pulse flips the pulse source flip-flop into the abnormal state.

During period III, then, $1'P_1$ and GP (and therefore either DP or SRP) cease to be emitted. Instead, a CPP is gated through F5 at the end of every addition time to produce a pulse designated by III P. III P cycles the program ring 1 stage per addition time during period III. Also, if the round-off switch has been set at RO, III P is gated through K4 or K5 (when the divider-square root and places switch is set respectively at a square-rooting or division point) to produce a round off pulse (ROP) at the end of every addition time in period III. Notice that ROP is emitted only if round off is to take place.

Period III is terminated when the program ring has been cycled through its 9 stages. Period IV is initiated when a CPP is gated through L50 to produce an F pulse and through E3 to produce an F' pulse. The F' pulse resets the pulse source flip-flop into the normal state so that in period IV (as in periods I and II) $1'P_1$, GP and SRP or DP are emitted.

6.2.3. The Interlock and Clear Circuit.

The F pulse sets the interlock coincidence flip-flop. Then the next CPP gated through J49 if the interlock switch is set at I and the interlock flip-flop[*] has been set as a result of the reception of an interlock input pulse is gated through H50 (controlled by the interlock coincidence flip-flop). The signal gated through H50 resets the interlock coincidence flip-flop and sets the clear flip-flop. The setting of the clear flip-flop results in the emission of a reset signal for the transceiver and the emission of the CL and CL' pulses.[**] The CL and CL' pulses are responsible for the condition of the program ring circuit, the place ring, the numerator ring, and the denominator flip-flop prior to the commencement of a divider and square rooter program (see Section 6.2.1).

---

* It is to be noted that the interlock flip-flop is insensitive to which of the 8 interlock input terminals has been pulsed. An interlock input pulse received at any of the interlock input terminals sets this flip-flop regardless of which program control on the divider and square rooter has been stimulated. This flip-flop is also insensitive, in some respects, to the time of reception of the interlock input pulse. An interlock input pulse received any time after the completion of one divider and square rooter program (and this may even be before the stimulation of the next divider and square rooter program) serves to flip the interlock flip-flop for the next divider and square rooter program.

** The only distinction between CL and CL' is that CL' is taken off before buffer E48 and CL after the buffer.

6.2.4. The Overdraft and Sign Indication Circuits.

The overdraft and sign indication circuits receive the information upon which they operate (in the case of the overdraft circuit, the sign of the contents of the numerator accumulator and in the case of the sign indication circuit, the sign of the denominator) by means of static leads from the numerator and denominator accumulators' PM counters. The N^- and N^+ lines carry sign signals if the contents of the numerator accumulator are respectively negative or positive. The D^- line delivers a signal to gate B1 of the sign indication circuits only if the denominator is negative.

The overdraft circuit consists of a numerator (binary) ring whose stages represent sign P and sign M and 4 gates (F1, F2, G1, G2). Each of the 4 gates receives one input from the numerator ring and the other from either the N^+ or N^- line. The gates F1, F2, G1, G2 may be thought of as (M, N^-), (M, N^+), (P, N^-), and (P, N^+) gates where the first symbol in a parenthesis designates the stage of the numerator ring and the second the numerator sign line to which the gate is connected.

The numerator ring clears to stage P at the end of a program and, in the midst of a program, can be cycled only during period I or at specific times in periods II and III. In period I, when the program ring is in stage B, a GP is gated through D6, the resulting signal is gated through K1 to cycle the numerator ring from stage P to M only if the numerator is negative. During period II and III, the numerator ring can be cycled only when L1 opens to pass a CPP. Gate L1, however, is open only when the S_α receiver is set and this receiver is set only after an overdraft has occured.

Thus, the 4 gates receive information about the current sign indication of the contents of the numerator accumulator over the static leads from the numerator accumulator's PM circuit. The numerator ring, on the other hand, registers the sign of the contents of the numerator accumulator before the denominator is either subtracted from or added to the contents of the numerator accumulator. The 4 gates in the overdraft circuit compare the current with the past sign of the contents of the numerator accumulator. The coincidence of signals to gate F1 (M, N$^-$) or G2 (P, N$^+$) leads to the emission of an NO signal. Similarly gate F2 or G1 emits an O signal upon the coincidence of signals on both inputs.

As long as an NO signal is emitted the basic operation sequence of period II is performed. When an O signal is emitted, the basic operation sequence is interrupted either by a shift sequence or by the initiation of period III. The O and NO signals produce these results by inhibitory actions since no inverters intervene between the gates of the overdraft circuit and the gates to which O and NO are delivered. When NO is emitted, gate D12 is closed and gate D11 passes a signal which gates a GP through D9. The resulting pulse is designated by P.[*] The P pulse, in period II, initiates the basic operation sequence; and in period III, initiates the 5 subtractions or additions of the denominator to the contents of the numerator accumulator by setting the Nγ receiver and either the D_S or D_A receiver. In period III, moreover, when NO is

---

[*]The P pulse is produced in other ways when the sensing of overdraft is irrelevant or unnecessary. At the end of period I in division, a signal from stage 1 of the program ring gates DP through B8 to produce a P pulse. Also, after shifting of the numerator accumulator's contents in period II, a signal from the N'γ receiver gates a GP through C9 to produce a P pulse. In period III, the P pulse is produced when a signal from stage B of the program ring gates an ROP through C8.

emitted, gate K12 passes a signal (emitted when a signal from stage 6 of the program ring opens gate J13 so that an ROP can pass) which activates the correction of the answer in accordance with the state of the divide flip-flop (see Section 6.2.4). When the O signal is emitted, gates D11 and K12 are closed and gate D12 passes a signal from the D_γ or Q_α receiver which, in turn, gates a CP through E9 to produce an S pulse. The S pulse motivates the shift sequence of period II or, when gated through E6 to produce an SS pulse (see Section 6.2.2) initiates period III.

The sign indication circuit is quite similar to the overdraft circuit in its components and functioning. This circuit consists of 4 gates (D1, D2, E1, E2) and a flip-flop, the denominator flip-flop. Each gate is connected to one of the 2 output leads from the denominator flip-flop and to either the P or M stage of the numerator ring. The denominator flip-flop is in the normal state when a program commences and can be flipped into the abnormal state to remember the fact that the denominator is negative at only one specific time[*] in the course of a divider and square rooter program. This one specific time is addition time 2 of period I when gate D6, held open by a signal from stage B of the program ring, passes a GP which can then pass through gate B1 to flip the denominator flip-flop if the contents of the denominator accumulator are negative. Once flipped, the denominator flip-flop remains in the abnormal state until reset by CL in period IV.

If the denominator is positive (and therefore the denominator flip-flop is in the normal state) and the contents of the numerator accumulator

---

[*]It is for this reason that the divider and square rooter is unable to find the real coefficient of i when the radicand is negative.

before a subtraction or addition of the denominator are positive or negative. (so that the numerator ring registers P or M respectively), then gates E1 or E2 respectively emits a like sign or unlike signal. Similarly, gates D2 and D1 emit a like or unlike sign signal respectively.

The like and unlike sign signals are also delivered to gates without the intervention of inverters so that these signals, like the O and NO signals, produce their effects by an inhibitory action.

The like sign signal closed gate B11 so that gate B10 passes a P pulse (see Section 6.2.4) which sets the D_S receiver. The unlike sign signal closes gate B10 so that gate B11 passes a P pulse which sets the D_A receiver. The coincidence of like or unlike sign signal and a signal from the round off flip-flop also determines which receivers of the internal - external programming circuits and of the numerical circuits are set in period III (see Section 6.2.7).

6.2.5. The External - Internal Programming Circuits.

A program input pulse delivered to a program pulse input terminal of the divider and square rooter immediately passes through the numerator and denominator accumulator switches whence it sets the N_α or N_β and D_α or D_β receivers. Thus, during addition time 1 of period I, the numerator and denominator accumulators receive their arguments if this reception is controlled by the divider and square rooter.* At the end of addition time 1, a CPP resets these receivers and they do not function again in any subsequent period of the program.

The $N\gamma$ and D_A or D_S receivers function during period II and, if round off is specified, during period III. The P pulse (see Section 6.2.4) sets the N_γ receiver at the same time that it sets the D_A or D_S receiver (depending on

---

* The arguments may of course, be received prior to this if their reception is controlled locally at the accumulators.

whether the unlike or like sign signal is being emitted. During period II, GP resets these receivers one addition time after they have been set. In period III of round off programs, the N_γ and D_A or D_S receivers remain set throughout addition times 3, 4, 5, 6, and 7. At the end of addition time 7 an ROP gated through D4 by a signal from stage 5 of the program ring resets these receivers. Thus, the denominator is subtracted from or added to the contents of the numerator accumulator 5 times in round off programs.

During period II, when DP or SRP is being emitted, the setting of the N_γ receiver leads, one addition time later, to the setting of the Q_α (if DP) receiver or the D_γ (if SRP) receiver. Simultaneous with the setting of the Q_α receiver, LP sets the +1 receiver if the D_S receiver was previously set or the -1 receiver if the D_A receiver was previously set. Similarly, in square rooting programs, the +2, or -2 receiver is set at the same time as the D_γ receiver is.

During period III of round off programs, the setting of the D_γ or Q_α receiver does not result from the setting of the N_γ receiver, but, instead, takes place if a ROP is gated through K12 because NO is emitted. The ROP is then routed to set either the D_γ or Q_α receiver by means of gates controlled by the round off flip-flop. This same ROP and other gates controlled by the round off flip-flop effects the setting of the +2 or -1 receiver (if the D_S receiver was set during addition times 3-7) or the -2 or -1 receiver (if the D_A receiver was previously set).

During period II, the emission of an O signal leads to the emission of an S pulse (see Section 6.2.4). The S pulse sets the S_α and N_{AC} receivers. A CPP gated through K7 as a result of the setting of the S_α receiver causes the setting of the S_{AC} and N'_γ receivers. Thus, in either division or square rooting, the shifting of the contents of the numerator accumulator one place to the left is provided for.

The S pulse also sets the D'_γ receiver and, gated through G9 or H9 by a signal from the +2 or -2 receiver respectively, sets the -1 or +1 receiver. The D'_γ receiver and the +1 or -1 receiver remain set for 2 addition times in period II for square rooting. They are reset when a CPP is gated through C13 after the NO state of affairs is restored in the overdraft circuit. Since the D'_γ and +1 or -1 receivers remain set for 2 addition times and, since the place ring is not cycled until the second addition time (see Section 6.3), the correction of twice the root as described in Section 6.0 (a change of one unit first in one decade place and then in a decade place one further to the right) takes place. It is to be noted that in period II for division, the D'_γ receiver is set but that there is nothing for the denominator accumulator to receive at the time since neither the +1 nor the -1 receiver is set in division. DP resets the D'_γ receiver in the division case one add. time after its setting.

At the beginning of period III, also, the S pulse sets the S_α and N_{AC} receivers and one addition time later the S_{AC} and N'_γ receivers are set. In period III, the D'_γ receiver is set and either the +1 or the -1 receiver is also set in the case of a square rooting program. It is to be noted, however, that III P resets the D'_γ receiver and the +1 or -1 receiver one addition time after their setting in period III so that twice the square root is corrected by only one unit in the last answer place.

When the clear flip-flop is set (see Section 6.2.3), Gate 62 in the transceiver emits a signal which has 3 effects: 1) passing through the answer disposal switch, it sets the answer disposal receiver (1, 2, 3, 4) specified

by the setting of this switch; 2) passing through the numerator and denominator
accumulator clear switches, it allows the carry clear gate to pass through gate ∴
A49 (if only the denominator accumulator is to be cleared), through gates A48
and B49 (if both the numerator and denominator accumulators are to be cleared),
or through gate B48 (if only the numerator accumulator is to be cleared); 3) it
gates a CPP through 68 to provide the transceiver's reset signal and a program
output pulse.

Thus clearing of the numerator and/or denominator accumulators takes
place a little prior to the emission of a program output pulse and answer disposal signal.

6.2.6. The Divide Flip-Flop.

The divide flip-flop is set or reset during period I of divider and
square rooter programs. In division programs DP flips this flip-flop into the
abnormal state (and turns on the corresponding neon); in square rooting programs,
SRP resets this flip-flop if it was previously flipped into the abnormal state
in a division program.

The effects of this flip-flop on the divider and square rooter's
common programming circuits become apparent in addition time 8 of period III
for round off programs when an ROP is gated through J13 by a signal from stage
6 of the program ring. If the signal from gate J13 is gated through K12 as a
result of the emission of the NO signal, then, in the division case, this signal
is gated through J10 to set the Q_α receiver and through gate J8. The signal
from gate J8 is gated through G8 to set the +1 receiver or through gate H8 to
set the -1 receiver when the like or unlike sign signal respectively is emitted.
Similarly, in the square rooting case, the D_γ receiver is set by a signal gated

TABLE 6-4

DIVISION - INITIAL SEQUENCE - PERIOD I

Requires three addition times: 1-3

Add. Time (and Prog. Ring stage)	Signal	Effect	Comment
0 (A)	1) Program input pulse	1) a) Sets transceiver in the divider b) Sets N_α or N_β and/or D_α or D_β receivers	1) a) b) The numerator and/or denominator are then received by the numerator and/or denominator accumulator respectively in add. time 1.
1 (A)	1) CPP	1) Gated through F4 by a signal from the pulse source flip-flop (in the normal state) produces a GP pulse.	1) This effect occurs in every subsequent add. time of a division program except during period III.
	2) GP	2) Gated through K6 or L6 produces a DP pulse.	2) This effect occurs in every subsequent add. time of a division program except during period III.
	3) DP	3) a) Gated through A10 by a signal from the program ring flip-flop, cycles the program ring to stage B. b) Sets the divide flip-flop if this flip-flop is in the normal state.	3) a) b) This turns on the divide flip-flop neon.
2 (B)	1) GP gated through D6 by a signal from stage B of the program ring.	1) Is then gated through gate K1 by the N⁻ signal so that the numerator binary ring is cycled to stage M in the event that the numerator is negative.	
	2) D⁻ signal	2) Is gated through B1 by the output of gate 6. Output of gate B1 sets the denominator flip-flop in the event that the denominator is negative	2) This turns off the denominator flip-flop neon.
	3) DP	3) Cycles the program ring to stage 1	
3 (1)	1) DP	1) a) Gated through B8 by a signal from stage 1 of the program ring produces a P pulse	
	2) P	2) a) Sets the N_γ receiver b) Gated through B10 when the like sign signal closes B11 sets the D_S receiver or gated through B11 when the unlike sign closes B10 sets the D_A receiver.	2) a and b) Then during add. time 4, the numerator accumulator receives either the complement of the denominator or the denominator. At the end of add. time 4, GP resets these receivers. The setting of these receivers is the event described (in the table for period II) as occurring in add. time d=3+2n for n=o.
	3) GP	3) a) Gated through W7 by a signal from stage 1, clears the program ring to stage A. b) Gated through B7 flips the program ring flip-flop.	3) a) b) The program ring flip-flop neon is turned off at this time.

+ ⬚ refers to "gate".

TABLE 6-5

DIVISION PERIOD II — BASIC DIVISION SEQUENCE

Requires two add. times: d+1 and d+2

Add. Time (and Prog. Ring Stage)	Signal	Effect	Comment
	For n=o, this add. time is counted as part of period I		
	For n>o, this add. time coincides with add. time s+2 of period II or add. time d+2 of period I		
d =3+2n for n=o or n>o see period. 1 (A)	1) P pulse derived from GP gated through D9 as a result of the coincidence of the NO signal and a signal from the Q_α receiver, or GP gated through C9 by a signal from the N'γ receiver, or (see period I) GP gated through E3 by a signal from stage 1 of the program ring.	1) a) Sets the Nγ receiver. b) Gated through B10 when the like sign signal closes A11, P sets the D_S receiver or gated through E11 when the unlike sign signal closes B10, P sets the D_A receiver.	1) During add. time d+1, then, the numerator accumulator receives either the complement of the denominator (when the numerator and denominator have the same signs) or the denominator (when the numerator and denominator have unlike signs). While these receivers are set, the corresponding neons are on. At the end of add. time d+1, these receivers are reset by a GP.
d+1 (A)	1) GP	1) a) Gated through L10 by a signal from the Nγ receiver, sets the Q_α receiver. b) Gated through G11 by a signal from the D_S receiver, sets the +1 receiver or, gated through K11 by a signal from the D_A receiver, sets the −1 receiver.	1) During add. time d+2, then, the quotient accumulator receives 1 in a given decade place if the denominator was subtracted from the numerator or receives the complement of 1 if the denominator was previously added to the numerator. The neons corresponding to these receivers are on as long as the receivers are set. The Q_α receiver is reset by a CPT and the +1 or −1 receiver is reset by a GP at the end of add. time d+2.

SHIFT SEQUENCE

Requires two add. times: s+1, s+2

Add. Time			
	This add. time coincides with add. time d+2 above		
	1) S pulse produced when a GP is gated through R9 as a result of the coincidence of an O signal and a signal from the Q_α receiver.	a) Sets the S_α and N_{AC} receivers. b) Sets the D'γ receiver. c) If gated through N6 as a result of the coincidence of signals from the places switch and place ring, produces an SS pulse (see Table 6-6).	a) During add. time s+1, the numerator is transmitted (with clearing) from the numerator accumulator and received in the shift accumulator. At the end of add. time s+1, a CPT resets the S_α receiver and N_{AC} receiver. b) There is no numerical effect on the division from the setting of the D'γ receiver since there is no data for the denominator accumulator to receive during add. time s+1. This receiver is reset at the end of add. time s+1 by a GP. c) SS pulse terminates period II and initiates period III.
s+1 (A)	1) Signal from the S_α receiver.	1) a) Gates 1'P₁ through L15 to produce 1'P₂ which cycles the place ring 1 stage. b) Gates a CPT through L1 so that the numerator binary ring is cycled 1 stage. c) Gates a CPT through H7 so that the N'γ and S_{AC} receivers are set.	1) a) b) As a result 0 ceases to be omitted and NO is emitted instead. c) Then the shift accumulator transmits (and clears) its contents to the numerator accumulator during add. time s+2. At the end of add. time s+2, a CPT resets the N'γ and S_{AC} receivers.

TABLE 6-6

DIVISION PERIOD III — ROUND OFF OR NO ROUND OFF

Items relevant only to the round-off case are circled
Requires 9 add. times: 1-9

Add. Time	Signal	Effect	Comment
		This add. time coincides with add. time d+2 of period II	
0 (A)	1) S pulse produced when a GP is gated through [E9] as a result of the coincidence of an 0 signal and a signal from the Q_α receiver.	1) a) Sets the S_α and N_{AC} receivers. b) Sets the D'γ receiver. c) Gated through [E6] as a result of the coincidence of signals from the places switch and place ring, produces an SS pulse.	1) a) During add. time 1, then, the numerator accumulator transmits (and clears) its contents to the shift accumulator. A CPP resets these receivers in add. time 1. b) Since during add. time 1, there is no numerical data on the tray from which the D_γ channel receives, there is no numerical result from 1 b).
	2) SS pulse	2) Sets the pulse source flip-flop.	2) At this time, the pulse source flip-flop neon is turned off.
1 (A)	1) CPP	1) a) Gated through [L1] by a signal from the S_α receiver, cycles the numerator binary ring. b) Gated through [K7] by a signal from the S_α receiver, sets the S_{AC} and N'γ receivers. c) Gated by [F5] produces a III P pulse.	1) a) So that NO ceases to be emitted and O is emitted by the sign indicating circuit. b) So that, during add. time 2, the numerator accumulator receives the number transmitted (with clearing) from the shift accumulator. At the end of add. time 2, these receivers are reset by a CPP. c) This pulse is produced in every subsequent add. time of period III.
	2) III P	2) a) (Gated by [K5] produces ROP.) b) Cycles the program ring to stage B c) Resets the D'γ receiver.	2) a) ROP is produced in every subsequent add. time of period III if round off is specified.
2 (B)	1) III P 2) ROP 3) P	1) Cycles program ring to stage 1 2) (Gated through [C8] by a signal from stage B of the program ring produces a P pulse.) 3) (Sets N_γ and D_γ or D_C receiver depending on whether unlike sign or like sign signal is emitted.)	1) 2) 3) These receivers remain set during add. times 3,4,5,6, and 7. (see below) They are reset at the end of add. time 7. Therefore, the numerator accumulator receives either the denominator or its complement five times.
3 (1)	1) III P	1) Cycles program ring to stage 2	
4 (2)	1) III P	1) Cycles program ring to stage 3	
5 (3)	1) III P	1) Cycles program ring to stage 4	
6 (4)	1) III P	1) Cycles program ring to stage 5	
7 (5)	1) ROP 2) III P	1) Gated through [C4] by a signal from stage 5 of the program ring, resets the N_γ and D_γ or D_C receivers. 2) Cycles the program ring to stage 6.	
8	1) ROP 2) III P	1) (Gated through [G13] by a signal from stage 6 of the program ring produces a signal which, if gated through [K12] by NO, passes through [U12] to set the S_α receiver and through [J8]. The signal from [J8] passes through [ ] when the like sign signal is emitted and sets the +1 receiver or passes through [ ] to set the -1 receiver when the unlike sign signal is emitted.) 2) Cycles the program ring to stage 7.	1) Thus, if the subtraction or addition of 5 times the denominator which takes place during add. times 3 through 7 does not produce an overdraft, during add. time 9 the quotient is increased (when numerator and denominator have like signs) or decreased (when numerator and denominator have unlike signs) by 1 unit in the last place at the right as specified by the setting of the places switch. At the end of add. time 9, III P resets and the +1 or -1 receiver and a CPP resets the Q_α receiver.

TABLE 6-7

SQUARE ROOT PERIOD I

Requires four add. times: 1-4

Add. Time (and Prog. Ring Stage)	Signal	Effect	Comment
0 (A)	1) Program input pulse	1) a) Sets transceiver in the divider and square rooter. b) Sets M_α or M_β receiver	1) b) The numerator is then received by the numerator accumulator during add. time 1.
1 (B)	1) CPP	1) Gated through [F4] by a signal from the pulse source flip-flop, produces a GP pulse.	1) This effect occurs in every subsequent add. time of a square root program except during period III.
	2) GP	2) Gated through [L3] or [K3] produces a SRP	2) This effect occurs in every subsequent add. time of a square root program except during period III.
	3) SRP	3) a) Gated through [A11] by a signal from the program ring flip-flop, cycles the program ring to stage B. b) Resets the divide flip-flop if this flip-flop is in the abnormal state.	3) b) This turns off the divide flip-flop neon.
2 (1)	1) GP gated through [D6] by a signal from stage B of the program ring.	1) Gated through [K1] by the Π signal cycles the numerator ring to stage N if the radicand is negative.	1) The divider and square rooter, however, does not find the real coefficient of 1 correctly if the radicand is negative.
	2) SRP	2) Cycles the program ring to stage 1.	
3 (A)	1) SRP	1) a) Gated through [K8] by a signal from stage 1 of the program ring, sets the D_γ receiver. b) Gated through [G7] by a signal from stage 1 of the program ring, sets the +1 receiver.	1) a and b) Thus, during add. time 4, the denominator (twice the root) accumulator receives 1 pulse in the 10^8 decade. At the end of add. time 4, a CPP resets the D_γ receiver and a CPP gated through as a result of the coincidence of the NO signal and a signal from the D_γ receiver, resets the +1 receiver.
	2) GP	2) a) Gated through [A7] by a signal from stage 1, clears the program ring to stage A. b) Gated through [B7] by a signal from stage 1 flips the program ring flip-flop.	2) b) The program ring flip-flop neon is turned off at this time.

TABLE 6-8

SQUARE ROOT PERIOD II — BASIC SQUARE ROOT SEQUENCE
Requires two add. times; r+1, r+2

Add. Time	Signal	Effect	Comment
		For n=o, this add. time coincides with add. time 4 of period I.	
		For n>o, this add. time coincides with add. time s+2 or r+2 of period II.	
r (=4+2n for n ≥ 0) (A)	1) P pulse derived from CP gated through L9 as the result of the coincidence of a signal from the D_γ receiver and an NO signal or CP gated through C9 by a signal from the N'$_\gamma$ receiver (after a shift sequence).	1) a) Sets the N$_\gamma$ receiver. b) Gated through B10 when the like sign signal is emitted, sets the D$_S$ receiver or gated through B11 when the unlike sign signal is emitted, sets the D$_A$ receiver.	1) a and b) Thus, during add. time r+1, the numerator accumulator receives the complement of the denominator (when N and D have like signs) or receives the denominator (when N and D have unlike signs). These receivers are reset by CP at the end of add. time r+1.
r+1 (A)	1) SRP	1) a) Gated through L9 by a signal from the N$_\gamma$ receiver sets the D$_\gamma$ receiver. b) Gated through C12 or B12 respectively by a signal from the D$_S$ or D$_A$ receiver sets the +2 or -2 receiver.	1) a and b) Thus, in add. time r+2, the denominator accumulator receives two in a given decade place of the complement of 2 if the denominator was previously subtracted or added respectively. The D$_\gamma$ receiver and the +2 and -2 receivers are reset by a CPP at the end of add. time r+2.

SQUARE ROOT — SHIFT SEQUENCE
Requires two addition times: s+1, s+2

add. Time	Signal	Effect	Comment
		This add. time coincides with add. time r+2.	
s (=4+2n for n ≥ 1) (A)	1) a pulse produced when a CP is gated through L8 as a result of the coincidence of an O signal and a signal from the D$_\gamma$ receiver.	1) a) Sets the S$_a$ and N$_c$ receivers. b) Sets the D'$_\gamma$ receiver. c) Gated through C9 by a signal from the +2 receiver, sets the -1 receiver or gated through B9 by a signal from the -2 receiver, sets the +1 receiver. d) If gated through L6 as a result of the coincidence of signals from the places switch and places ring produces an SS pulse (see Table 6-9).	1) a) As a result, the shift accumulator receives the numerator from the numerator accumulator which transmits and clears during add. time s+1. At the end of add. time s+1, a CPP resets these receivers. b and c) During add. time s+1, then, the denominator accumulator receives the complement of 1 or receives 1 in a given decade place if during the previous sequence, the denominator accumulator received +2 or -2 respectively in the same decade place. The D'$_\gamma$ receiver and the +1 or -1 receiver remain set through add. time s+2. d) SS pulse initiates period III. (See chart for period III.
s+1 (A)	1) signal from the S$_a$ receiver.	1) a) Gates 1'P$_1$ through L45 to produce 1'P$_2$ which cycles the place ring one stage. b) Gates a CPP through L1 so that the numerator binary ring is cycled 1 stage. c) Gates a CPP through L7 so that the N'$_\gamma$ and S$_{AC}$ receivers are set.	1) b) As a result O ceases to be emitted and NO is emitted instead. c) During add. time s+2, then, the numerator accumulator receives the contents of the shift accumulator which transmits and clears. At the end of add. time s+2, a CPP resets the N'$_\gamma$ and S$_{AC}$ receivers.
	2) See 1 c) of addition time s.	2) The D'$_\gamma$ and +1 or -1 receiver remains set.	2) Therefore, during add. time s+2, the denominator accumulator receives +1 or the complement of 1 but this time one decade place further to the right than during add. time s+1. At the end of add. time s+2, CP gated through C11 by a signal from the N'$_\gamma$ receiver resets the D'$_\gamma$ receiver and the +1 or -1 receiver.

TABLE 6-9

SQUARE ROOT PERIOD III - ROUND OFF OR NO ROUND OFF PERIOD
Requires nine add. times: 1-9
Items relevant to the round off case only are circled

Add. Time	Signal	Effect	Comment
		This add. time coincides with add. time r+2 of period $\overline{II}$.	
0 (A)	1) S pulse produced when a QP is gated through E9 as a result of the coincidence of an 0 signal and a signal from the Q_α receiver.	1) a) Sets the S_α and H_{AC} receivers. b) Sets the D'_γ receiver. c) Gated through G9 by a signal from the +2 receiver, sets the -1 receiver or gated through H9 by a signal from the -2 receiver sets the +1 receiver. d) Gated through F6 as a result of the coincidence of signals from the places switch and place ring produces an SS pulse.	1) a) During add. time 1, then, the numerator accumulator transmits (and clears) its contents to the shift accumulator. A CPP resets these accumulators in add. time 1. b and c) Thus, during add. time 1, the denominator accumulator receives the complement of -1 or +1 in a given decade place if in the previous square root sequence, +2 or its complement respectively was received in that decade place. At the end of add. time 1, III P (see below) resets the D'_γ and +1 or -1 receivers.
	2) SS	2) Sets the pulse source flip-flop.	2) At this time, the pulse source flip-flop neon is turned off.
1 (A)	1) CPP	1) a) Gated through L1 by a signal from the S_α receiver cycles the numerator binary ring. b) Gated through K7 by a signal from the S_α receiver, sets the S_{AC} and H'_γ receivers. c) Gated by K5 produces a III P.	1) a) So that NO ceases to be emitted and 0 is emitted instead. b) So that during add. time 2, the numerator accumulator receives the numerator from the shift accumulator which transmits and clears. At the end of add. time 2, a CPP resets these receivers. c) This pulse is produced in every subsequent add. time of period III.
	2) III P	a) Gated by K4 produces an ROP pulse. b) Cycles the program ring to stage B. c) Resets the D'_γ receiver and the +1 or -1 receiver.	2) a) ROP is produced in every subsequent add. time of period III if round off is specified.
2 (B)	1) III P	1) Cycles program ring to stage 1	1)
	2) ROP	2) Gated through C8 by a signal from stage B of the program ring produces a P pulse.	2)
	3) P	3) Sets H_γ receiver and D_A or D_S receiver if the unlike or like sign signal respectively is emitted.	3) These receivers remain set during add. times 3,4,5,6,7. They are reset at the end of add. time 7 (see below). Therefore, the numerator accumulator receives either the denominator or its complement five times.
3 (1)	1) III P	1) Cycles program ring to stage 2.	
4 (2)	1) III P	1) Cycles program ring to stage 3.	
5 (3)	1) III P	1) Cycles program ring to stage 4.	
6 (4)	1) III P	1) Cycles program ring to stage 5.	
7 (5)	1) ROP 2) III P	1) Gated through D5 by a signal from stage 5 of this program ring resets the H_γ and D_A or D_S receivers. 2) Cycles the program ring to stage 6.	
8 (6)	1) ROP	1) Gated through J13 by a signal from stage 6 of the program ring produces a signal which if gated through K12 by NO, passes through J9 to set the D_γ receiver and passes through J12. The signal from J12 passes through E13 when the like sign is emitted and sets the +2 receiver or passes through F13 when the unlike sign signal is emitted and sets the -2 receiver.	1) Thus, if the subtraction or addition of 5 times the denominator which occurs during add. times 3 through 7 does not produce an overdraft, during add. time 9, the quotient is increased (when N and D have like signs) or decreased (when N and D have unlike signs) by 2 units in the last place at the right as specified by the setting of the places switch. At the end of add. time 9, III P resets the +1 or -1 receiver and a CPP resets the D_γ receiver.

TABLE 6-10

PERIOD IV FOR EITHER DIVISION OR SQUARE ROOT — INTERLOCK OR NO INTERLOCK PERIOD

Requires 2 add. times: 1, 2.
Items relevant to the interlock case only are circled.

Add. Time	Signal	Effect	Comment
		This add. time coincides with add. time 9 or period III	
0 (7)	1) CPP	1) a) Gated through L50 by a signal from stage 7 or the program ring, produces an F pulse. b) Gated through E3 by a signal from stage 7 or the program ring produces an F pulse.	1)
	2) F	2) Sets the interlock coincidence flip-flop.	2) This turns on the interlock coincidence flip-flop neon.
	3) F'	3) Resets the pulse source flip-flop.	3) So that the pulse source flip-flop neon is turned on again.
1 (7)	1) CPP	1) Gated through F4 produces a GP.	Those three pulses continue to be produced every add. time of period IV but have no effect on the division or square rooting.
	2) GP	2) Gated through K6 or L6 produces a DP or through K3 or L3 produces a DRP.	
	3) 1'P	3) Gated through F6 produces 1'P$_1$.	
	4) CPP	4) Gated through K49 in the III case or gated through J49 in the I' case produces a signal which is gated through L50 to set the clear flip-flop and to reset the interlock coincidence flip-flop.	4) The clear flip-flop neon goes on at this time and the interlock coincidence flip-flop neon goes off.
2 (7)	1) CPP	1) Gated through F49 by a signal from the clear flip-flop, produces a CL' pulse.	
	2) CL'	2) a) Gated through L48 by a signal from the interlock switch, resets the interlock flip-flop. b) Clears the program ring to stage 2. c) After passing through buffer L48 becomes a CL pulse.	
	3) CL	3) a) Resets the clear flip-flop. b) Clears the numerator binary ring to stage F. c) Resets the denominator flip-flop. d) Clears the place ring to stage 1. e) Resets the program ring flip-flop.	
	4) Signal resulting from the coincidence of the transceiver's being set and the clear flip-flop's being set.	4) a) Allows the carry clear gate to pass to the numerator and/or denominator accumulator clear circuits if clearing is specified. b) Gates a CPP through 68 to provide a reset signal for the transceiver and a program output pulse. c) Gates a CPP to set one of the four answer disposal receivers.	c) Thus, during the add. time following the divider's program output pulse, the answer is disposed of in accordance with the setting of the answer disposal switch. At the end of add. time 3, the answer disposal receiver is reset by a CPP.

*If the interlock input pulse is not received until k addition times after add. time 0 of period IV, this event and all events listed next to add. time 2 occur k addition times later than that indicated in this table.

through J9 and either the +2 or -2 receiver on the coincidence of a signal from gate J12 and either the like or unlike sign signal respectively.

6.2.7. Chronological Description of the Common Programming Circuits.

Tables 6-4, 6-5, and 6-6 summarize the operation of the common programming circuits during periods I, II, and III respectively of a division program. The corresponding summaries for the square rooting case are found in tables 6-7, 6-8, 6-9. Table 6-10 summarizes the events of period IV for both square rooting and division.

Below the title, each table carries a statement indicating the number of addition times required to complete the events of the period. In some cases, the events which occur in the last addition time of the period are listed in the comment column beside the events of the next to the last addition time instead of on a separate line (e.g. the events of addition time 4, period I for square rooting in table 6-7). This is done when the event described occurs, not in the common programming circuits of the divider and square rooter, but rather in an associated accumulator.

The overlapping of periods is also indicated on the tables. For example, addition time 3 of period I for division overlaps with addition time d of period II for the first basic division sequence. Thereafter, addition time d overlaps with the second addition time of the basic division sequence or with the second addition time of the shift sequence.

It is recommended that tables 6-4 through 6-10 be compared, at this time, with the illustrative problems in tables 6-2 and 6-3.

From the tables, it appears immediately that the exact number of addition times required to complete any given division program[*] is

14+2 (p-2) + 2 (number of additions or subtractions of the denominator)

and that the number of addition times for any given square rooting program is

15 + 2 (p - 2) + 2 (number of additions or subtractions of the contents of the

denominator accumulator)

where p is the number of places specified by the setting of the divide-square
root. Since overdraft can never occur in division by zero, division by zero
consumes an infinite number of addition times. If denominator equal to zero is
a computational possibility, the operater should precede division programs by
discrimination programs with the purpose of avoiding such divisions.

6.3. NUMERICAL CIRCUITS

The 10 stage place ring in the divider and square rooter serves to
route the numerical data for the partial quotient or twice the square root
into particular decade lines at particular times. The stages of this ring
numbered 10, 1, 2, ..., 9 on PX-10-304 correspond respectively to decades 10,
9, ..., 1 of an accumulator. The place ring neons numbered 10, 9, ..., 1 on
PX-10-302 correspond respectively to stages 10, 1, 2, ..., 9 of the place ring.
It is to be noted that in period II for division or square rooting respectively,
$\pm$ 1 or $\pm$ 2 units are put into the 10^8 decade place of the answer first. A digit
different from zero (or the complement of zero if the quotient is negative)
occurs in the 10^9 decade place of the answer only if the divider and square
rooter puts in more than 10 pulses before the first shift sequence of period II

[*]Provided that the divider and square rooter need not mark time waiting for an
interlock input pulse.

or, if 10 pulses are put in before the first shift, and carry over from the addition of one or two pulses at the end of round off cause carry over to the 10th decade place. The neon numbered 10 on PX-10-302 never lights.

At the end of a divider and square rooter program this ring clears to stage 1. During the course of a program, the place ring can be cycled only during period II and then, only at the end of the first addition time $(s + 1)$ of each shift sequence. The cycling of this ring is accomplished by the $L'P_2$ pulse which is produced when the $1'P_1$ pulse (see Section 6.2.2.) is passed through L45 by a signal from the S_α **receiver**.

While the place ring has been classified as one of the numerical circuits, one of its functions is purely a programming function. Stages 3, 6, 7, 8, and 9 of the ring are connected respectively to gates C41, B41, A41, A42, and A43. The second inputs to these gates are connected respectively to points 4, 7, 8, 9, and 10 of the divide-square root and places switch. Upon the coincidence of a signal from the place ring and the divide-square root and places switch, the appropriate gate emits a signal which allows an S pulse to pass through gate E6. The resulting SS pulse terminates period II by flipping the pulse source flip-flop into the abnormal state.

The place ring carries out its numerical functions by its control of the 2 sets of answer output gates (B through L42, and B through L43). One gate from the group with No. 42 and one from the group with No. 43 is connected to each stage of the place ring. The second input to these gates comes from a line carrying digit pulses gated through the 1, 2, 2', 4, 9, and 1' pulse gates by the setting of the +1, -1, +2, or -2 receiver.

The routing of digit pulses into the appropriate decades by the place

ring can probably best be explained by means of numerical examples. Let us
assume that at some time in the course of a computation the place ring is in
stage 2 (this implies that one shift sequence has been completed thus far in
the computation) and that the +1 receiver is set at the end of some addition
time d+1 of period II. Then, in addition time d+2, gate L46 passes the 1P and
all of the other gates of this group are closed. This single pulse is delivered
to all of the gates B through L42. Since the place ring is in stage 2, however,
the only open gate of this group is J42. Therefore, one pulse is emitted in
decade place 8 (corresponding to the 10^7 decade of an accumulator) and no pulses
are emitted over any of the other leads of the answer output terminal.

Next, let us consider another case. Suppose that the place ring is in
stage 2 and that the -2 receiver is set at the end of some addition time r+1 of
period II. Then in addition time r+2, 7 pulses formed from the 1, 2, and 4P
passed through gates K47, J47, and H47 respectively are delivered to gates B
through L42, the 9P passed through gate G47 are delivered to the gates B through
L43 and to the PM lead of the answer output, and the 1'P passed through B46 is
delivered directly to the answer output lead for units decade. Since the ring
is in stage 2, gate J42 is the only open gate of the group B through L42 and
gate J43 is the only closed gate of the group B through L43. Thus, 7 pulses are
emitted over lead 8 of the answer output terminal and 9 pulses are emitted over
all of the other leads including the PM lead. In the first half of addition
time r+2, then, the denominator accumulator receives from the answer output
terminal of the divider and square rooter M 9 979 999 999. At the time of the
1'P during addition time r+2, the 1'P passed through B46 is put into the units
decade place of the answer output so that by the end of addition time r+2, the

No Load Box is used on this tray which carries pulses for the answer. No other units are to be connected into it.

Digit Trays with No Load Box

Digit Tray with Load Box

Quotient Acc. (*2)

Divider & Square Rooter

Numerator Acc. I (*3)

Numerator Acc. II (*4) (Used for 20 Digit Numerators or Radicands)

Denominator & Square Root Acc. I (*5)

Denominator & Square Root Acc. II (*6) (Used for 20 Digit Denominators)

Shift Acc. I (*7)

Shift Acc. II (*8) (Used for 20 Digit Numerators or Radicands Shift)

ITEM	DESCRIPTION	REFER TO
ST_1, SU_1	Accumulator Interconnector Terminals	PX-5-105
SU_2, SU_3, SV	Divider & Square Rooter Programming Terminals	PX-10-108
a	Special Cable from Digit Tray to ST_1 & SU_1 on Quotient Acc.	PX-5-134
b, c	Adaptors from SU_2 to Digit Tray or from SU_3 to Digit Tray	PX-4-114A, A & AC Adaptor / PX-4-114B, A & S Adaptor / PX-4-114C, AC & SC Adaptor
d	Special Cable from Digit Tray to ST_1 & SU_1 on the Denom. & Sq. Root Acc.	PX-5-136
e	Special Cable from Digit Tray to ST_1 & SU_1 on the Shift Acc.	PX-5-135
f	Special Cable from SV to ST_1 & SU_1 on the Numerator Acc.	PX-5-137

INTERCONNECTION OF DIVIDER & SQUARE ROOTER WITH ASSOCIATED ACCUMULATORS ~ PX-10-307

denominator accumulator receives from the divider and square rooter
M 9 980 000 000 which is the complement of 2 in the 10^7 decade place.

It is to be noted that in the divider and square rooter as in the high-
speed multiplier, standard transmitters have not been used in the answer output
circuit. Therefore, the numerical data for the answer must be delivered to the
quotient or denominator accumulator via either a digit tray used for no other
purpose or else by means of a special cable made for this purpose. No load box
is used on this digit tray.

6.4. INTERRELATION OF THE DIVIDER AND SQUARE ROOTER AND ITS ASSOCIATED ACCUMULATOR.

6.4.1. Interconnections for numerical data.

PX-10-307 shows the interconnections which must be made among the
accumulators associated with the divider and square rooter to carry out division
or square rooting programs when arguments of 10 or fewer places are involved.
Divisions involving arguments with from 10 to 20 places may be handled by interconnecting accumulators 3 and 4 (for 20 digit numerators) and accumulators 5
and 6 (for 20 digit denominators). In this case another digit tray is used to
connect the add output terminal of the right hand numerator accumulator to the
α input terminal of the right hand shift accumulator and a second additional
tray to connect the add output terminal of the right hand shift accumulator to
the γ input terminal of the right hand numerator accumulator. If the denominator has more than 10 digits, the add and subtract output terminals of the right
hand denominator accumulator are also connected into the latter tray.

It is to be noted that no mention has been made of interconnecting a
pair of accumulators to accumulate quotients or two-roots having between 10

and 20 places. The reason for this omission is that the divider and square
rooter is incapable of finding such answers in one operation because the place
ring has but 10 stages and the answer output terminal but 11 leads (and a ground).

Quotients with between 10 and 19 places can be found by performing
2 division programs serially. With the divide-square root and places switch
of the program control used for the first division set at 10, 9 or 10 places
(depending on the relative placement of the numerator and denominator in the
argument accumulators - see Section 6.4.3) of the answer are found. The round
off switch of the first program control should be set to NRO and the argument
accumulator clear switches to O. When the first division program is completed,
the quotient as thus far obtained is then transmitted from (and cleared out of)
the quotient accumulator to the left hand accumulator of a pair external to the
divider and square rooter system. The left hand accumulator of this pair should
be stimulated to receive this quotient through some input channel, say α. Then
the α input terminal of the right hand accumulator should not be connected to
the same tray as the A output terminal of the quotient accumulator. Because
of the setting of the round off and argument clear switches, the divider and
square rooter can then proceed on its second program, the division of the remainder from the numerator by the denominator. The quotient obtained in this
way contributes 9 more places of the answer. The number stored in the 10^8 decade
place of the quotient accumulator after the second division belongs in the 10^9
decade place of the right hand accumulator and the number stored in the 10^9
decade place of the quotient accumulator belongs in the units decade place of
the left hand accumulator. If the numerator and denominator before the first
division program have like signs, the remainder from the numerator after the

first program and the denominator have unlike signs so that the quotient obtained
by the second division program is necessarily negative. Therefore the second
quotient must be transmitted to the pair of interconnected accumulators with its
sign indication. The second quotient may be properly received in the pair of
accumulators if these accumulators receive the second quotient from the quotient
accumulator through an input channel different from the one used for receiving
the first quotient, say the β input channel and the β input terminals of both the
left and right hand accumulators should be connected to the tray to which the A
output terminal of the quotient accumulator is connected. Special adaptors and
shifters must then be used at the β input terminals of the right and left hand
accumulators. The right hand accumulator's β input terminal should have plugged
into it a shifter which shifts the data one place to the left. The left hand
accumulator's β input terminal should have an adaptor which connects the left
hand accumulator's PM input and 10^9, 10^8, ..., $10'$ decade place input leads
to the PM line of the digit tray and which connects the 10^0 decade place input
lead to the 10^9 decade place line of the digit tray.*

If 9 or 10 decade places of twice the root are found by a given square
rooting program, it is possible to find about as many places again of the <u>root</u>

---

*If it is known that the <u>numerator and denominator</u> for all division programs <u>will</u>
<u>always have like sign</u> and if the first division program is stopped after 9 places
instead of 10, then the denominator and the remainder from the numerator again
have like sign so that the quotient obtained from the second division is
positive. Under such circumstances the second quotient should be so shifted that
information from the 10^8 and 10^9 decade leads of the quotient accumulator add
output is received in the units and tens decade places of the left hand accumulator and the other digits of the second quotient are received in the right hand
accumulator shifted over two places to the left. The connections of the PM lead
of the output of the quotient accumulator to the PM and 10^9 - 10^3 decade place
leads of the input to the left hand accumulator may obviously be omitted.

(notice, not twice the root) by dividing the remainder from the radicand by twice the root as thus far found. The procedure for obtaining the final answer in a pair of interconnected accumulators external to the divider and square rooter system of accumulators is similar to that for the case discussed above for division. However, if it is desired to accumulate the root in the pair of interconnected accumulators, twice the root (resulting from the first program) should be multiplied by 0.5 before its reception in the left hand accumulator or, if it is desired to accumulate twice the root in the final accumulator, the quotient (resulting from the second program) should be multiplied by two before its reception by the pair of interconnected accumulators.

6.4.2. Interconnections for Programming Instructions.

PX-10-307 shows the interconnections which must be established between the divider and square rooter and its associated accumulators for the purpose of communicating programming instructions. For information about the wiring of the various program terminals on the divider and square rooter see PX-10-108, and for the wiring of the accumulator interconnector terminals which receive signals from the divider and square rooter program terminals see PX-5-105. On PX-10-108, SU_2 refers to the quotient accumulator and shift accumulator program terminal, SU_3 to the denominator-square root accumulator program terminal, and SV to the numerator accumulator interconnector terminal. ST_1 and SU_1 on PX-5-105 refer to the accumulator interconnector terminals designated by I_{L1}, and I_{L2} respectively on PX-5-301.

The numerator accumulator interconnector terminal on the divider and square rooter is connected directly to the left hand interconnector terminals on the numerator accumulator by means of the numerator accumulator interconnector cable shown on PX-5-132. The correspondence of the points α and β on the numerator accumulator switch and the α and β input channel receive circuits in the numerator accumulator is established by the wiring of the plugs of this cable.

Adaptors which will be discussed further below are plugged from the denominator-square root accumulator program terminal and from the quotient and shift accumulator program terminal to two different digit trays. The denominator-square root accumulator interconnector cable shown on PX-5-136 carries programming instructions to the denominator-square root accumulator's left hand interconnector terminals from the tray connected through an adapter to the divide-square root accumulator program terminal on the divider. The quotient accumulator interconnector cable shown on PX-5-134 and the shift accumulator interconnector cable shown on PX-5-135 carry instructions to the quotient and shift accumulators' left hand interconnector terminals respectively from the digit tray connected through an adaptor to the quotient and shift accumulator program terminal on the divider and square rooter.

The adaptors referred to in the preceding paragraph are shown on PX-4-114 A, B, and C. These adaptors may be used interchangeably at either the denominator-square root accumulator program terminal or at the quotient and shift accumulator program terminal. Leads 1-7 on the plug and socket of all the adaptors are wired in the same way; but, to provide flexibility in the meanings assigned to the points 1, 2, 3, and 4 on the answer disposal switch, some or all of leads 8, 9, 10, and 11[*] on the plug are wired in different ways

*Leads 8 and 10 on the quotient and shift accumulator program terminal correlate with points 1 and 2 of the answer disposal switch, and leads 8 and 10 on the denominator-square root accumulator program terminal correlate with points 3 and 4 of the answer disposal switch. Leads 9 and 11 on both program terminals are associated respectively with 8 and 10 for answer disposal instructions which involve clearing.

to leads on the sockets of the various adaptors.

When used with the standard quotient accumulator interconnector cable (PX-5-134) or denominator square root accumulator interconnector cable (PX-5-136) the adaptors referred to provide the following answer disposal options:

PX-4-114A	transmit additively without clearing / transmit additively with clearing
PX-4-114B	transmit additively / transmit subtractively
PX-4-114C	transmit additively with clearing / transmit subtractively with clearing

To illustrate the way in which these adaptors function let us consider a case in which adaptor PX-4-114A is plugged into the quotient accumulator and shift accumulator program terminal and adaptor PX-4-114C into the denominator-square root accumulator program terminal. Then the points on the answer disposal switch have the following meanings:

1 - transmit the quotient additively without clearing

2 - transmit the quotient additively with clearing

3 - transmit twice the root additively with clearing

4 - transmit twice the root subtractively with clearing

For computations in which other answer disposal option combinations than those provided by the 3 adaptors described above are needed, additional adaptors can be custom made.

6.4.3. Relationship between Alignment of the Arguments and the Answer.

The operator must exercise considerable care in the placement of the arguments in the argument accumulators for division or square rooting programs in order to make the most efficient use of the divider and square rooter.

TABLE 6-11

POSSIBLE PLACEMENT OF PAYMENT (also see Table 6-12)

Period / Time	Numerator (addend) Accumulator		Denominator (Two Root) Accumulator		Shift Accumulator	
	Receives	Stores after receiving	Receives	Stores after receiving	Receives	Stores after receiving
Example A						
1	P 0 900 000 000	P 0 900 000 000				
2						
3						
4			P 0 100 000 000	P 0 100 000 000		
5	P 9 900 000 000	P 0 800 000 000	P 0 200 000 000	P 0 300 000 000		
6	P 9 700 000 000	P 0 600 000 000	P 0 200 000 000	P 0 500 000 000		
7	M 9 700 000 000	P 0 500 000 000	P 0 200 000 000	P 0 700 000 000		
8	M 9 500 000 000	P 0 000 000 000	P 0 200 000 000	P 0 900 000 000		
9	M 9 300 000 000	M 0 300 000 000	P 0 200 000 000	P 0 500 000 000		
10			P 0 200 000 000	P 0 700 000 000		
11			P 0 200 000 000	P 0 100 000 000		
Example B						
shift 1	P 2 401 000 000	P 2 401 000 000	P 0 100 000 000	P 0 100 000 000	M 9 000 000 000	M 3 000 000 000
2			P 0 200 000 000	P 0 300 000 000		
3			P 0 200 000 000	P 0 100 000 000		
4			P 0 200 000 000	P 0 100 000 000		
5	P 9 900 000 000	P 2 301 000 000	P 0 200 000 000	P 0 100 000 000		
6		P 2 001 000 000	P 0 200 000 000	P 0 300 000 000		
7	M 9 700 000 000	P 1 501 000 000	P 0 200 000 000	P 0 500 000 000		
8	M 9 500 000 000		P 0 200 000 000	P 0 700 000 000		
9	M 9 500 000 000		P 0 200 000 000	P 0 900 000 000		
10			P 0 200 000 000	P 0 300 000 000		
11	M 9 900 000 000	P 2 901 000 000	P 0 200 000 000	P 0 100 000 000		
12		P 0 401 000 000	P 0 200 000 000	P 0 700 000 000		
13	M 9 300 300 000	P 0 801 000 000	P 0 200 000 000	P 0 900 000 000		
14	M 9 100 000 000	M 9 901 000 000	P 0 200 000 000	P 1 100 000 000		
shift 15			M 9 900 000 000	P 1 000 000 000		

Table 6-2

HISTORY OF SHIFT OF RADICANDS

Period Time	Add. Time	Numerator (radicand) Accumulator		Denominator (two-root) Accumulator		Shift Accumulator	
		Receives	Stores after receiving	Receives	Stores after receiving	Receives	Stores after receiving
Example	1	P 2 500 000 000	P 2 500 000 000				
	2						
	3						
	4	K 9 900 000 000	P 0 400 000 000	P 0 200 000 000	P 0 200 000 000		
	5						
	6						
	7	K 9 700 000 000	P 0 200 000 000	P 0 200 000 000	P 0 300 000 000		
	8						
	9	K 9 500 000 000	P 1 000 000 000	P 0 200 000 000	P 0 500 000 000		
	10				P 0 200 000 000	P 0 700 000 000		
	11	K 9 300 000 000	P 0 900 000 000				
	12			P 0 200 000 000	P 0 900 000 000		
	13						
	14	K 0 100 000 000	P 0 000 000 000	P 0 200 000 000	P 1 100 000 000		
Shift	15	K 8 900 000 000	(K 8 900 000 000)	P 0 200 000 000	P 1 300 000 000		
	16			P 0 200 000 000	P 1 500 000 000	K 9 000 000 000	
	17				P 1 500 000 000	K 9 000 000 000	(K 9 000 000 000)

From the fact that the divider and square rooter place ring allows one unit to pass to the 10^8 decade of the two root accumulator at the beginning of a square rooting program, it is obvious that the divider and square rooter proceeds on the assumption that the decimal point of the radicand occurs an even number of places (either right or left) from the PM place of the numerator accumulator. The operator therefore, must align the radicand in the numerator accumulator so that THE DECIMAL POINT OF THE RADICAND OCCURS AN EVEN NUMBER OF PLACES TO THE RIGHT OR LEFT OF THE NUMERATOR ACCUMULATOR'S PM POSITION.

A comparison between the square rooting example in Table 6-3 and the examples in Tables 6-11 and 6-12 also points to another consideration concerning the placement of the radicand. Examples A and B show radicands placed so that the correct answer will be obtained. Example C shows a radicand placed in such a way that the divider and square rooter cannot possibly obtain the correct answer. The examples in Tables 6-11 and 6-12 have all been carried through the first addition time of the first shift sequence since the reason for the impossibility of example C shows up at that time. In examples A and B (and also in table 6-3) when the remainder from the radicand is shifted the 9 at the extreme left is thrown away, This 9 (preceded by sign M) is not a significant figure since it is merely the complement of a non-significant zero at the left. In example C, however, the figure 8 at the far left of the remainder from the radicand is thrown away when shifting takes place. This figure (preceded by sign M), the complement of the digit 1, is a significant figure. Therefore, when the basic square rooting sequence is resumed after the completion of the shift sequence,,it will be resumed with an incorrect remainder from the radicand. A significant figure of the remainder from the radicand will be thrown away in the first shift sequence whenever the first two decade places at the extreme left of the radicand accumulator are occupied by the number 25 or any greater number. Therefore, in general, AT LEAST ONE ZERO SHOULD PRECEDE THE FIRST NON ZERO DIGIT (at the extreme left) OF THE RADICAND.

If the radicand's decimal point occurs n (positive to the right; negative to the left) decade places from the PM, the decimal point of twice the root occurs $\frac{n}{2} \pm \frac{1}{2}$ places from the PM. For example, in the computation of table 6-3, if the decimal point is considered to occur between the digits 1 and 3 of the radicand, then n is 4 and the decimal point of twice the root occurs 3 places to the left of the PM or after the digit 8. The rule given above may be derived from considerations arising out of the material in Table 6-1.

From the fact that the divider omits +1 or -1 unit in the 10^8 decade for every repetition of the basic division sequence until the first shift sequence of period I, it can be seen that if the first non-zero digit at the left of the denominator occupies the same decade place of the denominator accumulator as the second (from the left) non-zero digit of the numerator does in the numerator accumulator, then the first (from the left) non-zero digit of the quotient occupies either the first of second decade place to the left of the PM in the quotient accumulator (see Section 6.3). If the standard alignment of the denominator is defined to mean the alignment in which the first non-zero digit of the denominator occurs one decade place further to the right than does the first non-zero numerator digit, then shifting the denominator k places to the left or right of the standard alignment, results in shifting the alignment of the quotient k places to the right or left respectively of the position described above. Since with the standard alignment of the denominator, the first (from the left) non-zero digit of the quotient may occupy the extreme left decade of the quotient accumulator, it follows immediately that THE FIRST (from the LEFT) NON-ZERO DENOMINATOR DIGIT MUST NEVER OCCUR IN A DECADE PLACE TWO OR MORE TO THE RIGHT OF THE DECADE PLACE OF THE FIRST (from the LEFT) NON-ZERO DIGIT OF THE NUMERATOR or else the quotient may exceed the capacity of the quotient accumulator.

Another restriction on the placement of the denominator is that THE FIRST (from the LEFT) NON-ZERO DENOMINATOR DIGIT MUST NOT OCCUPY THE FAR LEFT DECADE PLACE OF THE DENOMINATOR ACCUMULATOR. The reason for this restriction is similar to the reason for not placing the first non-zero radicand digit in the extreme left hand decade place of the numerator accumulator (see Table 6-12). If this rule is violated, a significant figure of the remainder from the numerator may be discarded when the first shift sequence of period II occurs.

If the decimal points of the numerator, denominator, and quotient respectively occur n, d, and q̄ places from the PM place (where n, d, and q are positive when counted toward the right from the PM place), then q̄ may be predicted by the following formula:

$$q = n - d + 2$$

The following tabulation based on the example in table 6-2 illustrates this rule.

Numerator	n	Denominator	d	Quotient	q
P 0 209.070 000	4	P 0 2.30 000 000	2	P 0 091.000 000 3	4
P 0.209 070 000	1	P 0 23.0 000 000	3	P.0 091 000 000	0
P 0.209 070 000	1	P 0 230. 000 000	4	$(P.0\ 091\ 000\ 000) \times 10^{-1}$	-1

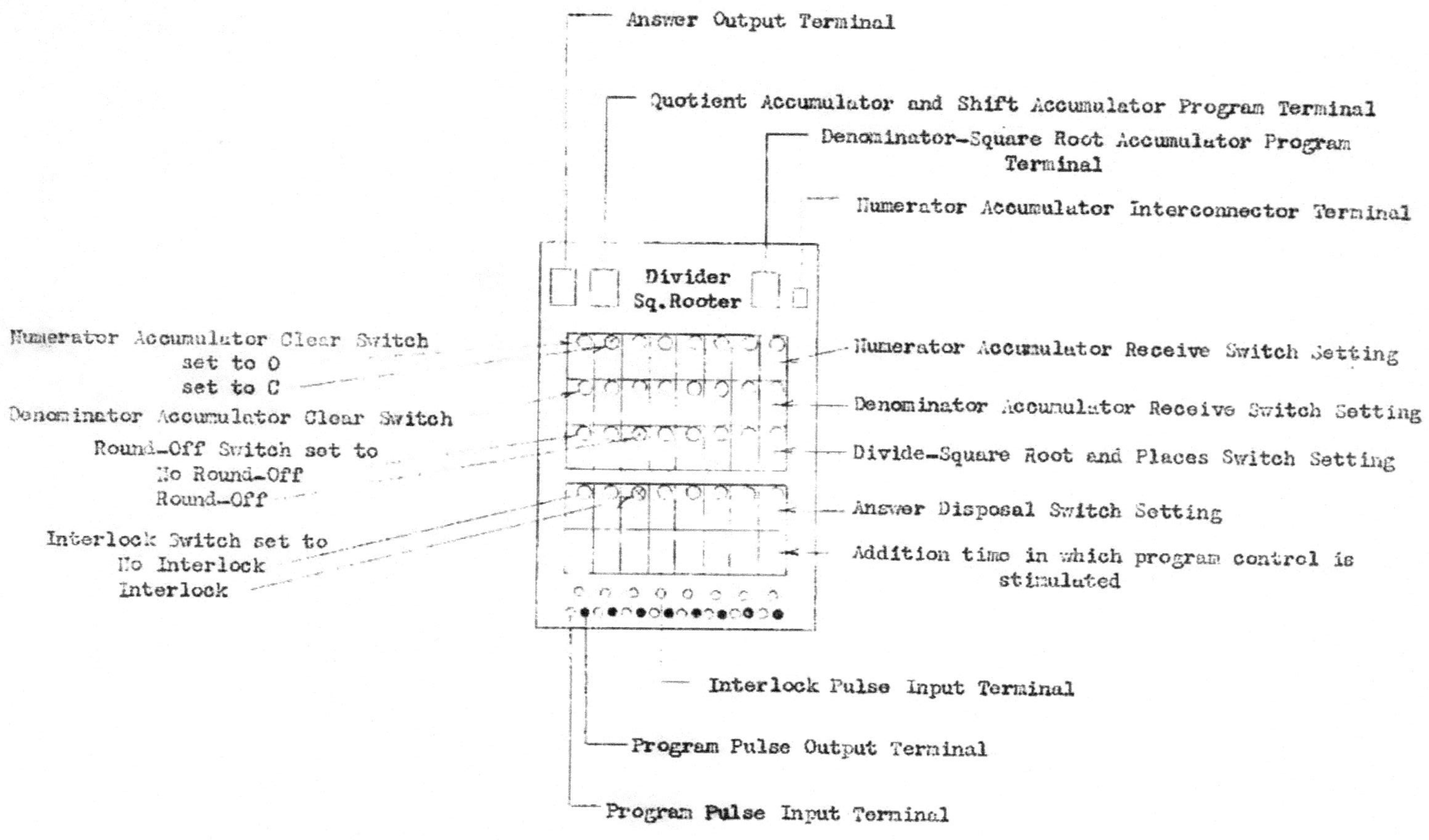

Figure 6-1

SYMBOLS USED FOR DIVIDER AND SQUARE ROOTER ON SET-UP DIAGRAM

Numerator Accumulator Clear Switch set to 0

Numerator Accumulator Clear Switch set to C

Denominator Accumulator Clear Switch

Round-Off Switch set to Round-Off

No Round-Off

Interlock Switch set to No Interlock

Interlock

Divider Sq. Rooter

Answer Output Terminal

Quotient Accumulator and Shift Accumulator Program Terminal

Denominator—Square Root Accumulator Program Terminal

Numerator Accumulator Program Terminal

Numerator Accumulator Interconnector Terminal

Numerator Accumulator Receive Switch Setting

Denominator Accumulator Receive Switch Setting

Divide—Square Root and Places Switch Setting

Answer Disposal Switch Setting

Addition time in which program control is stimulated

Interlock Pulse Input Terminal

Program Pulse Output Terminal

Program Pulse Input Terminal

6.5. ILLUSTRATIVE PROBLEM SET-UP

Table 6-13 contains instructions for setting up the units of the ENIAC to carry out a computation illustrating typical situations which arise when the divider and square rooter is used. The symbols used in this table with reference to accumulators and the high-speed multiplier have been previously taken up in chapters II and V. The master programmer is used in this set-up to route a program pulse received by it over a given program line (1-2) into 3 different program lines (2-4, 2-5, and 2-6) on 3 different occasions. For details concerning this use of the master programmer see Chapter X. The instructions to the master programmer appear in the double column immediately after the addition time column of Table 6-13. The first half of the double column shows the input terminal to which the program pulse from line 1-2 is delivered. The second half of the column designates the program output terminal (A_1o, A_2o, or A_3o) through which the master programmer delivers the program output pulse and the program line to which the program pulse output terminal is connected (2-4, 2-5, or 2-6).

The set-up table instructions given to the divider and square rooter occupy 5 levels. These instructions appear in the following order:

1) on the first level, i-j represents the program input pulse and ⓚ the program control number

2) on the second level,

the first pair of symbols represents the numerator accumulator receive and clear switch settings,

the second pair of symbols represents the denominator accumulator receive and clear switch settings, the last symbol represents the answer disposal switch setting (1, 2, 3, 4, or 0). The code for 1-4, which depends on the adaptor used, is given at the head of the divider and square rooter column.

3) on the third level,

the first pair of symbols represents the setting of the divide-square root and places switch,

the next symbol represents the round off switch setting.

4) on the fourth level the setting of the interlock switch (I or NI) is given. In interlock programs the program line from which the interlock pulse is received is noted in a parenthesis next to the symbol I.

5) on the fifth level, which is written on the line for the addition time* which represents the last one of the program, the program output pulse is written.

For example, the group of symbols shown at the left below describes the following instructions:

Add. Time	Divider 1 = AC 3 = AC 2 = SC 4 = SC	
I - 5	1-1 (5) αC OO 4 R8 RO I (2-6)	
End of div. program	↓ 1-3	
II - 1		

In addition time I-5 a program pulse from line 1-1 stimulates control 5 to carry out a square rooting program to 8 places with round off. The radicand is received via the α input channel of the numerator accumulator and the numerator accumulator is

*The practice adopted here with regard to counting addition times is to identify addition times by a roman numeral and arabic numeral. A new roman numeral is used when a division program is completed and addition times are then counted from arabic numeral 1 again.

cleared at the end of the program. The interlock pulse is received from
program line 2-6. At the end of the program a program output pulse is emitted
over line 1-3. Twice the square root is disposed of subtractively from the
denominator accumulator which is then cleared.

The conventions used with regard to the divider and square rooter in
set-up diagrams are explained in Figure 6-1 and those relating to the master
programmer in Figure 10-1 of Chapter X.

The computation described in Table 6-13 consists of forming X where

$$X = \frac{\sqrt{a} + \sum_{i=1}^{3} x_i^3}{b} + c \cdot d$$

It is assumed that the quantities a, 2b, c, d, x_1, x_2, and x_3 have been formed
before this computation begins and they are stored in the units indicated in
the table on the line corresponding to addition time zero. The ranges of these
quantities are indicated on the table and the fact that a quantity's decimal
point occurs n decade places from the PM is symbolized by [n] where n is positive
when counted toward the right.

The computation of $\sqrt{a}$ begins in addition time I-1 and the computation
of $\sum x_i^3$ proceeds in parallel with this. Only two program controls on the
high-speed multiplier are devoted to the 6 multiplications involved in forming
$\sum x_i^3$. To do this, however, 3 stages of master programmer stepper A (see
Chapter X) and 3 dummy programs (set up on program controls 5, 6, and 7 of
accumulator 9) are used. While approximately the same amount of equipment is
required as would be the case if 6 multiplier programs were used, this procedure
may be desirable in computations where so many multiplications are performed

that multiplier program controls are at a premium.

Program control (9) of the high speed multiplier is used for the computation of x_i^3. One addition time before this control is stimulated, however, the accumulator which stores the particular x_i needed is stimulated to transmit twice to the ier and icand accumulator. Since the high-speed multiplier is stimulated in time for only the second transmission, the ier and icand accumulators receive not $2x_i$ but only x_i.

x_i^3 is formed immediately after x_i^2 through the use of high-speed multiplier program control (10). The number x_i remains in the ier accumulator from the previous multiplication and x_i^2 is received in the icand accumulator from the final product accumulator. When this multiplication is completed, $2x_i^3$ is transferred to accumulator 12. The multiplier is made to stimulate the disposal of twice the product stored in the product accumulator by setting the product disposal switch at SC and connecting the SC output terminal on panel 3 of the multiplier to a program control on accumulator 13 which is instructed to transmit two times additively with clearing.

The master programmer in this problem serves to pick out the argument which is to be used whenever multiplier program control (9) is to operate and indirectly stimulates the performance or non-performance of the program set-up on multiplier control (9). The former action occurs because the master programmer's output pulse is delivered to a program control on the appropriate accumulator; the latter effect occurs because the master programmer's output pulse is delivered to dummy program controls whose output pulses, in turn, are

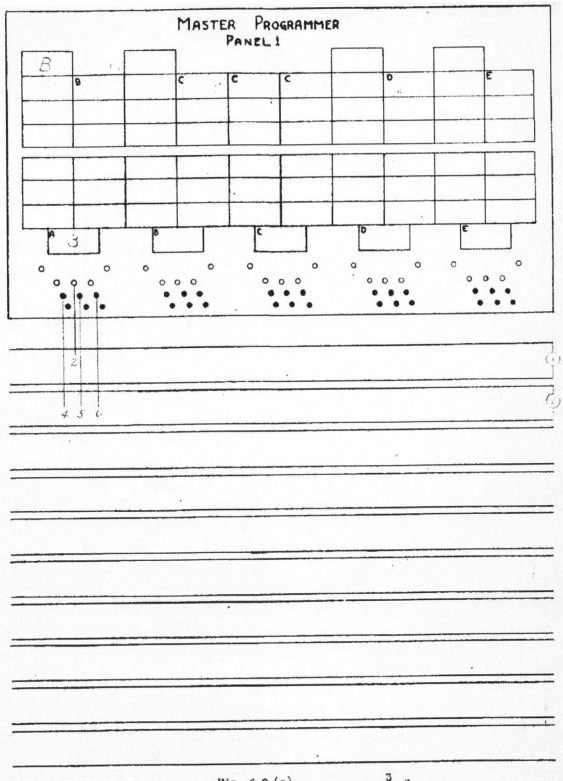

Fig. 6-2 (a)

SET-UP DIAGRAM FOR COMPUTATION OF $\dfrac{\sqrt{a} + \sum\limits_{i=1}^{3} x_i^3}{b} + cd.$

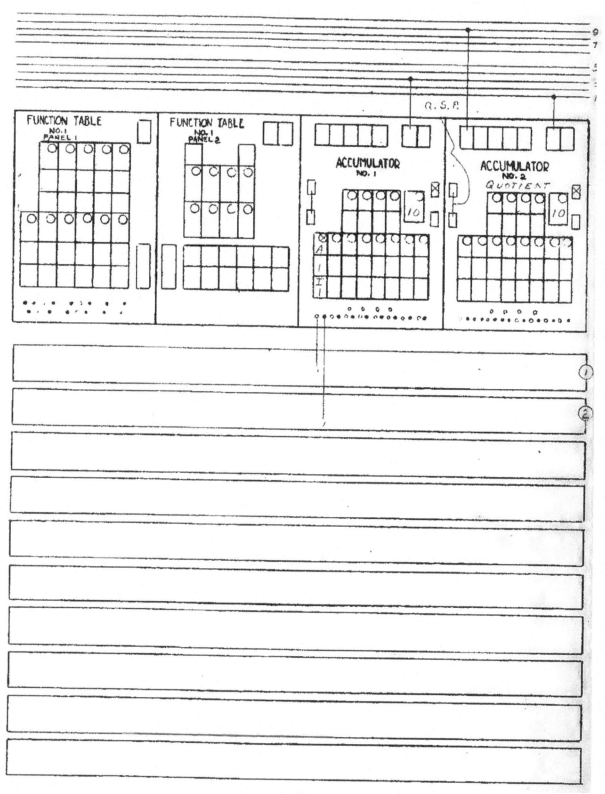

Fig. 6-2 (b)

SET-UP DIAGRAM FOR COMPUTATION OF $\dfrac{\sqrt{a} + \sum\limits_{i=1}^{3} x_i^3}{b} + cd$

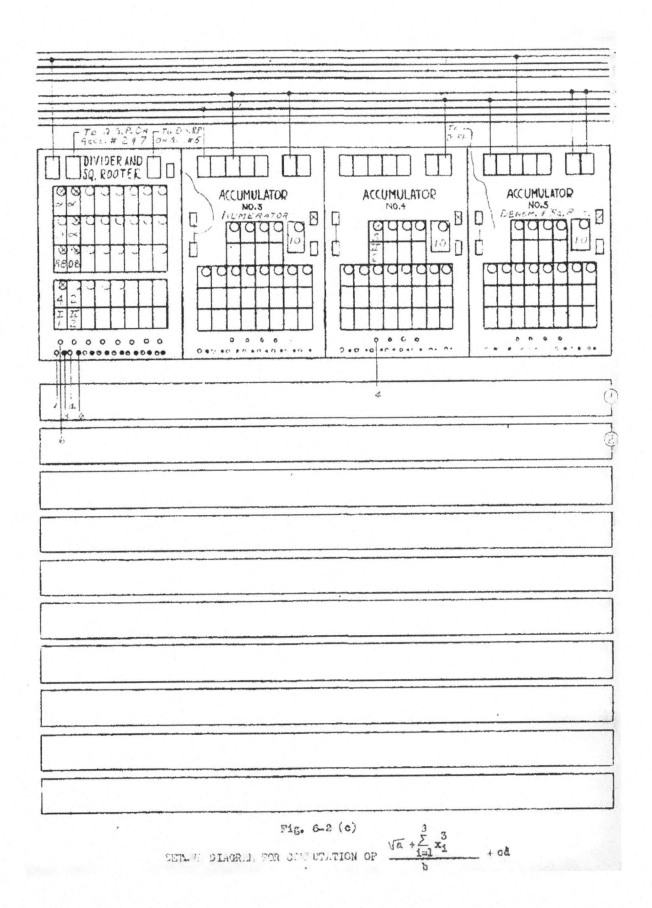

Fig. 6-2 (c)

SETUP DIAGRAM FOR COMPUTATION OF $\dfrac{\sqrt{a} + \sum\limits_{i=1}^{3} x_i^3}{b} + cd$

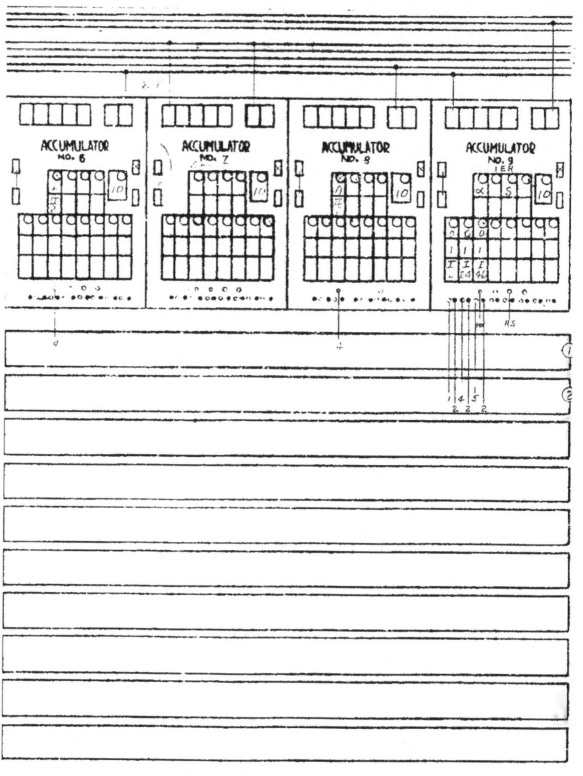

Fig. 6-2 (d)

SET-UP DIAGRAM FOR COMPUTATION OF $\dfrac{\sqrt{a} + \sum\limits_{i=1}^{3} x_i^3}{b} + cd$

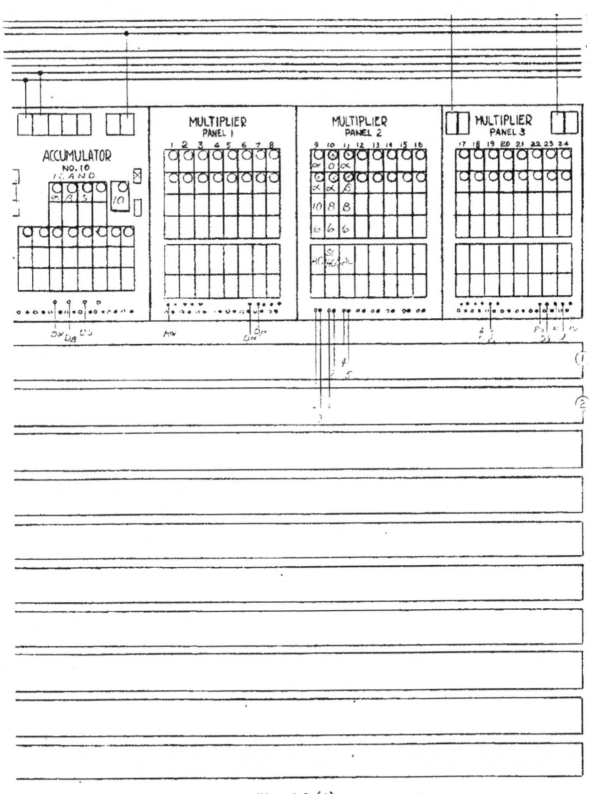

Fig. 6-2 (6)

SET-UP DIAGRAM FOR COMPUTATION OF $\dfrac{\sqrt{n} \cdot \sum\limits_{i=1}^{3} x_i^3}{0} + cd$

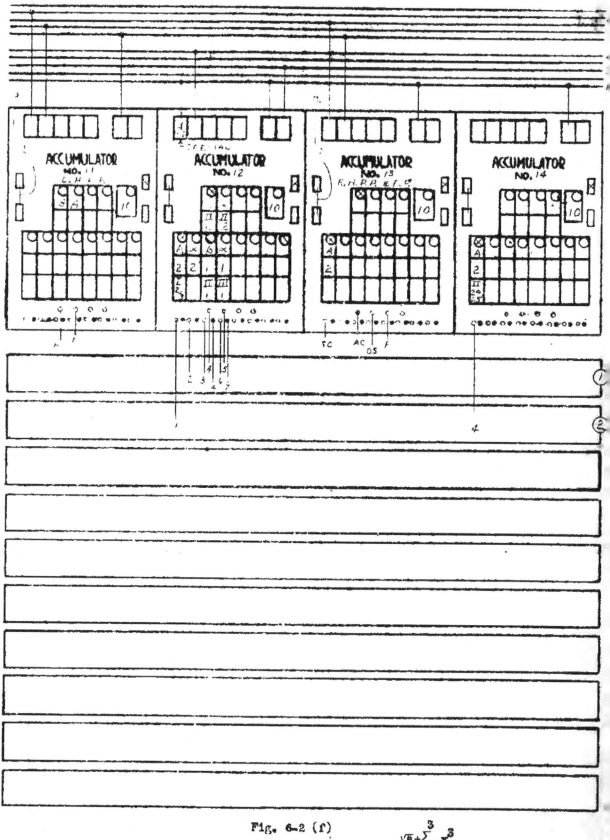

Fig. 6-2 (f)

SET-UP DIAGRAM FOR COMPUTATION OF $\dfrac{\sqrt{a}+\sum\limits_{i=1}^{3}x_i^3}{b}+cd$

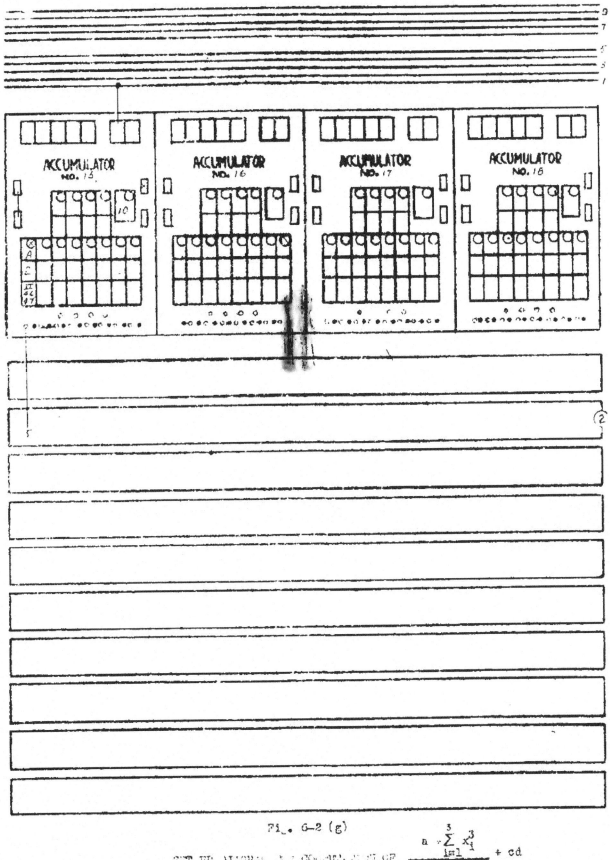

Fig. 6-2 (g)

SET-UP DIAGRAM FOR COMPUTATION OF $\dfrac{a + \sum\limits_{i=1}^{3} x_i^3}{b} + cd$

delivered to program control ⑨ as long as this multiplication program is to be repeated. After the third sequence of two multiplications has been performed, the output of the master programmer is delivered to the interlock pulse input terminal of the divider and square rooter to inform this unit that $2 \sum_i x_i^3$ has been formed and that the division of $2 \sqrt{a} + 2 \sum x_i^3$ by 2b can take place whenever the divider and square rooter has completed the formation of $2 \sqrt{a}$.

When the divider and square rooter has completed the computation of $2 \sqrt{a}$ the result is transmitted (during addition time II-1) to accumulator 12 which has been storing $2 \sum x_i^3$. In the next addition time, the divider and square rooter commences the division program (set up on program control ②) and the high speed multiplier begins the multiplication of c x d (set up on program control ⑪). When the multiplication program is completed, c x d is transferred to accumulator 12 which also receives $\frac{\sqrt{a} + \sum x_i^3}{b}$ when the division program is completed. Thus, by the end of addition time III-1, accumulator 12 stores χ and emits a program pulse (carried on line 1-7) which can be used to stimulate the next computation sequence if any.

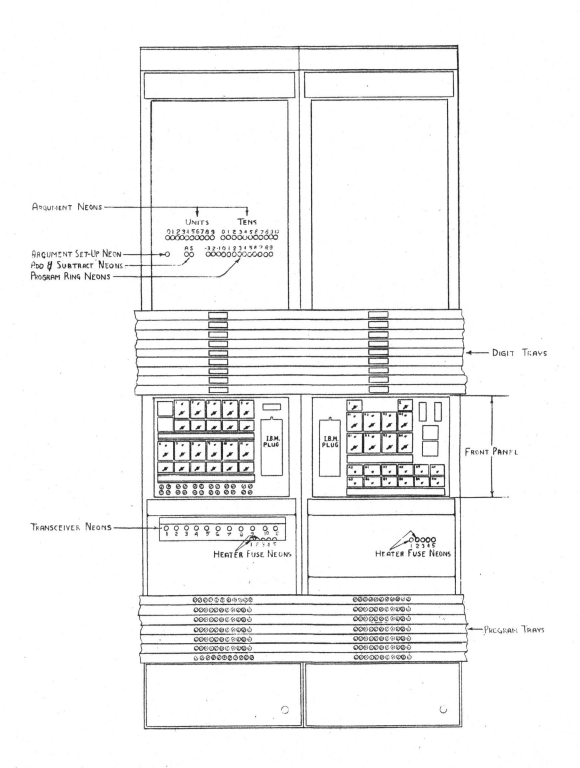

ARGUMENT NEONS

UNITS   TENS
0123456789 0123456789
○○○○○○○○○○ ○○○○○○○○○○

ARGUMENT SET-UP NEON
ADD & SUBTRACT NEONS
PROGRAM RING NEONS

AS   -3-2-10123456789
○   ○○   ○○○○○○○○○○○○

DIGIT TRAYS

I.B.M. PLUG   I.B.M. PLUG

FRONT PANEL

TRANSCEIVER NEONS

○ ○ ○ ○ ○ ○ ○ ○ ○ ○ ○
1 2 3 4 5 6 7 8 9 10 11
                12345
HEATER FUSE NEONS

○○○○○
12345
HEATER FUSE NEONS

PROGRAM TRAYS

MOORE SCHOOL of ELECTRICAL ENGINEERING
UNIVERSITY of PENNSYLVANIA

FUNCTION
TABLE
FRONT VIEW
PX-7-305

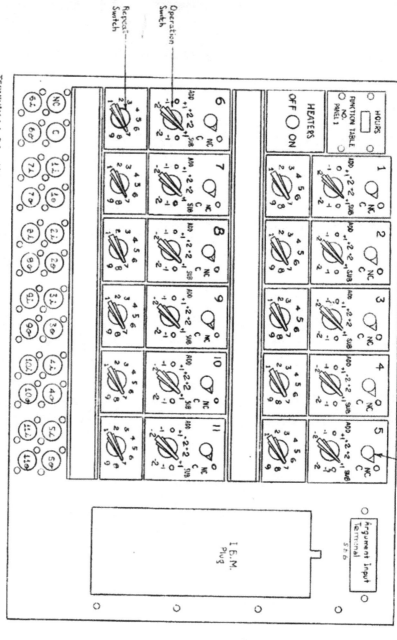

Repeat Switch

Operation Switch

FUNCTION TABLE NO. PANEL 1

HOURS

HEATERS
OFF ON

1 2 3 4 5
6 7 8 9 10 11

ADD +1 +2 -2 -1 SUB
C NC

I.B.M. Plug

Argument Input Terminal

Argument Clear Switch

Argument Clear Switch

TERMINALS 1,2,1...111
Program input pulse terminal, reprogram interrogation.

TERMINALS 10,20...110
Program output pulse terminal, reprogram interrogation.

TERMINAL NC
Program output pulse terminals associated with NC on argument clear switch.

TERMINAL C
Program output pulse terminals associated within on argument clear switch.

FUNCTION TABLE
FRONT PANEL NO. 1
PX-7-302 R

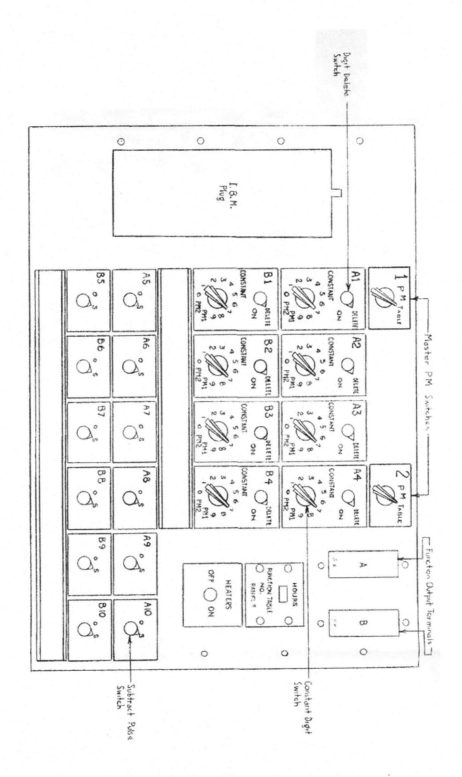

Digit Delete
Switch

Master PM Switches

I. B. M.
Plug

1 PM TABLE

CONSTANT
0 1 2 3 4 5 6 7 8 9
PM2 PM1
A1 DELETE ON

CONSTANT
3 2 1 0 4 5 6 7 8 9
PM2 PM1
B1 DELETE ON

CONSTANT
0 1 2 3 4 5 6 7 8 9
PM2 PM1
A2 DELETE ON

CONSTANT
3 2 1 0 4 5 6 7 8 9
PM2 PM1
B2 DELETE ON

CONSTANT
0 1 2 3 4 5 6 7 8 9
PM2 PM1
A3 DELETE ON

CONSTANT
3 2 1 0 4 5 6 7 8 9
PM2 PM1
B3 DELETE ON

2 PM TABLE

CONSTANT
0 1 2 3 4 5 6 7 8 9
PM2 PM1
A4 DELETE ON

CONSTANT
3 2 1 0 4 5 6 7 8 9
PM2 PM1
B4 DELETE ON

Constant Digit
Switch

Function Output Terminals

A

B

FUNCTION TABLE
NO.
PANEL

HOURS

HEATERS
OFF ON

B5
0 S

A5
0 S

B6
0 S

A6
0 S

B7
0 S

A7
0 S

B8
0 S

A8
0 S

B9
0 S

A9
0 S

B10
0 S

A10
0 S

Subtract Pulse
Switch

FUNCTION TABLE
FRONT PANEL NO.2
PX-7-303 R

VII FUNCTION TABLE

The ENIAC contains three function table units each of which can be used to store values of one or more functions tabulated against an independent variable and can be programmed to look up and transmit the values so stored. The function table is useful not only for storing and selecting values of a function (as the term is ordinarily defined) but also makes it possible to store and have readily available any numerical data which can be tagged with two digit numbers increasing monotonically between 0 and 99. Thus, a function table could be used to store the coefficients and constant terms of a system of simultaneous equations or programmatic information. The function table requires $r+4$ addition times to look up the value of a function and transmit it repetitively r times.

The following pages will be concerned with: program controls (7.1) common programming circuits (7.2); numerical circuits (7.3); storage of programming information in the   function table   (7.4); and illustrative problem set-ups (7.5). Reference will be made to the following diagrams:

Function Table Block Diagram	PX-7-304
Function Table Front View	PX-7-305
Function Table Front Panels	PX-7-302, 303

7.0. GENERAL SUMMARY OF THE FUNCTION TABLE

The function table can store 104 entries of one or more functions with each entry associated with an argument between -2 and 101. By an entry is meant 12 digits any one or all of which may vary from entry to entry and two signs, either variable or constant. In addition, 8 digits, constant throughout the range of the table, may be set up manually on switches.

If a is the argument (where $0 \leqq a \leqq 99$) and f (a) is the information stored in the function table line corresponding to value a of the argument, the function table can be programmed to look up $f(a-2)$, $f(a-1)$, $f(a)$, $f(a+1)$, $f(a+2)$, or the complement of any of the preceding and, furthermore, can be programmed to transmit the number looked up repetitively from one to nine times. Four addition times are required for looking up the value of a function and one more addition time is needed for each transmission of the functional value.

The function table can also exert some program control on the accumulator used to store the argument since it is capable of transmitting a program pulse to stimulate the argument accumulator to transmit the argument to the function table and then either to clear or not clear. In addition, the function table is capable of receiving a pulse which will stimulate it to carry out the operations noted above and then, of transmitting a program output pulse.

The physical appearance of the function table can be seen on PX-7-305. The function table has the two panels shown here and in addition, a portable function table (see ENIAC Floor Layout, PX-1-302) which extends into the center of the floor. As its name implies, the portable function table can be moved around and, any of the tables (A, B, C on PX-1-302) can be used with any one of the function tables. The portable function table will be discussed in greater detail in Sec. 7.3.

In its components and method of operation the function table is very much like the high-speed multiplier. The numerical circuits consist of a portable function table (analogous to the multiplication tables), argument counters, argument input gates (analogous to the ier selector gates), table output gates (analogous to the coding gates in the high-speed multiplier), and the 1, 2, 2', 4, and 9P gates.

There is a difference, however, between the high-speed multiplier and the function table in the way in which the argument is fed to the function table. Here, the argument is delivered in pulse form (rather than in the form of static outputs) to the function table where it is set up in the argument counters (a decade ring counter for units place with carry-over to the 11 stage counter used for tens place of the argument). The argument input gates are then set up by the static outputs of the argument counters in the function table.

The function table's numerical circuits also include 8 constant digit switches which have a purpose similar to that of the table output gates except that the former are used only for digits which remain the same throughout the table. A sign which remains constant over the whole table can be set up on one of the two master PM switches. The subtract pulse switches make it possible to transmit the 1'P over the leads for certain places when the function table transmits subtractively so that complements with respect to 10 can be emitted.

The common programming circuits of the function table consist of a 13 stage program ring analagous to the program ring in the high-speed multiplier, the argument correct gates (F-L44) which make it possible to look up f(a-2), f(a-1), f(a), f(a+1), f(a+2), the add and subtract gates and the flip-flops (C and D 46, 47) they control which make it possible for either the function or its complement to be looked up, and the argument flip-flop which controls the setting up of tens place of the argument in the argument selectors. There are also circuits for clearing the program ring and the argument counters, and for resetting flip-flops. The C and NC transmitters and their output terminals on front panel 1 which can deliver a pulse to the argument accumulators to stimulate transmission of the argument may also be counted among the common programming circuits.

The programming circuits mentioned above can be operated by any one of the function table's eleven program controls. Each program control includes a transceiver with program pulse input and output terminals on front panel 1 correlated with an operation switch, an argument clear switch, and a repeat switch.

The r+4 addition times required for the looking up of a function and its repetitive transmission r times are spent in the following way:

0   Program input pulse is received

1   Function table emits C or NC program output pulse to stimulate transmission of argument.

2   Function table receives digit pulses for the argument.

3   Argument stored in the argument counters of the function table is corrected to the value specified on the operation switch

4   Appropriate line of the portable function table is activated.

5   Functional value is transmitted for the first time.

4+r   Functional value is transmitted for the rth time and

a program output pulse is emitted after the rth trans-

mission.

7.1. PROGRAM CONTROLS

A pulse received at one of the 11 program input terminals of the
function table stimulates the function table to carry out the program set up
on the program switches of the control of which that input terminal is a part.
Each program control offers the operator options as to:

1) which of five "lines" of the table is to be entered for a given
   value of the argument,

2) whether the entry tabulated on the specified line or its
   complement is to be looked up and transmitted,

3) whether or not transmission of the argument to the function table
   is to be stimulated by the function table,

4) the number of times (from 1 to 9) in succession the function
   table is to transmit the value looked up.

The function table follows the program instructions set-up on the
control in a fashion similar to that discussed previously (see accumulator and
high-speed multiplier, for example). A pulse received at an input terminal
flips the flip-flop of the transceiver into the abnormal state. As a result,
signals from the transceiver (indirectly through inverters and/or buffers)
pass through the program switches and then proceed to cause the common program-

ming circuits (see Sec. 7.2.) to operate appropriately. As in units previously discussed, also, the reset signal for the transceiver's flip-flop comes from the unit's program ring and passes through the repeat switch of the control. After the function has been transmitted the number of times indicated by the setting of the repeat switch, the flip-flop is reset and a program output pulse is transmitted.

It is to be noted that the program output pulse is emitted <u>after</u> the function is transmitted. Therefore, the output pulse cannot be used to stimulate an accumulator to receive the function, but a pulse from some other source must be provided for this purpose four addition times after a function table transceiver is stimulated.

Program neons on front panel 1 (see PX-7-305) each correlated with a program control enable the observer to see which program control has been stimulated at a given time and, hence, which program should be in operation.

7.1.1. The Operation Switch

The operation switch has ten possible positions. The five left hand (add) positions are used when it is desired to transmit the value tabulated on a certain line; the five right hand (subtract) positions specify transmission of the complement. If a is the argument received in the function table (where $o \leq a \leq 99$), the setting -2, -1, ..., or 2 respectively specifies that line $a-2$, $a-1$, ..., or $a+2$ of the portable function table is to be entered.

The function table is especially well adapted to interpolation by means of algebraic interpolation polynomials of degree 1, 2, 3, or 4 since, by setting up several program controls, the operator can readily produce functional values for values of the argument surrounding the one for which the interpolation is being carried out. Interpolation of degree higher than the fourth can also be done. However, in order to obtain several of the entries required for such higher degree interpolation, the argument must be changed before its transmission to the function table. For example, to interpolate by means of the Newton Gregory forward interpolation formula out to sixth differences requires $f(a)$, $f(a+1)$, ..., $f(a+6)$. The entries $f(a)$, $f(a+1)$, $f(a+2)$ can be obtained in succession by using three program controls with operation switches set at 0, 1, 2, and by feeding a to the function table. The remaining entries may be produced by forming $a' = a+5$ in the accumulator in which the argument is stored and then using program controls set-up to produce $f(a'-2)$, $f(a'-1)$, ..., $f(a'+1)$.

7.1.2. Argument Clear Switch

The argument clear switch can be set at C, NC, or 0. If, on a given program control, the switch is set at C or NC, at the end of the first addition time, a program output pulse is transmitted from the correspondingly labelled terminal on front panel 1 (see PX-7-302). If, the argument clear switch is set at 0, no pulse is transmitted from either the C or NC program pulse output terminals.

The operator can utilize the C or NC pulse to stimulate transmission of the argument to the function table by connecting the C and NC terminals to suitably set up program controls on the argument accumulator or accumulators. If the argument for a given function table is always stored in one accumulator, the C terminal can be connected to a program control on the argument accumulator set up for transmission with clearing and the NC terminal, to a program control set-up for transmission without clearing. If, on the other hand, the argument for a given function table is stored sometimes in one accumulator and sometimes in another, the operator may find it convenient to use the C pulse to stimulate transmission of the argument from one accumulator and the NC pulse to stimulate transmission from the other argument accumulator.

When the argument clear switch is set at 0, the operator must provide, independently, for a program pulse to stimulate the transmission of the argument to the function table (unless the argument is to be zero). Such a pulse must be delivered to the argument accumulator one addition time after the program pulse which stimulates the function table program control since the argument must be received in the function table during the second addition time of a program.

7.1.3. The Repeat Switch

The purpose and use of the function table repeat switch is the same as that of the accumulator repeat switch. It enables the operator to secure, on any given program, repetitive transmission of the function looked up r times (where $1 \leqslant r \leqslant 9$) and causes a program output pulse to be transmitted when the last repetition has been accomplished, r+4 addition times after the reception of a program input pulse.

7.2. COMMON PROGRAMMING CIRCUITS

The device used to clock the advance of the function table through the sequence of suboperations involved in looking up and transmitting a functional value is the program ring counter (usually abbreviated as the program ring). This is a thirteen stage counter with the first stage labelled -3 (see PX-7-304) and the last 9. The program ring neons (shown on PX-7-305) are correlated with the 13 stages of the program ring.

The program ring clears to stage -3 when initial clearing takes place and whenever a function table program is completed. The reception of a program pulse by any transceiver results in opening a gate (D, E, or F49) which allows the ring to receive a CPP each addition time as long as the transceiver's flip-flop remains in the abnormal state. Each CPP then cycles the ring 1 stage. In this section, the program ring and its effect on associated gates and flip-flops are discussed (see Table 7-1 for a summary).

During the first addition time of a function table program (i.e. while the ring is in stage -3), gate J48 is opened so that the next CPP (after the one received by the transceiver) can pass through it and then cut through whichever of the gates H(46) or H(47) is open as the result of the setting of the argument clear switch to NC or C respectively. This pulse is the one referred to in Sec. 7.1.2. as the NC or C pulse.

Simultaneous with the transmission of the C or NC pulse, the program ring cycles to stage -2. During this addition time, the second of the program, a signal from stage -2, opens gates D42 and H42, the gates to the units and tens place argument counters to allow the argument to be received in the argument counters.

In the third addition time a signal from stage -1 allows 0, 1, 2, or 3 (depending on the setting of the operation switch) pulses to pass through gate E42 and be delivered to the argument counters so as to correct the argument to the value specified by the operation switch setting (see Sec. 7.3.2.) During this addition time, too, gate F47 is open so that the 1' pulse trans-

TABLE 7-1

CHRONOLOGICAL OPERATION OF THE FUNCTION TABLE'S
PROGRAMMING CIRCUITS

Add. Time	Stage of Program Ring	EVENT
End of 0	-3	1) Program input pulse is received
1	-3	1) Signal from stage -3 gates CPP through gate J48. Output of gate J48 gated through gate H46 or gate H47 by normally positive output of transceiver's flip-flop is emitted as C or NC pulse. 2) CPP gated through D, E, or F49 cycles program ring to stage -2.
2	-2	1) Signal from stage -2 opens gates D and H42 so that argument can be received in argument counters. 2) Program ring cycles to stage -1.
3	-1	1) Signal from stage -1 opens gate E42 to allow the argument correct pulses to pass through to the argument counter for units place. 2) Signal from stage -1 gates 1'P through gate F47. Output of gate F47 sets argument flip-flop. 3) Program ring cycles to stage 0.
4	0	1) Signal from stage 0 gates CPP through gate G48. Output of gate G48 gated through gate E47 or gate E46 by normally negative output of transceiver's flip-flop sets Add or Subtract flip-flop respectively. 2) Program ring cycles to stage 1
5	1	1) Signal from A or S flip-flop in the abnormal state allows 1, 2, 2', 4 and 9P to pass through certain of the pulse gates to provide the function table with the pulses for the functional value. 2) Program ring cycles to stage 2 unless the repeat switch is set at 1.
.	.	.
$4 + r$	r	1) Functional value is transmitted for the rth time. 2) Signal from stage r of the program ring passes through point r on the repeat switch to gate 62 in the transceiver. Signal emitted by gate 62 gates CPP through gate 68 to provide a reset signal for the transceiver and a program output pulse. 3) The signal from gate 62 also gates a CPP through gate C48 to provide a reset signal for flip-flops B, C, and D46-47 and gates a CPP through gate B48 and gate A48 which clears the program ring to stage -3 and the argument counters to zero.

mitted in this addition time is allowed to pass and thus to flip flip-flop B46--47 into the abnormal state. This provides a negative signal to turn off the tubes marked B11 and B, C, .., L1 and thus to allow the argument input gates to set up in accordance with the number registered in the argument counters. Flip-flop B46-47 is referred to as the argument flip-flop and its operation is correlated with the argument neon on front panel 1 (see PX-7-305).

During the fourth addition time the argument selector gates finish setting up. In this time, too, a signal from stage zero, opens G48 so that the next CPP can be passed through it (at the time of the fourth CPP after the one received by the transceiver). The pulse passed through gate G48 then passes through gate E46 or E47 (E46 is open if the operation switch is set at a subtract point; E47 is open if the operation switch is set at an add point) thus (in the fifth addition time) flipping the subtract or add flip-flop respectively into the abnormal state. The subtract and add flip-flops control the transmission of the complement of a function and the function respectively (see Sec. 7.4.). These two flip-flops are correlated with the add and subtract neons on PX-7-305.

In the fifth addition time the program ring is on stage 1. In this addition time and in every subsequent one until the transceiver's flip-flop is reset, the functional value which has been looked up is transmitted. The stages from 1 to 9 of the program ring are correlated with the points 1-9 respectively on the repeat switch. When the program ring reaches stage r, the number set up on the repeat switch, a signal from stage r passes through the repeat switch and opens the transceiver's reset gate (62). This results in the activation of the function table's clear circuits so that the ring is cleared to stage -3, the argument counters are cleared to zero, and the three programming flip-flops mentioned above are reset by the next CPP. The opening of the reset gate also results in allowing the next CPP (i.e. the $(4+\dagger)$th after the one that stimulated the program control) to pass through gate 68 and then to reset the transceiver's flip-flop and to be transmitted as a program output pulse.

7.3. NUMERICAL CIRCUITS

7.3.1. Storage: Portable Function Table, Master PM Switches, Digit Delete and Constant Digit Switches, Subtract Pulse Switches.

The function table can be set up to store 104 entries each consisting of 20 digits, and 2 signs. Twelve of the digits, variable from entry to entry, are tabulated on the switches of the portable function table. The remaining 8 digits must be constant throughout the range of the argument. These are set up on the constant digit switches. The signs may be either variable or constant. Function output terminals A and B on panel 2 are each responsible for the transmission of a sign, 4 constant digits, and 6 variable digits (see Table 7-2). Whenever the function table is stimulated, information is emitted simultaneously through both function output terminals.

The function table permits great flexibility in the way in which it is set up and used. One sign and as many as 20 digits may sometimes be used for a single function. The 2 PM's, one with k and the other with 20-k (where $0 \leq k \leq 20$) digits, can be used for 2 functions. As a matter of fact, more than 2 signed functions can be stored by setting up numbers zero and nine for sign indication P and M respectively on switches ordinarily used for digits provided that these switches are not required for digits. Of course, in cases where the digits for a single function are transmitted through both function output terminals, it may be necessary to use adaptors, shifters and/or deleters in order to receive the functional value properly lined up in another unit.

The portable function table is arranged with 26 rows and 28 columns of switches on each of its 2 faces. Each face, thus, has the switches for 52 entries with the 14 columns of switches for 26 entries appearing on the left half of the face and, those for the succeeding 26 entries on the right half. The sign and 6 digits set up on the first 7 switches (at the left) are emitted over terminal A; the next 6 digits and sign, over terminal B (see Table 7-2). Positive functional values are set up with sign P and the digits for the absolute value of the function. Negative values are set up as complements, i.e. with sign M and the digits for the absolute value subtracted from some power of 10.

The adjective "variable" is used to describe the type of function table discussed above in which the values of the function are set up manually on switches and which, with changed switch settings, can be used for storing different functions on different occasions. At present, one variable type is used with each function table unit. As the need arises, portable function tables of the fixed type in which the pattern of connections is permanently wired can be constructed and used in place of the fixed type. Such a permanent table would have the advantages of always being available for use without the necessity for tearing down a function already set up on switches, of being less expensive to build, and of being considerably smaller in size than the variable type.

Master PM switches 1 and 2 on panel 2 (see PX-7-303) of the function

TABLE 7-2

FUNCTION OUTPUT TERMINAL LEADS AND ASSOCIATED SWITCHES

Lead	Associated Switches for Terminal A		Associated Switches for Terminal B	
PM	Master PM Switch 1 and Portable Function Table Switch in Column 1		Master PM Switch 2 and Portable Function Table Switch in Column 14	
10	Constant Digit and Digit Delete Switches	A4	Constant Digit and Digit Delete Switches	B4
9	Constant Digit and Digit Delete Switches	A3	Constant Digit and Digit Delete Switches	B3
8	Constant Digit and Digit Delete Switches	A2	Constant Digit and Digit Delete Switches	B2
7	Constant Digit and Digit Delete Switches	A1	Constant Digit and Digit Delete Switches	B1
6	Portable Function Table Switch in Column 2	Subtract Pulse Switch A10	Portable Function Table Switch in Column 8	Subtract Pulse Switch B10
5	Portable Function Table Switch in Column 3	Subtract Pulse Switch A9	Portable Function Table Switch in Column 9	Subtract Pulse Switch B9
4	Portable Function Table Switch in Column 4	Subtract Pulse Switch A8	Portable Function Table Switch in Column 10	Subtract Pulse Switch B8
3	Portable Function Table Switch in Column 5	Subtract Pulse Switch A7	Portable Function Table Switch in Column 11	Subtract Pulse Switch B7
2	Portable Function Table Switch in Column 6	Subtract Pulse Switch A6	Portable Function Table Switch in Column 12	Subtract Pulse Switch B6
1	Portable Function Table Switch in Column 7	Subtract Pulse Switch A5	Portable Function Table Switch in Column 13	Subtract Pulse Switch B5

table are associated with the PM leads of terminals A and B respectively. These switches have the positions P, M, and Table. If the sign to be emitted over one of the terminals is constant throughout the range of the table, this constant sign may be set up on the associated master PM switch instead of on the 104 PM switches of the portable function table. For a sign varying from entry to entry however, the appropriate sign is tabulated in the PM column of the portable function table with each entry and the corresponding master PM switch is set at Table.

For each of the 8 decade places which can be filled with a constant digit, there is a digit delete switch with the positions "delete" and "on" and an associated constant digit switch with the positions 0, 1, ..., 9, PM1, and PM2. (See Table 7-2 for the decade place leads associated with these switches.)

With a digit delete switch set at delete, no pulses are transmitted over the decade place lead associated with the delete switch. With a delete switch set at on and the associated digit switch at d (where $0 \leq d \leq 9$), d or 9-d pulses are transmitted over the correlated decade place lead according as additive or subtractive transmission respectively takes place. With a digit delete switch set at "on" and the associated constant digit switch set at PM1 or PM2 the sign pulses emitted respectively over the sign lead of the A or B function output terminals are duplicated on the correlated decade place lead. This is true whether the pulses emitted over the sign lead are those specified on a portable function table PM switch or on the master PM switch.

When the function output of a terminal is to be received in an accumulator with the variable digits in decade places at the right and with no other information provided for b (where $1 \leq b \leq 4$) decade places at the left (such as constant digits or digits from another function output terminals), and when some or all function values emitted may be negative, the PM1 or PM2 setting of b of the constant digit switch provides a means of filling these decade places at the left with the nines needed to represent a negative number. If all entries associated with a function output terminal are tabulated as either positive or negative numbers (i.e. with the master PM switch set at P or M), the same end may be achieved by setting b constant digit switches at 0 or at 9 respectively. (See Table 7-3 which follows the discussion of the subtract pulse switches).

The digit delete switch correlated with a decade place lead is set at delete when it is desired to leave a decade place completely blank as is required, for example, if a variable digit from another function output terminal is to be inserted in that place.

The subtract pulse switches A and B 5-10 have the positions 0 and S. If a subtract pulse switch is set at S when subtractive transmission takes place (see Sec. 7.3.3.), the 1'P is emitted over the decade place lead associated with the switch (see Table 7-2) to make a 10's instead of a 9's complement. Complements with respect to 9 are emitted in the decade place leads associated with subtract pulse switches which are set at 0 (see Sec. 7.3.3.). In the usual applications of the function table, at most one of the A and/or one of the B subtract pulse switches would be set at S. There is, however, nothing in the design of this unit to preclude setting a greater number of these switches at S if the operator so desires.

7.3.2. Input to the Portable Function Table: Argument Counters and Table Input Gates.

During the second addition time of a program, the argument is received

TABLE 7-3

ILLUSTRATIONS OF THE USE OF SWITCHES ON PANEL 2 OF THE FUNCTION TABLE

LINE	SETTING OF PORTABLE FUNCTION TABLE SWITCHES
x	P 123 000 795 642 M
x + 1	M 764 000 421 508 M

EXAMPLE 1

Setting of Constant Digit Switches: (All Digit Delete Switches set at "On".)

A4 at PM1	B4 at PM2
A3 at PM1	B3 at PM2
A2 at PM1	B2 at PM2
A1 at 3	B1 at PM2

Subtract Pulse Switches: A8 at S   B5 at S (all others at O)

Transmit	For Argument	Number Emitted	
		Over Terminal A	Over Terminal B
Add.	x	P 0 003 123 000	M 9 999 795 642
Add.	x+1	M 9 993 764 000	M 9 999 421 508
Sub.	x	M 9 996 877 999	P 0 000 204 358
Sub.	x+1	P 0 006 236 999	P 0 000 578 492

EXAMPLE 2

Setting of Constant Digit Switches:

A3 at 0	B4 at 9
A2 at 0	B3 at 9
A1 at 0	B2 at 9
	B1 at 9

Digit Delete Switch A4 set at "Delete" (all others set at "On").
All Subtract Pulse Switches set at 0.

Transmit	For Argument	Number Emitted	
		Over Terminal A	Over Terminal B
Add.	x	P 0 000 123 000	M 9 999 795 642
Add.	x+1	M 0 000 764 000	M 9 999 421 508
Sub.	x	M 0 999 876 999	P 0 000 204 357
Sub.	x+1	P 0 999 235 999	P 0 000 578 491

in the function table's argument counters through the argument input terminal on front panel 1[*]. This terminal is so wired that UNITS AND TENS PLACE OF THE ARGUMENT MUST BE RECEIVED IN THE FUNCTION TABLE ON THE LEADS FOR THE DECADE PLACES 1 AND 2 RESPECTIVELY. This may be provided for by placing a shifter at the argument input terminal if arguments delivered to the function table will always require shifting the same number of places or, if at various times there will be different shifting requirements, by placing shifters at the argument accumulator's digit input terminals. The units and tens argument neons on front panel 1 are correlated with the stages of the argument counters as indicated on PX-7-305.

In the third addition time, the argument stored in the argument counters is corrected by from 0 to 4 pulses chosen from the 1, 2, and 2' pulses in accordance with the operation switch setting. The argument counters are so connected to the argument or table input gates that if x is the number registered in the argument counters, the table input gate for argument x-2 sets up (during the set up period from the middle of the third addition time through the fourth). Therefore, if the operation switch is set at -2 no correction pulses are added to the argument counters; if the operation switch is set at -1, one pulse is added to the number set up in the argument counters, etc.

The table input gates consist of 104 gates (each connected to a line of the portable function table corresponding to a value of the argument between -2 and 101). Each table input gate has as one of its inputs a signal from a stage of the units argument counter and as its other input a signal from a stage of the tens counter. When the argument counters receive the argument a from the argument accumulator and the operation switch of the control which has been

---

[*]The argument input terminal on the function table, like the digit terminals on accumulators, has 12 points. Only the leads for units and tens place, however, are operative.

stimulated is set at i (i = -2, -1, ..., +2), table input gate a + i emits a
signal to line a + i of the portable function table.

7.3.3: Function Output

The functional values transmitted from the A and B output terminals
on panel 2 are compounded out of the 1, 2, 2', 4, and 9P. These pulses are
admitted to the function table through the 1, 2, 2', 4, and 9P gates. The
pulses passed through these gates are delivered to the table output gates, the
constant digit switches, and the master PM switches. The gates and switches
mentioned above allow appropriate numbers of pulses to reach the A and B output circuits which include standard transmitters (see PX-7-304) and the digit
output terminals on front panel 2.

7.3.3.1. Transmission of Information Stored on Portable Function Table Switches.

Associated with each of the 12 digit columns of the portable function
table is a column* of table output gates for digits. Each of these columns has
10 gates, one for each digit from zero to 9 inclusive. A pair of PM table output gates, one for sign P and one for sign M, is associated with each of the 2
sign columns.

One input to the table output gates for digits comes from the circuits
containing the 1, 2, 2', 4, and 9P gates. These latter gates are so controlled
by the add. and sub. flip-flops (see Sec. 7.2.) and so connected to the table output gates that when additive transmission takes place (and the add. flip-flop is,
thus, in the abnormal state), d pulses reach the table output gates corresponding to digit d; when subtractive transmission takes place (and the sub. flip-flop

---

*The block diagram of the function table shows the table output gates rotated by
90° from their actual position in the function table where they are arranged in
rows. Refer to the cross section diagram for the position in the function table
itself.

is, thus, in the abnormal state), 9-d pulses reach the table output gates corresponding to digit d.

The signal from the table input gate corresponding to argument a+i, routed through the 12 digit switches on line a+i, holds open the table output gates corresponding to the digits set up on the line so that the pulses delivered to these gates from the 1, 2, 2', 4, and 9P gates can pass through.

The transmission of sign indication stored in the sign columns of the portable function table is accomplished similarly. The table output gate connected to point P on the sign switches receives 0 or 9 pulses from the 9P gate and the output gate connected to point M receives 9 or 0 pulses from the 9P gate according as the add or subtract flip-flop is in the abnormal state. The pulses passed by one of the pair of table output gates for sign are routed through "Table" on the associated master PM switch to be emitted over one of the PM leads.

With a master PM switch set at P or M (instead of table) the sign pulses emitted by one of the table output gates for sign cannot reach the output circuit. The transmission of a constant sign set up on one of the master PM switches takes place in the following manner: The same number of pulses are delivered to the points P and M respectively on the master PM switches as are delivered to the table output gates associated with digits 0 and 9. Thus, if a master PM switch is set at P, zero or nine pulses are passed through this switch to the associated function output terminal's PM lead according as additive or subtractive transmission takes place. The case where a master PM switch is set at M is taken care of similarly.

7.3.3.2. Transmission of Information Stored on Constant Digit Switches.

The 1, 2, 2'; 4, and 9P gates deliver d pulses (in additive transmission) or 9-d pulses (in subtractive transmission) to the point d (where $0 \leqslant d \leqslant 9$) on a constant digit switch. Thus, if one of these switches is set at d, d or 9-d pulses pass through it, then through the correlated digit delete switch to the associated decade place lead of a function output terminal.

The points PM1 and PM2 receive the pulses passed by master PM switches 1 and 2 respectively. In this way, a constant digit switch allows the same number of pulses as are transmitted over one of the PM leads to reach the decade place lead associated with the constant digit switch.

If a digit delete switch is set at "delete", the circuit from the correlated constant digit switch to the associated decade place lead is interrupted so that the pulses which arrive at the constant digit switch from the 1, 2, 2', 4, and 9P gates or from the master PM switch cannot reach the function output terminals.

7.3.3.3. Role of the Subtract Pulse Switches

The subtract flip-flop controls the gates A' and B' 64 so that these gates open to pass the 1'P when subtractive transmission takes place. The output of gates A' and B' 64 is routed through the subtract pulse switches set at S to the associated decade place leads of the function output terminals.

7.4. STORAGE OF PROGRAMMING DATA BY MEANS OF THE FUNCTION TABLE

When only a part of a total function table storage capacity (3744 variable digits and 624 variable signs for the 3 function tables) is required for the tabulation of numerical data, the remaining storage capacity can be used as

memory for programming instructions. This can be done either with a function
table operating in the same way as described in Sec. 7.3. when numerical functions
are stored and transmitted or, more conveniently, with a small change in the
circuits containing the 1, 2, 2', 4, and 9P gates.

First, let us consider the use of the unmodified function table for
programming memory. Suppose there are, say, 14 different programs $(P_1 - P_{14})$
one or more of which are to be stimulated at various times in a computation.
We could then assign one column on a portable function table to each of the 14
programs and assign one line of the portable function table to each occasion
on which it is necessary to make a choice as to which of the 14 programs is or
are to be stimulated. Then the switches on a given line of the portable function
table are set at P or 0 in the columns corresponding to programs which are not
to be stimulated and at M or a number different from zero in the columns corresponding to programs which are to be stimulated. An accumulator is set aside to
store the argument for the function table.

Now, when choice of program is required, a program pulse is sent to a
function table program control set up for additive transmission. In the fifth
addition time following the program input pulse, digit pulses are emitted over
function output terminals in the decade place leads corresponding to switch
settings different from P or zero. At the end of the fifth addition time a
program output pulse is emitted. The digit pulses are taken through adaptors
at the function output terminals to lines in program trays and then to dummy programs
for conversion to program pulses. The program output pulses of the dummy programs
are taken to the program controls on which are set up those of the 14 programs
which are to be stimulated (see Fig. 7-1). The function table's program output

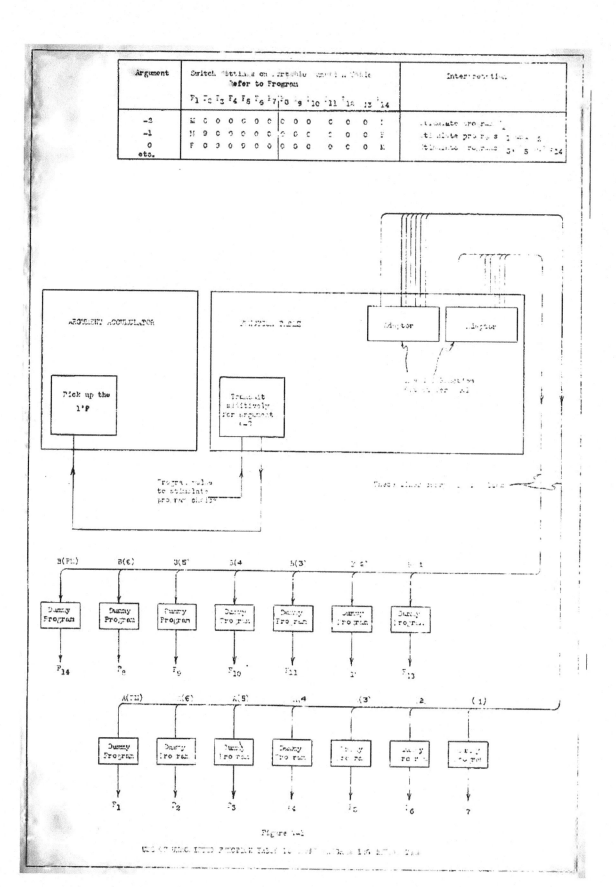

Figure 4-1

THE 47 MAGNETIZED PROGRAM TABLE TO STIMULATE PROGRAMS IN THE CHAIN

pulse can be taken to a program control of the accumulator containing the argument which is set-up for a "receive -C" program in order to increase the value of the argument by one.

In the example shown on Fig. 7-1, all 14 columns of switches on a program table are devoted to the storage of programming information. With the function table in its unmodified form, however, there is no reason why some of the columns cannot be used for numerical data and others for programming data (see Sec. 7.5.3.).

The disadvantage inherent in using the function table in its unmodified form to store programming information is the necessity for expending dummy programs to convert the digit pulses emitted from the function output terminals into program pulses (see Sec. 4.5.2.). With only a small amount of labor the function table can be adapted so that program pulses are transmitted from the function output terminals instead of digit pulses. The simplest way to make this change is to disconnect the 9P gates (B' and L'4) from the line in the synchronizing trunk which carries the 9P and to connect these gates, instead, to the line which carries the CPP. This may be done by means of an adaptor at the point where the synchronizing cable plugs into the back of panel 2. No wiring changes are necessary. The required adaptor is shown on PX-4-119. If this change is made, when the function table transmits additively, a CPP is emitted over the decade place leads corresponding to portable function table (or even constant digit switches) set at either M or 9. Notice, these CPP are emitted from the function table at the end of the fifth addition time. As always, no pulse of any kind is emitted over a decade place lead whose corresponding switch is set at P or 0. In this way, the necessity for converting digit pulses into program pulses is obviated. The pulses emitted from the function output terminals can be taken directly to the program controls on which are set up the various programs among which a choice is made.

It should be noted that a numerical function cannot be set-up alongside of programming data on a given portable function table when this modification is made unless the function is pathologic to the extent that its tabulated values never have the digit 9 or sign M.

The use of a modified function table to store programming information is illustrated in the problem described in Sec. 8.7.

In connection with this discussion of the role of the function table as programming memory, mention might also be made of the fact that the function table's program controls provide a convenient way of delaying a program pulse from 5 to 13 addition times. This use of the function table is also involved in the illustrative problem of Sec. 8.7.

7.5. ILLUSTRATIVE EXAMPLES OF THE USE OF THE FUNCTION TABLE IN INTERPOLATION

The function tables have been designed so as to make them particularly well suited for interpolation. One or more function tables or parts of them can be used to store the values of a function. The coefficients of the various terms of the interpolation formula used may either be stored in a function table or may be generated as needed by means of accumulators and the high speed multiplier. Various types of interpolation formulas can be employed with ease. There seems, however, to be a small advantage in using the Lagrangian formulas which involve functional values rather than formulas which involve differences since a pair of accumulators must always be tied up to find a difference unless storage space

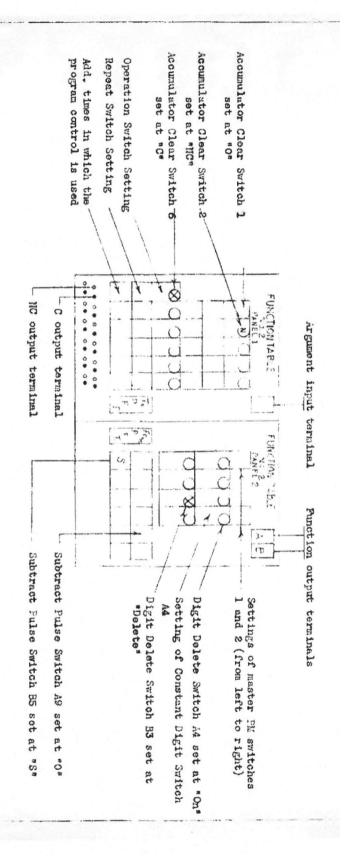

Accumulator Clear Switch 1
set at "O"

Accumulator Clear Switch 2
set at "NC"

Accumulator Clear Switch 6
set at "C"

Operation Switch Setting
Repeat Switch Setting

Add, times in which the
program control is used

Argument input terminal

Function output terminals

FUNCTION TABLE
No. 2
PANEL 1

FUNCTION TABLE
No. 2
PANEL 2

Settings of master PM switches
1 and 2 (from left to right)

Digit Delete Switch A4 set at "On"

Setting of Constant Digit Switch
A4

Digit Delete Switch B3 set at
"Delete"

Digit Delete Switch A9 set at "O"

Subtract Pulse Switch B5 set at "S"

C output terminal

NC output terminal

Subtract Pulse Switch

Figure 7-2

SET-UP DIAGRAM CONVENTIONS FOR THE FUNCTION TABLE

in the function table is used for the tabulation of differences.

In set-up tables, the following symbols are used for the function table:

1) On the first level i-j refers to the program input pulse, and (k) to the program control number.
2) On the second level,

    1st symbol (A or S) followed by a signed number (-2, -1, ..., or +2) is the operation switch setting.

    2nd symbol (C, NC, or O) is argument clear switch setting.

    3rd symbol (1, 2, ..., or 9) is repeat switch setting.

3) On the third level, at the right of the arrow tip i-j refers to the program output pulse.

When the function table is used for the storage of programming information, the connections from the decade place leads of the function output terminals to program lines are noted along the arrow from the second to the third level.

Thus, the symbol

$$4\text{-}3 \quad \textcircled{5}$$
$$A\text{-}2 \ NC \ 1$$
$$B(PM) \big| \ \text{to} \ 7\text{-}8$$
$$\downarrow$$
$$4\text{-}4$$

is interpreted as follows: The program pulse carried on lines 4-3 stimulates program control 5 so that the function table transmits f(a-2) once. The NC pulse stimulates transmission of the argument. Program control 5 emits a program output pulse to line 4-4. The output of the PM lead of function output terminal B is taken through an adaptor to program line 7-8.

Figure 7-2 shows the conventions used for the function table in set-up diagrams.

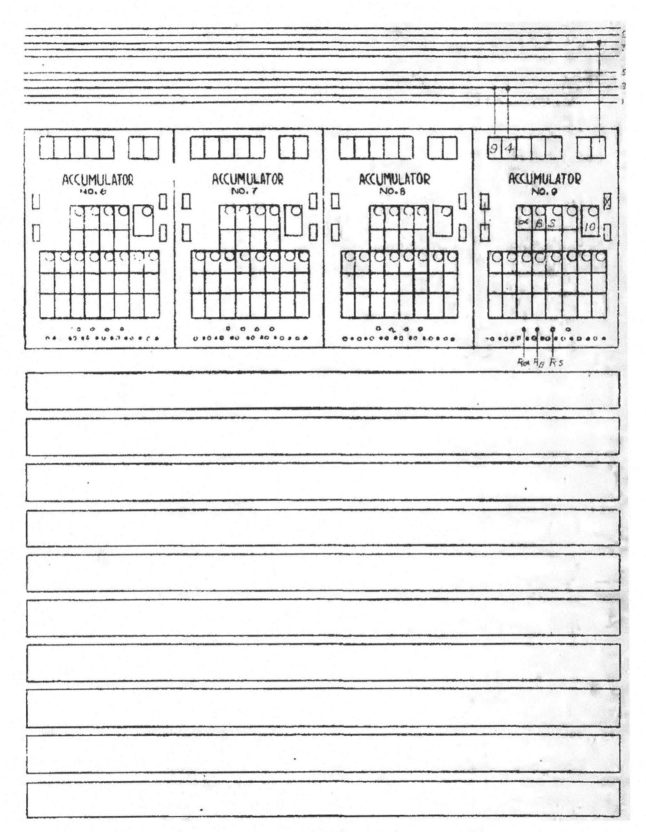

Fig. 7-3 (a)

Quadratic Lagrangian Interpolation – Set-Up Diagram

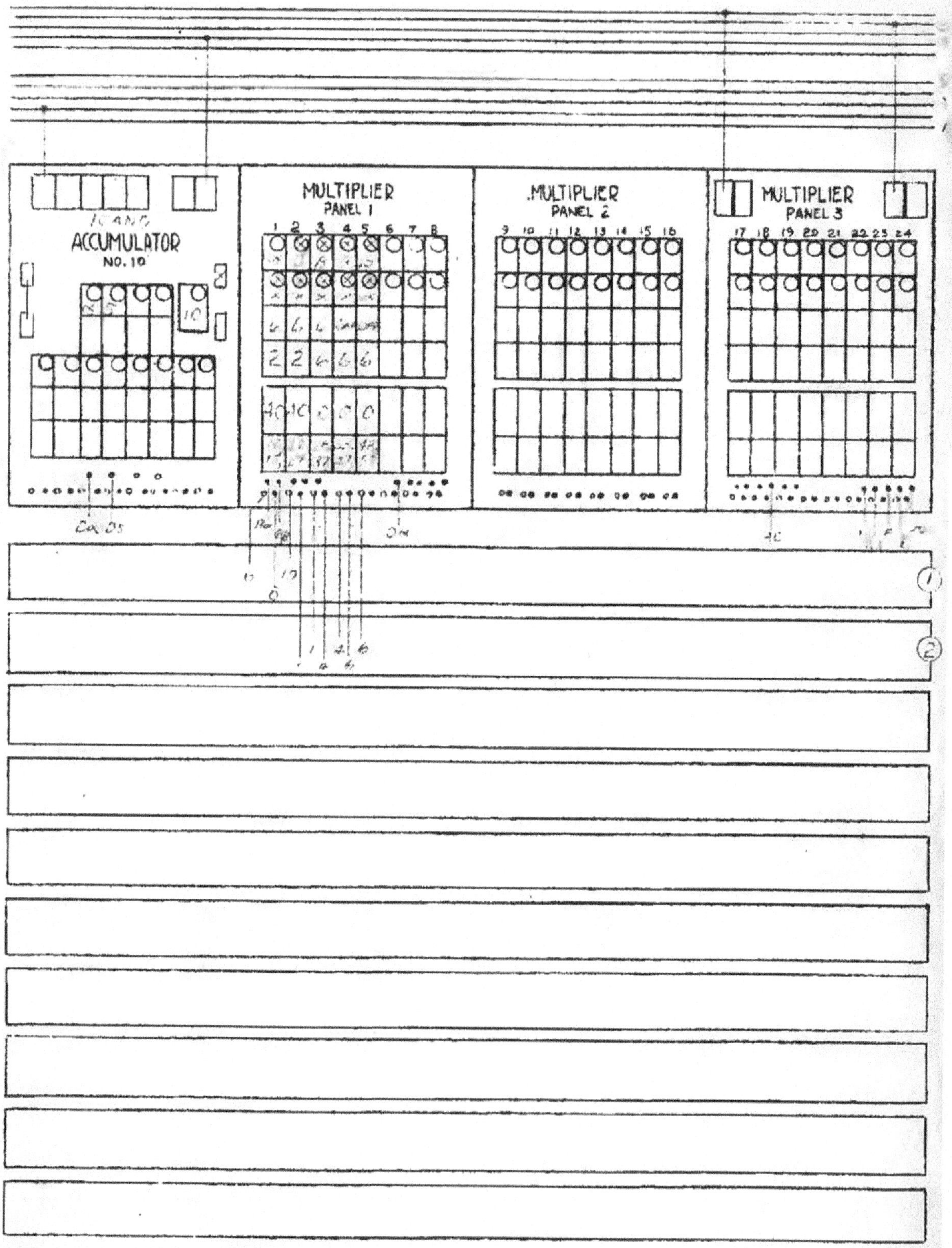

Fig. 7-3 (b)
Quadratic Lagrangian Interpolation – Set-Up Diagram

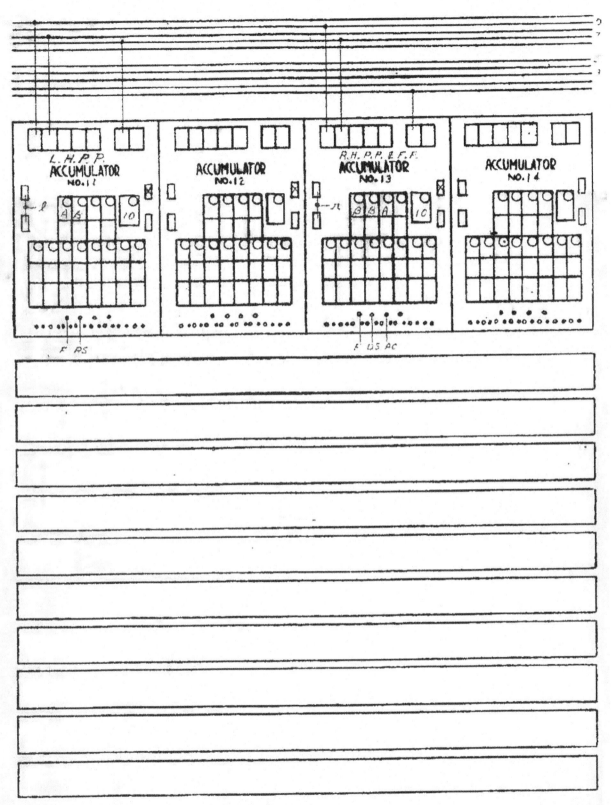

Fig. 7-3 (c)

Quadratic Lagrangian Interpolation – Set-Up Diagram

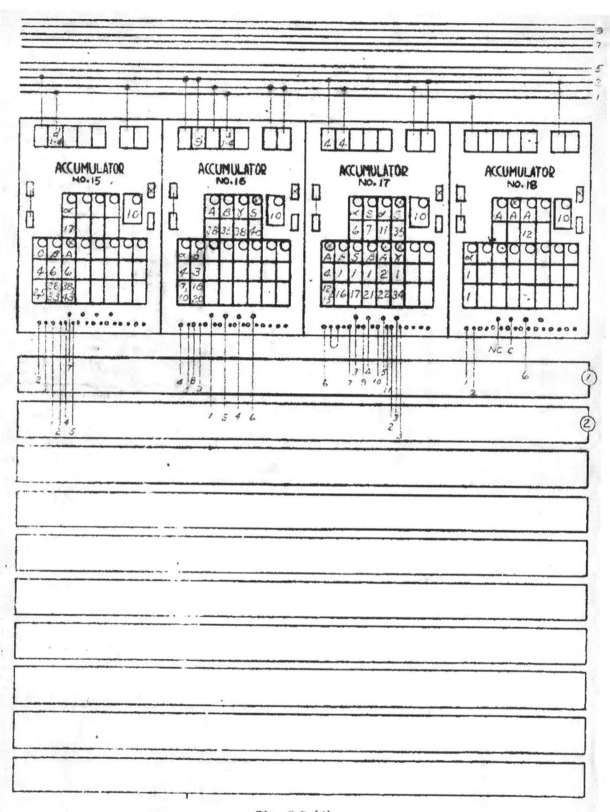

Fig. 7-3 (d)

Quadratic Lagrangian Interpolation — Set-Up Diagram

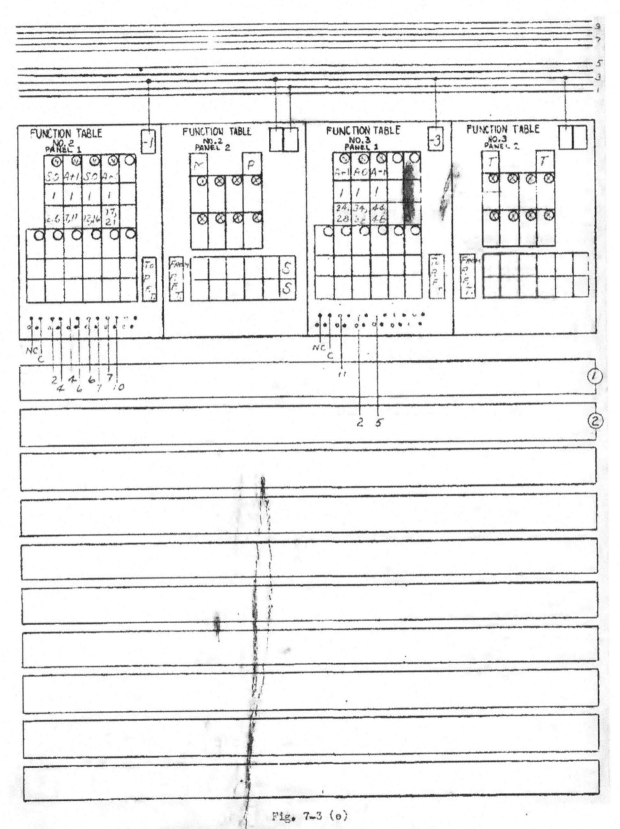

Fig. 7-3 (e)

Quadratic Lagrangian Interpolation — Set-Up Diagram

7.5.1. Quadratic Lagrangian Interpolation

In the following pages a set-up for quadratic Lagrangian interpolation for equal intervals is suggested. The interpolation formula is given by

$$f(x) = \sum_{i=-1,0,1} c^{(i)}(x_2,x_3,x_4) \cdot f_i(x_0,x_1)$$

where

$$x = \sum_{j=0}^{4} x_j \cdot 10^{1-j} \quad \text{and } 0 \leqslant x \leqslant 99$$

and where

$$f_i(x_0, x_1) = f_i(x_0, x_1 + i)$$

Even though it is cumbersome, the notation $x = \sum_{j=0}^{4} x_j \cdot 10^{1-j}$

is employed because it is useful in indicating the shifters and deleters required in certain phases of the problem.

The computation is described with the aid of Table 7-4, in which the set-up of the units involved is formulated, and Figure 7-3, which shows how to set up the units to carry out the instructions given in Table 7-4.

The values of $c^{(0)}$ and $c^{(1)}$ are stored in function table 2 in such a way that the former are emitted over the lines for decade places 1-6 of terminal A and the latter, over the lines for decade places 1-6 of terminal B. These coefficients are stored at intervals of 0.01 for $x_2 \cdot 10^{-1} + x_3 \cdot 10^{-2}$ starting with zero and ending with 1.00. Linear interpolation is used to find $c^1(x_2,x_3,x_4)$. The symbols $c_c^{(1)}$, $c_f^{(1)}$, and $\triangle c^{(i)}$ will be used as follows:

$$c_0^{(i)} = c^{(i)}(x_2,x_3,0)$$

$$c_1^{(i)} = c^{(i)}(x_2, x_3+1,0)$$

$$\triangle c^{(i)} = c_1^{(i)} - c_0^{(i)}$$

Thus, $c^{(i)}(x_2, x_3, x_4)$ is given by the formula

$$c^{(i)}(x_2, x_3, x_4) = c_0^{(i)} + \frac{1}{10} \cdot x_4 \cdot \triangle c^{(i)}$$

$c^{(-1)}$ has not been tabulated in a function table since it can be found readily from the relationship

$$c^{(-1)} = 1 - \sum_{i=0,1} c^{(i)}$$

$c^{(0)}$ and $c^{(1)}$, rather than a pair including $c^{(-1)}$ were chosen for tabulation on the portable function table to save a small amount of tabulation labor. For the range zero to one inclusive of the independent variable, $c^{(0)}$ and $c^{(1)}$, are both positive and have zero and one as their minimum and maximum values. Therefore, sign indication need not be tabulated with each entry but may, instead, be handled by setting the master PM switches to P. The co-efficient $c^{(-1)}$ has as its maximum value on this range of the argument, zero, and, as its minimum -0.12500. Were $c^{(-1)}$ tabulated, all entries would have to carry sign indication (and the master PM switch would be set to Table) in spite of the fact that the only non-negative functional entry is zero corresponding to argument zero. It might at first appear that zero could be tabulated as M 0 000 000 000, but if we recall that M 0 000 000 000 actually represents 10^{10} + P 0 000 000 000 it can be seen that this procedure would be incorrect.

$c^{(1)}$ and $c^{(0)}$, then, are tabulated on the portable function table associated with function table 2 on sides A and B respectively. Six decade places are used for each coefficient with the units place digit tabulated in the column for decade place 6 and the various decimal places (tenths place, etc.) occupying the remaining decade places, 5 through 1. The digit delete switches A4 – A1 and B4 – B1 are set to "delete" since there are no digits constant throughout the range of the argument for either $c^{(0)}$ or $c^{(1)}$. Since the coefficients $c^{(i)}$ find their way ultimately to the multiplier, it is desirable to have them located as far to the left as possible. The digit output of function table 2 is, therefore, shifted four places to the left before its reception in an accumulator. The shifter is designated by the number 4 in a box denoting a digit input terminal on Figure 7-3.

The function $f(x)$ is tabulated on the portable function table associated with function table 3. It is assumed, here, that only 6 variable digits are tabulated for this function and that these occupy the switches for decade places 1-6. Since f_i $(i= -1, 0, 1)$ too, enters into multiplications, the function output of function table 3 is also shifted 4 places to the left before its reception in the ier accumulator.

Accumulator 18 serves as the argument accumulator for both function tables. This set-up assumes that x is stored in this accumulator so that x_0 occupies the fifth decade place. A -1 shifter (which shifts a number one place to the right) is used at the argument input terminal of function table 2 to place x_2 and x_3 respectively in decade places 2 and 1 of the input and a -3 shifter is used at the argument input terminal of function table 3 to place x_0 and x_1 respectively in the proper decade lines of this input.

Detailed descriptions of the programs involved in the interpolation are given in Table 7-4. We wish, however, to call attention to the procedure used for stimulating the reception in an accumulator of functional values transmitted by the function table. Consider, for example, the programs involved in looking up $-c^{(0)}_0$. In addition time 12, program pulse 1-6 stimulates function table 2 to look up $-c^{(0)}_0$. Accumulator 17 is to receive this functional value when it is emitted during addition time 16. To provide for this reception, we take advantage of the fact that another program commences at the same time that function table 2 is stimulated, the program in which accumulator 17 transmits its contents to the multiplier. Even though only 1 transmission is required, the repeat switch on control 5 of accumulator 17 is set at 4 so that at the end of addition time 15 there will be a program pulse available to stimulate the reception of $-c^{(0)}_0$. This procedure saves the use of a special dummy program to delay a pulse until addition time 16.

The use of the high-speed multiplier in this computation is also worthy of note. During addition times 12 through 17 and 22 through 27 the multiplier is occupied in forming products required in the linear interpolation for $c^{(1)}$ and $c^{(0)}$ respectively. For each of these multiplications, the significant figures switch is set at 6. In view of the accuracy of the ier and icand and their positions in the ier and icand accumulators, the last significant figure of the product occurs in the eighth place from the left. These products, however, are added to numbers stored in either accumulator 16 or 15 which have their last significant figure 6 places from the left. The products referred to above are, therefore, rounded off to 6 significant figures and passed through deleters which delete decade lines 1-4 (counting units decade as 1) before reception in accumulator 16 or 15. This deleter is designated by d 1-4. Thus, by addition times 18 and 28 respectively, $c^{(1)}$ and $c^{(0)}$ appear in accumulators 16 and 15 respectively correct to 5 significant figures with the last significant figure appearing in decade 5 (from the right).

The products $f_i \cdot c^{(i)}$ (for $i = 1, 0, -1$) are formed during addition times 28-37, 38-47, and 48-57 respectively and are retained in accumulator 12 for collection to form $f(x)$. Since the coefficients $c^{(i)}$ will in general not exceed 5 significant figures, these products, too, will have no more than 5 significant figures with the last significant figure appearing in the sixth decade place from the left due to the positions of the ier and icand. Only the program in which $f_i \cdot C^{(1)}$ is formed, calls for round off to 6 figures, however, since the addition of five pulses in decade place 3 is required only once to produce the correctly rounded off sum of 3 products. For the other two multiplications $f_0 \cdot C^{(0)}$ and $f_{-1} \cdot C^{(-1)}$. The significant figures switch is set at "off".

It might be of interest to the operator to notice that of the 57 addition times required to carry out this quadratic Lagrangian interpolation routine, all but 15 are used for multiplications. In general, the principle that the number of multiplications involved in a computation determines approximately the duration of the computation is a reliable one.

7.5.2. Biquadratic Lagrangian Interpolation

Biquadratic Lagrangian interpolation can be carried out in a fashion similar to that described above for quadratic Lagrangian interpolation with a few minor alterations. The formula for biquadratic interpolation is

$$f(x) = \sum_{i=-2,}^{2} C^{(i)}(x_2; x_3, x_4) \cdot f_i (x_0, x_1)$$

Here, as in the quadratic interpolation, one of the coefficients need not be tabulated since

$$\sum_{i=-2}^{2} C^{(i)} = 1$$

The four coefficients needed may, as a matter of fact, be tabulated on one* portable function table to permit interpolation for $C^{(i)}(x_2, x_3, x_4)$

---

*This assumes that six decimal places for these coefficients will provide the required accuracy. If greater accuracy is required it is probably preferable to generate the coefficients rather than use up two function tables for storing them.

from a tabulation of $c^{(i)}(x_2, x_3, 0)$ since the $c^{(i)}$ need be tabulated only for $0 \leq x_2 \cdot 10^{-1} + x_3 \cdot 10^{-2} \leq .51$. For $0.5 \leq x_2 \cdot 10^{-1} + x_3 \cdot 10^{-2} < 1$, $f(x)$ may be computed by backward interpolation using the formula

$$f(x) = \sum_{i=-2,-1,\ldots,2} c^{(-i)}(x_2', x_3', x_4') f_i (x_0, x_1 +1)$$

where

$$x_2' \cdot 10^{-1} + x_3' \cdot 10^{-2} + x_4' \cdot 10^{-3} = 1 - (x_2 \cdot 10^{-1} + x_3 \cdot 10^{-2} + x_4 \cdot 10^{-3})$$

If the coefficients chosen for the tabulation are $c^{(i)}$ (for i = -2, -1, 1, 2), they may be set up on the portable function table as shown in Table 7-5.

To produce $c_0^{(i)}$ and $c_1^{(i)}$ for i = -2 or 2 the function table operation switches must be set at -2 and -1 respectively. Before $c_0^{(i)}$ and $c_1^{(i)}$, for i = 1 or -1, can be looked up, the argument (x_2, x_3), or (x_2', x_3') if backward interpolation is used, must be corrected to (x_2+5, x_3) or $(x_2' +5, x_3')$. The operation switches used in the programs of looking up $c_0^{(i)}$ and $c_1^{(i)}$, for i = 1 or -1, must be set at zero and 1 respectively.

If the suggested method of tabulating the interpolation coefficients and of carrying out the interpolation is followed, obviously two alternative interpolation routines, a forward and a backward routine, must be set-up.

The forward interpolation routine differs from the routine for quadratic Lagrangian interpolation only in that there are two additional product terms $f_i \cdot c^{(i)}$ to be formed. The backward interpolation routine must cover the use of the backward interpolation formula, the correction of the argument (x_0, x_1) to $(x_0, x_1 +1)$ and the correction of the argument (x_2, x_3, x_4) to

TABLE 7-5

TABULATION OF BIQUADRATIC LAGRANGIAN INTERPOLATION COEFFICIENTS ON THE

PORTABLE FUNCTION TABLE

Arg.	A OUTPUT Master PM switch 1 set at P. Decade places 1-6 used as shown below.	B OUTPUT Master PM switch 2 set at Table. PM place and decade places 1-6 used as shown below.
-2	$C^{(-2)}(00) = .000\ 000$	$C^{(2)}(00) = +\ .000\ 000$
-1		
.		
.	$0 \leq C^{(-2)} \leq .023\ 427$	$-\ .039\ 464 \leq C^{(2)} \leq 0$
.		
49	$C^{(-2)}(51) = .023\ 427$	$C^{(2)}(51) = -\ .039\ 464$
50	$C^{(1)}(00) = .000\ 000$	$C^{(-1)}(00) = +\ .000\ 000$
51		
.		
.	$0 \leq C^{(1)} \leq .480\ 016$	$-\ .155\ 767 \leq C^{(-1)} \leq 0$
.		
101	$C^{(1)}(51) = .480\ 016$	$C^{(-1)}(51) = -\ .155\ 767$

$(x_2', x_3'; x_4')$. The criterion for which routine is to be followed is a magnitude discrimination program to determine whether $x_2 < 5$ or $x_2 \geq 5$. In the former case, the forward interpolation routing is followed; in the latter case, the backward interpolation routine is used.

The disadvantage of the method suggested above for biquadratic Langrangian interpolation is that it requires a backward as well as a forward routine. This disadvantage is eliminated in an alternative method to be described below.

For the purpose of this discussion, we will abandon the notation used above and in section 7.5.2. Instead, x will be considered as $x = n + h$ where n is the integer closest to x and where $-.5 \leq h \leq .5$. The number n, thus, is an integer between 0 and 99 inclusive. In this notation f(x) is given by

$$\sum_{i=-2}^{2} c^{(i)}(h) \cdot f_i(n) \qquad \text{or} \qquad \sum_{i=-2}^{2} c^{(i)}(h) \cdot f(n+i)$$

To find n, the round off facilities of some accumulator are used and the number x + 0.5 is formed. Then n is the tens and units digits of x + 0.5. Now, the number x + 0.5 or n + k where k = h + 0.5 is stored in some accumulator.

Instead of tabulating coefficients $c^{(i)}(h)$ then, consider tabulating $B^{(i)}(k) = c^{(i)}(h)$ for the range $0 \leq k \leq 1$, where the coefficients $B^{(i)}(k) = c^{(i)}(k)$ have the following useful properties:

1) $\sum_{i=-2}^{2} B^{(i)}(k) = 1$ and 2) $B^{(-i)}(k) = B^{(i)}(1-k)$

We can then tabulate $B^{(i)}(k)$ for $0 \leq k \leq 1$ for two values of i. By property 2 above, $B^{(i)}(k)$ for two other values of i can be found, and the fifth value of B can be found by property 1.

7.5.3. The Drag Function of the Exterior Ballistics Equations

When the ENIAC is used for the computation of firing tables, the problem of tabulating the drag function (G) used in the exterior ballistics equations is likely to require considerable thought due to the behavior of this function in the region of the velocity of sound. It would appear that the drag function had best be tabulated against v^2 as is done for hand computation of trajectories to avoid the necessity for extracting square roots. It will also be necessary to use more than one portable function (or more than part of one portable function table) to list the values of the drag function since one portable function table will certainly have to be devoted to the values of G in the neighborhood of the velocity of sound. G before and after sound may be tabulated on one or two portable function tables depending on which G function is used and the accuracy requirements of the computation.

To determine what transformation to make on v^2, which function table to enter, and possibly, even which interpolation routine to follow, it will then be necessary to carry out a magnitude discrimination program on v^2 similar to the one used on y' in the printing discrimination sequence of problem 2 in Chapter X (Master Programmer).

An alternative and, probably, simpler method of determining which function table to enter for a given value of the argument can be used if this information is stored on portable function table switches not required for the tabulation of G. One column of a portable function table is required for each function table or portion of a function table used in tabulating G.

Here a preliminary transformation of variable which maps the entire range of the argument onto the interval 0 and 99 is made. The portable function table which stores program data is entered with this argument. The function out-

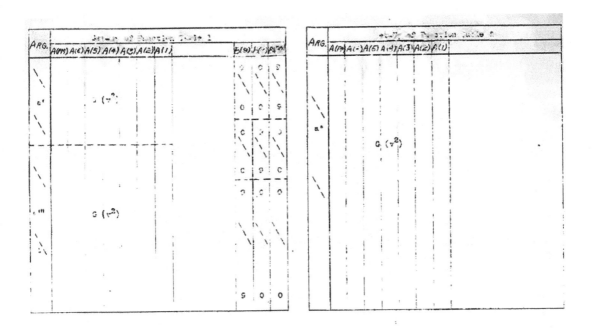

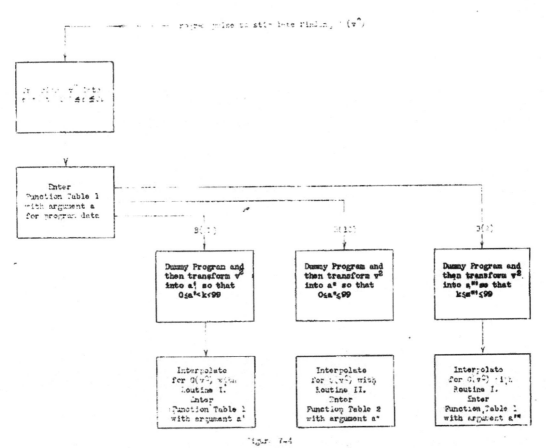

Figure 7-4

Storage of the G Function and Programming Instructions Regarding Use of the Tabulated Function

put of the decade place leads used for program choice are converted to a program pulse through the use of a dummy program. The resulting program pulse is then taken to a program control which initiates a suitable interpolation routine. (See Figure 7-4).

Another consideration which is likely to arise is that of making the most efficient use of the variable digits of the function table. Throughout the major part of the velocity of sound region, tenths place of the G function is occupied by the digit zero. However, for convenience in interpolation, it may be desirable to extend the tabulation on the portable function table devoted to the neighborhood of the velocity of sound so that some entries in which tenths place is occupied by the digit one instead of zero are also included.

If the obvious method of tabulation (PM column devoted to sign indication and variable digit columns to tenths, hundreds, etc., places) is followed, most of the entries will waste a place on the non-significant figure zero in tenths place in order to accommodate the few entries that have digit one in tenths place. However, since the G function does not change sign and since there is no reason for transmitting both the functional value stored and its complement, it is possible to resort to an artifice that will result in the storage of an additional significant figure without the use of an extra place of the portable function table.

The artifice consists of tabulating tenths place of the G function in one of the so called PM columns making sign P correspond to digit zero and sign M to digit one. The problem of converting the 9 sign pulses transmitted from the function table entries carrying sign M to a single digit pulse can be solved very simply by transmitting the PM channel of the function output to an unused transceiver input and then transmitting the transceiver's output to the digit input terminal channel devoted to tenths place at the unit receiving the functional value. Thus, when sign P is stored, no pulses will be transmitted from the PM channel of the function output terminal and therefore the transceiver, receiving no pulse, will transmit no output pulse so that the unit receiving the functional value will receive zero pulses in the decade channel devoted to tenths place. When sign M is stored, 9 sign pulses received by the transceiver cause the transceiver to emit one pulse which is received in tenths place by the unit receiving the function output of the function table. Obviously, if this strategem is resorted to, the program of receiving the functional value from the function table must be set up on an accumulator repeat program control whose repeat switch is set at 2 in order to allow time for the accumulator's reception of a pulse from the transceiver which converts the 9 sign pulses into a digit pulse.

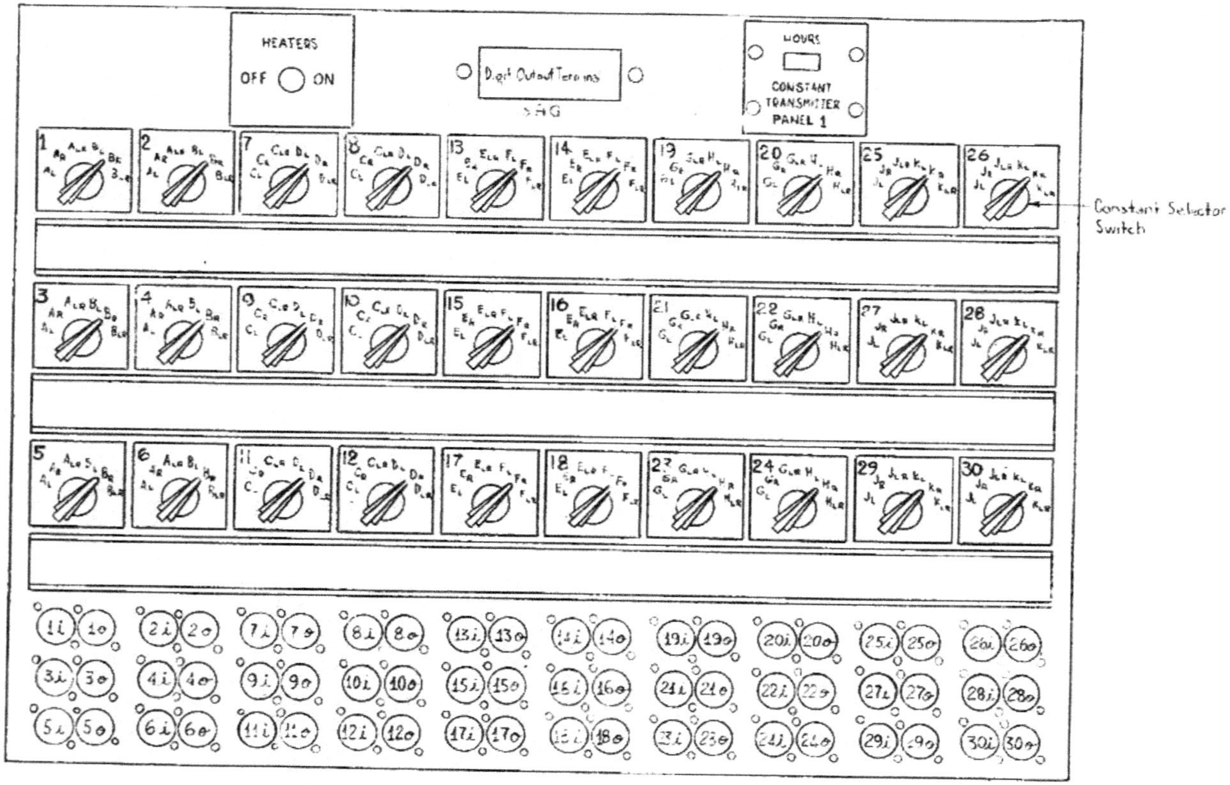

HEATERS OFF ON

Digit Output Terminals S-HG

CONSTANT TRANSMITTER PANEL 1

LIGHTS

Constant Selector Switch

TERMINALS 11, 21, ----301
Program input pulse terminals associated respectively with constant selector switches 1-30.

TERMINALS 10, 20, ----300
Program output pulse terminals associated respectively with constant selector switches 1-30.

CONSTANT TRANSMITTER
FRONT PANEL NO.1
PX-11-302 R

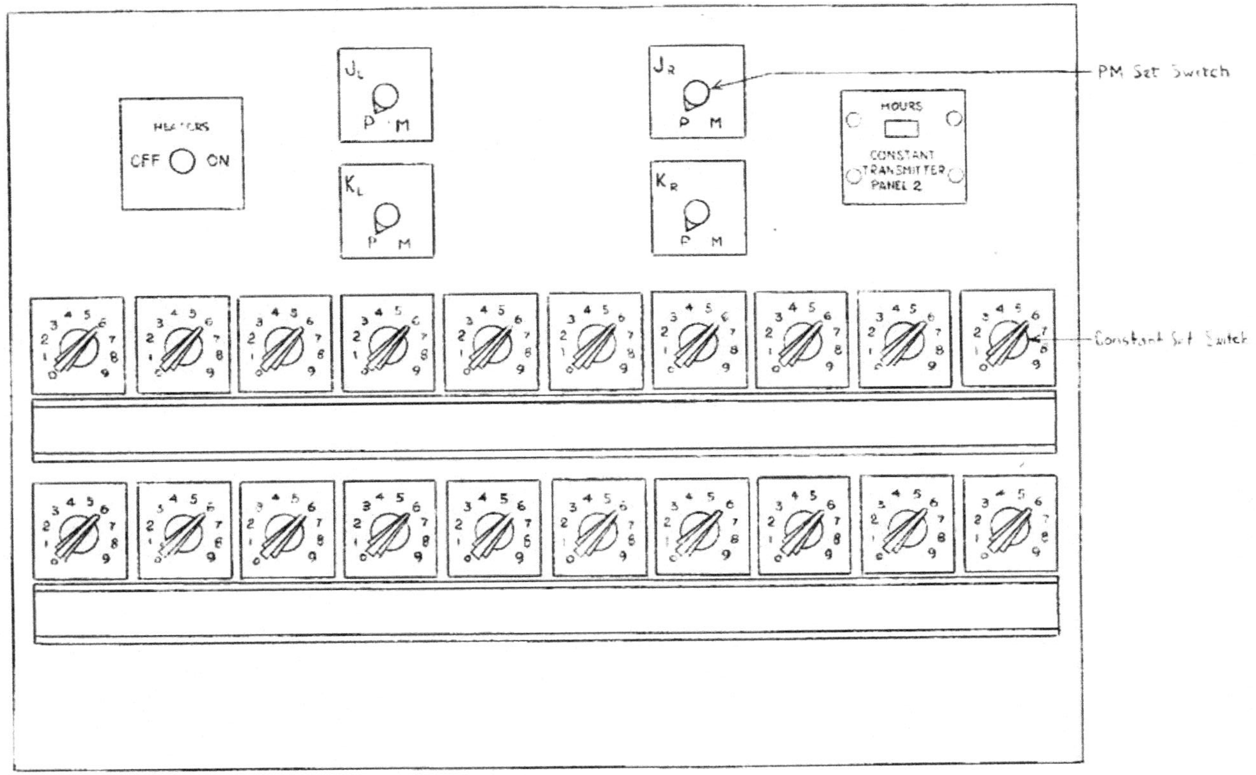

HEATERS

OFF ◯ ◯ ON

J_L
P M

K_L
P M

J_R
P M

K_R
P M

HOURS

CONSTANT
TRANSMITTER
PANEL 2

Constant Set Switch

PM Set Switch

CONSTANT TRANSMITTER NO. 2
FRONT PANEL NO. 2
PX-11-303 R

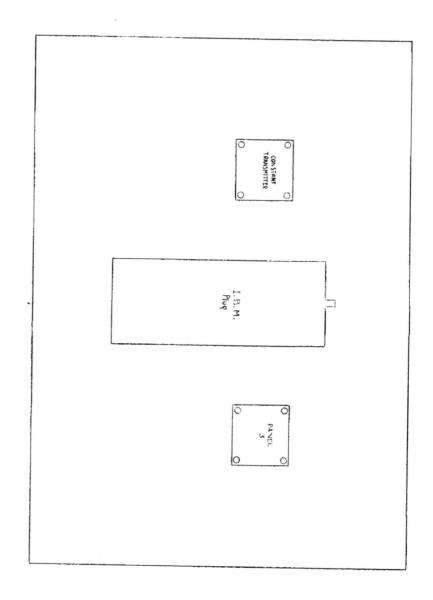

CONSTANT TRANSMITTER
FRONT PANEL NO. 3
PX-12-304 R.

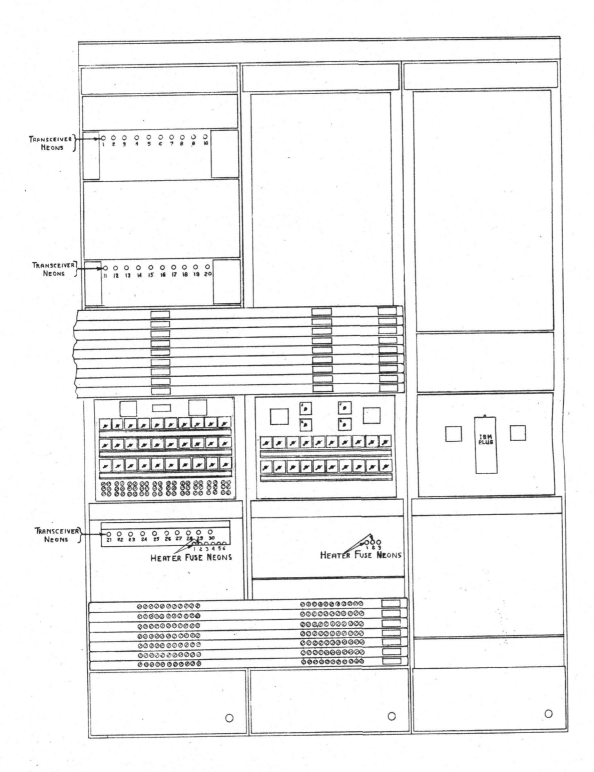

TRANSCEIVER NEONS → 1 2 3 4 5 6 7 8 9 10

TRANSCEIVER NEONS → 11 12 13 14 15 16 17 18 19 20

IBM PLUG

TRANSCEIVER NEONS → 21 22 23 24 25 26 27 28 29 30
1 2 3 4 5 6
HEATER FUSE NEONS

1 2 3
HEATER FUSE NEONS

MOORE SCHOOL of ELECTRICAL ENGINEERING
UNIVERSITY of PENNSYLVANIA

CONSTANT
TRANSMITTER
FRONT VIEW
PX-11-306

VIII. CONSTANT TRANSMITTER AND IBM READER

The constant transmitter operating in conjunction with an IBM card reader provides another form of memory for the ENIAC (see also, the function table and accumulator). The input rate for this memory is relatively slow; the output rate is rapid. The reader reads standard IBM cards at the rate of approximately 1/2 a second per card* and causes the data recorded on the card to be stored in relays located in the constant transmitter. The 80 digits which can be read from a card may be broken up into 5 digit or 10 digit groups with sign indication so that as many as 16 signed numbers may be read from a card. In addition, the constant transmitter can remember 20 digits and 4 signs set up manually on switches located on front panel 2 of this unit. These 20 digits may be broken up also into groups of either 5 or 10 digits with sign indication. Once stored in the relays or on the manual set switches of the constant transmitter, numerical data can be obtained in pulse form for use in any arithmetic unit of the ENIAC in one addition time.

The first four sections of this chapter are devoted to the IBM reader as follows: Section 8.1, program controls, Section 8.2, plug board, Section 8.3, programming circuits, and Section 8.4, numerical circuits. The program controls and numerical circuits of the constant transmitter are discussed in Sections 8.5, and 8.6, respectively. An illustrative problem set-up appears in Section 8.7.

In this chapter, reference will be made to the following drawings:

Constant Transmitter and Reader Cross Section	PX-11-309
IBM Reader Wiring	PX-11-119
IBM Reader Plug Board	PX-11-305

*The rate is 160 cards per minute when the reader reads continuously without stopping and may be either 120 or 160 cards per minute when the reader stops between readings.

Activation of IBM Reader Relays in
Reading a Detail-Master-Detail
Card Sequence   PX-11-308

Constant Transmitter Front View   PX-11-306

Constant Transmitter Front Panels   PX-11-302, 303, 304

Constant Transmitter Block Diagram   PX-11-307

Constant Transmitter Cross Section   PX-11-116

Initiating Unit - Front View   PX-9-305

Initiating Unit Front Panel   PX-9-302

8.0. GENERAL SUMMARY OF THE READER AND CONSTANT TRANSMITTER

8.0.1. IBM Cards

The IBM reader operates on standard IBM cards. These cards have 80
columns and each column has 12 positions. The first two positions (reading down
from the top) are designated by 12 and 11. The remaining ten positions correspond
to the numbers 0 to 9 and are printed to indicate this correspondence. Data is
stored on these cards by means of card punches. The group of columns used to
indicate the digits for a given number is called a field.

Any of the 80 columns on the card may be used to store either numerical
data or control data (i.e. information which instructs the reader how to dispose
of the numerical data stored on the card or on succeeding cards). A column used
for storing numerical data will have one of the positions zero to 9 punched.
Negative numbers are indicated by an 11 punch which can appear in addition to a
digit punch, in any one of the columns used for the various places of the number.
No sign indication punch is used for positive numbers. Columns used for control
purposes can have multiple punches. In addition, a column used for numerical
data can carry a 12 or 11 punch for control purposes provided that an 11 punch

does not appear in the same column for sign indication. The distinction between an 11 punch for control purposes and one for sign indication is made as a result of the wiring of the reader plug board (see Section 8.2.).

8.0.2. The Card Reader (refer to Px-11-309 and PX-9-302)

The IBM card reader scans cards and causes numerical data (with sign indication) located in any field of the card to be stored in any groups of constant transmitter storage relays specified by the operator (see Section 8.2. and group selection in Section 8.3.). The aforementioned operations are designated by the phrase card reading. True negative numbers on the cards are converted into nines complements in the process of being stored in the constant transmitter and into tens complements during transmission from the constant transmitter. Moreover, the IBM reader can recognize 2 classes of cards namely, master and detail cards. The reader causes numerical data read from a master card to be stored in constant transmitter storage relays and held until the next master card is read at which time the information read from the previous master card is dropped out and replaced by data on the new master card. Detail card information is dropped out whenever a new card, either master or detail, is read.

Certain controls for starting and stopping the reader are found on the initiating unit and others on the reader itself. The reader is stimulated to read a card which is in position to be read when the reader start button on the initiating unit is pressed at the beginning of a computation (see Chapter II, Section 2) or at the beginning or in the course of a computation when the reader program pulse input terminal (Ri) on the initiating unit is pulsed. Pushing the emergency start switch on the IBM reader itself also causes card reading to take place. When the reader is started initially and there are cards in its magazine but not in position to be read (see Section 8.1.), the initial start switch on the reader must be pushed to move a card into the reading position.[*] The reader stops reading when the cards in its magazine have been exhausted, or its hopper is filled, when the stop switch on the reader is pressed, or when the reader's motor generator is turned off (see Section 8.1.).

Also found on the initiating unit are a reader interlock pulse input terminal (Ri) and a reader program pulse output terminal (Ro). Since reading takes a not absolutely definite time for completion, the ENIAC has been so designed that an interlock pulse must be received and card reading must be completed before the reader will emit a program output pulse which can be used to initiate the phase of the computation which follows card reading. One exception to this statement is noted in Section 8.1.1.

8.0.3. Card Reading (refer to PX-11-309 and PX-11-119)

The operator specifies the criterion for master or detail cards and also the correspondence between positions on the card and storage relays in the constant transmitter by means of the setting of the polarity switch located on the reader and by the manner in which the reader plug board is wired (see Section 8.2.). The reader recognizes its instructions with regard to these matters through the punches made on the various cards.

The programming equipment (see Section 8.3.) in the reader which carries out the instructions consists of relays and cams which make and break contact at various times. The programming relays, in general, are used as follows: Each relay has either a pick-up (P) coil, a hold (H) coil or both[**] and 4 contacts some or all of which may be used. The hold coil of a relay is connected in series through one of its contacts, called the hold contact, to a timing cam.

---

[*] When cards are in position to be read, the initial start switch cannot stimulate card reading.

[**] Where one type of coil is missing, the functions of both types are performed by the one used.

Some stimulus, a particular punch on a card or the activation of another relay, perhaps, causes the P coil of a relay to pick up. The H coil then holds the relay through its hold contact until the cam with which the relay is in series breaks contact.

PX-11-119 shows the various relays and cams. The several components of a relay are often found on different parts of the diagram. The relay location chart at the top of PX-11-119 gives the location on the diagram of the P and H coils and the points of contact (A and B lower and upper). The timing cams are designated on this drawing by P1 - P10. The times at which the cams make and break contact are also noted here with M and B respectively identifying the make and break times. The times are given according to the IBM scale which divides the card reading cycle into 14 subdivisions designated by 14, 12, 11, 0, 1, ..., 8, 9, 13. The cycle begins half a unit before 14 and ends half a unit after 13. For the reader, the time divisions are approximately equal. More complete timing information about the cams is given on PX-11-309.

The cards are read by being passed under each of two continuous rolls. Eighty brushes located below the card make contact with the continuous roll where the card has been punched. The reader by means of the 80 brushes scans all 80 columns of a card simultaneously beginning at time 12 with line 12 in all columns and then the 11 line in time 11 and, finally, in time 9, the 9 line.

There are two continuous rolls each with a set of 80 brushes, roll No. 1 with the control brushes and roll No. 2 with the read brushes. Each card is read in two cycles. At the start of the ith card reading cycle, card i is in front of continuous roll No. 2 making contact with card lever contact No. 1 for continuous roll 2 (CR No. 2, CLC No. 1) and card i + 1 is in front of continuous roll No. 1 making contact with card lever contact No. 1 for continuous roll No. 1

(CR No. 1, CLC No. 1). During the ith reading cycle, card i is moved under roll No. 2 and scanned by the read brushes for numerical data. This data is ultimately delivered through the connections made on the plugboard to the lines which go to relays in the constant transmitter. While card i is passing under continuous roll No. 2, card i + 1 is passing under continuous roll No. 1 where it is read by the control brushes. The control brushes pick up instructions with regard to how card i + 1 is to be treated and deliver these instructions via plugboard connections to the programming circuits of the reader (see Section 8.3.) As card i + 1 moves under continuous roll No. 1, card i + 2 moves out of the magazine so that cards will be in position for the i + 1 st reading cycle. The second or numerical reading cycle for a card does not necessarily follow immediately after the first or control cycle. The second cycle takes place when the reader is stimulated to start reading. However, when a master card is read, the second cycle for the detail card immediately after the master card takes place without delay.

8.0.4. Storage of Card Data in the Constant Transmitter

The circuits involved in converting numerical data punches into a storage form usable by the Eniac itself are:

80 read brushes	(see PX-11-309, 11-119)	In the reader
Coding cams CB1, CB2, ..., CB9	(see PX-11-309, 11-119)	
16 groups of 8 coding relays each	(C_1, C_2, ..., C_8 on PX-11-116, 11-309)	
16 pairs of PM relays	(PM' and PM" on PX-11-116, 11-309)	In the Constant Transmitter
6 PM isolating relays	(labelled R on PX-11-116, 11-309)	
80 groups of 4 storage relays each	(the storage relays for the first group are labelled 1-1, 1-2, 1-2', and 1-4 on PX-11-116).	

Information from the 80 columns on the IBM card is ultimately stored in the 80 groups of storage relays. The 80 groups of storage relays control 80 groups of four constant selector gates each (see PX-11-307) and these gates in turn, control the gates which allow the 1, 2, 2', and 4 pulses respectively to pass when a constant is being transmitted from the constant transmitter.

Each 5 digit group with sign indication is set up in the storage relays and PM' and PM" relays as a result of the interaction of the coding cams, a contact on one of the 6 PM isolating relays, the pair of PM relays, a group of 8 coding relays, and the 5 leads from the read brushes which read the columns belonging to that group of 5 digits.

8.0.5. <u>Transmission of Data from the Constant Transmitter</u> (refer to PX-11-302, 11-303, 11-309, and 11-307)

On panel 1 (see PX-11-302) of the constant transmitter are found 30 program controls and associated neons (see PX-11-306). Each program control consists of a transceiver with program pulse input and output terminals and an associated constant selector switch. Each group of 6 program controls is concerned with the transmission of 20 digits. The program controls numbered 1-24 handle the 80 digits read from IBM cards and those numbered 25-30 the 20 digits set up manually on the constant set switches located on panel 2 (see PX-11-303). The letters A, B, ..., G, H on the constant selector switches refer to the 8 groups of 10 digits each which can be stored in the constant transmitter from IBM cards; J and K refer to the 20 digits set up manually on the set switches located on panel 2. Subscripts L and R refer respectively to the left and right hand groups of 5 digits (each with sign indication) of a 10 digit group. Ten digits with a single PM are designated by subscript LR. (See Section 8.2, for the correspondence between storage relay hubs on the plug board and the points A_L, A_R, ..., H_R on the constant selector switches.) The digit output of the constant transmitter is emitted through the output terminal on panel 1 (see PX-11-302).

Any or all of the 6 constant selector switches of a group may be set so as to call for the transmission of any one 5 digit or 10 digit signed number controlled by that group of switches. The only restriction is that if a constant selector switch be set so as to call for the transmission of either the L or R 5 digits of a 10 digit group, none of the other 5 switches may be set so as to call for the transmission of the same 10 digits as a group (LR). Conversely, if 10 digits are combined by an LR setting of a constant selector switch, the same 10 digits can never be broken up into 5 digit L or R groups on any of the remaining 5 constant selector switches.

The points on the constant selector switches are connected to the constant selector gates. For these gates the 2nd input comes from a storage relay or a constant set switch and may, in either case, be a digit or a PM.

The constant selector gates whose second inputs are numerical in nature, control the 1, 2, 2', and 4 pulse gates which allow suitable combinations of the 1, 2, 2', and 4 pulses to be passed over the 10 digit leads of the constant transmitter's digit output terminal (located on panel 1). The constant selector gates whose second inputs are derived from minus sign indication, control gates which allow the 9 pulses to pass over the PM lead and possibly the 5 left hand leads of the digit output terminal and which allow the 1' pulse (needed to produce a tens instead of nines complement) to pass over either the units place or 10^5 place lead of the digit output terminal.

8.1. PROGRAM CONTROLS OF THE IBM READER (Refer particularly to PX-11-119)

The reader program controls located on the reader are the initial start switch, the emergency start switch, the on-off switch and the green motor generator signal light, and a stop switch. Relay 3 in the reader is the start relay for the clutch magnets which cause the card feed mechanism to operate. Also inside the reader are certain circuit elements which function in conjunction with the program controls for starting the reader: magazine card lever contact (Mag CLC) and relay 1, card lever contact No. 1 for continuous roll No. 1 (CR No. 1, CLC No. 1) and relay 2, card lever contact No. 2 for continuous roll No. 1 (CR No. 1 CLC No. 2), and the card stacker switch. Card lever contact No. 1 for continuous roll No. 2 (CR No. 2, CLC No. 1) with relay 60, and relay 59 in the reader play a part in the emission of reset and finish signals by the reader and are discussed in greater detail in Section 8.3.3.

Located at the initiating unit (see PX-11-307) are other program controls for the reader: the reader start button, the reader program pulse input terminal (Ri) and start flip-flop, the reader interlock pulse input terminal (Rl) and flip-flop, the reader finish flip-flop, the reader synchronizing flip-flop, program output pulse transmitter, and program pulse output terminal (Ro).

The only program control for the reader that is housed in the constant transmitter is the reader start relay.

The green motor generator signal light goes on when the reader is plugged into a source of power provided that the on-off switch is on. The reader can be plugged into any of the a-c outlet terminals found at the base of each unit of the ENIAC. Power is supplied to the outlets below panel 2 of the printer and panel 3 of the constant transmitter only when the ENIAC's heaters are on; all

Table 8-1 — READER PROGRAM CONTROLS

Program Control	Location	Use
1) On-off switch	Reader	Turns reader's motor generator on or off. Green signal light is on when generator is running.
2) Initial Start Switch	Reader	Used to move first card of a deck into position for reading and to move last two cards through the reader.
3) R1 and start flip-flop and start relay.	Initiating Unit Constant Transmitter	When R1 is pulsed, start F.F. is set, start relay is activated, and card reading takes place subject to items 6, 7, and 8. Program output pulse is transmitted at the end of reading subject to items 9, 10, and 11.
4) Emergency Start Switch	Reader	Parallels the circuit of item 3. The reader continues to read subject to items 6, 7, 8 as long as this switch is closed. Does not usually cause the emission of a program output pulse when reading is completed since in the usual applications no interlock pulse is provided when this switch is used. It is chiefly used for testing the reader and constant transmitter.
5) Reader Start Button	Initiating Unit	Can be used to initiate the first card reading of a computation provided that the set-up does not call for a sequence in parallel with the first card reading. The initial start switch should be pushed immediately before or after the reader start button if all cards are in the magazine and there is not a card in position for reading.
6) Card Stacker Switch	Reader	Prevents operation of items 2-5 when card stacker is filled.
7) Mag. CLC and relay 1	Reader	Prevent card reading by items 3-5 when magazine is empty.
8) CLC No. 1 for CR No. 1 and relay 2	Reader	Prevent card reading by items 3-5 when there is no card before continuous roll 1.
9) CLC No. 1 for CR No. 2 and relay 60	Reader	Prevent reader from emitting a reset signal for the start F. F. and a finish signal if there is no card before continuous roll 2.
10) Relay 59	Reader	Prevents reader from emitting a reset or finish signal until the detail card following a master card passes under the read brushes associated with roll 2.
11) R1 and interlock flip-flop	Initiating unit	Note the reception of an interlock input pulse.
12) Finish flip-flop – Synchronizing flip-flop and R0.	Initiating unit	Provide for the transmission of a program output pulse when reading, initiated by item 3, is completed provided that an interlock pulse is received. For reading initiated by item 5, program output pulse is transmitted 2 addition times after reading is completed.

other outlets are alive even when the heaters are off. Switching the on-off switch to the off position turns the reader's power off completely; the reader can be prevented from reading temporarily by holding down the stop key.

The foregoing reader controls and others still to be discussed are summarized in table 8-1.

8.1.1. Program Input and Output Circuits

The usual method for stimulating the reader to read a card in the course of a computation is to deliver a program pulse to Ri. A pulse received at Ri sets the reader flip-flop and, thus, causes the start relay to be activated. Now, with contacts 1A and 2A closed and with the card stacker switch closed, the circuit to relay 3 is closed through a contact on the start relay (shown on PX-11-307). When relay 3 is energized, the clutch magnets which cause the card feed mechanism to operate are activated. Notice that relay 3 can be activated as the result of the setting of the start flip-flop only if there is at least one card in the magazine (so that relay 1 is activated through Mag CLC), there is a card waiting to be read by the control brushes (so that relay 2 is activated through CLC No. 1 of CR No. 1) and, the card stacker is not filled to capacity (so that the card stacker switch is closed).

During the period 12.0 - 12.5 which is about 1/7th the way through a reading cycle, the reader emits (via line 129) a reset signal for the start flip-flop in the initiating unit provided that a detail, and not a master card, is passing under the read brushes and provided that there is a card in contact with CLC No. 1 of CR No. 2 (see Section 8.3.3.). After the start flip-flop is reset, if another pulse is received at Ri, this flip-flop is capable of remembering that another reading cycle is to take place after the completion of the one in which the reader is engaged. The operator is cautioned that a pulse delivered to Ri

VIII - 11

before the start flip-flop has been reset is lost.

During the period 9.5 - 13.0, at the end of a card reading cycle, a finish signal is emitted by the reader (via line 127) provided that the card whose numerical reading is being completed is not a master card and provided that there is a card in front of continuous roll No. 2 waiting to be read (see Section 8.3.3.). The finish signal sets the reader finish flip-flop. When an interlock pulse is received and the interlock flip-flop, therefore, is set, gate 69 acting on the coincidence of signals from the finish and interlock flip-flops, emits a signal which allows a CPP to pass through gate 62. The output of gate 62 sets the reader synchronizing flip-flop. A CPP gated through gate 68 by the normally negative output of the synchronizing flip-flop resets the finish, interlock, and synchronizing flip-flops and passes through the reader program output transmitter to be emitted through Ro as a program output pulse.

Pushing the reader start button initiates the same actions as pulse input to Ri, but also sets the interlock flip-flop. Hence no interlock pulse need be provided to obtain a program output pulse for a reading initiated by this control.

The reader start button is intended for use at the start of a computation whose first program consists of card reading with no program sequence in parallel. Provision has been made for the setting of the interlock flip-flop by the reader start button since, with no parallel sequence for the first card reading, it would otherwise be impossible to provide the interlock pulse without which the reader does not emit a program output pulse (also see Section 8.1.3, for the procedure for reading the first card of a deck).

8.1.2. Emergency Start Switch

The emergency start switch parallels the operation of the circuit consisting of Ri, the start flip-flop, and the start relay. As long as this switch is closed, relay 3 is activated under the same restrictions as were noted above in the discussion for the circuit which this switch parallels. Just as in that case, card reading takes place and a reset and a finish signal are emitted. The reset signal has no effect since the start flip-flop is not flipped into the abnormal state. The finish signal does, however, set the finish flip-flop. If an interlock pulse is not delivered to R1 for a reading initiated by the emergency start switch, no program output pulse is emitted by Ro even though the finish flip-flop is set. Since no output pulse is transmitted, the finish flip-flop is not reset. Therefore, reading initiated by the emergency start switch does not leave the reader program controls in their normal state.

In a reading initiated by the controls discussed in Section 8.1.1, the reader stops after one detail card or after the detail card following one or more master cards. When the emergency start switch is used, the reader continues to read as long as this switch is held closed.

The emergency start switch provides a convenient means of testing the reader and constant transmitter. It has the advantage that no program tray connections are needed. If, moreover, there is a problem set up for computation on the ENIAC when the reader is tested, the use of the emergency start switch has the advantage that no program output pulse to stimulate other programs is emitted when reading is completed (unless an interlock pulse is received).

8.1.3. <u>Initial Start Switch</u> - Procedure for reading the first card of a deck.

Above it was pointed out that not only must the magazine have cards in it and the card stacker not be filled to capacity, but also, there must be a card in position before continuous roll No. 1 for card reading to be stimulated by pulse input to Ri, by the reader start button, or by the emergency start switch.

When the first reading is to be stimulated with cards in the magazine but no card in contact with CLC No. 1 of CR No. 1, the initial start switch is used. When the initial start switch is closed, relay 3 is activated through contact 2B which is closed because there is no card in contact with CR No. 1, CLC No. 1. The first card of the deck is thus pushed under continuous roll No. 1 and read by the control brushes. If the initial start switch alone is pushed, then the reader stops before this first card goes through a numerical cycle. If the start flip-flop is set(by the reception of pulse at Ri or by pushing the reader start button) after the initial start switch is pushed, relay 3 is then activated through contacts 1A and 2A so that the first card goes through a numerical reading cycle. Reset and finish signals are emitted in the course of this cycle provided that the first card is not a master card.

If desired, the start flip-flop may be set first and then the initial start switch can be closed. This switch then causes the first card to go through a control brush reading. Since there is no card in contact with CR No. 2, CLC No. 1, relay 60 is not activated and therefore, no reset or finish signals are emitted in this reading cycle. The start flip-flop thus remains activated, and, relay 3 is then activated through contacts 1A and 2A. A cycle in which the first card is read for numerical data follows immediately and, provided that card No. 1 is not a master card, reset and finish signals are emitted.

Notice that relay 3 can be activated as a result of pushing the initial start switch only through contact 2B or the upper B contact of relay 1. Thus, the initial start switch can be used only when all cards are in the magazine so that 2B is closed or, at the end, when the magazine is empty so that the upper B contact of relay 1 is closed.

If n cards are placed in the magazine at the beginning of a computation, the cycle in which card n-1 is read under continuous roll No. 1 and card n-2 under continuous roll No. 2 is the last cycle which can be initiated by pulse input to Ri, or by pushing either the reader start button or the emergency start switch. For, during this cycle, the nth card moves out of the magazine into position before continuous roll No. 1. With the magazine empty, Mag CLC does not make contact and relay 1, therefore, is not activated so that the reading of cards n-1 and n could be brought about only by holding down the initial start switch. The necessity for using this switch to cause the reading of the 2 final cards of interest to the computation can, obviously, be avoided by placing at least 2 dummy cards at the bottom of the deck (which becomes the top of the deck when the cards are placed in the magazine - see the note on PX-11-309).

If blank cards are used at the end of a deck and if they are not withdrawn by the use of the initial start switch before the magazine is refilled, the operator should anticipate difficulty if the set-up is one in which the reader's program output pulse stimulates the divider and square rooter to carry out a division program for which the denominator is derived from the card just read. For, when the magazine is refilled, the blank cards remaining from the last deck are the first cards read and the output pulse emitted when one of these has been read causes the divider to embark on an infinite process, division by zero. This difficulty can be circumvented by causing the reader's program output pulse to be suppressed for the dummy cards. If the plug board is wired so that the reader can recognize master cards and if the dummy cards are punched with master card instructions (see Section 8.2.), no program output pulse will be emitted as long as the dummy cards are read since the reader does not emit either a reset or a finish signal for a cycle in which a master card passes under continuous roll No. 2 (see Section 8.3.3.).

8.2. POLARITY SWITCH AND PLUG BOARD

The IBM plug board is a characteristic device belonging to IBM units. It is a detachable board containing a large number of single hole terminals called hubs. When the board is in place for operation, these hubs are connected to some line in the permanent wiring of the machine. Numerous small insulated lengths of wire are provided by which these hubs may be connected in pairs (occasionally in larger groups), thereby connecting in each case two or more lines in the permanent wiring. This process is called wiring the plug board. It may be done in an enormous variety of ways, thus achieving corresponding flexibility in programming. The possibility of detaching the board as a whole from the machine not only facilitates the process of wiring, but, by the use of spare boards, enables one to keep on hand a number of boards with programs wired up.

The wiring of the plug board establishes, among other things, the correspondence between columns carrying certain data on the cards and the relays storing the same data in the constant transmitter. It provides also for storage relay groups which may be used for negative numbers in order to isolate minus indications from numerical data.

There is on the reader a polarity switch whose setting, in conjunction with the wiring, contributes to program control. Among the more important types of programming accomplished by the wiring of the reader plug board are those for reset control and group selection.

The IBM plug board for the reader is shown on PX-11-305. The various hubs are labelled on this diagram but certain additional words of explanation may be helpful.

The No. 1 read brush hubs appear in lines 1-4 of the plug board. These

TABLE 8-2

CORRESPONDENCE BETWEEN STORAGE RELAY HUBS AND POINTS ON CONSTANT SELECTOR SWITCHES

Storage Relay Group	Point on C.S.Switch	Storage Relay Group	Point on C.S.Switch	Storage Relay Group	Point on C.S.Switch	Storage Relay Group	Point on C.S.Switch
1	A_L	2	B_L	3	C_L	4	D_L
5	E_L	6	F_L	7	G_L	8	H_L
9	A_R	10	B_R	11	C_R	12	D_R
13	E_R	14	F_R	15	G_R	16	H_R

```
 ---- 5 ----        #1 Read Brushes    ---- 15 ----              20
o   o   o   o   o   o   o   o   o   o   o   o   o   o   o   o   o   o   o   o
                25                  30                  35                  40
o   o   o   o   o   o   o   o   o   o   o   o   o   o   o   o   o   o   o   o
                45                  50                  55                  60
o   o   o   o   o   o   o   o   o   o   o   o   o   o   o   o   o   o   o   o
                65                  70                  75                  80
o   o   o   o   o   o   o   o   o   o   o   o   o   o   o   o   o   o   o   o
PL to 1 RB -- Plug to digit sel ------ Group Selection ------
o   o   o | o   o   o   o   o   o   o   o   o   o   o   o   o   o   o   o   o
          C  NC  1   2   3   4   5   6   7   8   9  10  11  12  13  14  15  16
o   o   o   o   o   o   o   o   o   o   o   o   o   o   o   o   o   o   o   o
 ------ Reset shunt ------    12 - 11- 0 ----- Digit selector - 6 - 7 - 8 - 9
o   o   o   o   o   o   o   o   o   o   o   o   o   o   o   o   o   o   o   o
|   |   |   |   |   |   |   |
o   o   o   o   o   o   o   o   o   o   o   o   o   o   o   o   o   o   o   o
PL to reset shunt ------      ---- Reset control ------
1o  2o  3o  4o  5o  6o  7o  8o  9o 10o 11o 12o 13o 14o 15o 16o  o   o   o   o

o   o   o   o   o   o   o   o   o   o   o   o   o   o   o   o   o   o   o   o
 ---- 5 ----        #2 Read Brushes    ---- 15 ----              20
o   o   o   o   o   o   o   o   o   o   o   o   o   o   o   o   o   o   o   o
                25                  30                  35                  40
o   o   o   o   o   o   o   o   o   o   o   o   o   o   o   o   o   o   o   o
                45                  50                  55                  60
o   o   o   o   o   o   o   o   o   o   o   o   o   o   o   o   o   o   o   o
                65                  70                  75                  80
o   o   o   o   o   o   o   o   o   o   o   o   o   o   o   o   o   o   o   o
Plug to 2 RB ------           ---- Minus control ------
o   o   o   o   o   o   o   o   o   o   o   o   o   o   o   o   o   o   o   o
1   2   3   4   5   6   7   8   9  10  11  12  13  14  15  16
o   o   o   o   o   o   o   o   o   o   o   o   o   o   o   o   o   o   o   o

o   o   o   o   o   o   o   o   o   o   o   o   o   o   o   o   o   o   o   o
Plug to 2 RB ------           ---- Group selection ------              4 ----
o C o   o   o   o     o C o   o   o   o     o C o   o   o   o     o C o   o   o   o
Plug to ST relays
o A o   o   o   o     o A o   o   o   o     o A o   o   o   o     o A o   o   o   o
Plug to ST relays
o B o   o   o   o     o B o   o   o   o     o B o   o   o   o     o B o   o   o   o
Plug to 2 RB ------           6 ----              7 ----              8 ----
o C o   o   o   o     o C o   o   o   o     o C o   o   o   o     o C o   o   o   o
Plug to ST relays
o A o   o   o   o     o A o   o   o   o     o A o   o   o   o     o A o   o   o   o
Plug to ST relays
o B o   o   o   o     o B o   o   o   o     o B o   o   o   o     o B o   o   o   o
Plug to 2 RB ------           10 ----             11 ----             12 ----
o C o   o   o   o     o C o   o   o   o     o C o   o   o   o     o C o   o   o   o
Plug to ST relays
o A o   o   o   o     o A o   o   o   o     o A o   o   o   o     o A o   o   o   o
Plug to ST relays
o B o   o   o   o     o B o   o   o   o     o B o   o   o   o     o B o   o   o   o
Plug to 2 RB ------           14 ----             15 ----             16 ----
o C o   o   o   o     o C o   o   o   o     o C o   o   o   o     o C o   o   o   o
Plug to ST relays
o A o   o   o   o     o A o   o   o   o     o A o   o   o   o     o A o   o   o   o
Plug to ST relays
o B o   o   o   o     o B o   o   o   o     o B o   o   o   o     o B o   o   o   o

o   o   o   o   o     o   o   o   o   o     o   o   o   o   o     o   o   o   o   o
 ---- Group 1 ----       ---- Storage Relays ----        ---- Group 4 ----
o   o   o   o   o     o   o   o   o   o     o   o   o   o   o     o   o   o   o   o
 ---- Group 5 ----       ---- Group 6 ----     ---- Group 7 ----    ---- Group 8 ----
o   o   o   o   o     o   o   o   o   o     o   o   o   o   o     o   o   o   o   o
 ---- Group 9 ----       ---- Group 10 ----    ---- Group 11 ----   ---- Group 12 ----
o   o   o   o   o     o   o   o   o   o     o   o   o   o   o     o   o   o   o   o
 ---- Group 13 ----      ---- Group 14 ----    ---- Group 15 ----   ---- Group 16 ----
o   o   o   o   o     o   o   o   o   o     o   o   o   o   o     o   o   o   o   o
```

IBM READER
PLUG BOARD
PX-11-305R

hubs connect to the control brushes and their numbering corresponds to that of the columns on an IBM card.

The two hubs on lines 5 and 6 which are above and below the letter C, are common, i.e., internally connected. One or both of these hubs may be used for control purposes. The hubs to the left of the C hubs are unused.

The single hub marked RC on line 6, the 16 reset shunt hubs which appear at the left of lines 7 and 8, and the reset control hubs on line 9 are used for the reset control programming instructions discussed below. The numbering of the reset control hubs corresponds to the numbering of the 16 five digit groups of storage relays in the constant transmitter (see Table 8-2).

The group selection hubs on lines 5 and 6 which are common hubs and those on lines 18-29 are used for group selection instructions as explained later in this section. The group selection hubs on lines 18-29 are arranged in 16 five digit groups. For each digit there are three hubs, C, A, and B. When group selection (see below) takes place the C and B hubs are internally connected; otherwise C and A are connected. Each of the group selection hubs above a number on line 5 is common with the hub below the same number on line 6. Each pair of hubs on lines 5 and 6 corresponds to the A-B-C group of the same number on lines 18-29.

The minus control hubs appear on lines 15 and 16. Each hub above a number is common with the one below the same number. Minus punch information is routed through these hubs to the PM' and PM" relays of the correspondingly numbered groups in the constant transmitter.

The No. 2 read brush hubs are the outputs of the No. 2 read brushes. Numerical data read from any of the 80 columns of an IBM card is delivered to the correspondingly numbered hub of this group.

The storage relay hubs on lines 31-34 connect to contacts on the constant transmitter's coding relays and ultimately to the storage relays. The correspondence between the numbering of the 16 five digit groups here and the labelling of the points on the constant selector switches is shown in Table 8-2.

The two kinds of programming instruction which the reader recognizes are reset control and group selection. The reset control instruction refers to distinguishing between master and detail cards. As long as detail cards are read, the reader causes information stored in the storage relays as a result of the reading of the previous detail card to be dropped out before new detail information is stored, and also causes information stored in the storage relays as a result of the reading of the last master card to be retained (provided the plug board is so wired). Reset control operates when a master card is read. This means that the reader causes all information, both master and detail, to be dropped out of the storage relays and new master information from the master card to be placed in storage. Also, when reset control takes place, the card following the master card (usually a detail card) is read immediately after the master card. No reset or finish signal is emitted until the reading of a card is completed.

The group selection instruction, which may be given for either a master or detail card, makes it possible for data from one field to be placed normally in certain storage relays, and, when group selection operates, in a different group of storage relays.

A second form of group selection instruction is used when it is desired to store in one set of storage relays information which normally occurs in a given field of the card, but which is found in a different field of the card when group selection is to occur.

The first form of group selection is convenient when using a set of cards, perhaps master and detail, which are so punched that the same field used for master information on the master card, on the detail card is used for detail information. The second form of group selection would be useful for a set of cards consisting of two subsets in which there appeared data for the same quantity sometimes in one field and sometimes in another.

The polarity switch has two positions, normal and abnormal. With the polarity switch in the normal position, programming instructions for reset control and/or group selection are always specified in a given column of the card with different instructions being specified by different punches. With the polarity switch in the abnormal position, programming instructions are given by a specific punch with the different instructions being distinguished by the different columns in which the specific punch appears. The polarity switch makes possible this flexibility by interchanging the connections to the source of power so as to make the polarity consistent with plug board wiring. It is important to note that the setting of the polarity switch must not be altered when the reader's motor generator is on (green signal light is on).

With the polarity switch in the normal position, the column which is to contain punches for programming instructions is specified by plugging from one of the C hubs to the No. 1 read brush hub corresponding to that column. If desired, the control punch may appear in either column i or j. This latter instruction is specified by plugging one of the common C hubs to the i hub and the other C hub to the j hub of the No. 1 read brushes.

The particular punch appearing in the given column (or columns) which is to signal for reset control is specified by plugging from the RC hub to the digit selector hub corresponding to the particular punch. A punch read no later

IBM READER PLUG BOARD

Illustrative plugging arrangement for Reset Control Instructions
with the Polarity Switch in the Normal Position.

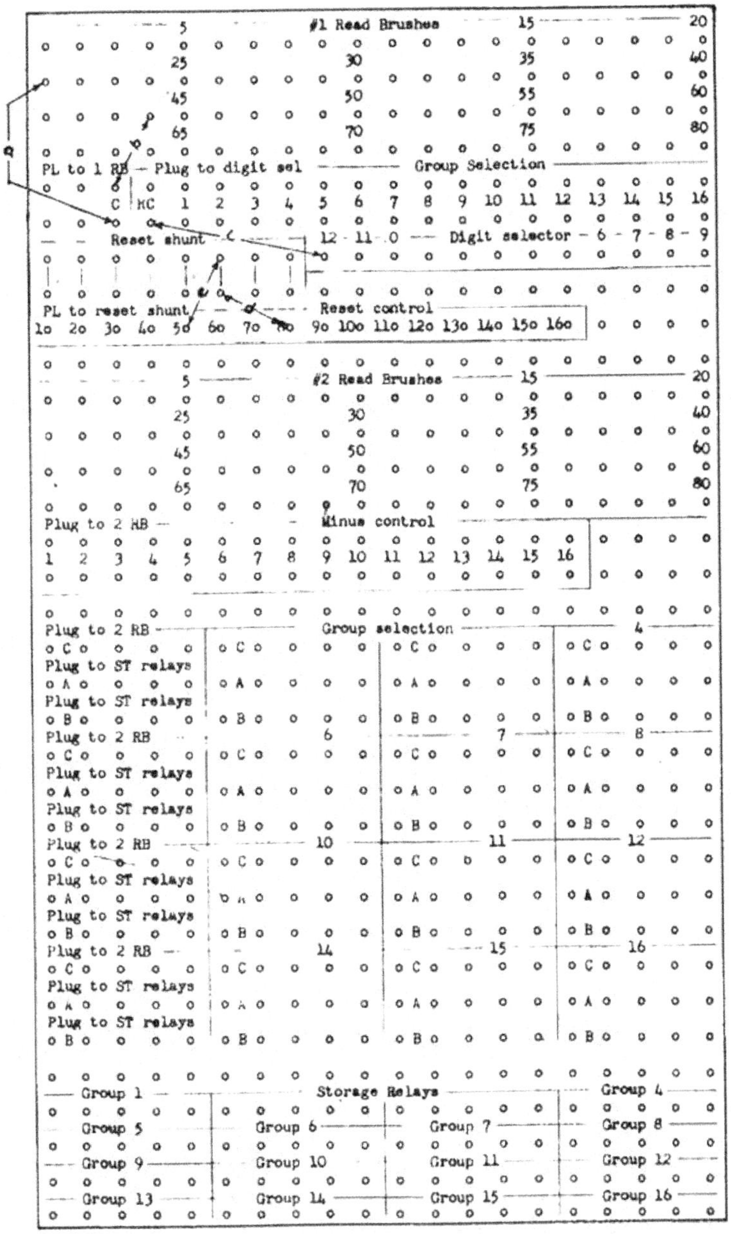

INSTRUCTIONS

(The line which carries the instruction appears in parenthesis)

When a 12 punch (c) appears in column 21 (a) or in column 44 (b), reset control is to operate (c).
The reset control consists of dropping out the master information stored in group 5 (e) and group
8 (d) storage relays.

in the card reading cycle than a 6 punch should be used to stimulate reset control in order to allow sufficient time for the reset control programming circuits to function properly (see Section 8.3.1.). Finally, the master information group[*] (or groups) is (or are) specified by plugging from the reset control hubs correlated with the group (or groups) to any of the reset shunt hubs. Drawing PX-11-305 R1 presents an illustrative plugging for reset control instructions when the polarity switch is in the normal position.

With the polarity switch in the normal position, the particular punch (in the column or columns specified by the plugging from C to the No. 1 read brushes) which gives a group selection instruction is specified by the plugging from the digit selector hubs to the group selection hubs immediately above. The card fields and storage relay groups involved in the group selection and the manner in which they are involved are designated by the plugging from the No. 2 read brushes to the group selection hubs on lines 18-29 (corresponding to the ones used on lines 5 and/or 6) and then from these hubs to the storage relay hubs. Group selection in which data from either of 2 fields on the card is placed in a single storage relay group is provided for by plugging the 5 hubs of the storage relay group to the C hub of the group selection hubs and by plugging the five No. 2 read brush hubs from which data is normally taken to the A hubs and the five No. 2 read brushehubs from which data is taken when group selection occurs to the B hubs of the group selection hubs on lines 18-29. Group selection in which data from one field on the card is ordinarily put in one group of storage relays but in another group when group selection takes place is specified by plugging the No. 2 brush hubs for the card field to the C hubs and the A hubs of the group selection relays to the usual storage relay hubs and the B hubs to the hubs of the storage relays used when group selection takes place.

---

[*]Master information group is used to mean the group of constant transmitter storage relays which stores information from a master card, releasing it only when a new master card is recognized.

IBM READER PLUG BOARD

Illustrative plugging arrangement for Group Selection Instructions
with the Polarity Switch in the Normal Position.

				5			#1 Read Brushes		15				20

PL to 1 RB — Plug to digit sel ——— Group Selection
C | RC 1 2 3 4 5 6 7 8 9 10 11 12 13 14 15 16
——— Reset shunt ——— 12 - 11 - 0 ← Digit selector - 6 - 7 - 8 - 9

PL to reset shunt ——— Reset control
1o 2o 3o 4o 5o 6o 7o 8o 9o 10o 11o 12o 13o 14o 15o 16o

#2 Read Brushes — 15
5   25   30   35
45   50   55
65   70   75
Plug to 2 RB — Minus control
1 2 3 4 5 6 7 8 9 10 11 12 13 14 15 16

Plug to 2 RB ——— Group selection ——— 4
o C o   o C o   o C o   o C o
Plug to ST relays
o A o   o A o   o A o   o A o
Plug to ST relays
o B o   o B o   o B o   o B o
Plug to 2 RB — 6 — 7 — 8
o C o   o C o   o C o   o C o
Plug to ST relays
o A o   o A o   o A o   o A o
Plug to ST relays
o B o   o B o   o B o   o B o
Plug to 2 RB — 10 — 11 — 12
o C o   o C o   o C o   o C o
Plug to ST relays
o A o   o A o   o A o   o A o
Plug to ST relays
o B o   o B o   o B o   o B o
Plug to 2 RB — 14 — 15 — 16
o C o   o C o   o C o   o C o
Plug to ST relays
o A o   o A o   o A o   o A o
Plug to ST relays
o B o   o B o   o B o   o B o

— Group 1 — Storage Relays — Group 4 —
— Group 5 — Group 6 — Group 7 — Group 8 —
— Group 9 — Group 10 — Group 11 — Group 12 —
— Group 13 — Group 14 — Group 15 — Group 16 —

INSTRUCTIONS

When a 0 punch (f) appears in either column 21 (a) or column 44 (b), the 5th digit of group 4 storage
relays (g) will come from column 20 of the card (j). Otherwise, the 5th digit of group 4 storage relays will come from column 40 of the card (h).

When a 6 punch (k) appears in either column 21 (a) or column 44 (b), the digit appearing in column 1
of the card (l), will be put in the storage relays for the first digit of group 13 (n); otherwise it
will be put in the storage relays for the first digit of group 1 (m).

Illustrative plugging arrangement for Reset Control and Group
Selection Instructions with the Polarity Switch in the abnormal
position.

#1 Read Brushes

```
              5                  #1 Read Brushes            15                    20
  o    o    o    o    o    o    o    o    o    o    o    o    o    o    o    o    o
              25                 30                         35                    40
  o    o    o    o    o    o    o    o    o    o    o    o    o    o    o    o    o
              45                 50                         55                    60
  o    o    o    o    o    o    o    o    o    o    o    o    o    o    o    o    o
              65                 70                         75                    80
  o    o    o    o    o    o    o    o    o    o    o    o    o    o    o    o    o
PL to 1 RB — Plug to digit sel —        Group Selection
  o    o    o    o    o    o    o    o    o    o    o    o    o    o    o    o    o
        C  NC   1    2    3    4    5    6    7    8    9   10   11   12   13   14   15   16
  o    o    o    o    o    o    o    o    o    o    o    o    o    o    o    o    o
        — Reset shunt —            12 - 11 - 0 — Digit selector - 6 - 7 - 8 - 9
  o    o    o    o    o    o    o    o    o    o    o    o    o    o    o    o    o
PL to reset shunt —            Reset control
 1o   2o   3o   4o   5o   6o   7o   8o   9o  10o  11o  12o  13o  14o  15o  16o   o    o
  o    o    o    o    o    o    o    o    o    o    o    o    o    o    o    o    o
              5                  #2 Read Brushes            15                    20
  o    o    o    o    o    o    o    o    o    o    o    o    o    o    o    o    o
              25                 30                         35                    40
  o    o    o    o    o    o    o    o    o    o    o    o    o    o    o    o    o
              45                 50                         55                    60
  o    o    o    o    o    o    o    o    o    o    o    o    o    o    o    o    o
              65                 70                         75                    80
  o    o    o    o    o    o    o    o    o    o    o    o    o    o    o    o    o
Plug to 2 RB —              Minus control
  1    2    3    4    5    6    7    8    9   10   11   12   13   14   15   16
  o    o    o    o    o    o    o    o    o    o    o    o    o    o    o    o    o
Plug to 2 RB —              Group selection
 o C o   o    o    o    o C o   o    o    o C o   o    o    o C o   o    o
Plug to ST relays
 o A o   o    o    o A o   o    o    o A o   o    o    o A o   o    o
Plug to ST relays
 o B o   o    o    o B o   o    o    o B o   o    o    o B o   o    o
Plug to 2 RB —        6                    7                  8
 o C o   o    o    o C o   o    o    o C o   o    o    o C o   o    o
Plug to ST relays
 o A o   o    o    o A o   o    o    o A o   o    o    o A o   o    o
Plug to ST relays
 o B o   o    o    o B o   o    o    o B o   o    o    o B o   o    o
Plug to 2 RB —        10                   11                 12
 o C o   o    o    o C o   o    o    o C o   o    o    o C o   o    o
Plug to ST relays
 o A o   o    o    o A o   o    o    o A o   o    o    o A o   o    o
Plug to ST relays
 o B o   o    o    o B o   o    o    o B o   o    o    o B o   o    o
Plug to 2 RB —        14                   15                 16
 o C o   o    o    o C o   o    o    o C o   o    o    o C o   o    o
Plug to ST relays
 o A o   o    o    o A o   o    o    o A o   o    o    o A o   o    o
Plug to ST relays
 o B o   o    o    o B o   o    o    o B o   o    o    o B o   o    o
— Group 1 —              Storage Relays              — Group 4 —
— Group 5 —     — Group 6 —      — Group 7 —       — Group 8 —
— Group 9 —     Group 10         Group 11          Group 12 —
— Group 13 —    Group 14         Group 15 —        Group 16 —
```

INSTRUCTIONS

When a 12 punch (a) appears in column 1 (c), reset control (c) takes place for the group 8 storage
relays (d).

When a 12 punch (a) appears in column 20 (k), then data from column 1 on the card (l) is put in the
first digit storage relays for group 13 (n). Otherwise data from column 1 is put in the storage relays for the first digit of group 1 (m).

PX-11-305 R2 illustrates plugging for both types of group selection if the polarity switch is in the normal position. It is to be noted, incidentally, that group selection for more than one group may be made to depend on the appearance of a given punch in the control column. For example, if group selection for groups 12 and 13 were desired on the presence of a 6 punch, this could be specified by making connection k as shown on PX-11-305 R2 and, in addition, cross connecting the other group selection hub 13 to either of the group selection hubs numbered 12.

With the polarity switch in the abnormal position, control is indicated by a specific punch and the different forms of control by the various columns in which the specific punch occurs. The particular punch is designated by plugging from one of the C hubs to the digit selector hub corresponding to that punch. The fact that reset control is to take place because this special punch occurs in a given column of the card is indicated by connecting the RC hub to the No.1 read brush corresponding to that column. A connection from a group selection hub to a read brush hub indicates that group selection is to take place when the particular punch appears in the column corresponding to the No. 1 read brush hub. PX-11-305 R3 shows a plug board arrangement for programming instructions when the polarity switch is in the abnormal position.

The No.2 read brush hubs associated with card fields used for positive numbers only may be plugged to the storage relay hubs directly or through the group selection hubs in any manner desired. Card fields which at some time carry negative numbers require special minus control wiring of the plug board so that minus sign indication can be delivered to the PM' and PM" relays in the constant transmitter and so that the digital information appearing in the same column can be delivered to the proper storage relays.

Minus control plugging consists of connecting the No.2 read brush hub associated with the column in which the minus punch appears to all the minus

ILLUSTRATIVE PLUG BOARD CONNECTIONS

For

CARD FIELDS STORING NEGATIVE NUMBERS

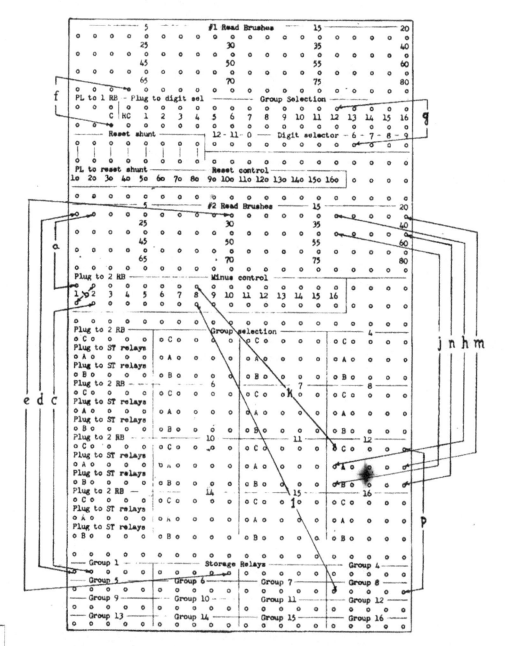

Lines (a), (b), (c), (d), (e) illustrate plugging for a 10 digit negative number which occupies group 1 and 2 storage relays. Since the minus punch is assumed to come from column 2 of the card, hub 2 of the #2 read brushes is connected to a minus control hub for group 1 (a). Because storage relay groups 1 and 2 are used for this number, the other minus control hub for group 1 is cross connected to a minus control hub for group 2 (b). The other minus control hub for group 2 is connected to the hub for the 2nd digit of group 1 storage relays. Lines (d) and (e) show the plugging for the first and last digits.

Lines (h), (j), (k), (l), (m), (n), (p) illustrate plugging for a 5 digit negative number, in which the minus punch appears in the same card column as the first digit and for which group selection occurs.

control hubs having the same numbers as the groups of storage relays in which the information from that card field is stored and then connecting from these minus control hubs to the storage relay hub corresponding to the storage position of the numerical data in the column containing the minus punch. The No.2 read brush hubs for the columns of the same field which do not carry a minus punch are plugged directly to the appropriate storage relays.

Where group selection intervenes between the No.2 read brushes and the storage relays, in the "C to No.2 read brushes - A and B to storage relay" type of group selection, minus control plugging is conveniently done from No. 2 read brush to minus control hub (or hubs) to C group selection hub and then from A or B hub to storage relay hub. In the "C to storage relay - A and B to No.2 read brush" type of group selection, minus control plugging may be carried out from C hub to minus control hub (or hubs) and then to storage relay hub. An illustrative plug board arrangement for minus control plugging is shown on PX-11-305 R4.

8.3. PROGRAMMING CIRCUITS OF THE READER (Refer to PX-11-119 and PX-11-309)

The programming circuits of the reader consist of the reset control, group selection, reset signal, and finish signal circuits. The discussion for the first 2 circuits will be made with the assumption that the polarity switch is in the normal position and that the plug board is wired accordingly.

8.3.1. Reset Control Circuits

Information remains stored in the 16 groups of storage relays in the constant transmitter by virtue of the signals delivered over lines 81-96 when the corresponding contacts on the storage holding relays 4-6 are closed. Relays 4-6 are activated during period 11.0 through 13.7 while cam P2 makes contact. When P2 breaks at 13.7, contacts on all the storage holding relays release so that at this time information is always dropped out of all storage relay groups for which a shunt connection has not been made from reset control hubs to reset shunt hubs on the plug board. The contacts on all the reset shunt relays 56-58 remain closed and thus cause the retention of information in the storage relay groups which they control by reason of plug board wiring. The contacts on relays 56-58 release to allow information in these storage relay groups to be dropped out only when relays 56-58 are activated.

When a master card is read relays 56-58 are activated through the interaction of the control brushes, the emitter, and reset control relay 23. The emitter has a moving arm which makes contact with the 12 digit selector hubs in synchronism with the reading of the corresponding punches on the card.

In reset control plugging, it is to be recalled, a connection is made between a control brush hub and the C hub which is internally connected to the pick up coil of R23 and to the RC hub and also between the RC hub and a digit selector hub which is internally connected to the emitter. The signal on this line when the reset control punch is read causes the pick up coil of R23 to be picked up. The hold coil of R23 holds until cam P5 breaks contact at time 13.7. While R23 is activated, contact B of this relay is closed so that relays 56-58 pick up when cam P8 makes contact at time 8. These relays hold until cam P9 breaks at 12.5. Thus, in the period that relays 56-58 are activated the contacts on these relays used for reset shunting are open so that information is dropped out of the storage relays holding master information as well as out of the detail information groups. The timing of the events discussed above is shown on PX-11-308.

The fact that relay 27 is activated when reset control takes place also has repercussions on the reset and finish signal circuits which will be discussed in Section 8.3.3.

From the time that Ri is pulsed for the reading of card i + 1 until 13.7 in the cycle for card i + 1 when data from card i is dropped out, the constant transmitter may be called on to transmit data from card i. This period can safely be taken as 50 addition times.

8.3.2. Group Selection Circuits

There are two sets of group selector relays, 7-22 and 24-55. Each of relays 7-22 controls a pair consisting of an even and the immediately succeeding odd numbered relay of the collection 24-55. Three contacts of each even numbered relay and two of each odd numbered relay of the collection 24-55 are used to produce a circuit between the B and C hubs (instead of between the A and C hubs) of a five digit group when one of the relays 7-22 and, thus, a pair of the relays 24-55 is activated.

Group selection plugging from a control brush hub to a C hub which is internally connected to the pick-up coils of relays 7-22 each of which, in turn, is connected internally to one of the group selector hubs (1-16) and, thence, by plug board connection to a digit selector hub and finally to the emitter allows the signal which occurs when a group selection punch is read to pick up the appropriate relay of the assemblage 7-22. Once picked up, such a relay (or relays) holds until cam P5 breaks contact at 13.7. While one of the relays 7-22 is activated the corresponding pair of relays of the 24-55 collection is activated through the B contact of its controlling relay when cam P6 makes contact at time 9.7. This pair of relays then holds until time 9.5 (when cam P7 breaks contact) of the reading cycle following the one in which the group selection punch is recognized. Thus, in the numerical reading cycle of a card for which group selection takes place, the circuit between read brushes for groups effected by group selection and storage relays is by the B-C route instead of the A-C route.

The timing of the events described above is shown on PX-11-308 where it is assumed that group selection is stimulated by some punch on master card m.

8.3.3. Reset and Finish Signal Circuits

Provided that relay 60 is activated and relay 59 is not, a reset signal is emitted via line 129 during the period 12.0 - 12.5 when cam P4 makes, and a finish signal is emitted via line 127 during the period 9.5 - 13 when cam P3 makes.

Relay 59 is activated when cam P1 makes (13.1 - 14.9) through contact R-57 AU provided that relay 57 has been activated; R59 holds until 13.0 when cam P10 breaks.   Now, in Section 8.3.1, it was pointed out that relay 57 is activated during the period 8.0 - 12.5 which is the end of the control reading cycle and the beginning of the numerical cycle for a master card. Thus, when cam P4 makes during 12.0 - 12.5 and a master card is entering its numerical cycle, no reset signal is emitted. Recalling the discussion in Section 8.1, concerning the reader program controls in the initiating unit, one can see that since the start flip-flop is not reset, the start relay remains activated (until a reset signal is emitted during 12.0 - 12.5 in the next reading cycle) and that the reader, therefore, proceeds with a cycle following the one in which numerical data is read from the master card before it stops.

Similarly, since relay 59 remains activated through time 13.0 of the numerical reading cycle for a master card, no finish signal is emitted and therefore no program output pulse can be emitted through Ro on the initiating unit until the reader has gone through a numerical reading cycle for the detail card following the master card.

The timing of the activation of the various elements involved in producing reset and finish signals when a sequence consisting of detail-master-detail

cards is read is shown on PX-11-308.

Relay 60 is not activated when there is not a card in position to move under continuous roll No. 2 (i.e. when CR No. 2, CLC No. 1 is open). This circumstance can arise when a card jams in passing under continuous roll No.1, when the reader is started (from rest) by pushing the reader start button or by the reception of a pulse at Ri and then depressing the initial start key (see Section 8.1.3.), or when the last card of a deck is passing under continuous roll No. 2.

The previous discussion may be summarized as follows: In general, when a detail card passes under continuous roll No. 2, the reader emits a reset signal during the period 12.0 - 12.5 of the cycle or when the card reading cycle is about 1/7th completed. This signal resets the start flip-flop so that subsequent to the reset signal, this flip-flop is capable of noting the reception of a program pulse by Ri. With a safety factor included, about 750 addition times should be allowed from the time that Ri is stimulated until it is stimulated again if all cards in a deck are detail cards. Also, a finish signal is emitted at the end of every cycle in which a detail card is scanned by the read brushes. Thus, about 2500 addition times elapse between the time when a detail card reading cycle commences and a program output pulse is emitted (provided that an interlock pulse has been received).

No reset or finish signals are emitted in the numerical cycle for a master card. These signals are, however, emitted during the numerical cycle for the detail card following a master card. When decks containing both master and detail cards are used, approximately 3200 addition times may elapse between the reception of a program input pulse at Ri and the resetting of the start flip-flop and a program output pulse may not be emitted until about 4400 addition times (as many as 2500 addition times for the reading of the master card and about 1900 for the detail card) after reading is stimulated.

No reset or finish signals are emitted if a card jams in passing under continuous roll No. 1 and no finish signal is emitted for the last card of a deck.

8.4. NUMERICAL CIRCUITS OF THE READER

The circuits in the reader which are used for numerical purposes are:

1) coding cams CB1-CB8 which emit signals to activate the coding relays in the constant transmitter via lines 115-122 (see PX-11-119)

2) coding cam CB9 which activates the constant transmitter's PM isolating relays by means of a signal carried on line 114

3) the read brushes which, by means of plug board wiring to the storage relay hubs, remit numerical indication signals over lines 1-80 to contacts on the coding relays and thence to the storage relays and which, by means of plug board wiring to the minus control hubs, remit minus indication signals over lines 97-112 to the PM' and PM" relays in the constant transmitter.

These circuits will be discussed in greater detail in Section 8.6, NUMERICAL CIRCUITS OF THE CONSTANT TRANSMITTER.

8.5. PROGRAM CONTROLS AND PROGRAMMING CIRCUITS OF THE CONSTANT TRANSMITTER

The 30 program controls (see PX-11-307 and 11-302) of the constant transmitter, each consisting of a transceiver, program pulse input and output terminals, and a constant selector switch, are subdivided into 5 groups of 6 program controls each. Groups 1 through 5 respectively consist of the following program controls 1-6, 7-12, 13-18, 19-25, and 25-30. The 30 transceiver neons associated with the program controls are shown on PX-11-306.

Each constant selector switch of a group of 6 is connected in parallel with the other 5 switches of the group to the programming circuits which elect for transmission a signed 5 or 10 digit number from among the 4 signs and 20 digits controlled by that group. For example, any of the first six switches can be used to select for transmission either of the signed ten digit numbers A_{LR} or B_{LR} or one of the 4 signed five digit numbers, A_L, A_R, B_L, or B_R. However, because of the way these six switches are connected in parallel, it is not possible to elect the transmission of a signed 5 digit L or R group on one switch and the transmission of the signed 10 digit LR group having the same letter on another switch.

For each 5 digit group (whether read from cards or set up manually) there are 20 constant selector gates (4 gates per digit). For the first 5 digits in the storage relays, for example, these gates are numbered B' - L' 1 and B' - L' 21 (see PX-11-307). These gates emit a signal on the coincidence of a signal from a constant selector switch and the activation of the storage relay to which the constant selector gate is connected or on the coincidence of a signal from a constant selector switch and a signal from one of the constant switches.

Also associated with each 5 digit card group is a minus selector gate and a complement correction selector gate. Each 5 digit group that can be set up on the switches located on panel 2 of the constant transmitter has a minus selector gate but not a complement correction selector gate.

These gates emit signals on the coincidence of a signal from a constant selector switch and a signal from either a minus setting on a PM set switch or from an activated PM' or PM" relay. The minus selector gates control the putting in of the 9P for sign indication when a negative number is transmitted and the complement correction selector gates control the putting in of the 1'P needed to make a tens complement when a number punched on a card as a negative number

TABLE 8-3

GATES CONTROLLED BY POINTS ON FIRST 6 CONSTANT SELECTOR SWITCHES.

POINT	GATES CONTROLLED BY FIRST DECK	FUNCTION OF GATE	GATES CONTROLLED BY SECOND DECK	FUNCTION OF GATE
A_L	A'1 (2nd input from PM relay for A_L group)	L M S	B' - L' 1	constant selection for group A_L
	A'21 (2nd input from PM relay for A_L group)	L C C S	(BI) - L' 21 (2nd inputs from storage relays)	
A_R	A'41 (2nd input from PM relay for A_R group)	R M S	B' - L' 41 B' - L' 61	constant selection for group A_R
			A' 61 (2nd input from PM relay for A_R group)	R C C S
A_{LR}	A'1	L M S	B' - L' 1 B' - L' 21	constant selection for group A_L
			B' - L' 41 B' - L' 61	constant selection for group A_R
			A' 61	R C C S
B_L	A'2	L M S	B' - L' 2 B' - L'' 22	constant selection for group B_L
	A'22	L C C S		
B_R	A'42	R M S	B' - L' 42 B' - L' 62	constant selection for group B_R
B_{LR}	A' 2	L M S	B' - L' 2 B' - L' 22	constant selection for group B_L
			B' - L' 42 B' - L' 62	constant selection for group B_R
			A' 62	R C C S

is emitted from the constant transmitter. Negative numbers are set up as tens complements on the switches of panel 2 so that no complement correction selector gates had to be provided for these groups.

Associated with the five-digit groups having subscript L are left minus selector (LMS) and, in the case of card groups, left complement correction selector (LCCS) gates; while the groups with subscript R have right minus selector (RMS) and right complement correction selector (RCCS) gates. The 10 digit LR groups have LMS gates and RCCS gates. The LMS gates control the passing of the 9P to only the PM lead; the RMS gates, to the PM lead and 5 left hand places as well. The LCCS gates or RCCS gates respectively control the putting in of the 1'P in the 5th or 10th decade place from the left.

When a constant transmitter program control is stimulated, signals from the 2 decks of the control's constant selector switch are delivered to the appropriate constant, minus, and complement correction selector gates. Table 8-3 illustrates how the points on the first 6 constant selector switches are connected to the various selector gates. The question of how the selector gates affect the digit pulses emitted from the digit output terminal will be taken up in Section 8.6.2.

The constant chosen for transmission is emitted through the digit output terminal on panel 1 of the constant transmitter during the 20 pulse time p e r i o d   following the reception of the program input pulse. The program control used emits a program output pulse at the end of the addition time in which the constant is transmitted.

The constant transmitter can be stimulated to transmit a constant stored on the manual set switches at any time in the course of a computation. Constants read from a given card can be called for any time in the period between the program output pulse emitted by the reader when that card is read and 50 addition times after the reader is stimulated to read the succeeding card (see Section 8.3.1).

In general, only one program control on the constant transmitter can be stimulated in a given addition time. Circumstances may, however, arise in which the operator would desire to stimulate two program controls simultaneously.

Consider, for example, a set-up in which the following rather particularized conditions are found:

1) accumulator program controls are nearly exhausted

2) 5 digit numbers are used

3) both arguments for a multiplication program are derived from the constant transmitter.

If the normal method of using the constant transmitter were used, both the ier and icand for the multiplication could not be transmitted simultaneously from the constant transmitter and received in the argument accumulators by means of the semi-permanent programming connections (Rα-Rε and Dα-Dε). Therefore, an additional program control on one of the argument accumulators would have to be expended. Under certain specialized conditions which do not conflict with the way in which the leads of the digit output terminals are used (see Section 8.6.2.1), two constant transmitter program controls can be stimulated simultaneously provided that a total of no more than 10 digits and a PM are called for.

Another special case which can arise is that the constant transmitter's program controls may not be adequate in number for some set-up. Under certain circumstances (see Section 8.6.2.1.) the LR setting of a constant selector switch makes it possible to obtain 2 five digit constants at the expense of only one program control.* This procedure, however, must never be used if at any other time in

---

*Another way to circumvent a shortage of constant transmitter program controls is, of course, to make use of the master programmer.

the computation the L or R group identified by the same letter A, B, ..., K is called for separately as mentioned earlier in this section.

8.6. NUMERICAL CIRCUITS OF THE CONSTANT TRANSMITTER

8.6.1. Storing Information from Cards in the Constant Transmitter

Digital information is stored in five-digit blocks each using 5 groups consisting of 4 storage relays each. PM indication for each 5 - digit block is stored in the associated PM' and PM" relays. Each storage relay bears the designation i-j where i identifies the particular one of 80 digits and where j has the value 1, 2, 2' or 4 of the pulse code in which the digits are transmitted from the constant transmitter. The digits read from a card are coded in the 1, 2, 2', 4 code by means of coding cams in the reader and the PM, isolating PM' and PM", and coding relays in the constant transmitter before being put in storage.

The pick up coils of the 6 PM isolating relays are connected via line 114 to coding cam CB9 which makes contact while PM punches are read (see PX-11-307). The PM' and PM" relays for each 5-digit block are connected through a contact on one of the PM isolating relays (labelled R on the schematic diagram shown on PX-11-116) to the line (97-112) which carries the minus indication signal for that block of digits. If a minus punch is read for the group, the PM' and PM" pick up and hold until information is dropped out when a new card is read or when reset control takes place. Since the isolating relay contact is closed only during the period 14.5 - 11.5, digit information punched in the same column as a minus punch cannot activate the PM' and PM" relays.

The pair of PM relays serves not only to remember sign indication, but also aids in converting true negative numbers on the cards to nines complements. When the PM relays are activated by a minus punch, the coding relays (C_1-C_8) used

TABLE 8-4 — ACTIVATION OF CONSTANT TRANSMITTER STORAGE RELAYS

Punch	Energized Coding Cams	Activated Coding Relays	Activated Storage Relays
0	none		
-0	CB1 CB3 CB5 CB7	C_1 or C_2 C_3 or C_4 C_5 or C_6 C_7 or C_8	1 2 2' 4
+1	CB2	C_1 or C_2	1
-1	CB3 CB5 CB7	C_3 or C_4 C_5 or C_6 C_7 or C_8	2 2' 4
+2	CB4	C_3 or C_4	2
-2	CB1 CB3 CB7	C_1 or C_2 C_3 or C_4 C_7 or C_8	1 2 4
+3	CB2 CB4	C_1 or C_2 C_3 or C_4	1 2
-3	CB5 CB7	C_3 or C_4 C_7 or C_8	2 4
+4	CB8	C_7 or C_8	4
-4	CB1 CB7	C_1 or C_2 C_7 or C_8	1 4
+5	CB2 CB8	C_1 or C_2 C_7 or C_8	1 4
-5	CB7	C_7 or C_8	4
+6	CB4 CB8	C_3 or C_4 C_7 or C_8	2 4
-6	CB1 CB3	C_1 or C_2 C_3 or C_4	1 2
+7	CB2 CB4 CB8	C_1 or C_2 C_3 or C_4 C_7 or C_8	1 2 4
-7	CB3	C_3 or C_4	2
+8	CB4 CB6 CB8	C_3 or C_4 C_5 or C_6 C_7 or C_8	2 2' 4
-8	CB1	C_1 or C_2	1
+9	CB2 CB4 CB6 CB8	C_1 or C_2 C_3 or C_4 C_5 or C_6 C_7 or C_8	1 2 2' 4
-9	none		

for a five digit block are connected to the odd numbered coding cams. Otherwise the coding relays are connected to the even numbered coding cams.

Each of the 4 coding cams CB1, CB3, CB5, and CB7 or CB2, CB4, CB6, and CB8 is connected through contacts on the PM' and PM" relays to the pick up coils of a pair of coding relays (one even numbered and one odd numbered relay). Various combinations of the coding cams make contact as the different digit punches are read by the read brushes (see the coding cam time table and Table 8-4). When a coding cam makes contact it activates the pair of coding relays to which it is connected. The coding relay picks up and holds as long as the associated coding cam makes contact.

A signal for a punch appearing in one of the first 3 places of a 5-digit block is delivered to one contact on each of the odd numbered coding relays and a signal for either of the 2 remaining places of the block to a contact on the even numbered coding relays. Only the contacts on relays activated at the particular time when the punch is read are closed so as to allow the punch signals to reach the storage relays.

A signal carried on the i lead (i=1, 2, ..., 80) and passing through a contact on coding relay C_1 or C_2 sets up the i-1 storage relays; a signal through a contact on coding relays C_3 or C_4, the i-2 relays; a signal through a contact on C_5 or C_6, the i-2' relay; and a signal through a contact on C_7 or C_8, the i-4 relay. Table 8-4 shows which coding cams are energized as the different punches are read, the coding relays that are activated as a result, and the storage relays which are set up when a given line is passing over the read brushes if such a punch appears in a column of the card. The hold contacts on the storage relays for groups A_L through H_R are connected to lines 81-96 respectively so that, once set up, these relays hold until a new card is read or until reset control takes

TABLE 8-5

USE OF DIGIT OUTPUT LEADS FOR CONSTANT SELECTOR SWITCH SETTINGS L, R, or LR

Lead	L	R	LR
PM	0 or 9 sign pulses	0 or 9 sign pulses	0 or 9 sign pulses
10	digit pulses	0 or 9 sign pulses	digit pulses
9	digit pulses	0 or 9 sign pulses	digit pulses
8	digit pulses	0 or 9 sign pulses	digit pulses
7	digit pulses	0 or 9 sign pulses	digit pulses
6	digit pulses and 1'P for negative L group	0 or 9 sign pulses	digit pulses
5		digit pulses	digit pulses
4		digit pulses	digit pulses
3		digit pulses	digit pulses
2		digit pulses	digit pulses
1		digit pulses and 1'P for negative R group	digit pulses and 1'P for negative LR group

place.

8.6.2. Transmitting Information from the Constant Transmitter

In general, only one signed 10 digit or signed 5 digit number can be transmitted from the constant transmitter in an addition time. The digit output terminal on panel 1 of the constant transmitter has 10 digit leads and a PM lead. Each of the 10 digit leads is fed by 4 coding gates, the 1, 2, 2', and 4P gates. The digit leads for the fifth and tenth decade places from the left can also receive pulses from a gate which passes the 1'P. The PM lead and the digit leads for the first five decade places from the left are connected to gates which pass the 9P (see PX-11-307 and Table 8-5).

8.6.2.1. Constants read from a card

The 1, 2, 2' and 4P gates for the first decade place from the left are controlled by the 4 constant selector gates which receive one input from the 1, 2, 2' and 4 storage relays for the first digit of the L group, and the 2nd input from an L or LR point on a constant selector switch; the 1, 2, 2', and 4 pulse gates for the second decade place from the left are controlled by the constant selector gates which receive one input from the 1, 2, 2' and 4 storage relays for the second digit of the L group and the 2nd input from an L or LR point on a constant selector switch, etc.

The gates which allow the 1' pulse to pass to the 5th or 10th from the left decade place leads respectively are controlled by the left or right complement correction selector gates. The gates, which allow the 9P to pass to the PM lead or to the PM lead and the first 5 decade place leads from the left, are controlled respectively by the left or right minus selector gates.

When a constant transmitter program control is stimulated, the selector gates chosen by the setting of the constant selector switch (see Table 8-3) emit a

TABLE 8-6

SIMULTANEOUS STIMULATION OF TWO CONSTANT TRANSMITTER PROGRAM CONTROLS

A_L refers to a group A_L storing a positive number; $\bar{A}_L$ to a group A_L storing a negative number. D.P. is used for the phrase "digit pulses".

Switch set-tings	A_L and B_R			A_L and B_R			$\bar{A}_L$ and B_R			A_R and B_R		
Lead	0	gp		0	gp	gp	0	gp	gp	0		
PM												
10	D.P. for A_L			D.P. for A_L			D.P. for A_L			D.P. for A_L		
9	A_L and B_R set up in storage relays	A_L and B_R set up in storage relays	where only A_L and B_R are set up in storage relays	where only A_L and B_R are set up in storage relays	where only A_R and B_R are not up in storage relays	where only A_L up in storage relays						
8	Impossible since gp for sign of B_R are emitted over loads 6-10	Impossible since gp for sign of B_R are emitted over loads 6-10				Impossible since gp for sign of A_R are emitted over loads 6-10						
7	"	"	"	"	"	"	"	"	"	"		
6	"	"	"	"	"	"	"	"	"	"		
5	D.P. for B_R	and 1'P	D.P. for B_R	D.P. for B_R	D.P. for B_R	D.P. for A_R	D.P. for B_R	D.P. for B_R				
4	"		"	"	"	"	"	"				
3	"		"	"	"	"	"	"				
2	"		"	"	"	"	"	"				
1	"		and 1'P	and 1'P	and 1'P	"	and 1'P					

Comment

Simultaneous stimulation of two program controls set up for A_L and B_R transmission is possible when:

1. A_L and B_R are always positive

or 2. A_L may be $\bar{A}_L$ but B_R is always B_R provided that the accumulator which receives B_R has a deleter for suppressing sign.

Simultaneous stimulation of 2 program controls set up for A_L and B_R transmission is possible when only 5 digit A_L and B_R groups are set up in the storage relays and then:

1. A_L and B_R are both always positive or both always negative

or 2. A_L may be $\bar{A}_L$ but B_R is always B_R provided that the accumulator which receives B_R is supplied with a deleter for suppressing sign.

Simultaneous stimulation of two program controls set up for $\bar{A}_L$ and B_R transmission is possible when only 5 digit A_L and B_R groups are set up in the storage relays and then:

1. A_R and B_R are both always positive

or 2. B_R is always B_R and $\bar{A}_R$ is always A_R provided that the accumulator which receives A_R has a PM deleter and provided that the 1'P is supplied at the accumulator which receives B_R.

Simultaneous stimulation of two program controls set up for A_R and B_R transmission is possible when only 5 digit A_R and B_R groups are set up in the storage relays and when:

1. A_L and B_R are both always positive

or 2. A_L and B_R are both always negative provided that the negative provided that the 1'P is put in at the accumulator which receives A_L

or 3. A_L may be $\bar{A}_L$ but B_R is always B_R provided that a PM deleter is used at the accumulator which receives B_R.

signal if their corresponding relays have been activated. The signals thus emitted open the gates controlled by such selector gates and allow appropriate numbers of pulses to be transmitted over the 11 leads of the digit output terminal. The leads of the digit output terminal transmit information as shown in Table 8-5.

In Section 8.5, the statement was made that two constant transmitter program controls could be simultaneously stimulated or 2 five digit constants could be transmitted simultaneously provided that no logical conflict existed in the demands thus put on the leads of the digit output terminals.

Consideration of Tables 8-3 and 8-5 shows the cases in which the simultaneous stimulation of two program controls is possible. Certain possible cases are tabulated in Table 8-6 (cases not shown can be argued similarly). The illustrations of Table 8-6 involve groups A and B but any other pair of groups (with both not necessarily being controlled by the same group of 6 constant selector switches) can be treated in the same way.

Similarly, it can be seen that a 5 digit L and a five digit R subgroup of the same ten digit group can be called for simultaneously by the stimulation of one constant transmitter program control set up for LR transmission when:

1) Both subgroups are always positive

2) The left subgroup is always positive and the right subgroup always negative provided that the sign of the right subgroup is corrected at the receiving accumulator. This involves picking up the 1'P in units decade of some accumulator and then transmitting it to the PM decade of the accumulator which receives the R group.

3) Both subgroups are always negative provided that the 1'P needed for a tens complement is provided at the accumulator which receives the left subgroup.

8.6.2.2. Constants set up on set switches

The transmission of the J and K groups of constants is similar to that for groups A-H except that there are no complement correction selector gates for these constants and the other selector gates receive one input from the set switches instead of from storage relays.

Notice that since no provision has been made for converting negative numbers into complements in the case of the J and K groups, negative numbers must be set up on these switches as complements and, since no complement correction gates have been provided for these groups, tens complements must be set up.

8.7. ILLUSTRATIVE PROBLEM

A problem illustrating the use of both the reader and constant transmitter is discussed in this section.

In set-up tables, the symbol $\frac{i-j}{Ri}$ is written on the line corresponding to the first addition time of a reading program. For example, a reading program which is stimulated by the program pulse 2-3 emitted at the end of addition time 6 is written on the line for addition time 7. Similarly $\frac{i-j}{Rl}$ is used to indicate the reader interlock pulse. The symbol $\frac{Ro}{i-j}$ designates the program output pulse which the reader emits and is written on the line corresponding to the addition time in which reading is completed. On set-up diagrams Ri, Rl, and Ro have been drawn in the same relative position as they appear on PX-9-302. The reader start button is circled for a computation initiated by it.

The instructions for the constant transmitter are given in a double column on set-up tables. The left half shows the program input pulse and program control number on the first level, the setting of the constant selector switch on the second level, and the program output pulse on the third level. In the right

TABLE 3-8

Computations to form $_tN_k$, the tth term of Quantity N_k, where k = 0, 1, ..., and 5.

t = 1, 2, 3, 4, 5	t = 6, 7, 8, 9, 10
(1) $= x_{r+1,2} x_{r+2,3}$	(1) $= x_{r+1,2} x_{r-2,3}$
(2) $= x_{r+3,4} x_{r+4,5}$	(2) $= x_{r-3,4} x_{r-4,5}$
(3) $=$ (1) . (2)	(3) $=$ (1) . (2)
(4) $= x_{r,1}$. (3) $= {_tD_0}$	(4) $= x_{r,1}$ (3) $= - {_tD_0}$
(5) $= a_r$. (3) $= {_tD_1}$	(5) $= a_r$. (3) $= - {_tD_1}$
(6) $= x_{r,1}$. $x_{r+2,3}$	(6) $= x_{r,1}$. $x_{r-2,3}$
(7) $=$ (2) . (6)	(7) $=$ (2) . (6)
(8) $= a_{r+1}$. (7) $= {_tD_2}$	(8) $= a_{r-1}$. (7) $= - {_tD_2}$
(9) $= x_{r+1,2}$. $x_{r,1}$	(9) $= x_{r-1,2}$. $x_{r,1}$
(10) $=$ (2) . (9)	(10) $=$ (2) . (9)
(11) $= a_{r+2}$. (10) $= {_tD_3}$	(11) $= a_{r-2}$. (10) $= - {_tD_3}$
(12) $= x_{r+2,3}$. $x_{r+4,5}$	(12) $= x_{r-2,3}$. $x_{r-4,5}$
(13) $=$ (9) . (12)	(13) $=$ (9) . (12)
(14) $= a_{r+3}$. (13) $= {_tD_4}$	(14) $= a_{r-3}$. (13) $= - {_tD_4}$
(15) $= x_{r+3,4}$: $x_{r+2,3}$	(15) $= x_{r-3,4}$. $x_{r-2,3}$
(16) $=$ (9) . (15)	(16) $=$ (9) . (15)
(17) $= a_{r+4}$. (16) $= {_tD_5}$	(17) $= a_{r-4}$. (16) $= - {_tD_5}$

t	r*
1	1
2	2
3	3
4	4
5	5

t	r*
6	5
7	6
8	7
9	8
10	9

* all subscripts
r, r+1, ..., r-1,
..., are mod 5

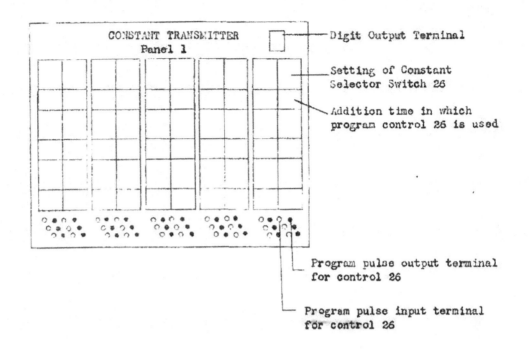

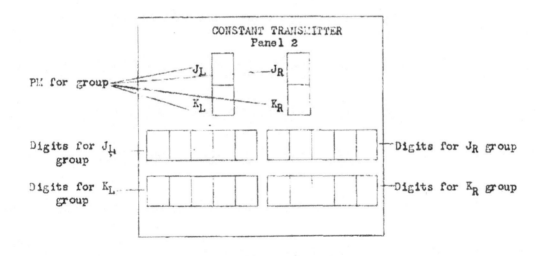

Fig. 8-1

SET-UP DIAGRAM CONVENTIONS FOR CONSTANT TRANSMITTER

TABLE 6-7
TABLE OF $\tilde{x}$

No.	t = 1	t = 2	t = 3	t = 4	t = 5	t = 6	t = 7	t = 8	t = 9	t = 10
M_0	$x_{11}x_{22}x_{33}x_{44}x_{55}$	$x_{21}x_{32}x_{43}x_{54}x_{15}$	$x_{31}x_{42}x_{53}x_{14}x_{25}$	$x_{41}x_{52}x_{13}x_{24}x_{35}$	$x_{51}x_{12}x_{23}x_{34}x_{45}$	$-x_{11}x_{52}x_{43}x_{34}x_{25}$	$-x_{21}x_{12}x_{53}x_{44}x_{35}$	$-x_{31}x_{22}x_{13}x_{54}x_{45}$	$-x_{41}x_{32}x_{23}x_{14}x_{55}$
M_1	$a_1\,x_{22}x_{33}x_{44}x_{55}$	$a_2\,x_{32}x_{43}x_{54}x_{15}$	$a_3\,x_{42}x_{53}x_{14}x_{25}$	$a_4\,x_{52}x_{13}x_{24}x_{35}$	$a_5\,x_{12}x_{23}x_{34}x_{45}$	$-a_5\,x_{42}x_{33}x_{24}x_{15}$	$-a_2\,x_{12}x_{53}x_{44}x_{35}$	$-a_3\,x_{22}x_{13}x_{54}x_{45}$	$-a_4\,x_{32}x_{23}x_{14}x_{55}$
M_2	$x_{11}\theta_2\,x_{33}x_{44}x_{55}$	$x_{21}\theta_3\,x_{43}x_{54}x_{15}$	$x_{31}\theta_4\,x_{53}x_{14}x_{25}$	$x_{41}\theta_5\,x_{13}x_{24}x_{35}$	$x_{51}\theta_1\,x_{23}x_{34}x_{45}$	$-x_{51}\theta_4\,x_{33}x_{24}x_{15}$	$-x_{21}\theta_1\,x_{53}x_{44}x_{35}$	$-x_{31}\theta_2\,x_{13}x_{54}x_{45}$	$-x_{41}\theta_3\,x_{23}x_{14}x_{55}$
M_3	$x_{11}x_{22}\theta_3\,x_{44}x_{55}$	$x_{21}x_{32}\theta_4\,x_{54}x_{15}$	$x_{31}x_{42}\theta_5\,x_{14}x_{25}$	$x_{41}x_{52}\theta_1\,x_{24}x_{35}$	$x_{51}x_{12}\theta_2\,x_{34}x_{45}$	$-x_{51}x_{42}\theta_3\,x_{24}x_{15}$	$-x_{21}x_{12}\theta_5\,x_{44}x_{35}$	$-x_{31}x_{22}\theta_1\,x_{54}x_{45}$	$-x_{41}x_{32}\theta_2\,x_{14}x_{55}$
M_4	$x_{11}x_{22}x_{33}\theta_4\,x_{55}$	$x_{21}x_{32}x_{43}\theta_5\,x_{15}$	$x_{31}x_{42}x_{53}\theta_1\,x_{25}$	$x_{41}x_{52}x_{13}\theta_2\,x_{35}$	$x_{51}x_{12}x_{23}\theta_3\,x_{45}$	$-x_{51}x_{42}x_{33}\theta_2\,x_{15}$	$-x_{21}x_{12}x_{53}\theta_4\,x_{35}$	$-x_{31}x_{22}x_{13}\theta_5\,x_{45}$	$-x_{41}x_{32}x_{23}\theta_1\,x_{55}$
M_5	$x_{11}x_{22}x_{33}x_{44}\theta_5$	$x_{21}x_{32}x_{43}x_{54}\theta_1$	$x_{31}x_{42}x_{53}x_{14}\theta_2$	$x_{41}x_{52}x_{13}x_{24}\theta_3$	$x_{51}x_{12}x_{23}x_{34}\theta_4$	$-x_{51}x_{42}x_{33}x_{24}\theta_1$	$-x_{21}x_{12}x_{53}x_{44}\theta_2$	$-x_{31}x_{22}x_{13}x_{54}\theta_3$	$-x_{41}x_{32}x_{23}x_{14}\theta_4$

hand half the constant transmitted is specified. The symbols are written on the line for the addition time in which the constant is transmitted.

The set-up diagram conventions for the constant transmitter are shown on Figure 8-1.

The master programmer is also used in the illustrative problem of this section. In most cases, the symbols used are explained where they appear. For further details see Chapter X.

The illustrative problem of this section consists of forming the six quantities N_0 through N_5 each of which is the sum of the 10 terms shown on Table 8-7. We assume that the N_k are to be evaluated for 100 different sets of values x_{ij} but that the a_i do not vary from set to set. We assume, also, that the numbers x_{ij} and A_i are 5 digit numbers between 0.1 and 1.0 and, further, that the numbers x_{ii} are non-negative for all sets.

The numbers a_2, a_3, a_4, and a_5 will be stored on the constant set switches. The numbers x_{ij} and a_1 are to be introduced into the ENIAC by means of punched cards. The subject of storing those numbers will be treated in more detail presently. At this point, however, we wish to describe the routine which will be used to form the numbers N_k.

Table 8-8 presents a sequence of multiplication programs which could be used to find the one term for each of the numbers N_k. From one value of t to another, the most striking change in the computations consists of using different sets of the x_{ij}. One distinction between the computations for $t = 1$ through 5 and those for $t = 6$ through 10 consists of the fact that in the former the A_i are required in ascending order of subscript and in the latter, in descending order of subscript. A second point of difference is that in the first class we are interested in the terms (4), (5), (8), (11), (14), and (17) and in the second class, in the negatives of them. The operations of forming terms (1) through (17) will be referred to as the multiplication sequence. In order to provide for the differences noted above this sequence will be modified as multiplication sequence A or B for $t = 1$ through 5 or $t = 6$ through 10 respectively. The quantities N_0 through N_5 will be found by repeating each of the modifications of the multiplication sequence 5 times.

Now we return to the matter of storing the numbers x_{ij} and a_i. In all, 26 numbers are to be introduced from punched cards. Since, only 16 five digit constants can be obtained in one card reading, at least 2 readings are required for each system of equations. Since, furthermore, the constants are needed repeatedly in different combinations, either they must be read repeatedly from cards on which they occur in different combinations, or at least 10 of them must be read from 1 card and stored in accumulators to be available when the card containing the remainder of them is read. The latter course is adopted here. The constants needed to form the terms listed in columns $t = 1$ and $t = 6$ (see Table 8-7) are read from a card and transferred to accumulators. Then, computations start for these values of t and meanwhile the reader scans the card containing the remaining numbers. As it turns out, only 8 accumulators are available for storing the 10 numbers read from the 1st card. Therefore, in each of 2 accumulators, we store a pair of numbers, one in the 5 left hand decades and the other in the five right hand decades. The 2 pairs of numbers are chosen from the x_{ii} terms, since it is easiest to store two positive numbers in one accumulator.

One further consideration influences the manner in which the constants are stored. The x_{ij} and a_i are all destined to go to the multiplier unit and we wish the resulting products to be similarly located in the decades of the product accumulator. One way to accomplish this is to align the numbers similarly in the argument accumulators, let us say at the extreme left. This, then, requires that

TABLE 8-9

STORAGE OF CONSTANTS

FIRST CARD			SECOND CARD		
Constant Transmitter Group	Constant	Accumulator to which constant is transferred	Constant Transmitter Group	Constant	Accumulator to which constant is transferred
A_L	x_{22}	1L	A_L	x_{12}	
A_R	x_{11}	1R	A_R	x_{21}	
B_L	x_{44}	2L	B_L	x_{32}	
B_R	x_{33}	2R	B_R	x_{31}	
C_L	a_1	8L	C_L	x_{52}	
C_R	x_{55}	3R	C_R	x_{41}	
D_L			D_L	x_{14}	
D_R	x_{51}	4R	D_R	x_{13}	
E_L	x_{24}	5L	E_L	x_{34}	
E_R			E_R	x_{23}	
F_L			F_L	x_{54}	
F_R	x_{15}	6R (clear at end of 3rd. M.S.)	F_R	x_{43}	
G_L			G_L	x_{53}	6R (after third M.S.)
G_R			G_R	x_{25}	
H_L	x_{42}	7L (clear at end of 3rd M.S.)	H_L	x_{35}	7R (after fifth M.S.)
H_R			H_R	x_{45}	
J_L	a_2		J_L	a_2	
J_R	a_3		J_R	a_3	
K_L	a_4		K_L	a_4	
K_R	a_5		K_R	a_5	

TABLE 8-10

SET-UP ANALYSIS FOR EVALUATION OF THE NUMBERS N_k

INITIAL SEQUENCE: Read

1-1[*]   Transfer constants from constant transmitter to accumulators

2-1   Read in parallel with sequence 2.1 and 2.2

     2.1-1 Multiplication Sequence A

        Form Terms (1) - (17) for i = 1
        Receive Terms (4), (5), (8), (11), (14), and (17) from product
          accumulator's A output via α input channel of accumulators
          14, 16, 17, ..., and 20 respectively.

     2.2-1 Multiplication Sequence B
        Form terms (1) - (17) for i = 6
        Receive terms (4), (5), (8), (11), (14), and (17)
          from product accumulator's S output via β
          input channel of accumulators 14, 16, 17, ..., and 20
          respectively.

3-1   Send Interlock Signal to Reader

4-4   Multiplication Sequence

     4.1-1 A for i = 2, 3, 4, 5 in turn
     4.2-1 B for i = 7, 8, 9, 10 in turn.

5-1   Read and, in parallel, print and then selective clear

[*]The number following a dash indicates how many times the sequence identified by
the number preceding the dash is to be repeated.

numbers stored in the right hand side of an accumulator or a constant transmitter group be shifted to the left upon reception in an argument accumulator and that those stored at the left, not be shifted. Then, to make the computations for all ten columns precisely alike, all numbers which are used in the same programs from one multiplication sequence to another must be similarly located with regard to side left or right of storage facility. This plan calls for storing x_{ij} for j even at the left and for j odd at the right. This necessitates moving certain x_{ij} with odd j out of left hand constant transmitter groups (where they are temporarily located for want of free right hand groups) into right hand accumulator. groups when the latter become available because the numbers they store at first are no longer needed. Table 8-9 shows a plan for the storage of constants required in this computation.

We return to a broad discussion of the plan for the computation. For each set of numbers x_{ij}, one card containing 10 of them is read. These numbers are put in storage in accumulators. Immediately, computation of the terms in columns $t = 1$ and $t = 6$ of table 8-7 starts and the reading of a card with 16 more numbers begins. When the reading of the 2nd card is completed, computation for the terms in the remaining columns of table 8-7 is carried out. As the various terms of the N_k are computed they are emitted from the product accumulator both additively and subtractively. In multiplication sequence A, these products emitted additively are received in accumulators 14, 16, 17, ..., 20; in multiplication sequence B, the products emitted subtractively are received in these same accumulators. After 10 repetitions of the multiplication sequence, the 6 numbers N_k are stored in the accumulators mentioned above. The values are printed, and the accumulators which store N_k are then selectively cleared. While printing takes place, the first card for the next set of x_{ij} is read. This plan is summarized in table 8-10.

TABLE 6-4
SET-UP TABLE

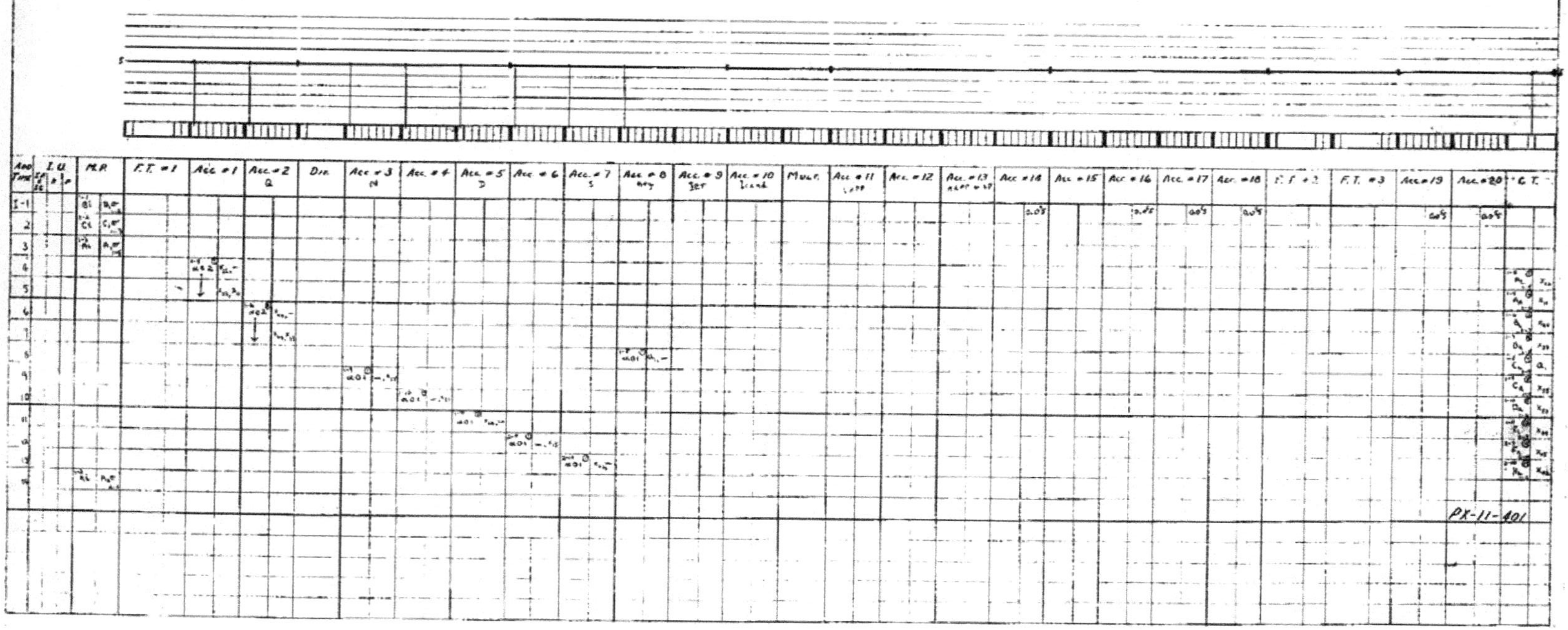

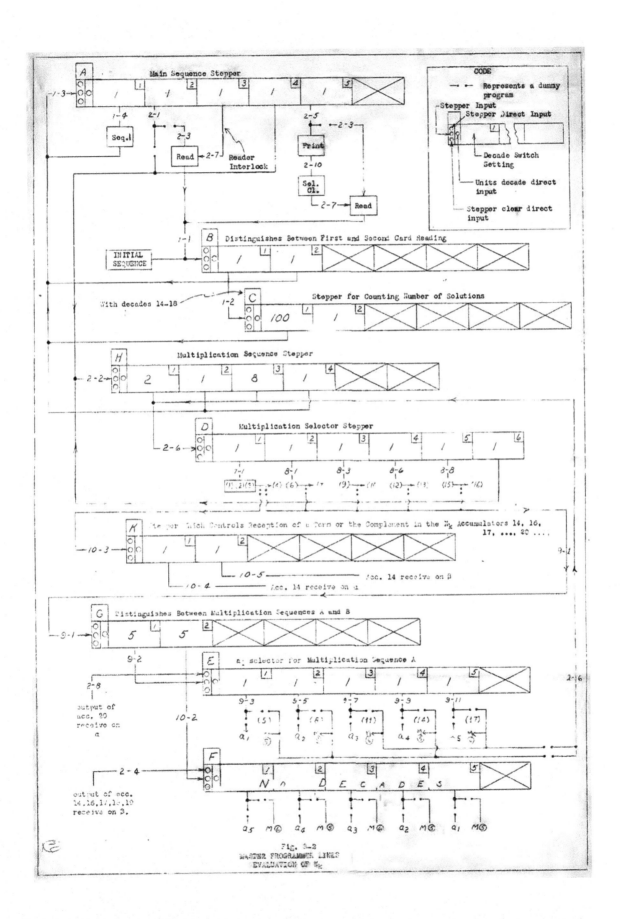

Fig. 3-2
MASTER PROGRAMMER LINES
EVALUATION OF M_k

Figure 8-2 shows how the main program sequences are linked together by the master programmer. Stepper B is used to determine whether reading is the first for a system of equations (stage 1) or the second (stage 2). For the first reading, stepper B shifts control to stepper C which counts the number of solutions and then . routes control to stepper A which directs the main sequences of the problem.

The output of stage 1 of stepper A stimulates the sequence in which constants from the first card are put in storage in accumulators. The output of stage 2 stimulates the reader and also goes to stepper H which controls the multiplication sequence. The output of stage 3 provides an interlock pulse for the reader. Control is shifted to stepper H again by the output of stage 4. The output of stage 5 stimulates the reader and printer. The output of the reader goes back to stepper B, etc.

Specific details for the set-up of sequence 1 are given in Table 8-11. On the line for addition time I-1, the symbol 0.0^55 in the contents column for accumulators 14, 16, 17, ..., 20 which will store the N_k terms indicates that the decimal point occurs one decade place to the right of the PM counter and that these accumulators clear to 5 in the 6th decade from the PM place. During addition times 4-13, the constants x_{ii} (for i = 1-5), x_{51}, x_{24}, x_{15}, x_{42}, and a_i are transferred from the constant transmitter to accumulators 1-8. Notice that constant transmitter program controls ① and ② set at A_L and A_R respectively are used serially for the transmission of x_{22} and x_{11} instead of one control set at A_{LR} as would be possible since both constants are positive. The reason this must be done is that when the second card is read, we must enter A_L and A_R separately for x_{12}, x_{21} (see Table 8-9) which may or may not be positive.

The multiplication sequence of the problem which is repeated once as

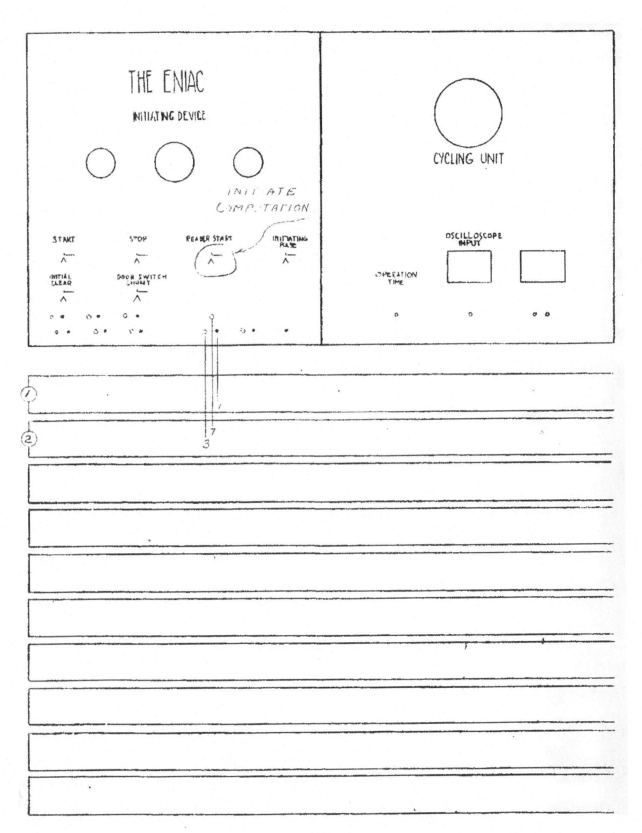

Fig. 8-3 (a)

SET-UP DIAGRAM FOR SEQUENCE 1 AND SEQUENCE 2.1

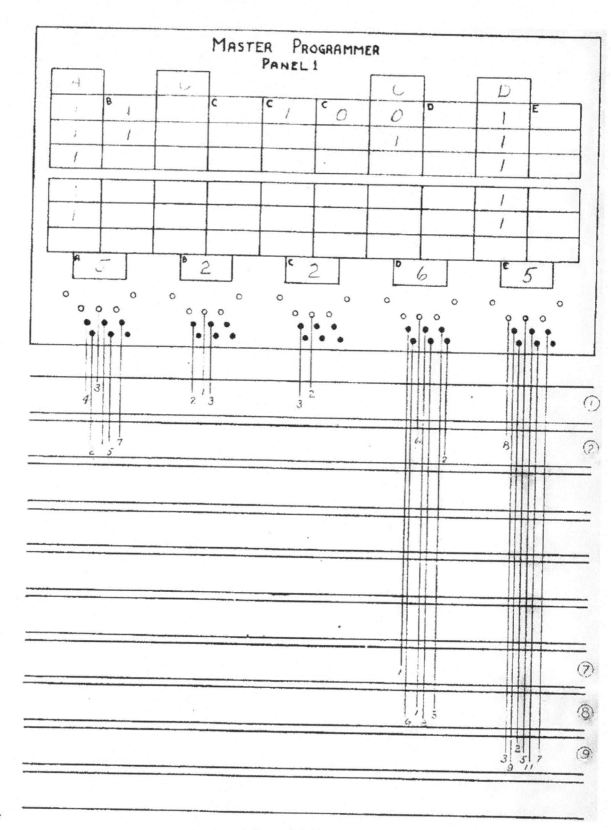

Fig. C-3 (b)

SET-UP DIAGRAM FOR SEQUENCE 1 AND SEQUENCE C.1

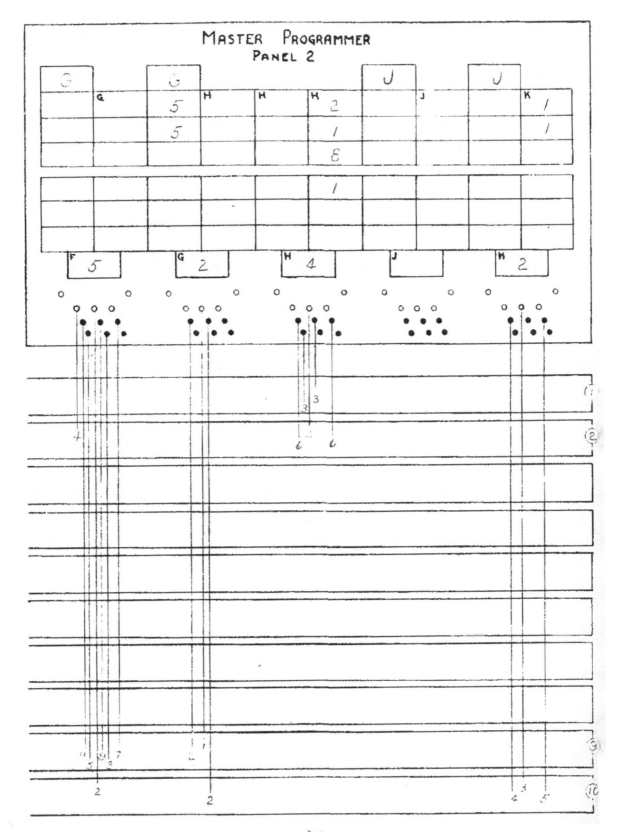

Fig. 6-3 (c)

SET-UP DIAGRAM FOR SEQUENCE 1 AND SEQUENCE 2.1

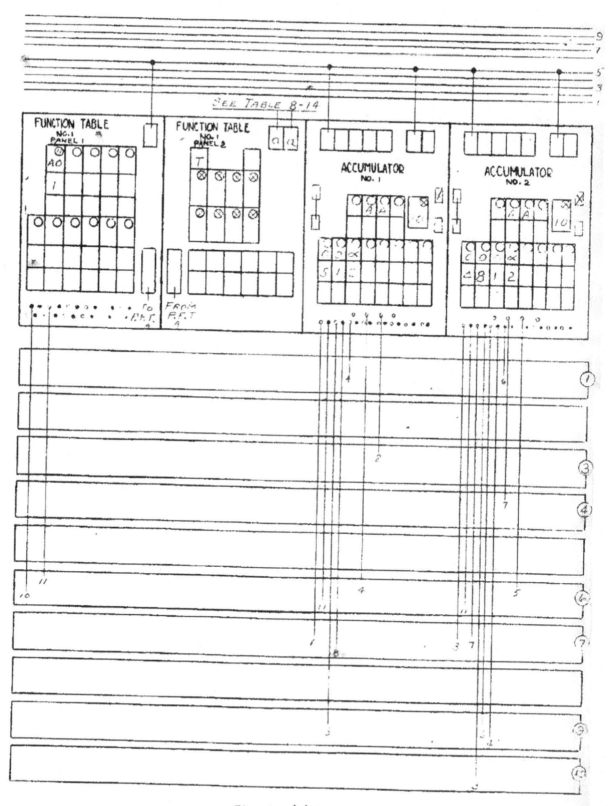

Fig. 8-3 (d)

SETUP DIAGRAM FOR READINGS 1 AND SEQUENCE 8.1

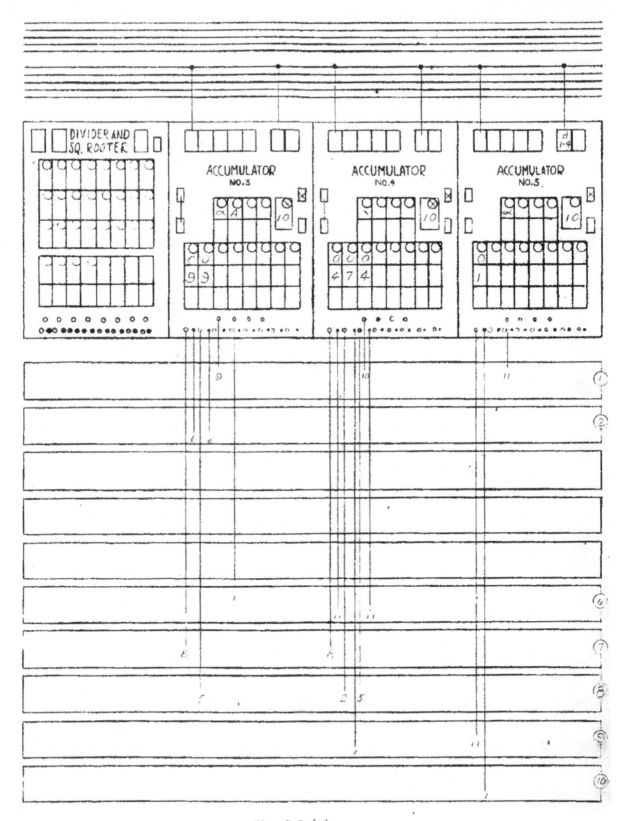

Fig. 8-3 (e)

SET-UP DIAGRAM FOR SEQUENCE 1 AND SEQUENCE 2.1

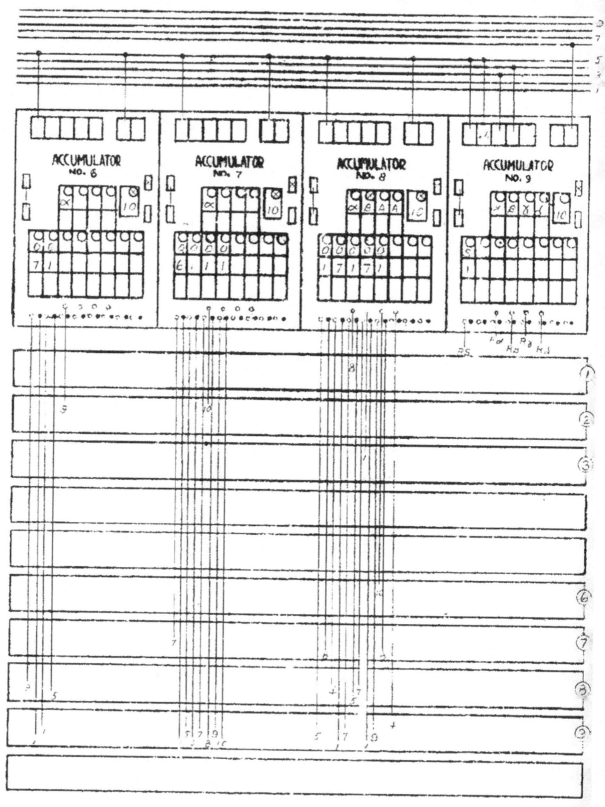

Fig. 4-5 (f)

SET-UP DIAGRAM FOR SEQUENCE 1 AND SEQUENCE 2.1

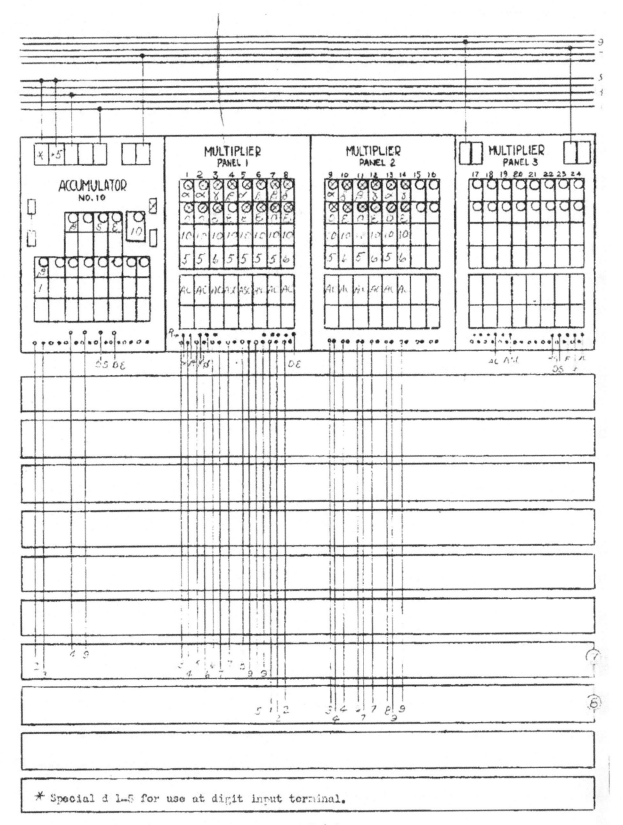

* Special d 1-5 for use at digit input terminal.

Fig. 3-3 (B)

SET-UP DIAGRAM FOR SCHEDULE 1 AND SEQUENCE 2.1

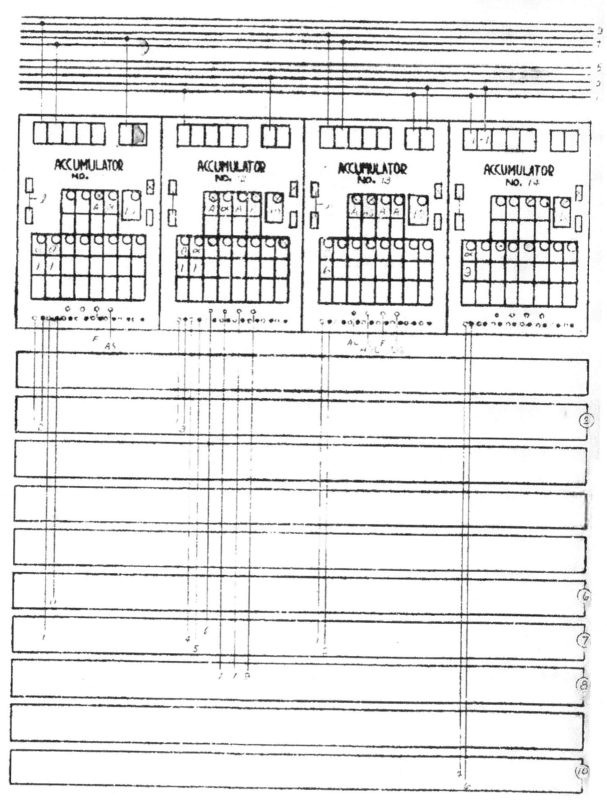

Fig. 3-3 (h)

SET-UP DIAGRAM FOR SEQUENCE 1 AND STATEMENTS

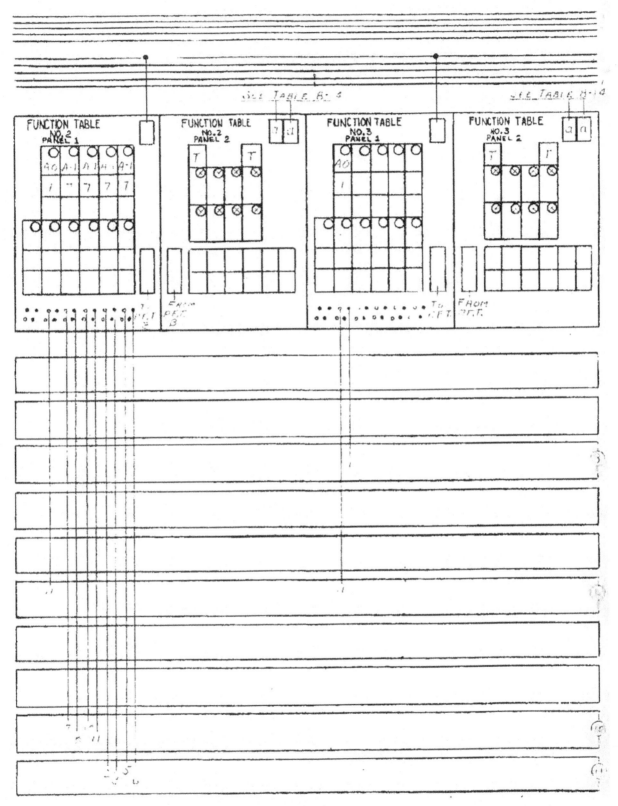

Fig. 8-5 (j)

WIR-UP DIAGRAM FOR SOLUTION 1 AND SEQUENCE 2.1

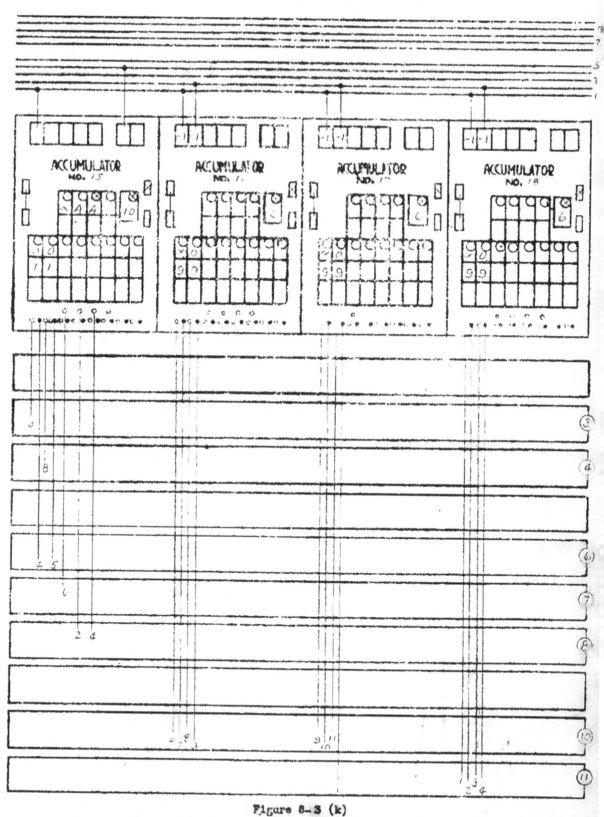

Figure 8-3 (k)
SET-UP DIAGRAM FOR SEQUENCE 1 AND SEQUENCE 2.1

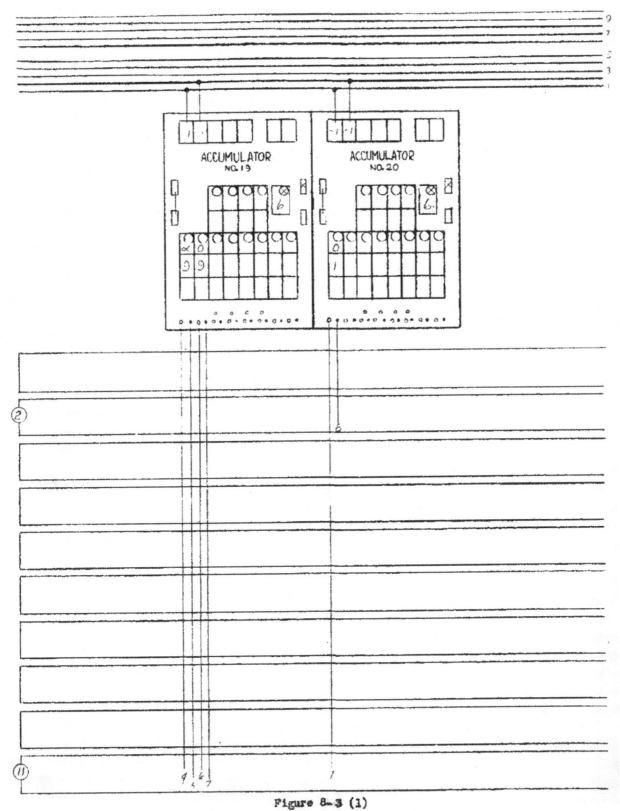

Figure 8-3 (1)

SET-UP DIAGRAM FOR SEQUENCE 1 AND SEQUENCE 2.1

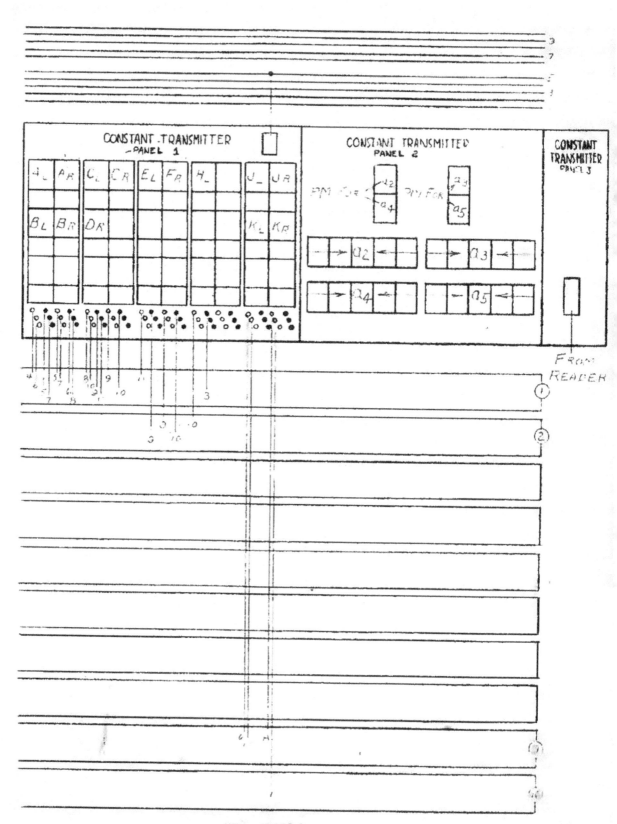

Fig. 8-3 (m)

SET-UP DIAGRAM FOR SEQUENCE 1 AND SEQUENCE 2.1

2.1, once as 2.2, four times as 4.1, and four times as 4.2, is described with the aid of the following tables and figures:

Table 8-8   Computations to form $_t N_k$

Table 8-9   Storage of Constants

Table 8-13   Set-Up Table for Sequence 2.1

Table 8-14   Set-Up of Function Tables for Programming Transmission of Constants

Figure 8-2   Master Programmer Links

Figure 8-3   Set-Up Figure for Sequences 1 and 2.1

Table 8-9 shows that the $x_{i,2n}$ and a_{2n} are stored either in left hand constant transmitter groups or in the five left hand decades of accumulators and that the $x_{i,2n+1}$ and a_{2n+1} are stored at the right. Therefore, to make the most efficient use of the high-speed multiplier, the $x_{i,2n+1}$ are shifted five places to the left when they are received in the ier or icand accumulators. A +5 shifter (which shifts numerical data 5 places to the left) is used at the β input terminals of the ier and icand accumulators and arguments of the form $x_{i,2n+1}$ are received over the β input channel. Also, because certain accumulators store 2 numbers, it is necessary to delete the five right hand digits of an icand received from a left hand group when the icand is of the form $x_{i,2n+1}$. A d 1-5 deleter is used at the α input terminal of the icand accumulator for this purpose. A similar deleter is not needed at the ier accumulator since the high-speed multiplier uses only as many places of the ier as specified on the places switch.

Examination of Table 8-8 shows that the 17 multiplications of the multiplication sequence fall into three groups with characteristics as shown below:

All 17 multiplications are arranged in a predominant sequence with

TABLE 8-12

ANALYSIS OF MULTIPLICATION SEQUENCE

Group	Multiplications	Characteristics
A	(3), (7), (10), (13), and (16)	Arguments derived from same source and products received from product accumulator in same way for all 10 repetitions.
B	(1), (2), (6), (9), (12) and (15)	Arguments located in different places for the various repetitions. Products received from product accumulator in same way for all repetitions.
C	(4)	Ier located in different places from repetition to repetition. Product received from A or S output of product accumulator on alternate repetitions.
D	(5), (8), (11), (14) and (17)	Ier located in different places for the various repetitions. Furthermore, ier must be received sometimes on α and sometimes on β input terminal of ier accumulator. Products transmitted respectively from A or S output of product accumulator are received through α or β input channels of accumulators 14, 16, 17, ..., 20 on alternate repetitions.

TABLE 8-14

SET-UP OF FUNCTION TABLES* FOR PROGRAMMING TRANSMISSION OF CONSTANTS

FUNCTION TABLE 1

Arg. \ Load	PM1	A5	A6	A7	A8	A9	A10	B5	B6	B7	B8	B9	B10	PM2
0	9													
1		M												
2		M												
3			9											
4			M											
5				9										
6														
7 etc.														

Use													
	x11 x22	x11 x12 x13	x13 x14	x15	x21	x23	x23	x24	x25	x31	x31	x32 x33

FUNCTION TABLE 2

PM1	A5	A6	A7	A8	A9	A10	B5	B6	B7	B8	B9	B10	PM2	PM1	A5
	9	9	9												
		9													
		9	9												

Transmit

| x33 x44 | x33 x34 | x35 | x41 | x42 | x43 | x43 | x45 | x51 | x51 | x52 | x53 | x53 | x54 | x55 |

FUNCTION TABLE 3

A6	A7	A8	A9	A10
		9		
			9	

Replace

| x15 x42 by x53 in sec. 6R | x42 x53 by T1 in sec. 7L | x35 in sec. 7R |

Use

| (i) imme-diately or (d) with one odd, one delay | 1 | d | d | 1 | d | 1 | 1 | d | 1 | d | 1 | d | 1 | d | d | 1 | d | d | 1 | d | d | d | 1 | d | 1 | d | 1 | 1 |

| pro gram line used for signal | 3-2 | 3-3 | 3-4 | 3-5 | 3-6 | 3-7 | 3-8 | 3-9 | 3-10 | 3-11 | 4-1 | 4-2 | 4-3 | 3-3 | 4-5 | 4-6 | 4-7 | 4-8 | 4-9 | 4-10 | 4-11 | 5-1 | 5-2 | 5-3 | 5-4 | 4-5 | 5-6 | 5-7 | 5-8 | 5-9 | 5-10 | 5-11 | 6-1 | 6-2 | 6-4 |

* It is assumed here that the function tables have been modified for the storage of programming data as suggested in Sec. 7.4. Furthermore, an adapter is used at the function output terminals to take information from digit terminals to program terminals.

multiplication (1) leading to multiplication (2) etc. For group A, the predominant sequence also procures the arguments and stimulates accumulators to receive the products. The program pulses for this predominant sequence are carried in program trays 7 and 8. For group B, the predominant sequence includes the stimulation of the high-speed multiplier program controls used and also the stimulation for receiving products from the product accumulator. An auxiliary program sequence (carried in program trays 3-6) obtains from function tables 1, 2, and 3 programming instructions for procuring the arguments for the multiplications of group B. Group C is handled in the same way as group B except for the manner of stimulating reception of the product which is described below. The predominating sequence goes to steppers G and either E or F for instructions as to which argument to use and which high-speed multiplier program control to stimulate for a multiplication in group D (the program pulses in this sequence are carried on lines 9-1 through 10-2). A third auxiliary sequence (whose program pulses are carried in trays 10 and 11) stimulates the reception of the products from the product accumulator for groups C and D. Stepper K of the master programmer controls this third sequence.

The set-up shown in Table 8-13 actually lists the events of sequence 2.1. Sequence 2.2 in which the terms $_6N_k$ are computed resembles sequence 2.1 except for the constants chosen for the multiplications of groups B, C, D, and E and the fact that reception of terms for the various N_k in accumulators 14, 16, 17, ..., 20 is through the β input channel. Sequence 4 is carried out in the same way as sequence 2 with the multiplication sequences A and B alternating. Sequence 5 in which the final results are printed is described in Section 9.5.

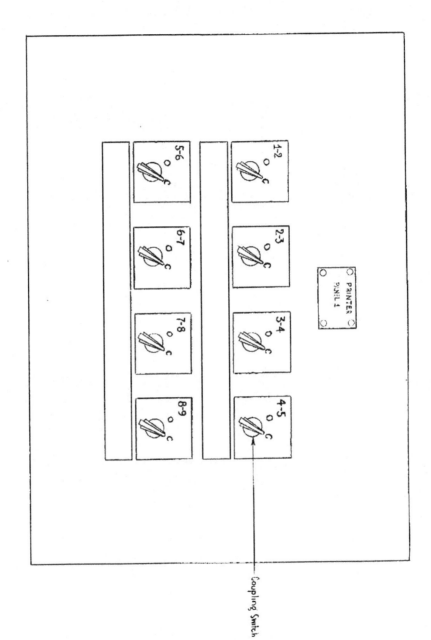

Coupling Switch

PRINTER
FRONT PANEL NO.1
PX-12-301R

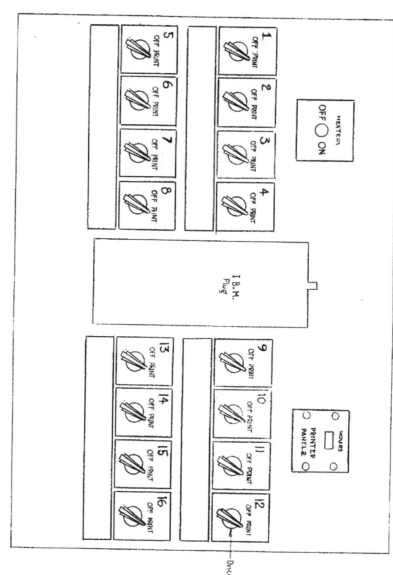

PRINTER
FRONT PANEL No.2
PL-12-302 R

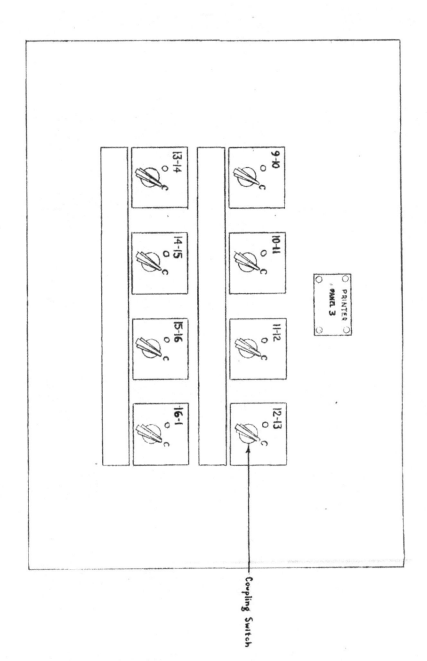

PRINTER
PANEL 3

9-10 10-11 11-12 12-13

13-14 14-15 15-16 16-1

Coupling Switch

PRINTER
FRONT PANEL NO.3
PX-12-303R

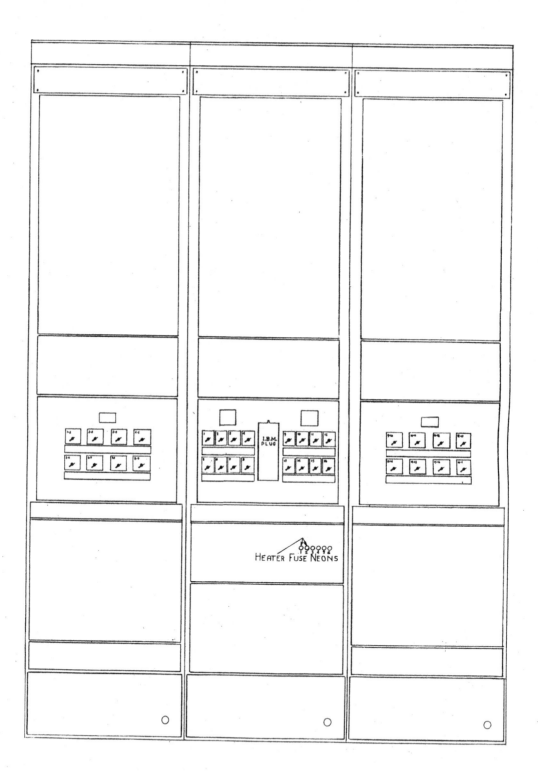

I.B.M.
PLUG

HEATER FUSE NEONS

MOORE SCHOOL of ELECTRICAL ENGINEERING
UNIVERSITY of PENNSYLVANIA

PRINTER
FRONT VIEW
PX-12-306

IX. PRINTER AND IBM GANG PUNCH

The ENIAC records 80 digits with as many as 16 signs on a standard IBM card (see Chapter VIII) by means of the printer which is connected to a modified IBM gang punch. Data to be recorded is delivered from the static outputs of master programmer decades and accumulator counters to the printer. Cards may be punched at the rate of approximately 100 per minute. When printing takes place, the counters from which data is recorded are tied up for about 150 ms. or 750 addition times which is only part of the total printing time (0.6 sec.).

The printer and IBM gang punch will be discussed in this chapter along the following lines: Sec. 9.1, programming circuits; Sec. 9.2, plug board of the IBM gang punch; Sec. 9.3, numerical circuits; Sec. 9.4, units connected to the printer. An illustrative problem is discussed in Sec. 9.5. The following diagrams will be referred to:

IBM Card Punch	PX-12-112
Printer Block Diagram	PX-12-307
Printer Front Panels	PX-12-301, 302, 303
Printer Front View	PX-12-306
IBM Punch Plug Board	PX-12-305
Initiating Unit Front View	PX-9-305
Initiating Unit Front Panel	PX-9-302

9.0 GENERAL SUMMARY OF THE IBM PUNCH AND PRINTER

Data stored in electronic counters of certain units of the ENIAC (see Sec. 9.4 for a list) is taken to an array of tubes in the printer by static output leads which run along a trough at the top of the ENIAC.

For each 5 digit group (of the total of 80 digits which can be punched on one card) there are 5 rows of 10 tubes each for the input of digital data. These tubes are labelled by a letter from A to E followed by a number between 0 and 9 inclusive. In addition, for each 5 digit group, there are 3 tubes for recording minus indication belonging to the group. Associated with each input tube is a printer relay. The printer relays for digits are labelled in the same way as are the tubes. The relays for minus sign indication are labelled M1, M2, and C_o. The last relay, C_o, is referred to as the carry-over relay. A printer relay is activated when its associated tube goes "on". The hold contacts on these relays are connected to the holding cam in the punch (see PX-12-112) so that when this cam breaks at time 9.5 in the card punching cycle[*] the printer relays release.

It is to be noted that the input tubes and printer relays are set up in accordance with the digital information as it is stored in the accumulators connected to the printer, i.e. complements[**] are set up as such. Complements are converted to negative numbers before punching takes place through the intervention of relays C_1 through C_5, the PM relays, M1 and M2, and the carry-over relay, C_o. The carry-over cam in the punch (see PX-12-112) also plays a part in this conversion.

In the IBM punch, as in the reader, there is an emitter with 12 stages (12, 11, 0, ..., 9 with stage 11 the minus punch stage). Certain stages of the emitter are connected through so called PM transfer contacts on the minus relays (M1 and M2) to contacts on the printer relays which

---

[*] The card punching cycle is divided into 14 units as is the card reading cycle discussed in Sec. 8.0.3.

[**] In this chapter, the word complement is restricted to mean the complement of a positive number.

register digital information. The latter, in turn, are connected through transfer contacts on the relays C_1 through C_5 to lines which carry signals for punches in the various columns to the computer result exit hubs on the IBM punch plug board (see PX-12-305). By means of plug board wiring, these signals can be delivered to the punch magnets (see PX-12-112) for any desired column of the card.

Each of the 80 punch magnets operates a lever with a little head on it. When a punch magnet is activated, the lever moves forward and a hammer bar in the punch hits the head of the lever against a punch shaft. Thus, a hole is punched in the column with which the lever is associated. Since, throughout the punching, the card moves forward in synchronism with the emitter, the hole is punched in the digit row corresponding to the activated printer relay for that column.

Data may be punched in all 80 columns of the card or, if desired, certain columns or 5 digit groups may be left blank. If the print switch of a 5 digit group (see PX-12-302), which has the positions "print" and "off", is set at off, the printer input tubes for the group of numbers do not set up and punch signals for that group are not delivered to the IBM punch (see Secs. 9.2 and 9.4). No punch is made in a column for which there is no plug board connection between computer result exit hub and punch magnet hub.

The total of 80 digits can be broken up into signed 5, 10, 15, ..., or 80 digit groups by means of the coupling switches on panels 1, and 3 of the printer. The numbering on these switches corresponds to the numbering of the printer relay groups (see Secs. 9.2 and 9.4). When a coupling switch is set at C, the 2 five digit groups whose numbers appear on that coupling

switch are considered as one for sign indication purposes and for complementation. If two adjacent coupling switches are set at C, the three groups
whose numbers appear on the switches are considered as a single 15 digit
group, etc. The use of PM adaptors is also involved in the coupling or
isolation of five digit groups (see Sec. 9.4).

Certain programming circuits for both the printer and punch are
located in the initiating unit of the ENIAC and others are in the punch
itself. Located at the initiating unit (see PX-12-307 and 9-302) are the
printer program pulse input terminal, start flip-flop (68, 69), finish
flip-flop (64, 65), synchronizing flip-flop (67, 68), program output pulse
transmitter (70 - 72) and terminal. Neons correlated with these flip-flops
are shown on PX-9-305. The start flip-flop operates a printer start relay
located in the printer.

On the punch there are start and stop switches and a master-
detail switch (which should, however, always be set at master). Inside the
punch are found a start relay (R10), the motor hold relay (R9 and H.D. No. 1
motor relay, relays 1 and 3 which are associated respectively with the die
card lever contact (Die CLC on PX-12-112) and the magazine card lever
contact (Mag. CLC .), and relay 23. The program controls in this and the
preceding paragraph have to do with starting and stopping the printer and
punch and will be discussed at greater length in Sec. 9.1.

In addition to the switches and relays mentioned above, two of
the cams in the punch, the interlock and reset cams, act as programming
circuits. The timing for these cams is shown on PX-12-112 and 12-307.
When the interlock cam makes contact, and when the starting relay located
in the printer (see PX-12-307) is activated as a result of the reception of

a program pulse by the printer program pulse input terminal, the input tubes are connected to 20V, which allows all groups with print switch set at print to set up. When the interlock cam breaks (12.8-13.3), the input tubes cannot set up. The reset cam which makes in the period 11.2 to 11.8 provides a reset signal for the start flip-flop (68, 69) and sets the printer finish flip-flop (64, 65) which results, finally, in the transmission of a program output pulse by the printer (see Sec. 9.1).

9.1 PROGRAMMING CIRCUITS OF THE PRINTER AND IBM PUNCH

A program pulse received at the printer program pulse input terminal on the initiating unit flips the printer start flip-flop (68, 69) into the abnormal state. The resulting signal from the start flip-flop energizes the start relay in the printer.

Provided that there is at least one card in the magazine (so that Mag. CLC is closed and relay 3 is activated) and provided that there is a card in the punch position (so that Die CLC is closed and relay 1 is activated), the signal from the printer start relay carried to the punch over circuit I-11 activates R23. As long as the printer stop switch is not thrown and under the conditions noted above for Mag. CLC and Die CLC the circuit to the punch start relay (R10) through R23 BL is now closed so that R10 is activated. Now, with contact R10 BL closed, the motor hold relay (R9) and the H.D. No. 1 motor relay in parallel with it are activated so that the drive motor starts up. Also, with R10 BU closed the printer clutch is activated so that a card is pushed through the punching apparatus. R10 holds through its hold contact R10 AL until cam P5 breaks at time 9 in the punch cycle.

With all the cards in the magazine and no card in the punch position, the printer cannot be started by the procedure described in the previous paragraph since Die CLC is open when there is no card in the punch position. If the start switch on the punch is depressed first, one or more cards (depending on how long this switch is depressed) move out of the magazine so that subsequently the punch and printer can be stimulated to operate by a program pulse received at Pi on the initiating unit.

The chronological operation of the punch, once the printer start relay is activated[*], is summarized in Table 9-1.

The signal from the reset cam (during 11.2-11.8) is taken back to the printer program control circuit in the initiating unit via line 38. This signal resets the printer start flip-flop and sets the printer finish flip-flop. With the printer finish flip-flop in the abnormal state, a CPP is gated through 66 so that the printer synchronizing flip-flop is set. Thus, gate 69 is opened to allow a CPP to pass to the program output pulse terminal. Notice that the printer start flip-flop is reset so that it can recognize that a new printing program is to take place if another program input pulse is received and a program output pulse is transmitted about 750 addition times after Pi is stimulated or about 1/4 through the punching cycle.

If the printer is engaged in a printing program and another program input pulse reaches Pi before the start flip-flop is reset, naturally, the reception of this second program input pulse is not noted. Therefore, if printing programs are to follow closely on one another,

[*]About 10 ms elapse between the reception of a program pulse at Pi and the beginning of the card punch cycle.

TABLE 9-1

CHRONOLOGICAL OPERATION OF PUNCH

Time in Card Punch Cycle	Event
D = 13.5	Punch starts - interlock cam is making contact
14.5	Holding cam makes
12.8	Interlock cam breaks
11.0	Minus punches are made
11.2	Reset cam makes
11.8	Reset cam breaks
0 . . . 9	Digit punches are made
9.5	Holding cam breaks so that printer relays release
13.3	Interlock cam makes again so that input tubes can set up for next printing
13.5	Punch stops unless Pi received program pulse during period 11.2 - 13.5

the programming sequences that culminate in a pulse to Pi should be initiated by a program output pulse from Po, the printer's program output pulse terminal, so that there will be no danger of the printer's receiving a program input pulse while the start flip-flop is in the abnormal state.

If the printer receives a program input pulse while engaged in printing but after the start flip-flop has been reset, then the start flip-flop is again flipped into the abnormal state. The printer and punch continue with the punching cycle in which they are engaged. Since the interlock cam breaks at time 12.8 (before the start flip-flop is reset) the printer input tubes cannot set up for the second printing program until at least time 13.3 in the punch cycle when the interlock cam once again makes contact (see Sec. 9.3 and Table 9-1). When the first punch cycle is completed, the printer and punch immediately start a second cycle in the event that Pi is pulsed between the resetting of the start flip-flop and the completion of the cycle.

When the interlock cam breaks at time 12.8 (without a safety factor, about 150 ms after Pi is stimulated) the printer input tubes drop out their information so that the units which are connected statically to the printer are free for computing purposes again. Before this time, such units cannot be called upon for computational programs. Program sequences which require computations in units connected to   printer groups whose print switches are in the print position and which partly parallel printing should be initiated by the program output pulse from the printer, so that there will be no danger on this score. Units not connected to the printer are, of course, not affected by printing programs and can be used for computing programs throughout printing if such a set-up is desired.

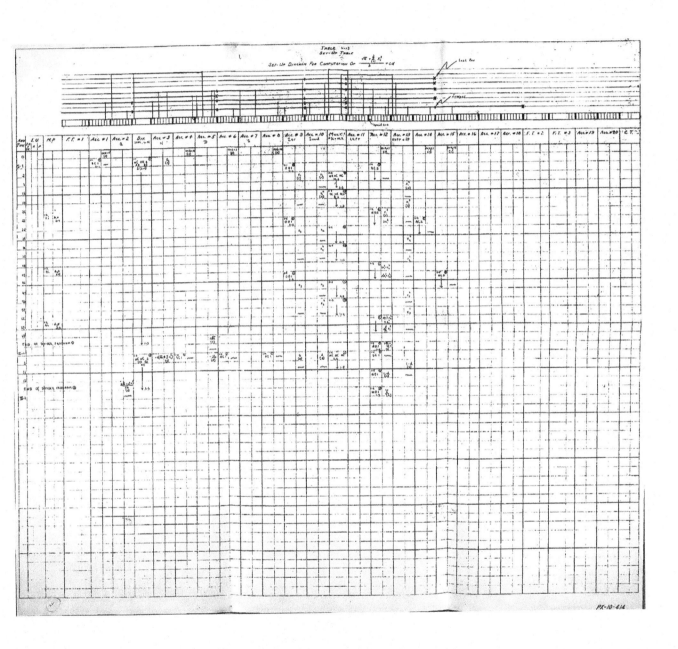

Table No. 3
Set-Up Table

Set-Up Diagram For Computation Of $\frac{\sqrt{x} + \frac{a}{(x)} x_1^2}{2} + r\,c\,d$

PX-10-414

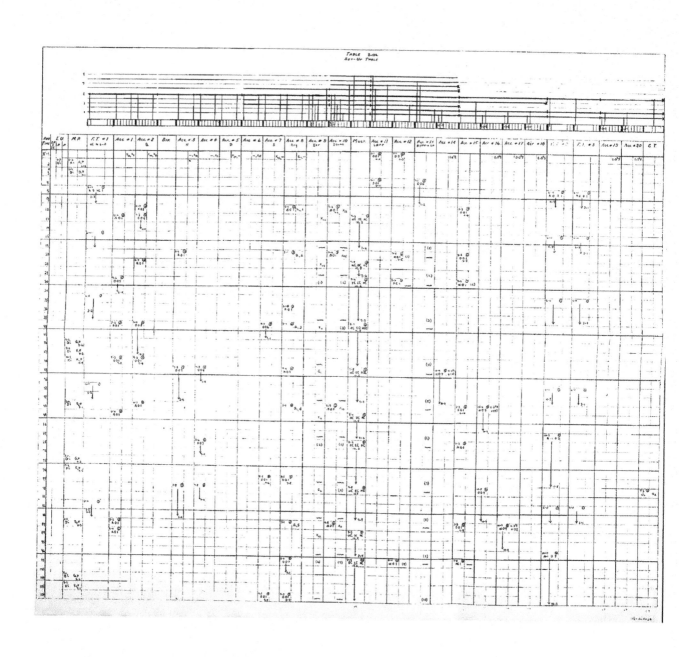

Table 3-132
Set-Up Table

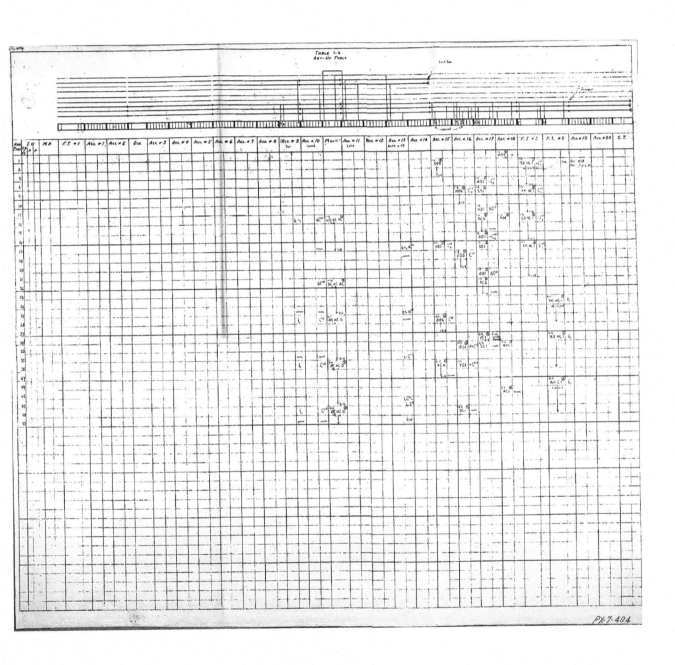

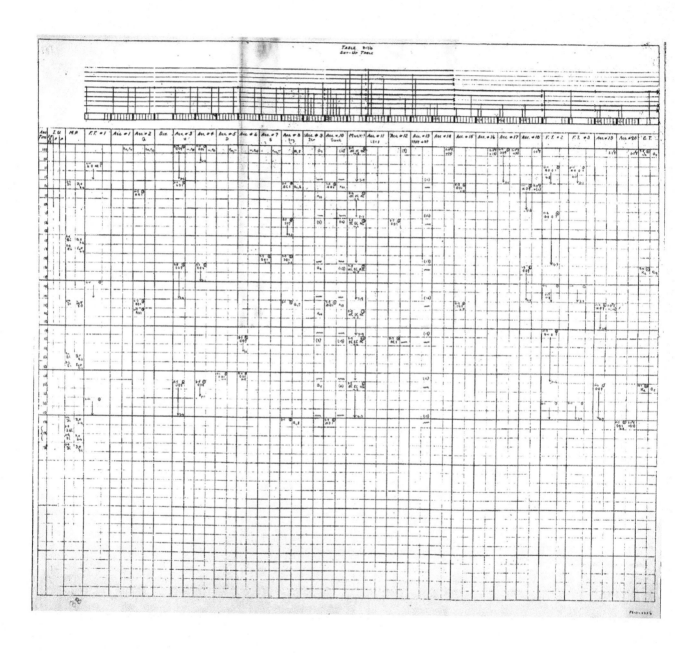

Table 2-136
Set-Up Table

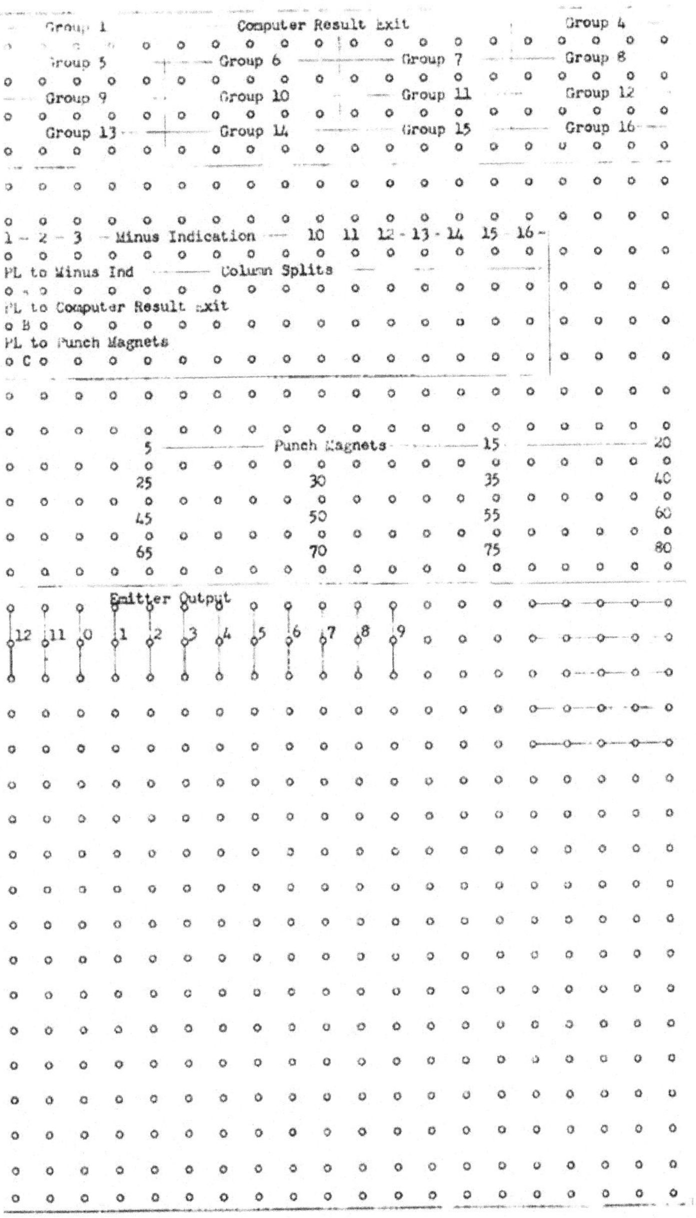

Group 1   Computer Result Exit   Group 4

Group 5   Group 6   Group 7   Group 8

Group 9   Group 10   Group 11   Group 12

Group 13   Group 14   Group 15   Group 16

1 — 2 — 3 — Minus Indication — 10 11 12 - 13 - 14 15 16 —

PL to Minus Ind ——— Column Splits —

PL to Computer Result Exit

o B o   PL to Punch Magnets

o C o

5 ——— Punch Magnets ——— 15   20

25   30   35   40

45   50   55   60

65   70   75   80

Emitter Output

12 11 0 1 2 3 4 5 6 7 8 9

When the interlock cam makes contact again at time 13.3, the printer input tubes do not set up again in a given punch cycle unless Pi receives a program input pulse during the period 11.2-13.5 since the input tubes are connected to the interlock cam through a contact on the start relay.

In the printer, as in the reader, a design is used in which a pulse stimulates successively the unsynchronized flip-flop, a gate, the synchronizing flip-flop, another gate, and the transmitter. This insures the emission of a program output pulse synchronized with the pulses in the rest of the ENIAC and of the proper shape.

It is to be noted that in this discussion a number of elements in the punch such as R22, R7, R8, R2, and R14 have not been mentioned. Discussion of these relays which, in a standard summary punch are functionally significant, has been omitted since in the card punch, as it has been modified for connection with the printer, they serve no logical purpose.

9.2 IBM GANG PUNCH PLUG BOARD

The IBM gang punch plug board is shown on PX-12-305. The computer result exit hubs appear at the top. These hubs are classified in 16 groups of 5 hubs each. The numbering of the groups here corresponds to the numbering of the groups of printer tubes and associated relays in the printer (see Sec. 9.4 for a list of the units connected to the various printer groups). From the printer relays that store digital information the computer result exit hubs receive signals via the cable that connects the printer to the punch. Each minus indication hub receives a signal from a contact on the M2 relay of the printer group bearing the same number as appears above the minus indication hub, if that printer group stores a complement.

PLUG BOARD FOR GANG PUNCH

PLUGGING FOR NEGATIVE NUMBERS

The 10 digits stored in the printer relays for groups 1 and 2 are to be printed in the columns 1-10 of the card (b,....,d). Minus sign indication for these digits (a) is to be punched in column 1 (c).

The digits for the first and second places of printer group 12 (f and h) are to be punched in columns 96 (h) and 17 (g) respectively. The minus punch for group 12 (e) is to appear in column 17 (g).

The 16 groups of 3 column split hubs on the gang punch plugboard are similar in operation to the group selection hubs on the reader plugboard but differ from the group selection hubs in purpose. On PX-12-112, it can be seen that there is normally a circuit from the B to C hubs but that when the column split relays (R11, R12, R17, and R18) are activated at the time when cam P2 makes (13.0-11.6) the circuit is from the A to C hubs. Thus, while minus punches are made there is a circuit from A to C, and while digit punches are made, there is a circuit from B to C.

The 80 punch magnet hubs are connected to the punch magnets each of which has responsibility for one of the 80 columns on the card.

The computer result exit hubs for printer groups which will always be used for recording positive numbers may be connected directly to the punch magnet hubs for the columns in which those numbers are to be punched. Special plugboard connections must be made for printer groups that record numbers which may or may not be complements. For such a printer group, the correspondingly numbered minus indication hub should be connected to an A hub of the column split hubs. The computer result exit hub which receives a signal for the digit to be punched in the same column as the minus punch for the group is connected to the B hub below the A hub chosen. The C hub is then connected to the punch magnet hub corresponding to the column in which both the digit and minus punch are to be made. Connections are made directly from computer result exit hubs to punch magnet hubs for the columns in which the minus punch does not occur. An example of the plugging required for the first and last digits of a ten digit negative number when the minus punch is to appear in column 1 is shown on PX-12-305 R1. Notice that while 2 printer groups record this number, only one minus indication

PLUG BOARD FOR GANG PUNCH

USE OF THE EMITTER OUTPUT HUBS AND COMMON TERMINALS

Line a: A zero punch is to be made in column 61.

Lines b,c,d,e,f: A 12 punch (b) is to be made in columns 30 (c), 40 (d), 60 (e), and 80 (f).

hub is connected to an A hub of the column splits. This minus indication hub could just as well have been the group 2 hub instead of the group 1 hub as shown on PX-12-305 R1.

Corresponding to each of the 12 stages of the emitter there are 3 hubs. If an emitter output hub is connected to a punch magnet hub, the digit corresponding to the emitter output hub is punched in the column associated with the punch magnet hub whenever a card is punched. By means of connections from emitter output to punch magnet hub, a given digit punch can be made in as many as three columns.

To the right of the emitter output hubs are 5 groups of common terminals. All 5 terminals connected by a horizontal line are common. By plugging from an emitter output hub to one of a group of 5 common terminals and from each of the other four common terminals of the group to punch magnet hubs, the punch is instructed to punch the digit selected in 4 columns (see the illustrative example of PX-12-305 R2).

9.3 NUMERICAL CIRCUITS OF THE PRINTER AND PUNCH

If the print switch of a 5 digit group is in the print position, at the beginning of the card punching cycle while the interlock cam is making contact, the cathodes of all 53 printer input tubes for the group are connected through a contact on the printer start relay to a source of the required voltage for allowing the set up of these tubes. Thus when a program input pulse is received at Pi, the digit tubes connected through the static leads to the stages of counters in the abnormal state go on. The tubes associated with relays M1, M2 and C_o are connected to the static lead from the M stage of the PM counter of the unit from which the digits for the group come so that these tubes go on only if the number to be printed is a complement. Thus if the number M 1 234 500 000 is stored in an accumulator which has its PM counter and five left hand decade counters connected to group 1 of the printer, the minus tubes M1, M2, and C_0 and the digit tubes A1, B2, C3, D4, and E5 go on at this time. The "on" tubes activate the relays associated with them.

In addition to the hold contacts, two contacts for each of the digit relays, in other words, a total of 100 contacts for a 5 digit group, are arranged in a 10 by 10 array. PX-12-307 shows these contacts arranged so that the horizontal lines $2i-1$ (where $i = 1, 2, ..., 5$ and where $i = 1$ identifies the bottom line) have the contacts for the relays used to represent the digits 9, 8, 7, ..., 0 and the horizontal lines $2i$ have the contacts for relays used to represent the digits 0, 9, 8, ..., 1 reading from left to right. Each vertical column of relay contacts is connected to one of 2 stages of the emitter through a PM transfer contact on either relay M1 or M2. The labelling on PX-12-307 indicates how these vertical lines are connected to stages j or $9-j$ of the emitter (reading from left to right $j = 9$ to 0) according as the PM relays M1 and M2 are in the normal state (when the group is a positive number) or the abnormal state (when the group is a complement).

In this manner the process of converting a complement into a negative number by subtracting the digits in each decade place from 9 is provided for. To complete the conversion, it is necessary to subtract from 10 instead of 9 the extreme right hand digit of the complement or the first from the right non zero digit of the complement and to leave the zero digits to the right of the first non zero digit. For this purpose, the relays C_1 through C_5 are used. If the coupling switches of a given 5 digit group are in the 0 position, and the number set up in the printer relays for that group is a complement (so that relay C_0 is activated), then, when the carry over cam makes (13.6-9.4), the relay C_5 which is associated with the first place at the right of the 5 digit group is activated. Relay C_4 is activated only if C_5 is activated and contact EO is closed (as is the case when the first from the right digit of the group is a zero). Similarly, C_3 is activated only if C_5 and C_4 are and contact DO is closed, etc. The case in which two or more 5 digit groups are coupled together by means of the C setting on one or more coupling switches is similar to this except that it is the C_5 relay for the group of highest number which is activated if the number registered in the printer groups is a complement. The C_4, C_3, ... relays for this highest numbered group are activated or not depending on the presence or absence of zeros in the right hand places of the complement.

Now either an odd (reading from the bottom up) line or its immediate even successor is connected through a transfer contact (on one of the relays C_1 through C_5) to a line which carries a punch signal back to the computer result exit hubs. An even numbered line is connected to a punch signal line only when the relay C_1, C_2, ..., or C_5 corresponding to that punch signal line is activated; otherwise punch signals come from the odd numbered lines.

A signal for a digit punch results from the establishment of a circuit from an emitter stage through a PM transfer contact, through a contact on a digit relay through a transfer contact to a computer result exit hub. A signal for a minus (11) punch reaches a minus indication hub as a result of a circuit from stage 11 of the emitter through a contact on relay M2.

Table 9-2 illustrates the process of converting data stored in the printer relays into punches on an IBM card. It is assumed that the coupling switch for the printer relay group in which the numbers are stored

TABLE 9-2

OPERATION OF NUMERICAL CIRCUITS OF PRINTER AND PUNCH
Coupling Switches set at 0

NUMBER to be PUNCHED	EMITTER STAGE	is connectd through PM TRANSFER CONTACT	to a Contact on RELAY	which is connected through TRANSFER CONTACT	to COMPUTER RESULT EXIT HUB
P 13057	0	M1	C0	C_3	3
	1	M1	A1	C_1	1
	3	M1	B3	C_2	2
	5	M2	D5	C_4	4
	7	M2	E7	C_5	5
M 13057	11		Minus punch is made		
	3	M2 (A)	E7	C_5 (A)	5
	4	M2 (A)	D5	C_4	4
	6	M1 (A)	B3	C_2	2
	8	M1 (A)	A1	C_1	1
	9	M1 (A)	C0	C_3	3
M 13570	11		Minus punch is made		
	0	M2 (A)	E0	C_5 (A)	5
	3	M2 (A)	D7	C_4 (A)	4
	4	M2 (A)	C5	C_3	3
	6	M1 (A)	B3	C_2	2
	8	M1 (A)	A1	C_1	1

is in the 0 position. The symbol (A) after a relay number indicates that the relay is activated. The table is arranged to indicate the chronological order in which the punches are made. The punching of the first number P 13057 is a straightforward example of what happens when a positive number is punched. The case, M 13057, illustrates the conversion of a complement into a negative number, and the case, M 13570, illustrates the conversion of a complement with at least one zero at the far right.

9.4 UNITS CONNECTED TO THE PRINTER

The static outputs of the counters in any accumulator or in the master programmer can be connected to the printer input tubes. To deliver information for five digits and a sign to the printer, a 55 conductor cable is used. Each of 50 leads connects the static outputs of 1 stage of one of the 5 decade counters to a printer input tube . Another lead delivers the static output of the M stage of the PM counter to the minus indication tubes associated with the 50 printer tubes for the 5 digits*. The 16 cables used for the 80 digits and 16 minus signs that can be punched are carried in a trough which runs along the top of the ENIAC.

At the time of writing of this report, the following connections have been established between units of the ENIAC and printer groups:

*When 10 digits and sign are printed from a given accumulator, the static output of stage M is connected to the PM load in each of 2 static output cables through the use of adaptor A on PX-12-114. When 5 digits without sign indication are printed from an accumulator or from the master programmer, no connection is made to the PM load in the static cable, and adaptor B shown on PX-12-114 is connected to the socket in the printer which goes to the PM tubes of the 5 digit group.

Printer Groups	Connected to
1*	Master Programmer decades 14 - 18
2 and 3	Accumulator 13 - 10 decades and PM
4 and 5	Accumulator 14 - 10 decades and PM
6	Accumulator 15* - decades 6-10 and PM
7 and 8	Accumulator 16 - 10 decades and PM
9 and 10	Accumulator 17 - 10 decades and PM
11 and 12	Accumulator 18 - 10 decades and PM
13 and 14	Accumulator 19 - 10 decades and PM
15 and 16	Accumulator 20 - 10 decades and PM.

The static outputs of decades 1-5 of accumulator 15 are also delivered to the printer in the static output trough but the leads are not plugged into the printer input sockets. If it is desired to print 10 digits from accumulator 15 and none from the master programmer, the leads from the master programmer should be pulled out and those from accumulator 15 plugged in instead. Notice that a ten digit negative number cannot be printed from accumulator 15 since there is no way to couple together groups 6 and 1. It is, however, possible to print either of the following from accumulator 15:

1) A ten digit positive number
2) Two five digit numbers with the left hand number having any sign and the right hand number only a plus sign.

The connections made to the printer make it possible to use the printer in a moderately flexible way. For example, even though ten decades of an accumulator are connected to the printer, it is not necessary that all ten columns be punched when data from this accumulator is printed. If there are five or fewer significant figures of a result to be printed from an accumulator which has 10 decades connected to the printer and if these figures are located in the five left hand or five right hand decade places of the accumulator, the punching of columns in which the non-significant figures are located can be avoided by setting the print switches of the higher or lower numbered five digit group respectively to off. If the significant figures are at the left of the accumulator the coupling switch which carries the numbers of the 2 printer groups connected to that accumulator must certainly be set at 0 so that complementation will be carried out correctly. If the significant figures are at the right of the accumulator, the coupling switch may be set at either C or 0.

Another method which eliminates the punching of non-significant zeros consists of omitting plug board connections between punch magnets and those computer result exit hubs which receive the non-significant zeros.

Another procedure which is possible under certain circumstances consists of printing two five digit numbers from an accumulator which has 10 decades and its PM connected to the printer. When the two numbers stored in the accumulator always have the same sign, the standard PM adaptor labelled A on PX-12-114 which connects stage M of the accumulator's PM counter to the static leads which go to the printer PM tubes for both five digit groups is used. The coupling switch for the two printer groups is set at 0 so that tens complements are taken in converting each number into a negative number when the common sign is M.

When one of the five digit numbers is always positive and the other may be either positive or negative, the static connection from the accumulator's PM counter to the PM tubes for the positive group is broken for, otherwise, complements would be taken for both five digit groups and both groups would be printed as negative numbers. In this case, moreover, the adaptor labelled S on PX-12-114 is connected to the socket in the printer which goes to the PM tubes of the positive group. This adaptor grounds the grid of the PM tubes. The coupling switch associated with the two printer groups is set at 0 so that a tens complement will be taken in converting numbers with sign M into negative numbers.

If both five digit numbers may have different signs and if one of the five digit numbers is not known to be always positive, there is no way to print both numbers correctly from one accumulator.

9.5 ILLUSTRATIVE PROBLEM SET-UP

The printing sequence of the problem discussed, in part, in Chapter VIII is taken here to illustrate the use of the printer. The problem may be summarized briefly as follows: Six numbers, N_k (for $0 \leqslant k \leqslant 5$), are formed in accumulators 14 and 16-20 by the end of sequence 4 (see Tables 8-8 and 8-10. Since the significant figures switches on these accumulators are set at 6 (see Figure 8-3), the values are correct to 6 figures. The four irrelevant right hand digits, however, have not been deleted. Master programmer decades 14-18 (associated with stepper C) store the identification number for the results.

In sequence 5, the numbers N_k are printed and the reading of constants for the next computation proceeds in parallel. When printing is completed, selective clearing takes place. The program output pulse from a selective clearing transceiver provides a reader interlock pulse. The reader program output pulse goes back to the master programmer (see Figure

PLUG BOARD FOR GANG PUNCH

PLUGBOARD WIRING FOR PRINTING IDENTIFICATION NUMBERS AND VALUES OF N_k

Lines a, b, c: wiring for identification number

Lines d, e, f, g: wiring for first and last digits of N_0

Lines h, i, j, k, l: wiring for first and last digits of N_5

8-2 from which will come a program output pulse to stimulate the computations for the next system of equations.

The set-up for this sequence, sequence 5, is shown on Table 9-3 and Figure 9-1 (a and b) is a set-up diagram for this sequence. Master programmer decades 14-18 are connected to printer group 1 and, therefore, the coupling switches 1-2 and 16-1 are set at 0 (see Figure 9-1). Since 6 digits are being printed from accumulators 14, 16, 17, ..., 20, coupling switches 4-5, 7-8, 9-10, 11-12, 13-14, and 15-16 are set at C. All other coupling switches are set at 0. The print switches for the 13 printer groups used here are set at print with all others set at off.

A possible plug board wiring for printing the numbers involved is shown on PX-12-305 R3. Notice that even though 10 digits are set up in the printer groups for each value of N_k, only 6 digits are printed since connections from computer result exit hubs to punch magnet hubs for the four digits at the right in each pair of five digit printer groups are omitted.

TABLE 9-3

SET-UP FOR SEQUENCE 5 – EVALUATION OF W_K

Add. Time	Selective Clear	Reader	Printer	Accumulator 14	Accumulator 16	Accumulator 17	Accumulator 18	Accumulator 19	Accumulator 20
V-0				$N_1+0.05_5$	$N_1+0.05_5$	$N_2+0.05_5$	$N_3+0.05_5$	$N_4+0.05_5$	$N_5+0.05_5$
V-1		2-5 P₁	2-5 / 001 / 2-3						
2		2-3 R₁							
VI-1			Po 2-10						
2	2-10 C₁ 2-7	2-7 R₁							
3									
VII-1		Ro 1-1							

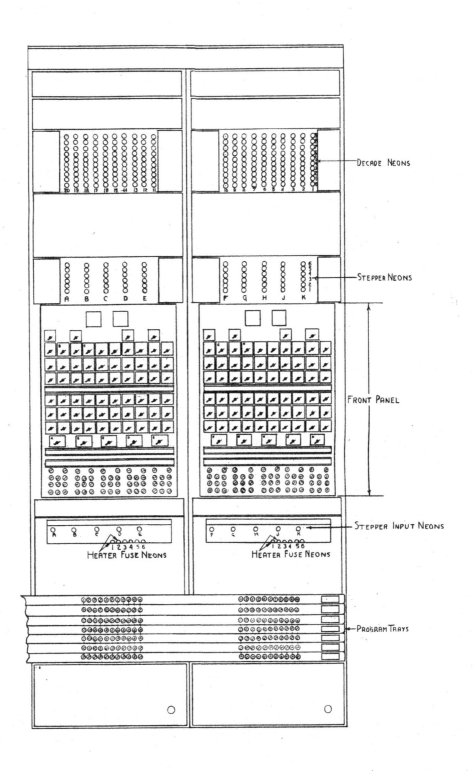

Decade Neons

Stepper Neons

Front Panel

Stepper Input Neons

Heater Fuse Neons

Program Trays

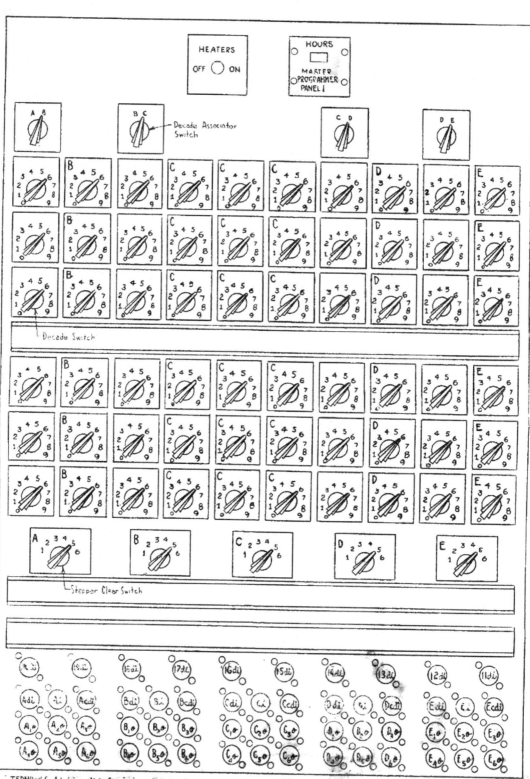

TERMINALS Ai, bi --- Ki - Stepper input
TERMINALS Adi --- Kdi - Stepper direct input
TERMINALS Acdi --- Kcdi - Stepper clear direct input

TERMINALS A$_1 o$, A$_2 o$, ---, A$_6 o$
Stepper output terminals associated
respectively with stages 1, 2, ---, 6

MASTER PROGRAMMER
FRONT PANEL NO. 1
PX-8-301R

TERMINALS 1di, 2di---, 20di — Decade direct input terminals associated
respectively with decades 1,2, ---,20.(counted from right to left).

MASTER PROGRAMMER
FRONT PANEL NO. 2
PX-8-302R

X. MASTER PROGRAMMER

The master programmer is a central programming unit whose primary function is to direct and stimulate the performance of the program sequences of various levels which enter into a computation. While the master programmer is capable of stimulating the performance of individual programs, it is usually not required for this purpose. It is, however, essential to use the master programmer to accomplish the iteration of a program sequence into a chain (see Section 1.4.) or to link together chains and program sequences. The master programmer can link programs together either serially or on the basis of magnitude discrimination. The master programmer may also be used as a counter in that it is capable of storing numbers (without sign, however) and also of adding by counting pulses. This latter feature enables the operator to store values, say of the independent variable, in the master programmer. Certain decades of the master programmer have been connected to the printer so that a number stored in these decades can be printed.

Sections 1, 2, and 3 of this chapter are concerned with the components of the master programmer. The programming of the master programmer is discussed in Section 4, and the uses of the master programmer are considered in Section 5. Illustrative set ups involving the master programmer are found in Section 6. Reference will be made to the following diagrams:

Master Programmer Front View	PX-8-303
Master Programmer Front Panels	PX-8-301, 8-302
Master Programmer Block Diagram	PX-8-304

10.0 GENERAL SUMMARY

The master programmer has ten steppers (identified by the letters A-K on PX-8-301 and 302). The basic property of a stepper is that it has one input and 6 outputs. By means of the 6 output terminals, a pulse received at a stepper input terminal from a given program line can be routed to one of 6 program lines.

Each stepper has a 6 stage counter. The output terminal through which a pulse is emitted when a stepper input is stimulated depends on the stage of the stepper counter at the time when the pulse is transmitted.

The master programmer also includes 20 master programmer decades (numbered 1-20 beginning with the extreme right hand decade on panel and ending with the extreme left hand decade on panel 1). By means of decade associator switches as many as five decades can be combined into a group, and, as a group, associated with a stepper.

The group of decades associated with a stepper counts one each time the stepper is pulsed. Each decade has associated with it 6 decade switches, one for each stage of a stepper counter. When the stepper counter is in stage s and when the decades associated with a stepper register the number set up on the decade switches belonging to stage s of the associated stepper, the stepper advances from stage s to stage s+1 and the decades associated with the stepper clear to zero. Thus, the decades and decade switches make it possible for a stepper to emit a pulse from the output terminal associated with stage s of the stepper on the number of occasions specified by the settings of the stage s decade switches and then to emit a pulse from the output terminal associated with stage s+1 of the stepper counter.

Besides the preceding there are other features of the master programmer which provide means of controlling the stepper counters and decade counters. Each decade counter has a direct input (labelled by the decade number followed by di). Each pulse received at a decade direct input terminal cycles the decade counter one stage. Similarly each pulse received at a stepper direct input terminal (di preceded by the stepper letter) cycles the stepper counter 1 stage. A stepper is cleared to stage 1 by pulse input to its clear direct input. (cdi preceded by the stepper letter). A stepper clear switch associated with each stepper unit makes it possible to use a stepper counter as a c stage counter where $1 \leq c \leq 6$.

10.1. DECADE ASSOCIATOR SWITCHES

Certain decades are permanently associated with one another and, as a group, with a particular stepper. For example, decades 15, 16, and 17 are permanently associated with one another and with stepper C. Other decades (decades 12, 14, 18, and 20 on panel 1, for example) can be associated by means of a decade associator switch with either of the 2 steppers whose identifying letters appear on the switch and thus, with the other decades permanently connected to that stepper. Notice that steppers A and F may be used without any associated decades.

The decades of a group are connected to one another for the purpose of carry-over and, as a group, are associated with a stepper to provide one of the signals which can cycle the stepper counter at certain times (see Section 10.2.2.).

10.2. MASTER PROGRAMMER DECADES

The master programmer decades will be described with reference to the diagram for decade 11 on PX-8-304. Each master programmer decade consists of 6 decade switches each with an associated inverter (B41, 42, or 43), and a decade ring counter with a clear circuit (inverters 1[*] and B45 and gate B44), a carry over circuit (gate 28 and tubes 30), and an input circuit containing pulse standardizer 25-27 and buffer 31. Neons associated with stages 0 through 9 of the decade counters are shown on PX-8-303.

10.2.1. Decade Counter: Input and Carry Over Circuits

Decade counter D (where $1 \leq D \leq 20$) can be cycled by input to its decade direct input terminal, from the carry over circuit of decade D-1 (if there is a decade D-1 associated with it), or, in the case of units decade of a group associated with a stepper, from the stepper input circuit (see Section 10.3.1.) Pulse input to the decade direct input cycles the decade counter immediately, but there is a one addition time delay between the pulsing of the stepper input and the cycling of the decade counter which results (see Section 10.3.1.).

When a given decade counter is cycled to stage 9, gate 28 (in the case of decade 11) opens so that the next pulse delivered to the decade not only cycles the counter back to stage zero, but also passes through the gate and tubes 30 to be delivered to the next decade at the left if there is one. The time between successive digit pulses is not sufficient to allow safely for the carry over process. For this reason digit pulses should not be fed to the decade direct input terminal (also see Section 10.2.2.). Input to the decade derived from pulsing the stepper input terminal (see Section 10.3.) comes at the time of the CPP so that there is sufficient time for carry over.

*Tube 1 and the decade ring counter are mounted in a plug-in unit.

10.2.2. Decade Switches and Decade Counter Clear Circuits

Each decade switch is correlated with one of the 6 stages of the stepper counter associated with the decade. A decade switch in the top row is associated with stage 1; a switch in the bottom row, with stage 6.

The operator sets up on the decade switches corresponding to stage s of a stepper the number which the decades associated with the stepper must register for the stepper to advance from stage s to stage s+1 and for the decade counters to be cleared back to zero. For example, if decades 12 and 11 are associated with stepper E and if the switches in the second row from the top are set at 3 and 8 respectively, then stepper E will advance from stage 2 to 3 and the decades will clear back to zero when this pair of decades stores the number 38.

Each point on a decade switch is connected to the normally positive output of one of the stages of the decade counter. The negative signal from a stage in the abnormal state turns off the inverter associated with a switch set at the corresponding number. All inverters for the stage s decade switches are connected to the stage s stepper cycling gate (see Section 10.3.2.) of the associated stepper. When the stepper counter is in stage s, the stage s stepper cycling gate emits a signal provided that all the inverters for stage s switches of decades associated with the stepper are turned off.

The output of the stepper cycling gate is taken (through an inverter) to the gates numbered 44 (preceded by B, C, ..., or L) of the decades associated with the stepper. The CPP passed through these gates clears the decade counters associated with the stepper. The output of the stepper cycling gates also goes (through inverter 64) to gate 63 in the stepper. The CPP which is thus allowed to pass through gate 63 causes the stepper counter to cycle one stage at the same time that the associated decades are being cleared. The necessity for providing sufficient time for gates 44 and 63 to set up before the arrival of the CPP they are to pass is a second reason for feeding only program pulses to the decade direct input terminals (also see Section 10.3.2.2.)

10.3. STEPPERS

Each of the 10 steppers (A-K) consists of a 6 stage stepper counter, a stepper-counter input, a stepper clear circuit, a stepper input (as distinguished from the stepper-counter input), and 6 outputs. For convenience, the elements of these circuits will be identified with reference to the drawing for stepper E.

The stepper input circuit consists of a stepper input terminal, an input flip-flop (66, 67) and input gate (69), buffers (65 and 70) and an inverter (68). Each of the 6 outputs consists of an output gate (61-69), a standard transmitter, and an output terminal.

The stepper-counter input circuit includes a pulse standardizer (21-23) an inverter (61) and buffer (62) and can be entered either through the stepper direct input terminal and buffer 61 or through the circuit containing the stepper cycling gates (B, C 48-50), inverter 64, and gate 63.

The stepper clear circuit contains an inverter (C46), the stepper clear direct input terminal and buffer B46, the stepper clear switch, inverter B46 and gate B47.

10.3.1. Stepper Input and Output Circuits

A program pulse received at the end of addition time t or a group of digit pulses received early (see below) in addition time t+1 by the stepper input terminal sets the input flip-flop. The normally negative output of this flip-flop then opens gate 69 so that a CPP passes through at the end of addition time t+1. It is to be noted that if <u>digit pulses</u> are <u>fed</u> to the <u>stepper input</u>, they <u>must be pulses which begin to be emitted before the 4P</u> (i.e. no later than pulse time 6) in order to allow time for gate 69 to set up and pass the CPP which arrives at the end of the addition time. Since, in general, one does not know in advance the magnitude of a number, this restriction on the digit pulses which may be delivered to the stepper input is equivalent to saying that the only digit pulses which may be brought to a stepper are sign pulses since the 9P for sign begin to be emitted early enough in the addition time cycle.

The output of gate 69 has three effects:

1) It resets the input flip-flop*.

2) Passed through inverter 68, cathode follower 70, and buffer A43, it causes the associated group of decade counters to be cycled one stage in units place.

3) Passed through inverter 68 and cathode follower 70, it is delivered to the stepper output gates.

Each of the 6 output gates is controlled by the normally positive output (through an inverter) of a stage of the stepper counter. Thus the pulse from cathode follower 70 is passed through the gate and the transmitter corresponding to the stage in which the stepper counter is at the end of addition time t+1.

If, when the stepper counter is in stage s, the stepper input alone is pulsed, the output pulse is thus emitted from the terminal associated with stage s. It is, however, possible to pulse both the stepper input and stepper direct input

---

*Since this flip-flop is reset at the end of addition time t+1, a stepper input must not be pulsed in successive addition times. The same restriction is also pertinent to the use of program controls on other units.

terminal (see Section 10.3.2.1.) at the same time. If this is done, the output pulse is emitted from the terminal corresponding to the stage to which the stepper counter is cycled by the end of addition time t+1 as a result of the pulses delivered to the stepper direct input terminal.

10.3.2. Cycling a Stepper Counter

A stepper counter which has associated decades can be cycled either by pulses received at the stepper direct input terminal or as a result of the fact that the decades have counted to the number set on the decade switches corresponding to the stage in which the counter is. A stepper without decades (steppers A and F can be used in this way) can be cycled only by pulse input to the stepper direct input terminal.

10.3.2.1. Stepper Direct Input

A pulse received at a stepper direct input terminal is delivered through tubes 61 and 62 and the pulse standardizer to the stepper counter. Each pulse, whether program or digit, delivered to the stepper direct input causes the counter to be cycled one stage immediately. Notice, no output pulse is emitted when a stepper direct input is pulsed.

10.3.2.2. Stepper Cycling Gates

Each stepper cycling gate receives as one input, the normally positive output (through an inverter) of a stage of the stepper counter and as its second input, the outputs of the inverter tubes connected to s stage decade switches of all the decades associated with the stepper. These inverter tubes have their plates connected in parallel to a common load resistor. The circuit containing the inverters and stepper cycling gates is such that even if only one of the inverters connected to a switch is on, the gate remains closed. In this way, a stepper cycling gate, emits a signal only if, when the stepper counter is in stage s, all the associated decade counters have reached the stages specified by their s stage decade switches.

The output of a stepper cycling gate causes a CPP to be passed through each of the gates 63 and 44 (preceded by B, C, ..., or L). The output of gate 63 causes the stepper counter to be cycled one stage, and the output of the gates 44 (preceded by B, C, ..., L) clears the associated decade counters.

Notice that the clearing of the decade counters and stepping of the stepper takes place one addition time after the decade counters arrive at the number specified by the decade switch settings whether the decades arrive at this number because of pulse input to the decade direct or stepper input terminal. Thus, if the stepper input is pulsed at the end of addition time t or early in addition time t+1 and the decade counters, as a result, reach the setting of the decade switches at the end of addition time t+1, the decade counter clears to zero and the stepper counter advances one stage at the end of addition time t+2. But, if the decade counters reach the switch settings as a result of pulsing the decade direct input at the end of addition time t, the stepping and clearing takes place at the end of addition time t+1.

10.3.3. Clearing a Stepper Counter

A stepper counter clears back to stage one as the result of pulse input to its clear direct input terminal or as the result of receiving a pulse when it is in stage c (the number set up on the stepper clear switch).

10.3.3.1. Stepper Clear Switch

Each point of the stepper clear switch is connected to the normally negative output of a stage of the stepper counter. If c is the setting of the stepper clear switch, then, when the stepper counter reaches stage c, the signal which passes through the clear switch opens gate B47. In this way, the next

TABLE 10-1

PROPERTIES OF MASTER PROGRAMMER INPUTS

t = addition time when terminal is pulsed unless otherwise noted.
s = stage of stepper counter before a pulse is received.
d_s = number set up on decade switches associated with stage s of stepper counter.
c = number set up on stepper clear switch

INPUT TERMINAL	PULSE INPUT	EFFECT OF RECEPTION OF A PULSE	ADDITION TIME EFFECT OCCURS
Stepper Input	Program pulse at end of add. time t or PM pulses during add. time t+1.	1. Output pulse is transmitted through output terminal corresponding to stage s of stepper counter.	t + 1
		2. Decade counters cycle 1 stage in units place	t + 1
		3. If input cycles decade counters to d_s a. decade counters clear to zero b. stepper counter cycles to (s+1) mod c	t + 2 t + 2
Stepper Input A or F with decades dissociated	Program pulse at end of add. time t or PM pulses during add. time t+1.	1. Output pulse is transmitted through output terminal corresponding to stage s of stepper counter.	t + 1
		2. (No decade counters)	
		3. (No decade counters)	
Stepper Direct Input	Digit or program pulse	1. No output pulse is transmitted	
		2. Decade counters do not cycle	
		3. Stepper counter cycles 1 stage for each pulse received.	immediately
Stepper Direct Input A or F with decades dissociated	Digit or program pulse	1. No output pulse is transmitted	
		2. (No decade counters)	
		3. Stepper counter cycles 1 stage for each pulse received.	immediately
Stepper Input	Program pulse at end of add. time t	1. Output pulse is transmitted through output terminal associated with stage (s+p) of stepper counter.	t + 1
and Stepper Direct Input	Program pulse at end of add. time t or p digit pulses during add. time t+1.	2. Decade counters cycle 1 stage in units place.	t + 1
		3. Stepper counter cycles 1 stage for each pulse received at stepper direct input terminal.	immediately
		4. If decade counters are cycled to stage d_{s-p} a. decade counters clear to zero b. stepper counter cycles to (s+p+1) mod c.	t + 2 t + 2
Stepper Input	Program pulse at end of add. time t	1. Output pulse is transmitted through stage (s+p) mod c.	t + 1
and Stepper Direct input A or F with no decades	Program pulse at end of add. time t or p digit pulses during add. time t+1.	2. (No decade counter)	
		3. Stepper counter cycles 1 stage for each pulse received.	immediately
Decade Direct Input	Program pulse	1. No output pulse is transmitted	
		2. Decade counter cycles one stage	immediately
		3. If decade counters are cycled to stage d_s a. decade counters clear to zero b. stepper counter cycles to stage (s+1) mod c	t + 1 t + 1
Stepper Clear Direct Input	Program pulse or digit pulses	1. Stepper counter clears to stage 1	immediately

pulse from buffer 62, whether derived from the stepper cycling gate circuit or from pulse input to the stepper direct input, is gated through B47 after passing through inverter B46. The output of gate B47 inverted by C46 clears the stepper counter back to stage 1.

The circuit containing the stepper clear switch and gate B47 requires more time than that between successive digit pulses if it is to operate reliably. For this reason, if digit pulses are ever brought to a stepper direct input terminal, the stepper clear switch must be set at 6. With the stepper clear switch set at 6, clearing to stage one results from the fact that the stepper counters are ring counters.

10.3.3.2. Stepper Clear Direct Input

Pulse input to the stepper clear direct input terminal passes through buffer B46 and inverter C46 and immediately clears the stepper.

If another pulse attempts to cycle the stepper at the same time that the stepper clear direct input is pulsed, the clearing action will predominate because the clear circuit spreads its signal out in time sufficiently for this purpose.

10.4. PROGRAMMING THE MASTER PROGRAMMER

One aspect of master programmer control is provided by the switch settings (decade associator, decade, and stepper clear). The other aspect is the input terminal (decade direct, stepper, stepper direct, or stepper clear direct) which is pulsed. Table 10-1 summarizes the properties of the master programmer inputs.

It is to be noted that in the master programmer, each stepper with its associated decades functions as a unit independently of the other steppers and decades. For this reason, it is possible to stimulate some or all of them simultaneously.

It is even permissible to pulse more than one of the input terminals of a given stepper-decade combination simultaneously. For example, a decade direct input terminal and a stepper input terminal may be pulsed simultaneously because the cycling of the decade counters due to the former is completed before that due to the latter begins. A stepper input and stepper direct input terminal may also be pulsed simultaneously because the latter affects only the stepper counter and does so immediately while the former affects the decade and, if it affects the stepper counter, does so two addition times after the input. On the other hand, the stepper direct input should not be pulsed two addition times after the stepper input or one addition time after a decade direct input because of the conflict that would arise if the decade counters were thus cycled to the settings of the decade switches.

10.5. USES OF THE MASTER PROGRAMMER

The program controls of the master programmer make this unit suitable for link or digit program control of sequences or chains, for accumulating values of an independent variable (or even serial numbers), and for extending the program control facilities of other units.

10.5.1. Link Program Control

The master programmer's contribution to the link programming of sequences, sequences iterated into a chain, chains of chains and various other program hierarchies is the program output pulses which can be transmitted through any of its 60 output terminals.

10.5.1.1. The stimulation of sequences

The operator can provide for the stimulation of any given sequence by connecting the input terminals of the first program controls used in the sequence to the same program line that one or more program output terminals of the master programmer are connected. To stimulate that particular sequence, then, a pulse must be delivered to a stepper input at a time when the stepper counter will be in the stage associated with one of the master programmer output terminals mentioned in the previous sentence. Control of the stage of the stepper counter may be exercised through the settings of the decade switches or by pulsing the stepper direct input or stepper clear direct input. The pulse which must be delivered to the stepper input terminal in order to obtain a program output pulse may be derived from the program output terminal of one of the transceivers used in the last program of the sequence (see problem 1, Section 10.6.) or, in more complex problems, may even be obtained from another master programmer output terminal (see problem 2, Section 10.6.)

10.5.1.2. Iteration of the sequences of a chain

To secure the iteration of the sequence of a chain n times the master programmer must be set up to transmit a program output pulse through an output terminal which feeds to the initial programs of the sequence n times and then to transmit a pulse through an output terminal which does not feed to that sequence. This can be accomplished by setting at n the decade switches associated with the stepper output terminal which feeds to the first programs of the sequence and by delivering to the stepper input the terminal pulse of the sequence. A pulse to initiate the chain must be delivered to this stepper input. Then on each of n successive occasions whenever the stepper input receives a pulse, a pulse will be transmitted to stimulate the sequence. The nth pulse delivered to this stepper input will, moreover, clear the decade counters to zero and cycle the stepper counter 1 stage so that the delivery of another pulse to the stepper input will result in the transmission of an output pulse through a terminal other than the one which, above, was described as being connected to the first program controls of the sequence.

10.5.1.3. The stimulation of program hierarchies

In general one stage of a stepper counter must be devoted to the stimulation of a single sequence or to the stimulation of a chain of iterated sequences. To link together a number of different sequences (where some or all of the sequences may be chains) requires the use of a stepper with one stage of the stepper counter devoted to each sequence or chain. A number of sequences, each consisting of several subsequences of the kind referred to in the previous sentence, requires the use of one stepper for the main sequences and one stepper for each of the subsequences.

A stepper must have associated with it by means of a decade associator switch sufficient decades to count the maximum number of iterations involved in any chains controlled by that stepper. If for any reason, there are not sufficient decades for this purpose, the decade switches correlated with several successive stages of a stepper may be set so that the sum of the decade switch settings is the required number and the corresponding outputs hooked together to the same program line.

The clear switch of the stepper must be set to the number of sequences (or sequences of chains) to be controlled by the stepper. If the number of sequences to be linked exceeds 6, several steppers may be used sequentially.

10.5.2. Digit Program Control

If it is desired to use two or three function tables to list the values of a single function instead of merely one, digit control of the program of looking up a function is needed so that the table appropriate to the value of the independent variable may be entered. This control can be supplied very easily by using the master programmer.

For illustrative purposes, let us say that three function tables are to be used (the case in which only two are used may be treated similarly except for minor details). Then a transformation of the independent variable will be made which will cause its values to lie between zero and 299 inclusive. The program P_i (for i = 1, 2, 3) is defined as the program of entering function table i for a tabular value. The problem, then, is to stimulate the performance of P_i if the digit in hundreds place of the independent variable is i - 1.

The operator must connect three successive program output terminals of a stepper to three program lines which are in turn connected, one each, to the program input terminals on function tables 1, 2, and 3 respectively and must provide for the pulsing of the stepper direct input by digit pulses from the hundreds decade line of the accumulator storing the independent variable. The digit pulses may be those transmitted out of the accumulator's add or subtract output. Which stepper output terminals are made to correspond to programs P_1, P_2, and P_3 respectively depends on whether digit pulses from the add or subtract output terminal are used. The stepper input must also be pulsed (either at the end of the addition time just before the stepper direct input receives the digit pulses or some time subsequent to that) so that an output pulse will be transmitted by the stepper through the output terminal associated with the stage to which the stepper has been cycled by the digit pulses. And finally, the stepper clear direct input should be pulsed after the digit discrimination has been completed so that the stepper will be ready for use in the next digit discrimination program when needed.

A conceivable motive for pulsing the stepper direct input with digit pulses from the subtract output might be avoidance of tying up the accumulator's add output. If digit pulses from the subtract output are used, 9, 8, or 7 pulses will be received at the master programmer's stepper direct input if the hundreds place digit of the argument is respectively 0, 1, or 2. Then the stepper output terminals corresponding to stages 4, 3, and 2 (with the stepper clear switch set at 6) respectively of the stepper counter should be so connected as to deliver the stimulating program pulses for programs P_1, P_2, and P_3 respectively. If digit pulses from the add output terminal are used, then the stepper output terminals corresponding to stages 1, 2, and 3 respectively of the stepper counter should be so connected as to deliver the stimulating pulse for programs P_1, P_2, and P_3 respectively.

Steppers A or F with zero decades associated are especially suited to digit discrimination programs. Any other stepper, however, may be used. If a stepper with decades is employed, two alternative methods for setting the decade switches exist:

1) the decade switches corresponding to stage 1 of the stepper counter may be set at a number exceeding the number of times the digit discrimination program will occur;

2) the decade switches corresponding to the various stages of the stepper may all be set at 1.

Whether a stepper with or without decades is used, provision must be made for clearing the stepper counter back to stage one sometime before the next digit discrimination program occurs. This may be done by pulsing the stepper clear direct input. If the stepper input is pulsed in addition time t,

TABLE 10-2

SET-UP FOR STIMULATING PROGRAM P_i

($i = 0, 1, \ldots, 9$) if digit i appears in k^{th} decade of Accumulator 12

Unit Add Time	Acc. 12	Acc. 14 (clears to 5 in decade k)	Master Programmer Master — Input	Master Programmer Master — Output
1	1-1 ① A 0 1	1-1 ⑤ α 0 1 1-2		
2		1-2 ⑥ A 0 1 $\boxed{A(k+1)}$ to 2-1 $\boxed{A(k)}$ to 2-2 2-3	Edi 2-1 Adi 2-2 Fdi 2-2	
3			2-3 Ei	$\overbrace{\quad}$ E_1^o $\quad$ E_2^o * 2-4 $\qquad$ 2-5
4	2-4 ⑤ 2-5 ⑥ 0 0 2		2-4 $\quad$ 2-5 Fi $\quad$ Ai	F_1^o to $^1P_1$ F_2^o to $^2P_2$ F_3^o to $^3P_3$ F_4^o to $^4P_4$ F_6^o to $^6P_0$ $\qquad$ A_1^o to $^1P_5$ A_2^o to $^2P_6$ A_3^o to $^3P_7$ A_4^o to $^4P_8$ A_5^o to $^5P_9$
5	↓ 2-6			
6			2-6 A, E, and F cdi	

*Braces are used here to mean "or".

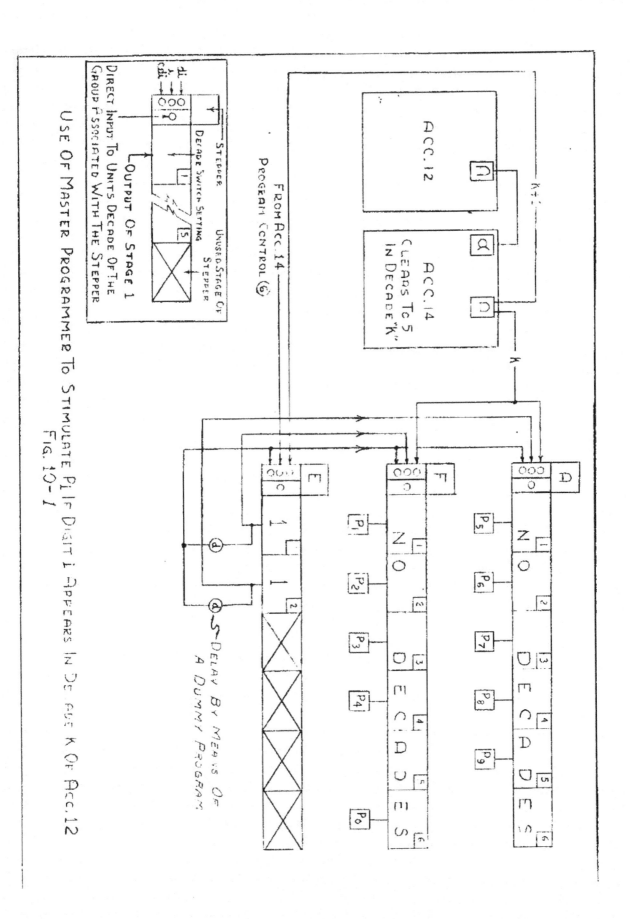

Use Of Master Programmer To Stimulate Pi If Digit i Appears In Decade K Of Acc.12

Fig. 10-1

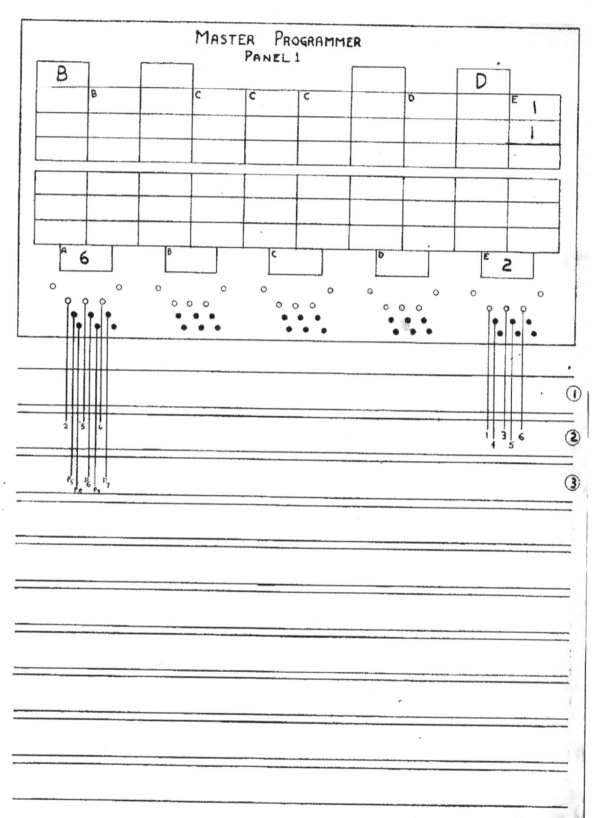

Fig. 10 - 2 (a)
Digit Discrimination Program
To stimulate P_i if digit i appears in decade k of
accumulator 12.

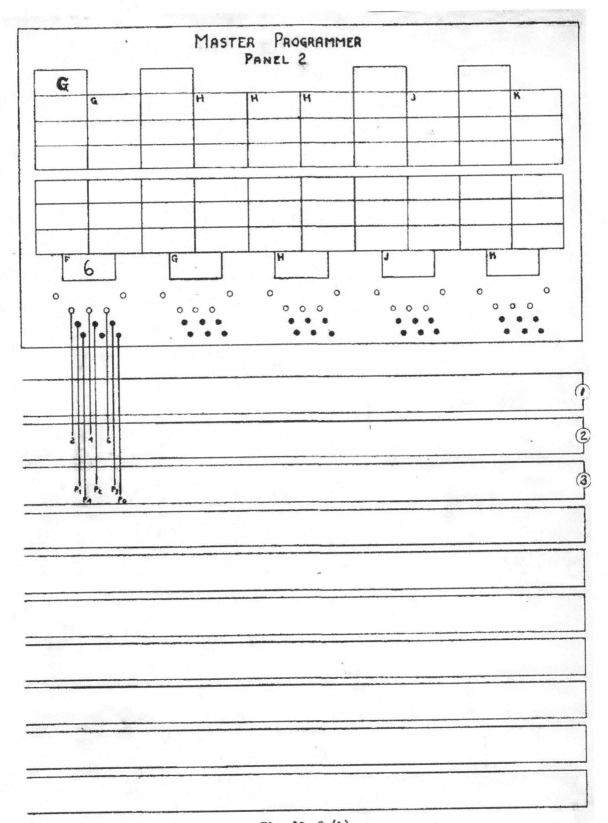

Fig. 10- 2 (b)
Digit Discrimination Program
To stimulate P_1 if digit i appears in decade k of acc.12

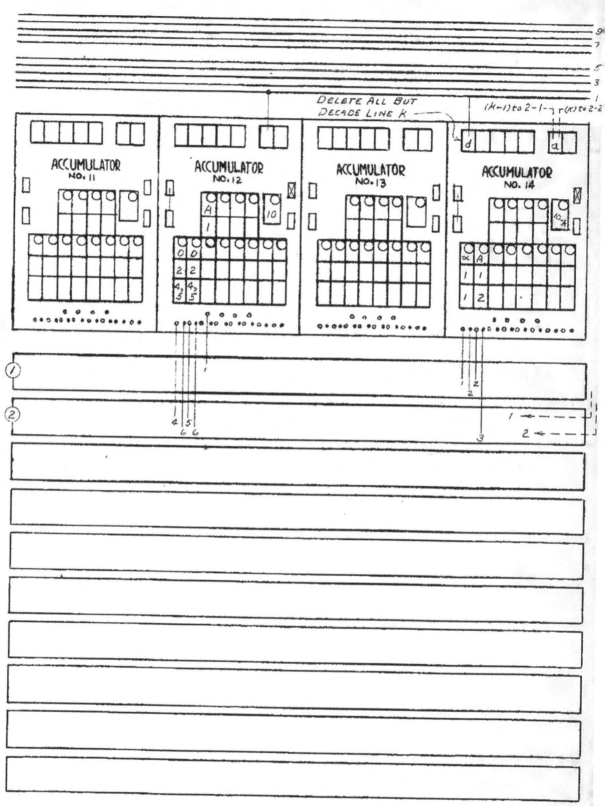

FIG. 10-2(c)

DIGIT DISCRIMINATION PROGRAM TO STIMULATE p_i
IF DIGIT i APPEARS IN DECADE k OF ACC. 12

the stepper clear direct input may be pulsed in addition time t+1 when a stepper without decades is used or when a stepper with decades whose stage one decade switches have been set at a number greater than the number of times digit discrimination occurs is used. This allows sufficient time for the stepper to emit a program output pulse from the output terminal corresponding to the particular stage to which the digit pulses cycled the stepper. If there are decades associated with the stepper used for digit discrimination and if the decade switches of the various stages used are set at 1, the stepper counter should not be cleared to stage 1 sooner than the end of addition time t+2 since, in addition time t+2, a pulse will try to cycle the stepper counter due to the fact that the decade counter has been cycled to stage 1.

A digit discrimination program where the possibilities are limited to 6 consecutive digits may be treated in a fashion similar to that described above except for obvious modifications. A digit discrimination program calling for the stimulation of P_i if digit i (where $0 \leq i \leq 9$) appears in decade k requires more extensive modification.

This problem may be handled in two steps: 1) discriminate to determine whether the digit is between zero and four inclusive or between 5 and 9 inclusive; 2) using two different steppers for the two ranges mentioned above, discriminate among 5 consecutive digits.

Table 10-2 shows one possible method of carrying out this problem and Figure 10-1 presents a visual summary of this set-up. Figure 10-2 (a, b, and c) shows the program and digit connections and switch settings required to carry out this digit discrimination program. The notation for the master programmer in Table 10-2 and in Figure 10-2 is explained at the beginning of Section 10.6.

Step 1 of this digit discrimination program is handled by transmitting the number stored in accumulator 12 to accumulator 14 where it is received through a special deleter which eliminates all of the decade lines except decade k. The significant figure switch on accumulator 14 is set to 10-k so that this accumulator clears to 5 in decade k. Now, if the digit stored in decade k of accumulator 12 does not exceed 4, decade k+1 of accumulator 14 will store zero; if the digit stored in decade k of accumulator 12 is between 5 and 9 inclusive, decade k+1 of accumulator 14 stores 1.

The next step of the program consists of transmitting the addition output of decade line k+1 from accumulator 14 to the direct input of stepper E and simultaneously the digit pulses of the output of decade line k to the direct inputs of steppers A and F. The program output pulse from the program control on accumulator 14 used for the previously mentioned program is delivered to the input terminal of stepper E. If the digit stored in decade k of accumulator 12 does not exceed 4, the output terminal corresponding to stage 1 of stepper E delivers a pulse to Fi. Stepper F, acting on the information which it received from the addition output of accumulator 14, then transmits an output pulse to stimulate program P_0, P_1, ..., or P_4. If the digit stored in decade k of accumulator 12 exceeds 4, the output terminal corresponding to stage 2 of stepper E delivers a pulse to A_i. Stepper A then emits a pulse to stimulate P_5, P_6, ..., or P_9.

The pulse output from the terminals corresponding to stages 1 and 2 of stepper E is also taken to a program control on accumulator 12 whose repeat switch is set at 2. The output pulse from this transceiver is used to clear steppers A, E, and F back to stage 1.

10.5.3. Accumulating Values of an Independent Variable

The master programmer is a convenient unit for accumulating, storing and printing values of the independent variable. This may be done by delivering to a decade direct input, the number of pulses by which the value of the independent variable is to be increased at a given time or by pulsing a stepper input. In the latter case, the stepper input must be pulsed in several different addition times if the independent variable is to be increased by more than 1 unit at a time. At the present time, decades 14 through 18 inclusive, are connected to the printer. Therefore, it is desirable to choose from among these the decades to be used for the accumulation of the independent variable.

The decade switches associated with the stepper counter stage involved in accumulating the independent variable should be set to a number one higher than the maximum value of the independent variable to be counted so that the decade counters will not clear to zero before printing is accomplished (see Section 10.2.2.). After the last printing takes place, the decade counters may be cleared to zero by feeding one more pulse to either the decade direct input or to the stepper input after printing. In the event that the criterion for printing the final result is something other than a certain value of the independent variable (see Problem 2 of Section 10.6.), it may be necessary to include a program sequence designed to clear the decade counters.

10.5.4. Extending the Program Control Facilities of Other Units

Should the number of program controls on a particular unit prove inadequate for some computation, the master programmer may be employed so as to make possible the repeated use of program controls on that unit at various times in the set-up.

One way to accomplish this is to deliver the final pulse of the sequence which precedes the program set-up on a repeatedly used program control . to that control. Then the program output pulse of the program which is used repeatedly goes to the master programmer stepper which determines which sequence to stimulate subsequently.

Let us suppose, for example, that program control 26 on the constant transmitter is to be used twice in a computation, with programs P_0 and P_1 respectively preceding and following the first use of this constant transmitter control and with programs Q_0 and Q_1 respectively preceding and following the second use of the same constant transmitter control. By delivering the program output pulse of the controls on which programs P_0 and Q_0 are set up to the program pulse input terminal of control 26 on the constant transmitter, provision is made for stimulating this control on each occasion. If, however, the program output pulse of program control 26 must stimulate program P_1 once and the next time, program Q_1, this cannot be done directly. Instead, the output of program control 26 is taken to a master programmer stepper which determines whether to stimulate program P_1 or Q_1.

When high-speed multiplier or divider and square rooter program controls are used repeatedly in this way, the problem of stimulating the accumulators which store the arguments to transmit may arise. The function table or another master programmer stepper may be used to provide for this stimulation. The illustrative problem of Section 8.7. illustrates the repeated use of high-speed multiplier program control through the use of the master programmer (see Figure 8-2 with particular attention to the use of steppers D-K).

In Section 4.5.2. the use of dummy programs set up on accumulators for the delay of a program pulse was suggested and, in Section 7.4. the use

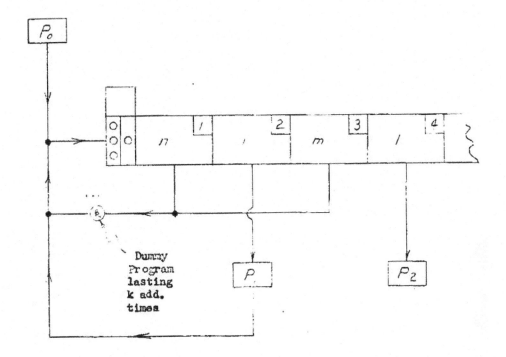

Program Sequence P_1 follows P_0 after a delay of $n(k+1)+1$ addition times

Program Sequence P_2 follows P_1 after a delay of $m(k+1)+1$ addition times

Fig. 10-3

USE OF MASTER PROGRAMMER TO DELAY A PROGRAM PULSE

of a function table program to achieve a longer delay than is possible with a single accumulator control was mentioned. An alternative method of delaying a program pulse, and one which is practicable for long delays, can be achieved through the use of the master programmer. This use of the master programmer is illustrated in Figure 10-3.

10.6. ILLUSTRATIVE PROBLEM SET-UPS

Two problems are offered in this section to illustrate the use of the master programmer in central programming. Problem 1 uses only link control to stimulate its sequences. Problem 2 is more complex involving both link and magnitude control and the use of the master programmer to accumulate the independent variable.

Both problems are described with reference to a set-up analysis table, a figure showing the master programmer links, and a set-up diagram. For problem 2, moreover, there is a set-up table.

In the set-up analysis tables a decimal notation is used to identify the program sequences and subsequences. The number separated from the sequence identification decimal by a dash indicates the number of times the sequence is to be iterated into a chain. For example, the symbols

$$2-6$$
$$2.1 - 10 \text{ integrate}$$
$$2.2 - 1 \text{ print}$$

are used to mean that sequence 2, which consists of a subsequence, 2.1, to be iterated into a chain by its successive performance 10 times and another subsequence, 2.2, to be performed only once, is itself to be iterated 6 times.

In set-up tables, (see Table 10-5) instructions for the master

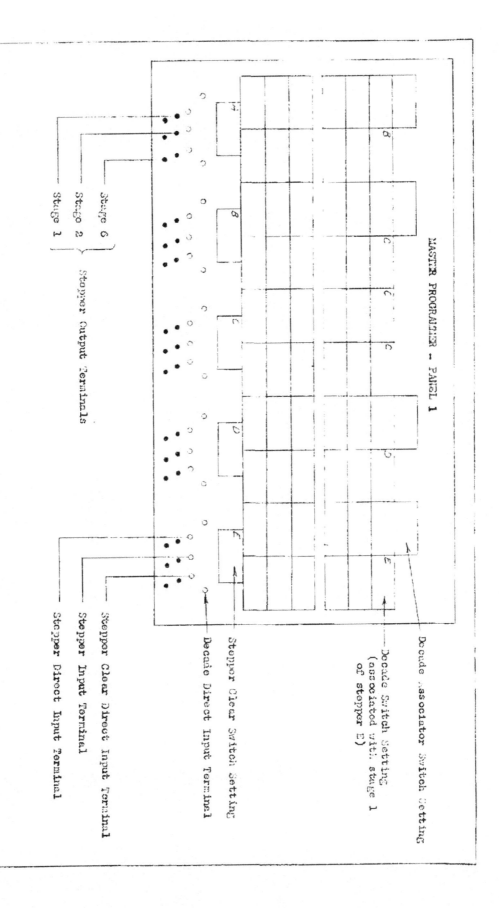

MASTER PROGRAMMER — PANEL 1

Fig. 10—4

MASTER PROGRAMMER SET-UP DIAGRAM CONVENTIONS

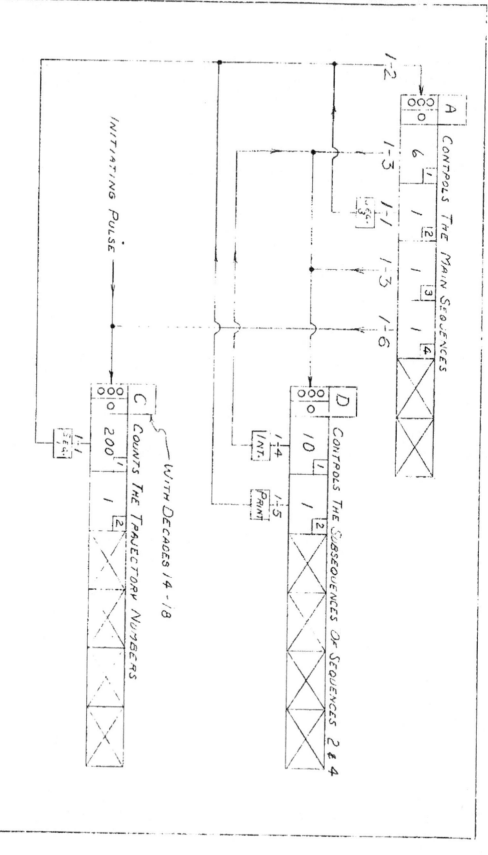

MASTER PROGRAMMER LINKS — PROBLEM 1

FIG. 10-5

programmer are given in a double column. The input terminal and program line from which it receives a pulse appear in the left hand half of the column. The program line designation appears above or below the symbol for the input terminal according as the line carries a program pulse or digit pulses. The output terminal through which a program output pulse (if any) is transmitted and the program line to which the output pulse is delivered appear in the right hand half of the column.

The set-up diagram conventions for the master programmer are shown in Figure 10-4.

The master programmer link diagrams are essentially block diagrams designed to summarize the way in which the various program sequences of a problem are tied together by the master programmer. The conventions used in these diagrams appear at the lower left of Figure 10-1. On these diagrams, we have used two different symbols for dummy programs, namely ——— •——— and (d) . This is done to distinguish between the purposes for which the dummy programs are used. A dummy program used to isolate program pulses is symbolized by ——— •———; one used to achieve a delay of d addition times by (d) .

10.6.1. Problem 1

Problem 1 suggests a possible method of setting up the ENIAC to compute the trajectories needed to make an anti-aircraft table. The number of trajectories to be computed has arbitrarily been taken as 200. The number of integration steps performed before printing has also been arbitrarily taken as 10, and it is assumed here that 60 integration steps will adequately cover the required range. Obviously, numbers other than these could be chosen at the operator's discretion and convenience. Sequences 3 and 4 (see Table 10-3 and Figure 10-5) together constitute a test run.

TABLE 10-3

SET-UP ANALYSIS -- PROBLEM 1

1-1 Selective clear
     Read
     Transmit from Constant Transmitter to Accumulators

2-6

    2.1 - 10 integrate

    2.2 - 1 print

3-1

    Selective clear
    Read
    Transmit from Constant Transmitter to Accumulators

4-1

    4.1 - 10 integrate

    4.2 - 1 print

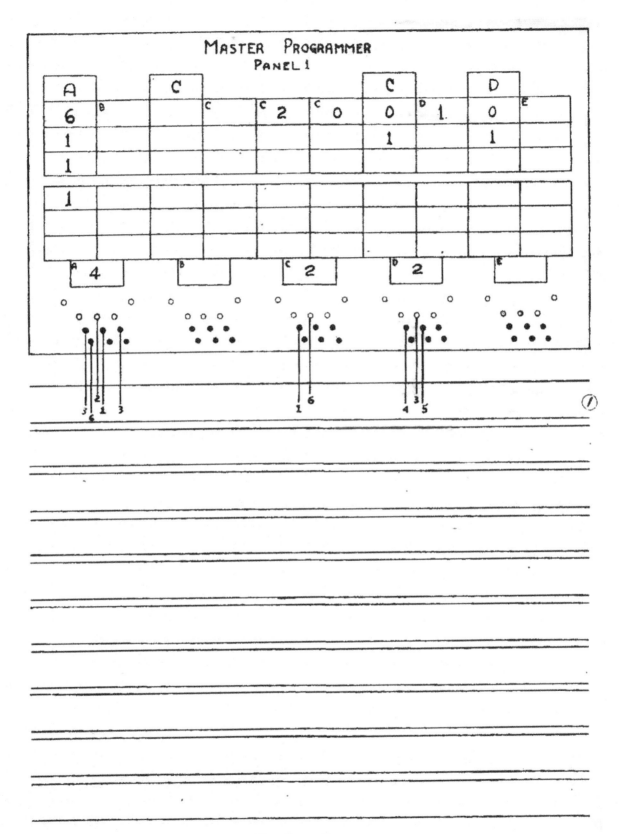

Fig. 10 - 6
Set-Up Diagram - Problem 1

In sequence 3, this set-up assumes that the initial conditions for the test run will be read from an IBM card different from the one which held the initial conditions for the previous trajectory. This is not meant to indicate that such a procedure is the only possible one. Depending on the amount of information to be put on the IBM cards or to be set up on the constant set switches of the constant transmitter, the initial conditions of the test run could be put on the same IBM card as those for the previous trajectory or set-up manually on the constant transmitter.

Stepper C (with decades 14-18 associated) is used to count the number of trajectories (see Section 9.4.). After 200 trajectories have been computed further computation sequences will not be initiated. As stepper C is set up here, the 200th card will be punched with serial number zero.

Four stages of stepper counter A are used to advance the computation through its four main sequences. Stage 1 of stepper counter D is devoted to the chain of 10 integrations (2.1-10 and 4.1-10) and stage 2 to the printing sequence (2.2-1 and 4.2-1).

10.6.2. Problem 2

This problem set-up again involves the sequential computation of a number of trajectories. Here, however, the set-up is one that would be suitable for ground gunfire trajectories. Results are printed not after a constant number of integration sequences (and thus, at even intervals of time if time is the independent variable) but, instead, only in the neighborhood of the summit and ground. This is accomplished by following each integration sequence with a test to determine the magnitude of y' or y. When the projectile goes below ground, computations cease, a test run is performed, and then the next trajectory is initiated.

TABLE 10-4

SET-UP ANALYSIS — PROBLEM 2

1-1   Initial Sequence
       Read IBM card and selective clear
       Transmit initial conditions from constant transmitter to accumulators.

2-   Until $y+c_2 < 0$ (see Seq. 2.5) below.

   2.1-1   Integrate

   2.2-   Repeat as long as $y'-c_1 \geqslant 0$

           Test $y'-c_1$ and then integrate

   2.3-   Repeat as long as $y'+c_1 \geqslant 0$

           Test $y'+c_1$, print, and then integrate

   2.4-   Repeat as long as $y - c_2 \gtrless 0$

           Test $y - c_2$ and then integrate

   2.5-   Repeat as long as $y + c_2 \gtrless 0$

           Test $y + c_2$, print, and then integrate

3-1   Print

4-1   Clear the decades of the master programmer which have been accumulating

       the independent variable and clear all other steppers which require

       clearing in preparation for the next trajectory computation.

5-1   Test run

   5.1-1   Transfer initial conditions from constant transmitter to
           accumulators[*]

   5.2-10 Integrate

   5.3-1   Print

---

[*]It is assumed here that the initial conditions for the test run are set up on
the constant set switches of the constant transmitter or read from the IBM card
for the previous trajectory so that a new card need not be read for the test
run's initial conditions.

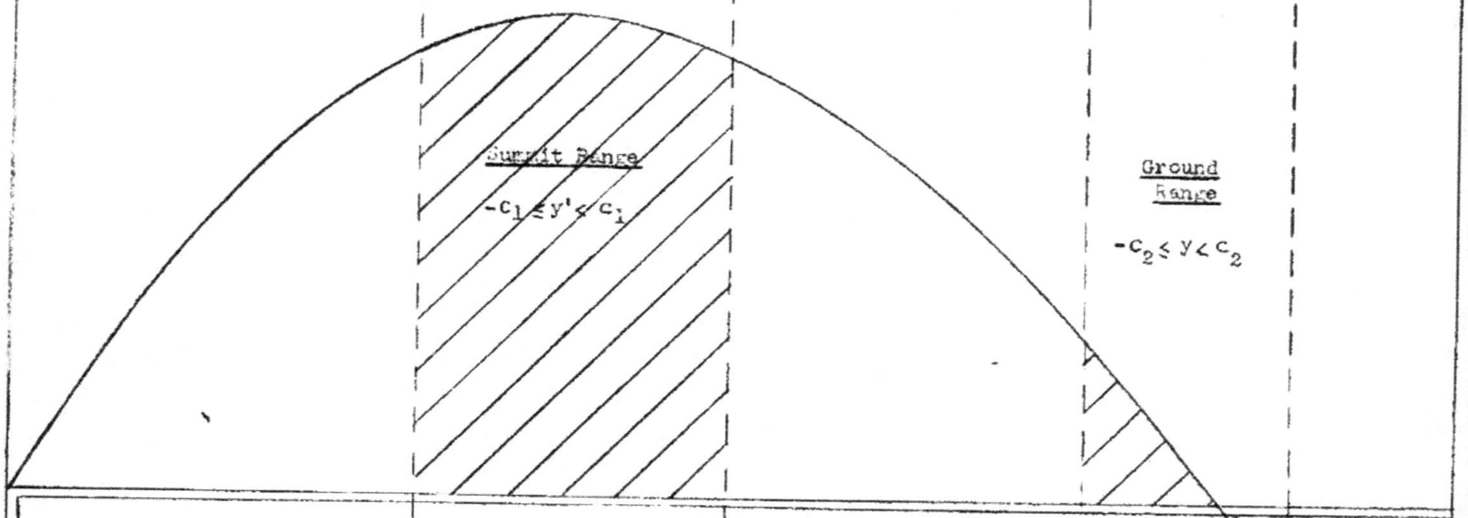

Result of Discrimination	$y' - c_1 \geq 0$	$y' - c_1 < 0$	$y' + c_1 < 0$	$y - c_2 < 0$	$y + c_2 < 0$
		$y' + c_1 \geq 0$	$y - c_2 \geq 0$	$y + c_2 \geq 0$	
Program Sequence Performed	Test $y' - c_1$ and then Integrate	Test $y' + c_1$ / Print / Integrate	Test $y - c_2$ and then Integrate / Integrate	Test $y - c_2$ / Print and then Integrate	Initiate Sequence 2

Summit Range
$-c_1 \leq y' < c_1$

Ground Range
$-c_2 \leq y < c_2$

FIGURE 10-7

SUBSEQUENCES OF SEQ.2—PROBLEM 2

The sequences of this problem are defined in table 10-4. Sequences 1 through 3 cover the computations for a trajectory. The breakdown of sequence 2 into its component subsequences is shown pictorially in Figure 10-7.

It is assumed in this set-up that the value of the independent variable is stored in and printed from decades 14-18 (associated with stepper C) of the master programmer. Computation, for a given trajectory, ceases, not at a fixed value of the independent variable, but when the projectile has gone past ground range (see Figure 10-7). This means that the decade switches associated with stage 1 of stepper counter C must be set at a number safely in excess of the highest value of the independent variable that can be expected in any of the trajectory computations. (For the problem under discussion, we will arbitrarily take this number to be 80.0 with tenths place registered in master programmer decade 14). Furthermore, we cannot depend on clearing decades 14-18 as a result of arriving at the setting of the decade switches associated with stage 1 of stepper C. For this reason, sequence 4 is included in the set-up. The details for carrying out this sequence will be explained in section 10.6.2.2.

Sequence 5 constitutes a test run. The plan of the problem calls for a test run after each trajectory has been completed.

The master programmer links for this problem are shown in Figure 10-8. Steppers A, C, D. E, and F are used.

Stepper A controls the main sequences of the computation with the output of stage i stimulating sequence i+1. Stepper C records the value of the independent variable and steppers C and D have been so interrelated as to make possible the clearing of decades 14-18 after the projectile goes below ground. The same integration sequence is performed as a subsequence of both sequence 2 and sequence 5. Stepper E is used to choose the routine to be performed after

In sequence 2, however, the integration sequence is accompanied by programs concerned with accumulating the independent variable. In Sequence 5, we do not record the independent variable.

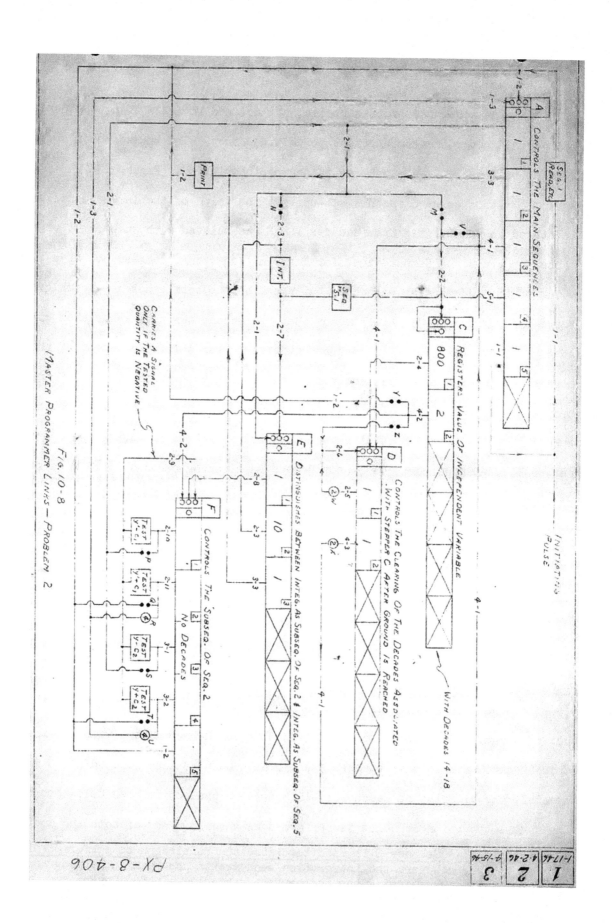

FIG. 10-8
(MASTER PROGRAMMER LINKS — PROBLEM 2)

PX-8-406

integration, with stage 1 motivating the routine in sequence 2, and either

stage 3 or 4, the routine in sequence 5. Stage one of stepper E routes control

to stepper F. This stepper participates in sequence 2, determining which of

the subsequences of sequence 2 is to be performed at any given time.

10.6.2.1. Sequences 1, 2, and 3.

The initiating pulse, at the very beginning of a computation, and

thereafter, the output of stage 5 of stepper A stimulates the performance of

sequence 1 and thus initiates the computations for a trajectory and its test

run.

The final pulse of sequence 1, pulse 1-2, goes to stepper A. Pulse 2-1,

delivered by A_1O, stimulates the performance of sequence 2.1 (integration) and

also causes the value of the independent variable to be increased. It is assumed

here that the increment to the independent variable is 0.2 (see Section 10.6.2.2.).

Pulse 2-1, thru dummy program M goes to the direct input of decade 14 and to Ci

to produce the required increment. Dummy program M is used to isolate the pulse

which goes to Ci and to 14 di from the pulse which stimulates the integration

sequence since, in sequence 4, we shall desire to stimulate Ci and 14 di without

stimulating the other programs initiated by pulse 2-1 (also see Section 10.6.2.2.).

Dummy program N intervenes between 2-1 and the pulse which stimulates the

integration sequence, pulse 2-3, since, in sequence 5, it is necessary to stim-

ulate the integration sequence without stimulating the associated programs of

sequence 2. Pulse 2-1 is also taken to E cdi to return stepper E to stage 1

as long as sequence 2 is performed.

The terminal pulse of the integration sequence, pulse 2-7, goes to Ei

and the output of E_1O stimulates Fi. Before the summit range, stepper F is in

stage 1 so that pulse 2-10 is emitted. This pulse stimulates the performance of the test on $y'-c_1$ (see Section 10.6.2.4. for details of the tests in sequences 2.2-2.5) and through dummy program P, brings the computation back to 2-1 which initiates the programs discussed in the previous paragraph. Dummy program P isolates the integration sequence from the test of $y'-c_1$ so that later (as in sequence 2.4) the integration maybe performed with a different test. As long as $y'-c_1$ remains non-negative stepper F remains in stage 1. When $y'-c_1$ is negative for the first time, the test on this quantity yields pulse 2-9 which advances stepper F to stage 2. While the test on $y'-c_1$ goes on, the pulse emitted by dummy program P, initiates the integration sequence.

When the integration sequence is completed, pulse 2-7 is emitted, and then pulse 2-8. This time, stepper F is in stage 2 so that pulse 2-11 is emitted by stepper F. Pulse 2-11 stimulates the test on $y'+c_1$ and, through dummy program Q, causes the emission of pulse 1-2. Since pulse 1-2, given out as the terminal pulse of sequence 1, advances stepper A to stage 2, this time, pulse 1-2 causes stepper A to emit pulse 3-3 (and advance to stage 3). This pulse stimulates printing. Pulse 2-11 is also taken to dummy program R for a delay of 4 addition times. Dummy program R emits pulse 1-3 which clears stepper A back from stage 3 to stage 1 so that when the printing is completed with the emission of pulse 1-2, stepper A again emits pulse 2-1 (and advances to stage 2). Pulse 2-1 stimulates the performance of the integration sequence and associated programs. Sequence 2.3 is then repeated until $y'+c_1$ becomes negative. At that time stepper F advances to stage 3. Whenever integration is completed in this phase of sequence 2, pulse 3-1 is given out. This pulse stimulates the test on $y-c_2$ and, through dummy program S, stimulates the integration sequence as was described above for sequence 2.2.

When $y-c_2$ becomes negative, stepper F is advanced to stage 4. In this part of sequence 2, pulse 3-2 stimulates the test of $y+c_2$ and, through dummy programs T and U, stimulates printing and then integration as described above for sequence 2.3.

When $y+c_2$ is negative for the first time pulse 2-9 is given out so that stepper F advances to stage 5.

Thus, when the integration initiated after the test which yields $y+c_2 < 0$ has been completed, pulse 1-2 is emitted by F_5O.

Pulse 1-2 finds stepper A in stage 2 so that pulse 3-3 is given out and printing is stimulated. This completes sequence 3.

We note that at the end of sequence 3 the following state of affairs exists in the master programmer:

Stepper	Stage of Stepper	Stage of associated decades
A	3	0
C	1	d $<$ 800
D	1	0 (see Section 10.6.2.2.)
E	2	0
F	5	no decades.

10.6.2.2. Clearing the Decades which Store the Independent Variable: - Sequence 4

In the course of sequence 2, we have been increasing the value of the independent variable by 2 in decade 14 with every repetition of the integration sequence. Pulse 2-2, taken to the decade direct input, accounts for an increase of 1 unit and, taken to Ci, accounts for an increase of one more unit. Pulse 2-2 also causes pulse 2-4 to be emitted. This pulse goes to Di causing stepper D to advance to stage 2 and pulse 2-5 to be emitted. This pulse, delayed for two addition times by dummy program W, restores stepper D to stage 1 as long as sequence 2 is in progress.

At the end of sequence 3 (the last printing for a trajectory), pulse 1-2 is delivered to Ai. Pulse 4-1 is then given out by A_3O and stepper A advances to stage 4.

Pulse 4-1 advances stepper D to stage 2 and, through dummy program V, goes to both Ci and 14 di. Since we assumed that the settings of the decade switches associated with stage 1 of stepper C safely exceeded the maximum value of the independent variable, stepper C is found in stage 1 at this time. Thus 2-4 is given out to stimulate Di and, because 4-1 advanced stepper D to stage 2, pulse 4-3 is emitted. One addition time after pulse 4-3 is given out stepper D cycles back to stage 1. However, pulse 4-3, delayed for two addition times by dummy program X, yields 4-1. Pulse 4-1 then causes the repetition of the programs described at the beginning of this paragraph.

Now, let us assume that the last printing for a trajectory takes place when the independent variable has the value 10^{-1} (800 -2m). Then, the output of A_3O causes the decades of stepper C to register 800 -2 (m-1) and, finally, causes dummy program X to emit a pulse for the 1st time. This, in turn causes the decades of stepper C to advance to 800-2(m-2) and causes dummy program X to emit pulse 4-1 for the 2nd time etc. The (m-1) st pulse emitted by dummy program X causes decades 14-18 to reach 800 and also causes the emission of 2-4 which results, finally, in the emission of pulse 4-1 by dummy program X for the mth time. Stepper C advances to stage 2 and its decades clear to zero before the mth pulse from dummy program X causes Ci to be pulsed again. Therefore, this time pulse 4-1 causes pulse 4-2 to be emitted from C_2O. Pulse 4-2 goes to F cdi to restore this stepper to stage 1. Since the mth pulse emitted by dummy program X steps D to stage 2, it is necessary also to clear stepper D in preparation for the

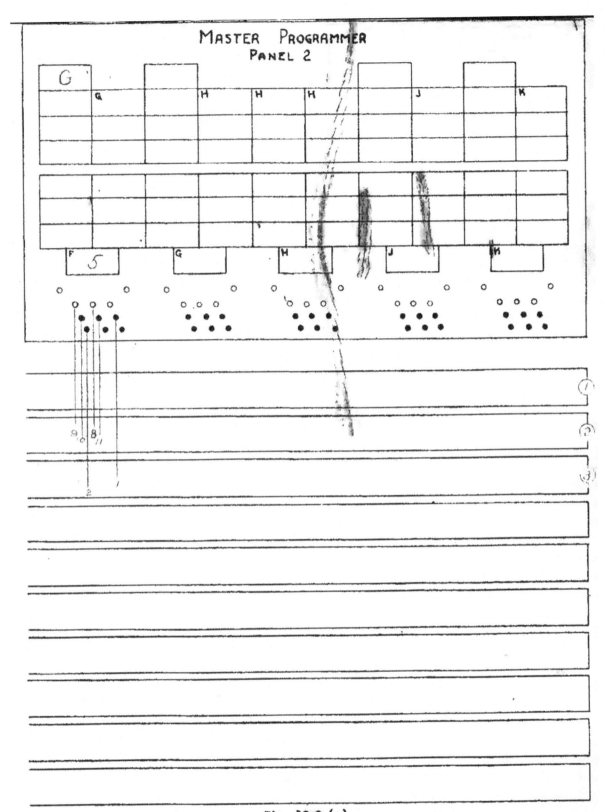

Fig. 10-9 (a)
Set Up Diagram For Tests on y and y' -- Problem 2

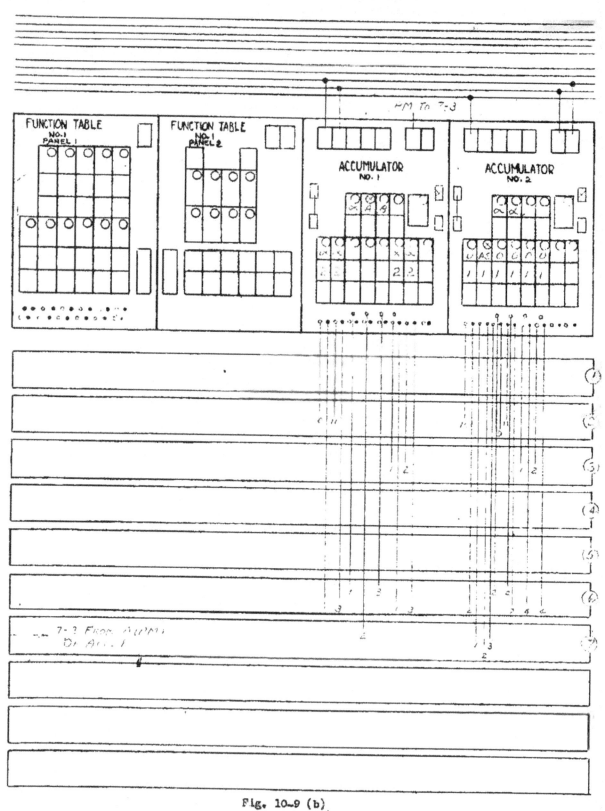

Fig. 10-9 (b)

Set-Up Diagram For Tests on y and y' - Problem 2

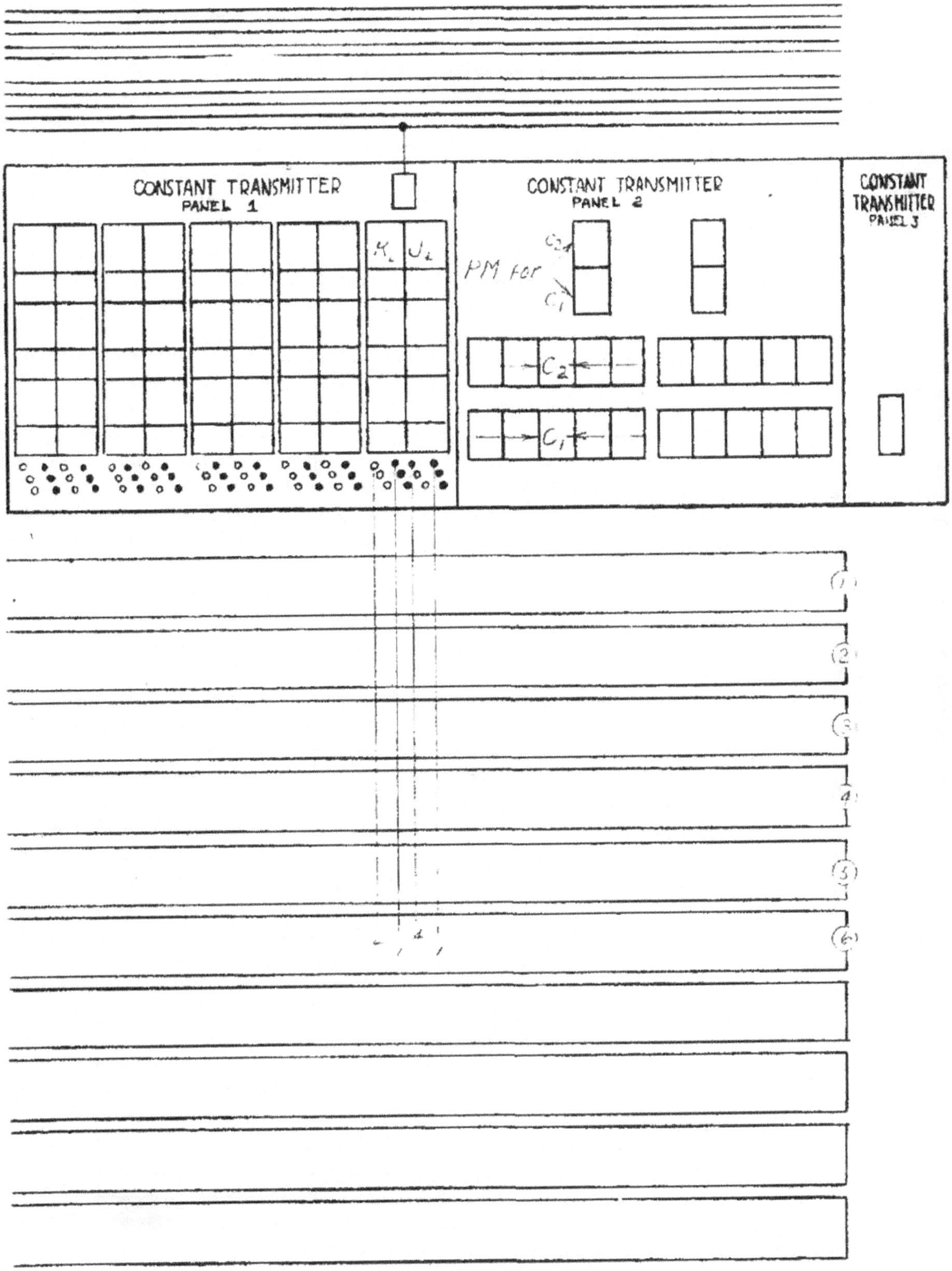

Fig. 10-9 (c)

Set Up Diagram For Tests on y and y' - Problem 2

TABLE 10–5

SET-UP TABLE FOR TESTS ON y' AND $\bar{y}$ – PROBLEM 2

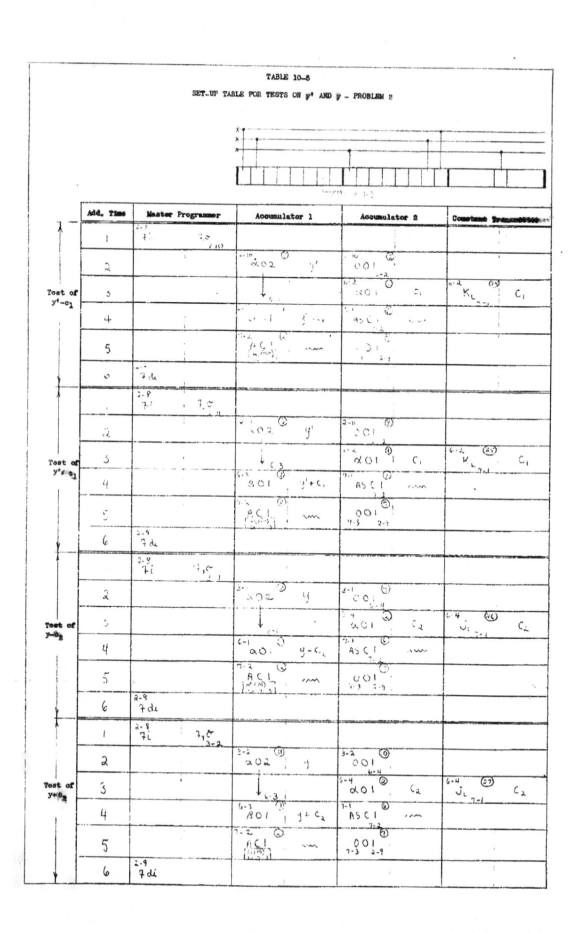

	Add. Time	Master Programmer	Accumulator 1	Accumulator 2	Constant Transmitter
	1	7. 7.0			
	2		α02 y'	001	
Test of $y'-c_1$	3		↓	α01 c_1	K_L C_1
	4		$y'-$	A5C1	
	5		β C1	001	
	6	7 d$_i$			
	1	7.1 7.0			
	2		α02 y'	001	
Test of $y'+c_1$	3		↓ c_3	α01 c_1	K_L C_1
	4		801 $y'+c_1$	A5C1	
	5		AC1	001	
	6	7 d$_i$			
	1	7$_i$ 7$_1$c			
	2		α02 y	001	
Test of $y-θ_2$	3		↓	α01 c_2	J_L C_2
	4		α01 $y-c_2$	A5C1	
	5		AC1	001	
	6	7 d$_i$			
	1	7$_i$ 7$_1$c			
	2		α02 y	001	
Test of $y+θ_2$	3		↓	α01 c_2	J_L C_2
	4		801 $y+c_2$	A5C1	
	5		AC1	001	
	6	7 d$_i$			

trajectory to follow the test run. This is done by the output of dummy program Z. Pulse 4-2, through dummy program Y, yields 1-2 which goes to Ai. Pulse 5-1, the output of A_4O, initiates sequence 5.

It is to be noted that the method described above for clearing stepper C requires that the settings of the decade switches for stages 1 and 2 be multiples of the increment to the independent variable.

10.6.2.3. Sequence 5.

The output of A_4O stimulates the performance of sequence 5-1 in which the accumulators used for integration and printing are cleared and in which the initial conditions for the test run are transferred from the constant transmitter to accumulators. The last pulse of sequence 5.1, pulse 2-7, is delivered to Ei. Pulse 2-3, emitted from E_2O, stimulates the performance of the integration sequence. After 10 integrations have been stimulated, E advances to stage 3 so that pulse 2-7, delivered to Ei at the end of the 10th integration, causes 3-3 to be emitted. Pulse 3-3 stimulates printing and the output of the printing , pulse 1-2, causes stepper A to emit pulse 1-1 from A_5O and then to return to stage 1. Pulse 1-1 initiates the computations for the next trajectory. No provision has been made for counting the number of trajectory computations and terminating computations after a specified number. Instead, we rely upon the exhaustion of the cards in the reader's magazine to terminate computation (see Chapter VIII).

10.6.2.4. Tests on y and y'

The tests on $y'-c_1$, $y'+c_1$ etc. included in sequence 2 are described with the aid of Table 10-5 and Figure 10-9 (a-c). All 4 tests have been planned in such a way as to use the same program controls wherever possible. In table 10-5 the program controls used in each of the 4 tests are stimulated by pulses carried in program tray 7; those controls common to only 2 of the tests are stimulated by pulses carried in program tray 6.

XI. SYNCHRONIZING, DIGIT, AND PROGRAM TRANSMISSION SYSTEMS AND SPECIAL EQUIPMENT

There are three principal types of dynamic communication between units of the ENIAC: 1) communication of the synchronizing pulses and gates, 2) digit pulse communication, and 3) program pulse communication. These three types of communication are accomplished through the use of conductors mounted in trays, which, except for their outlets, are identical for all three purposes. Each tray has a ground and 11 conductors separated from one another by metal shields and has the dimensions 8 ft. x 9 in. x 1.25 in. Since each panel of the ENIAC is two feet wide, each tray extends the length of 4 panels. Found at both ends of a tray is a 12 point terminal. Trays can be connected serially to one another by jumper connections between these end terminals. Communication of types 1 and 2 above is by means of so called digit trays. These have twelve point terminals at 2 foot intervals. The digit tray is shown on PX-4-102. Program trays which have a set of 11 two point (1 wire and ground) outlets at 2 foot intervals are used for communication of type 3. The units of the ENIAC are connected into these trays by means of digit or program cables.

The synchronizing, digit, and program transmission system and associated equipment such as load resistors, shifters, deleters, etc. are discussed in the following sections: Transmission of Synchronizing Pulses and Gates, Section 11.1; Transmission of Digit Pulses, Section 11.2; and Transmission of Program Pulses, Section 11.3. Pulse amplifiers which may be used in either the digit or program transmission system are discussed in Section 11.4.

The semi-permanent connections between accumulators and the printer, high-speed multiplier, and divider and the interconnection of accumulators are treated in Section 11.5.

A portable control box which parallels certain controls on the initiating and cycling units is discussed in Section 11.6.

11.1. SYNCHRONIZING TRUNK

Nine digit trays connected in series by jumpers from the synchronizing trunk which delivers to the other ENIAC units the 9 trains of pulses and the carry clear gate emitted by the cycling unit and the selective clear gate emitted by the initiating unit. The synchronizing trunk runs around the back of the ENIAC below the ventilating panels from the initiating unit up until (but not including) panel 3 of the constant transmitter. The lines marked (1) through (11) on PX-4-102 are used for the following pulses or gates:

(1) CPP   (6) RP

(2) IP   (7) 1'P

(3) 9P   (8) CCG

(4) 10P   (9) 2P

(5) SCG   (10) 2'P

               (11) 4P

A cable with a 12 point plug at either end is used to bring into each unit the fundamental pulses and gates.

11.2. DIGIT TRANSMISSION

11.2.1. Digit Trunks

Seventy-two digit trays (in addition to the 9 trays for the synchronizing trunk) have been built for the ENIAC. These trays can be stacked on a shelf above the switch panels of the units from panel 1 of function table 1 to panel 2 of the constant transmitter inclusive. As many as 8 trays on one level can be

REVISIONS

Drawing numbers was
PX4-13A Now PX-4-104A

Semi-final revision
R. F. Shaw   7/3/45   [1]

MATERIAL
/

FINISH
/

Drawn by:
H.S.M.
OCT 26 1944

Checked by:
A. [illegible]
C. [illegible]

Approved by:
[illegible]
10/30/44

SCALE
/

MOORE SCHOOL OF ELECTRICAL ENGINEERING
UNIVERSITY OF PENNSYLVANIA

SHIFTER (-2 & +2)

PX-4-104A

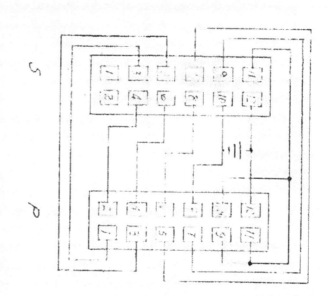

−2 SHIFTER

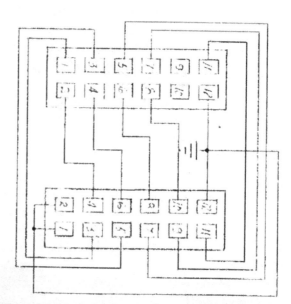

+2 SHIFTER

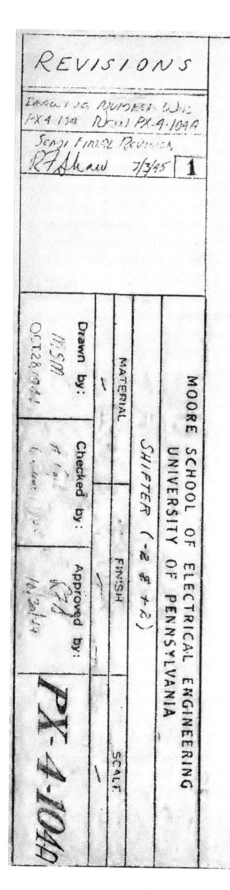

connected by jumpers. The load resistor (or load box) shown on PX-4-103 is plugged into an unused terminal usually on either the first or last tray of a set of jumper connected trays (certain exceptions to this statement are noted in Section 11.2.4.). The digit input and output terminals on the various units are connected into the digit trays by means of digit cables. A three-way plug is used at a digit tray terminal when more than one digit terminal of a unit is connected to a particular digit tray terminal. The term digit trunk is used to refer to a set of jumper connected digit trays, the load box at one end, and the digit cables which connect units to the set of digit trays.

In digit trunks, the lines marked 1 through 10 on PX-4-102 carry the digit pulses for decade places 1 through 10 respectively and line 11 carries the PM pulses (also see Section 11.2.2.).

11.2.2. Shifters, Deleters, and Adaptors

Shifters, deleters, or adaptors, used between digit cables, and digit terminals on the units, when it is desired to establish a special relationship between the decade place leads of the transmitting and receiving digit terminals, consist of specially wired 12 point plug and socket assemblies. Shifters are used to effect multiplication by powers of 10, deleters to eliminate digit pulses on certain decade place leads, and adaptors for other special purposes such as taking digital information to program lines.

The shifters which have been constructed at present are shown on PX-4-104 A-E. While in some cases special shifters could be built for use at digit output terminals, these shifters are for use only at digit input terminals. The terminology used here is that a +n shifter (for n positive) multiplies a number by 10^n (or shifts data n places to the left); a -n shifter multiplies a number by 10^{-n} (or shifts data n places to the right).

The following connections are made between the socket (S) and plug (P) leads of the +n shifters:

S [PM] ⟶ P [PM]

S [n left hand decade places] ⟶ Not connected to anything

S [decade places i] ⟶ P [decade places i + n] respectively

Ground ⟶ P [n right hand decade places]

The connections established in the -n shifters are the following:

S [PM] ⟶ P [PM and n left hand decade places]

S [decade places i] ⟶ P [decade places i - n] respectively

S [n right hand decade places] ⟶ Not connected to anything

Notice that connections in the shifters for translating numbers n places to the right are made in such a way as to duplicate the PM pulses in the n left hand decade places of the receiving unit. Thus, for example, the number carried in a digit tray as M 4 823 000 000 is received through a -3 shifter in an accumulator as M 9 994 823 000. Because of the necessity of duplicating sign pulses in the n left hand decade places when a negative number is shifted to the right, a right hand shifter could not be designed for use at a digit output terminal for such a shifter would cause the PM transmitter to be loaded with the capacity of two or more lines in the digit trunk and would tie these lines together, thus making the trunk a special purpose trunk.

From the description of the +n and -n shifters above, it can be seen that if a +n shifter were used at a digit output terminal, the shift with regard to the n left hand decade places transmitted would be equivalent to that which results when a -n shifter is used at a digit input terminal. However, this interchange cannot be made because, in the case of a negative number, sign pulses

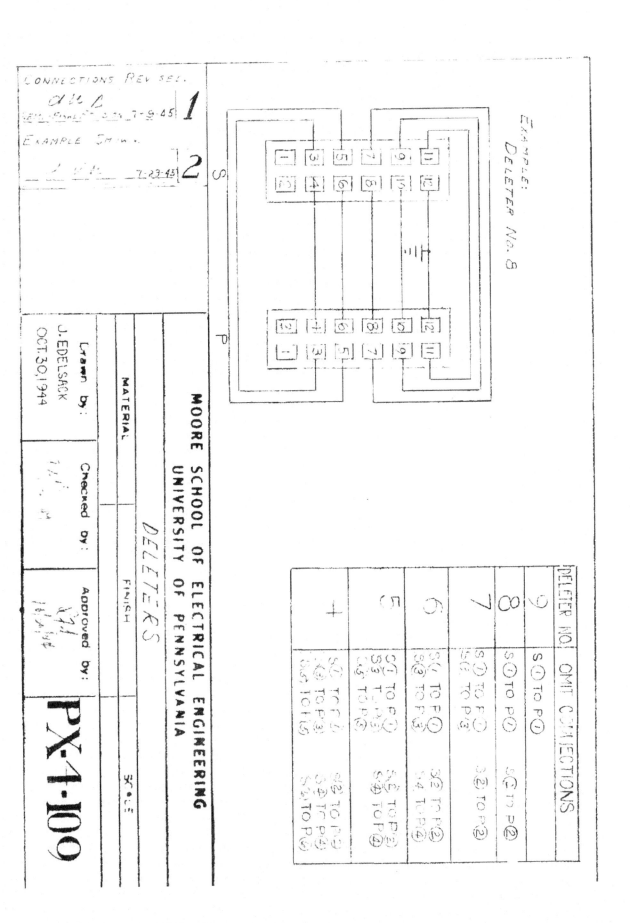

EXAMPLE:
DELETER No. 8

CONNECTIONS REV SEL.
all L
REV & FINAL 3-23 7-9-45 │ 1
EXAMPLE SHOWN
_2_ [signature]   7-23-45 │ 2

MATERIAL

DELETERS
FINISH

Drawn by:
J. EDELSACK
OCT. 30, 1944

Checked by:

Approved by:

MOORE SCHOOL OF ELECTRICAL ENGINEERING
UNIVERSITY OF PENNSYLVANIA

SCALE

PX-1-100

DELETER NO.	OMIT CONNECTIONS		
9	S① TO P①		
8	S① TO P①	S② TO P②	
7	S① TO P①	S② TO P②	S③ TO P③
6	S① TO P①	S② TO P②	S③ TO P③
	S③ TO P③	S④ TO P④	
5	S① TO P①	S② TO P②	S③ TO P③
	S③ TO P③	S④ TO P④	S⑤ TO P⑤
+	S① TO P①	S② TO P②	S③ TO P③
	S③ TO P③	S④ TO P④	S⑤ TO P⑤
	S⑤ TO P⑤	S⑥ TO P⑥	

are not duplicated in the n left hand decade places. Similarly a -n shifter
cannot be used at a digit output terminal to accomplish a shift to the left
because the n right hand decade place leads at the receiving end are not grounded.

The deleters which have been constructed are tabulated on PX-4-109.
The deleters omit socket to plug connections for the leads associated with the
decade places which are deleted. The deleters on PX-4-109 are designed for use
at digit output terminals. Special deleters could be built for use at digit
input terminals. Such deleters would ground the plug leads for the deleted
decade places.

Certain special adaptors which combine shifting and deleting characteristics have also been constructed. These are shown on PX-4-117. These adaptors
have the following properties:

3A	5 place to the right shifter with sign deletion
5A	5 left hand and PM place deleter
8A	1 place to the right shifter with sign deletion
4A	5 place to the left shifter with output of decade place 5 brought also to the PM lead
6A	3 place to the left shifter with sign deletion
10A	PM deleter
7A	5 place to the right shifter with sign deletion.

Adaptors for use at 12 point terminals on the divider and square rooter
which function in a programming capacity are described in Section 6.4.2.

11.2.3. Load Units for Digit Trunks

The capacity to ground of any line in a tray is approximately 120
micro-farads. This capacity, plus that of the short jumper used to connect
one tray to the next, is called a load unit. The capacity of a three foot cable

for connecting a digit input or output terminal to a digit tray is roughly equal to a load unit. Adaptors have negligible capacity. In order to obtain pulse rise times within the proper limits for safe and reliable operation of the ENIAC, the total number of load units (which equals the number of jumper connected trays plus the number of digit cables plugged into the trays) of a given digit trunk must not exceed 60 (also see Section 11.4.)

11.2.4. Special Uses of Digit Trays Without Load Boxes

A load box is used on all digit trunks formed by connecting digit trays together. Because the trays have been designed so that the load resistor is plugged into the unused terminals of one of the end trays of a trunk, the flexibility of being able to connect varying numbers of digit terminals to the trunks is possible.

In a few special cases, the resistance has been built into circuits of the units and certain single digit trays connected to these units by digit cables are used without load boxes. No other units may be connected in parallel into these trays.

In the case of the divider and square rooter (see PX-6-311), the following associated digit trays are used without load boxes:

1) the single digit tray[*] which carries components of the answer from the answer output terminal to the quotient accumulator's α input terminal and to the denominator accumulator's γ input terminal.

2) the digit tray[**] which carries programming instructions from the

---

[*]Running from the divider and square rooter to accumulator 5. A special short cable connects this digit tray to the α input terminal on the quotient accumulator and another cable connects this tray to the γ input terminal of the denominator accumulator.

[**]A single tray running from the divider and square rooter to accumulator 5 is used. Special cables (see PX-10-307) are plugged from this tray to the interconnector terminals on accumulators 2 and 7.

quotient and shift accumulator program terminal on the divider and square rooter to interconnector terminals on accumulators 2 and 7

3) the <u>digit</u> tray which carries <u>programming</u> instructions from the denominator and square root accumulator program terminal to accumulator 5.

In the case of the high-speed multiplier, a digit tray without load box is used to connect each of the three partial products output terminals LHPP II, RHPP I and II to the appropriate accumulator. A special short digit cable without load connects the LHPP I terminal to accumulator 11 and, for safest operation, the three lowest digit trays are used for the other three partial products.

11.3. PROGRAM TRANSMISSION

11.3.1. Program Lines

Eighty one program trays have been constructed for the ENIAC. These trays, like the digit trays, are 8 feet long, have 11 wires and a ground, and at either end, have 12 point terminals so that a number of program trays can be jumper connected to form a program trunk. The program trays, however, have a group of eleven 2 point terminals spaced at 2 foot intervals instead of the 12 point terminals found on digit trays. A program pulse input or output terminal of a unit is connected to a program tray by means of a program cable which has a **two** point plug on each end (1 wire and a shield). In general, a load box (see PX-4-103) is plugged into an unused terminal at one end of program trunk. The term <u>program line</u> is used to refer to one conductor running the length of a set of jumper connected program trays and the program cables plugged into the conductor.

Fifty digit - program adaptors have been made. Each of these consists of a box with a 12 point digit plug connected to a group of 11, 2-point program sockets. These adaptors make it possible to use digit trays as program trays.

11.3.2. Special Program Cables

In addition to the standard program cables, a number of special U and Y program cables have been assembled. The U cable has a 2 point terminal on either end and a built in load. It is used to connect two program terminals on the same unit or on adjacent units without going into a program tray. The Y cable has three 2 point plugs. This latter type is used when it is desired to connect 2 program terminals on the same unit and also to connect to a program line.

11.3.3. Load units for Program Trays

In the case of program lines, as in the case of digit trunks, the number of load units must be restricted in order to provide suitable time constants for safe and reliable operation of the ENIAC. For program lines which carry only program pulses the total number of load units (number of jumper connected program trays through which the line runs and program cables plugged into the line) must not exceed 120. A program line which carries digit pulses, a case which can arise in magnitude discrimination programs for example, must not have more than 60 load units. The more stringent restriction of load units is made for lines carrying digit pulses particularly because the short interval between successive digit pulses makes necessary an especially short rise and fall time for digit pulses for safe resolution of these pulses. Also, the digit pulses are slightly broader than the program pulses so that even in the case where only 1 digit pulse is transmitted in a given addition time, for the most reliable operation, it is best to restrict the number of load units to 60.

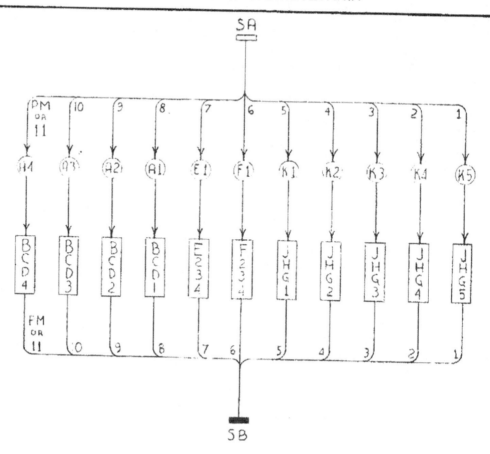

SA

SB

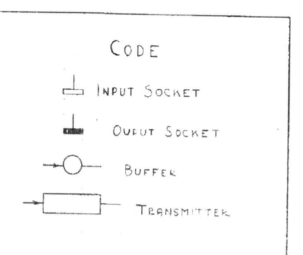

CODE

⊥ INPUT SOCKET

▬ OUTPUT SOCKET

→○→ BUFFER

→▭→ TRANSMITTER

DRAWN BY H. Crosswaite Lewis

CHECKED BY

APPROVED BY

PULSE AMPLIFIER
BLOCK DIAGRAM

SCALE

PX-4-301

11.3.4. Special Program Lines Without Load Resistor

Program lines without a load resistor are used to carry stimulating signals to the following program input terminals:

I_S and R_S on the initiating unit (see PX-9-302)

PA, 1A, and Cont. on the cycling unit (see PX-9-303).

If desired, special program cables without resistance load may be used instead of lines in program trays. Also, see Section 11.6. for a discussion of the portable control box which can be used to parallel these terminals.

11.4. PULSE AMPLIFIER

Three pulse amplifier units (and chassis for two more) have been constructed. The pulse amplifier unit provides a means of circumventing the load limit restriction (see Sections 11.2.3. and 11.3.3.) on the total number of digit terminals or program terminals that can be connected for communication with one another and also is capable of being used to isolate program pulses.

This device contains eleven identical circuits, each consisting of a buffer and transmitter (see PX-4-301). A signal delivered to the pulse amplifier by way of one of the leads of the 12-point terminal at the left of its front face, passes through the associated buffer and transmitter and is emitted from the output terminal on the right side. Power for the pulse amplifier is obtained by connecting the terminal on the left face to one of the four 12-point terminals at the bottom of the diagonally placed panels at either end of the wall containing the high-speed multiplier.

If two trays are connected by a pulse amplifier, each tray may have as many as the maximum number of load units specified for that type (digit or program). Furthermore, data transmitted through the tray connected to the input

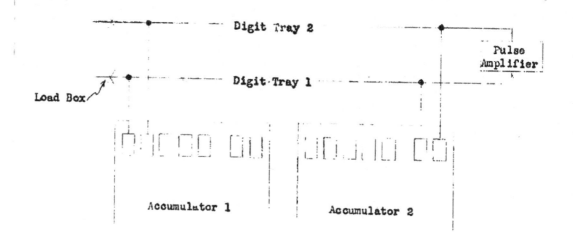

Fig. 11-1

DIGIT TRAYS CONNECTED BY PULSE AMPLIFIER

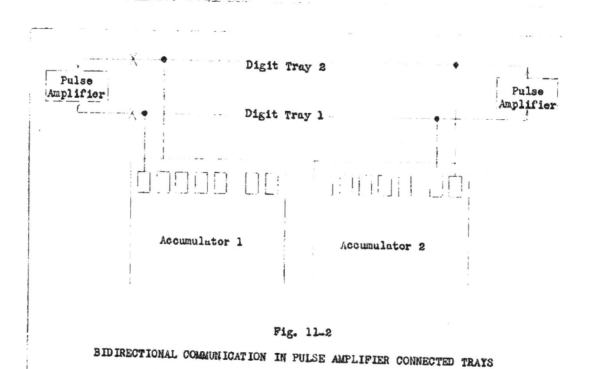

Fig. 11-2

BIDIRECTIONAL COMMUNICATION IN PULSE AMPLIFIER CONNECTED TRAYS

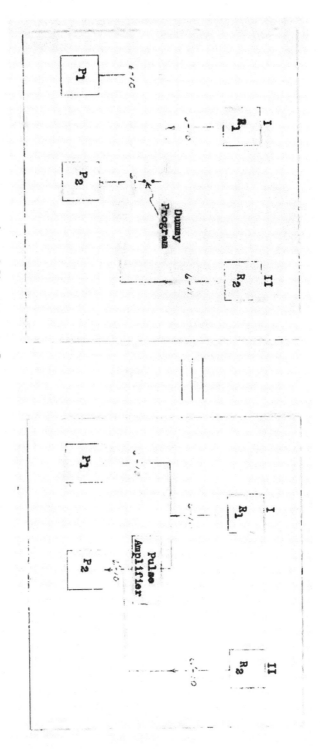

I: Programs P_1 and P_2 follow program R_1.

II: At some other time in the computation, program P_2 (without program P_1) follows program R_2.
Program tray 6 is connected to the input and 6' to the output of a pulse amplifier.

Fig. 11-3

ISOLATION OF PROGRAMS THROUGH THE USE OF A PULSE AMPLIFIER

of the pulse amplifier is communicated to the tray connected to the pulse amplifier's output. Data carried on the tray connected to the pulse amplifier's output, however, is not communicated to the tray connected to the input. For example, in Figure 11-1, the α input of accumulator 1 can receive from only the A output of accumulator 2; the β input of accumulator 2 can receive from both the A and S outputs of accumulator 2.

Through the use of 2 pulse amplifiers, two trays can be connected so that there is bidirectional communication between them. In Figure 11-2, for example, both the α and β inputs on accumulator 1 can receive from either the A or S outputs of accumulator 2.

The unidirectional communication in one of two trays connected by a pulse amplifier provides a means of using a pulse amplifier instead of one or more dummy program controls to isolate program pulses. In Figure 11-3, the schematic drawing shows two set-ups that are logically equivalent: one uses a dummy program control; the other, a pulse amplifier.

11.5. SPECIAL INTERCONNECTION OF UNITS

11.5.1. Connections to the Printer

The units whose static outputs are delivered to the printer so that data stored in them can be recorded are listed in Section 9.4. The reader is also referred to the following diagrams:

Static Output Cable	PX-4-111
Printer Adaptors	PX-12-114

11.5.2. The High-Speed Multiplier and Its Associated Accumulators

The accumulators connected to the high-speed multiplier for the communication of digital and programming information are discussed in Section 5.4.

Reference is also made to the following diagrams:

Interconnection of High-Speed Multiplier with Associated Accumulators	PX-6-311
Static Output Cable	PX-4-111
Accumulator Interconnector Cable (Multiplier)	PX-5-131

11.5.3. The Divider and Square Rooter and Its Associated Accumulators

The connections established between the divider and square rooter and its associated accumulators are described in Section 6.4. The interconnection of these units is pictured on PX-10-307 and, on this same drawing, reference is made to the drawings of special cables and adaptors used.

11.5.4. Interconnection of Accumulators

In Section 4.4.2, the interconnector terminal connections for using one accumulator as a 10 decade accumulator or for using 2 accumulators as a 20 decade accumulator are discussed. The following diagrams are relevant to that discussion:

Accumulator Interconnector Terminal Load Box	PX-5-109
Accumulator Interconnector Cable (Vertical)	PX-5-121
Accumulator Interconnector Cable (Horizontal)	PX-5-110
Accumulator Program Front Panel	PX-5-105

11.6. PORTABLE CONTROL BOX

Certain initiating unit and cycling unit controls which are particularly useful in testing the operation of the ENIAC have been described in Chapters II and III. These controls include:

Initial Clear Switch   Section 2.1.2.

Reader start switch and terminal R_S

which parallels the switch   Section 2.2.

Initiating Pulse Switch and terminal

I_S which parallels the switch   Section 2.2.

Operation selector switch for switching

from 1P to either 1A or continuous operation,   Section 3.2.

and the terminals 1A and Cont. which parallel

this switch

1 Pulse or 1 Addition Time Switch and the

terminal PA which parallels this switch   Section 3.2.

In Chapters II, and III there was described the direct operation
of these controls at the initiating and cycling units or, except for the
initial clear control, from anywhere in the ENIAC room with the aid of special
program lines without load resistor.

The portable control box provides a third and more convenient means
of operating these controls and the initial clear button. By means of a cable
the portable control box is connected directly into the circuits of the controls
mentioned above. This cable is long enough to permit the use of the control box
anywhere in the ENIAC room. The controls on the box reading from top down are:

1) Operation selector switch for switching to 1 addition time or
continuous operation when the operation selector switch on
the cycling unit is set at 1 pulse time.

2) Initial clear button which, when pushed, causes initial clearing to take place. (Operation selector switch must be set at Cont. when initial clear button is pushed.)

3) Reader start button which is used to stimulate the reading of a card. Terminal R_0 emits a pulse when reading initiated in this way is completed, without the reception of an interlock pulse at R1.

4) Initial pulse button which, when pushed, causes a program output pulse to be emitted from terminal I_0 on the cycling unit.

5) 1 Pulse - 1 Addition push button. With the operation selector switch set at 1P or 1A respectively, one pulse or the 1 addition time sequence of pulses is given out each time this button is pushed.

The mechnical torpedo data computer provided firing solutions for U.S. Navy submariners during the first half of WWII. This Mark 3 manual provides a fascinating glimpse inside this mechanical wonder.

Designed by Swedish cryptographer Boris Hagelin, the M-209 Converter was a portable mechanical cipher machine. This M-209 Technical Manual describes the operation and care of this fascinating device and provides a fascinating glimpse into mid-level encryption technology circa 1944.

Also now available!
www.PeriscopeFilm.com

CPSIA information can be obtained
at www.ICGtesting.com
Printed in the USA
BVOW04s1054211217
503380BV00004B/172/P